A BRIEF HISTORY
OF FRANCE

A BRIEF HISTORY OF FRANCE

PAUL F. STATE

Checkmark Books®
An imprint of Infobase Publishing

A BRIEF HISTORY OF FRANCE

Checkmark Books
An imprint of Infobase Publishing
132 West 31st Street
New York, NY 10001

Library of Congress Cataloging-in-Publication Data
State, Paul F., 1950–
  A brief history of France / Paul F. State
    p. cm.
  Includes bibliographical references and index.
  ISBN 978-0-8160-8181-3 (hardcover: acid-free paper)
  ISBN 978-0-8160-8328-2 (pbk: acid-free paper) 1. France—History. I. Title.
  DC37.S73 2010
  944—dc22   2009052607

Checkmark Books are available at special discounts when purchased in bulk quantities for businesses, associations, institutions, or sales promotions. Please call our Special Sales Department in New York at (212) 967-8800 or (800) 322-8755.

You can find Facts On File on the World Wide Web at http://www.factsonfile.com

Text design by Joan M. McEvoy
Composition by Hermitage Publishing Services
Maps by Dale Williams
Cover printed by Yurchak Printing, Landisville, Pa.
Book printed and bound by Yurchak Printing, Landisville, Pa.

Printed in the United States of America

This book is printed on acid-free paper.

This book is dedicated to my mother, Ruth Mary Louise,
who delights in her French heritage,
in love and gratitude for her unstinting support

CONTENTS

LIST OF ILLUSTRATIONS

LIST OF MAPS

ACKNOWLEDGMENTS

I would like to express my sincere appreciation to the staffs of the Bibliothèque Nationale, the Library of Congress, the New York Public Library, and the Consulate General of France in New York for their kind assistance. Jennifer Belt at Art Resource proved helpful in securing images. Special thanks to Claudia Schaab, peerless in her skill as editor.

INTRODUCTION

A mong the world's nations, France has an especially long history, and so its record is filled with more than an ordinary share of great dramatic events and larger-than-life personalities. At the same time, its status as western Europe's largest country territorially, and for hundreds of years demographically, ensured that many among the events occurring, and decisions taken, here would have an impact far beyond its borders.

Although the nation's boundaries—except for the one in the north—conform to well-defined natural features, France is, in fact, an artificial creation, deliberately and painstakingly welded together out of a welter of disparate territories over many centuries by those among its monarchs who possessed the will, talent, and resources to build a successively stronger realm. Only after these rulers had crafted a kingdom unified politically and religiously—both attributes deemed essential for the security of the monarchy—did the regime under which modern France is governed emerge at the end of the 18th century. It did so by revolutionary action of the French people, who, inspired by ingenious ideas of liberty and theories of democracy, transformed what had been a state in which they had been the ruled into a nation in which they were the rulers. Because they were the first people in Europe to do so and because France was then the predominant continental power, the French imparted that legacy, both by example and by conquest, to the rest of the Continent.

Europe's premier pacesetter for political change in the 19th century, France has experienced a troubled modern history, stemming, partly, from the succession of very different ruling systems—aristocratic monarchy, constitutional monarchy, empire, republic—that left in their wake stakeholders anxious to retain or restore their power and position, and, partly, from political actors unable to reconcile competing conceptions of liberty and equality. "France" and "republic" are taken as self-evident today, but this particular form of government has, since 1789, either proved troublesomely unstable or failed altogether to survive. Only with the fifth and last of the regimes to be established has the nation found a highly workable republican formula.

Widespread economic growth throughout much of the preceding 60 years has made France a prosperous country, and it is today one of the world's wealthiest. While a fully modern nation in every respect, at the same time the links to its past—so evident in the splendid architectural legacy on display everywhere in the physical landscape—endure. Varying cultural, social, and linguistic differences among the French people that persisted well into modern times are reflected today in distinctive regional characteristics, including in language, dress, cuisine, and other customs. Food, fashion, and transportation are only several among an array of fields in which the French have won, and continue to earn, renown. Active overseas since the 17th century, the nation became a major colonial power, a status that has bequeathed a lingering presence for France, today largely economic and cultural, in places across the globe.

The French historical tapestry is remarkably rich. Monarchies, dictatorships, and democracies have ruled here. Civil conflicts of every kind have raged. Wars have brought sweeping, prideful victories and stinging, humiliating defeats. Innovative trends and theories and technological and scientific advances of international import have been launched.

The designation *great power* is highly subjective by definition, and nations rise and fall according to parameters of strength over time. Still, at various periods in its lengthy history and judged by a wide range of standards—the might of its armies, the wealth of its rulers, the impact of its political principles, the influence of its culture, the achievements of its artists and intellectuals, the well-being of its inhabitants—France has qualified in every way.

The Land

Metropolitan France, including the island of Corsica, encompasses 212,910 square miles (551,553 sq. km). The country's status as western Europe's largest nation in area is reflected in its varied physical geography and climatic divisions. The long period of territorial growth beginning in the first millennium has given modern France national borders that are nearly all natural ones. Except for the country's level to hilly northern frontier, whose barrier-free geography fittingly enough served as the gateway to invasions, physical features, namely, the Alps, the Jura, and the Rhine River; the Pyrenees; the Mediterranean Sea; the Atlantic Ocean; and the English Channel, define the boundaries of the six sides of the "hexagon" (*l'hexagone*)—a term that, since the 1960s,

Topographical Map of France

North Sea

THE NETHERLANDS

UNITED KINGDOM

GERMANY

Strait of Dover

Calais
Dunkirk
Lille
BELGIUM

English Channel (La Manche)

LUXEMBOURG

Channel Is. (U.K.)
Guernsey
Jersey

Île d'Ouessant

Brest

Seine Bay

Caen

Gulf of Saint-Malo

St-Lô

NORMANDY

Amiens

Somme R.

Rouen

Seine R.

Reims

Marne R.

Verdun

Metz

Meuse R.

Moselle R.

BRITTANY

Mont-St-Michel

Versailles

Paris

Strasbourg

VOSGES

Rhine R.

Rennes

Chartres

Seine R.

Lorient

Orléans

Loire R.

Loire R.

PLATEAU DE LANGRES

Mulhouse

Belle-Île

Angers

Tours

Blois

Besançon

Île de Noirmoutier

Nantes

Chinon

Cher R.

Dijon

Saône R.

JURA

Île d'Yeu

Poitiers

Bourges

BURGUNDY

Doubs R.

SWITZERLAND

ATLANTIC OCEAN

Île de Ré

La Rochelle

FRANCE

Lake Geneva

Île d'Oléron

Vichy

A L P S

Limoges

Clermont-Ferrand

Mont Blanc 15,780 ft.

Gironde R.

Cognac

Lyon

Chambéry

Bay of Biscay

Bordeaux

Dordogne R.

MASSIF CENTRAL

St-Étienne

Isère R.

Grenoble

ITALY

LANDES

Garonne R.

Lot R.

Rhône R.

Drac R.

Aveyron R.

Bayonne

Adour R.

GASCONY

Tarn R.

Toulouse

Montpellier

Nîmes

Avignon

Durance R.

Nice

MONACO

Lourdes

Garonne R.

Ariège R.

Aude R.

Aix-en-Provence

Cannes

Marseille

Côte d'Azur

Narbonne

Gulf of Lion

Toulon

N

P Y R E N E E S

SPAIN

ANDORRA

Bastia

Corsica

Ajaccio

0   100 miles
0   100 km

Mediterranean Sea

© Infobase Publishing

French commentators have made synonymous with the country. France sits at the territorial and climatic crossroads of northern Europe and the Mediterranean lands. The country consists of five geographic regions.

In the northwest, flat and rolling terrain stretches in a wide arc from the Vendée and lower Loire River regions through Picardy to Champagne. It includes the Paris basin, a level to hilly area that rises outward from its center at the city of Paris in a series of ridges and scarps, which, in the west, end in cliffs along the English Channel. Elevations are generally fewer than 700 feet (210 m), and the basin is bordered in the extreme northwest by the Armorican Massif, an upland plateau that forms the peninsular areas of Brittany and Normandy.

In the northeast, plateaus and limestone slopes predominate in Burgundy. Prominent upland areas include the Vosges, a range of rounded hills near the border with Germany that vary in height from 1,200 feet (365 m) to almost 4,700 feet (1,430 m), and the Ardennes Plateau, a very old, deeply eroded highland of which a small portion extends into France from southeastern Belgium.

The southwest features a combination of plains, hills, and plateaus. It includes the Aquitaine basin, a triangular-shaped lowland that is smaller and less hilly than the Paris basin, to which it is connected by a strip of land labeled the "Gate of Poitou." South of the Gironde estuary along the Atlantic Ocean lies the flat, sandy area known as the Landes.

The southeast comprises a patchwork of contrasts. Limestone plateaus broken by flatlands and valleys mark the Limousin, while coastal lowlands stretch along the Mediterranean littoral from Languedoc-Roussillon to Provence, and they break into the interior along the Rhône-Saône valley, the only north-south corridor in rugged southeastern France.

Mountain areas make up the fifth distinctive geographic region. Much of southern France is covered by the Alps and the Pyrenees, whose highest peaks remain capped with snow year-round. The Alps run from the Italian border westward to the Rhône River valley, with elevations increasing generally from south to north. Many summits exceed 12,000 feet (3,650 m) above sea level; at the point where French, Swiss, and Italian frontiers meet, Mont Blanc, at 15,771 feet (4,807 m), is the highest mountain in western Europe. France is linked to Italy through Alpine passes, including Mont Cenis and Little Saint Bernard. The Pyrenees rise dramatically from the plains of southernmost France. Because of their height—elevations rise as high as 10,820 feet (3,048 m) at the Pic de Vignemale—and their length—running from the Bay of Biscay to the Mediterranean Sea—they provide a formidable barrier between France and Spain. Along the French-Swiss border north of the Alps lie the Jura Mountains, which, though linked geologically with the former, feature gentler inclines and rounded, lower summits (fewer than 6,000 feet [1,800 m]). The Massif Central slopes gradually upward from the Paris and Aquitaine basins to occupy the south-central part of the country. Elevations of 2,500 to 3,000 feet (760 to 900 m) are general, although the remnants of ancient volcanoes rise sharply above the surrounding landscape to heights that reach more than 6,000 feet (1,800 m). The eastern and southern edges of the massif are marked by steep escarpments, most notably the Cévennes, which comprise nearly a sheer wall that overlooks the lower Rhône valley.

Most of the country lies within the drainage basins of four major rivers—the Seine, Loire, Rhône, and Garonne. The Seine drains most of the Paris basin. The Loire spans the center of France, running in a broad arc from its headwaters in the Cévennes to empty into the Bay of Biscay at Saint-Nazaire. At 625 miles (1,006 km), it is the nation's longest river. Rising in the Pyrenees, the Garonne, together with tributaries flowing from the Massif Central, constitutes the central river system of the Aquitaine basin. The Rhône River enters the country from Switzerland and empties into the Mediterranean. Because it drains the Alpine region, the Rhône, together with tributaries such as the Isère and Saône, carries massive volumes of water, which have been dammed to provide hydroelectric power. The Meuse and the Moselle Rivers are prominent arteries in the northeast, while France shares the commercially busy Rhine River with Germany. There are no large natural lakes though numerous small ones are found in the Alps, and small lakes have been made by damming in the Rhône River system and the Massif Central. Saltwater lagoons and marshes are scattered in the Landes region and in the Camargue area west of the Rhône estuary.

The climate of France is marked by distinct regional variations that center around two major divides. The primary division is between the cool north and the warm south, and the secondary one separates the maritime west from the continental east. Atlantic coastal winters are mild (January temperatures average 40° to 45°F [4° to 7°C]), and summers are cool (July temperatures average 60° to 65°F [16° to 18°C]). In the inland east, seasons are more distinct with colder winters and warmer summers. Precipitation is uniform across northern France, with heavier amounts in summer. Some snow falls in winter, especially in the Massif Central and the Vosges. The Mediterranean coast is markedly milder (January temperatures average 45° to 50°F [7° to 10°C], and July temperatures attain an average of 75° [24°C]). Sunny weather is abundant, and rain, which because it can be sparse gives rise to wildfires, falls mostly in the non-summer months. In winter, a cool, dry wind called the mistral blows down the Rhône valley. Very cold winters and cool summers with significant rain and snow characterize the weather in the Alps and the Pyrenees.

While plains and hills account for approximately two-fifths of the total land area, forests cover about one-fifth of the national territory, largely in the mountain areas and the Massif Central. Deciduous trees, including various types of oak, European beech, and poplar, prevail at lower elevations, while conifers, primarily pine, spruce, and fir, spread along mountain slopes. Pine forests are also a feature of the Landes, while maquis, a scrubby vegetation of low evergreen shrubs and small trees, is a defining plant cover along the Mediterranean coast together with holm oaks and cork oaks. Over the centuries, the plains areas were cleared of natural vegetation for farming, and grasses and patches of woodland mark the uncultivated areas here.

Fertile, brown forest soils predominate in France since most of the country experiences cool to warm temperatures with moderate rainfall. Thinner, less fertile soils are found in the wetter climates in the extreme west and in colder locales, especially in the high uplands and mountain areas. The fertile soils of northern France rest on deposits of loess (limon). In about a third of the country limestone-based soils are found, both in lowland areas, most especially in parts of the Paris basin where they are light and easy to fertilize, and in the high plateaus of southern France and the mountain regions, where they are of poor cultivable quality. The distinctive red-colored soils of the Mediterranean region depend on irrigation for agricultural yields. Following centuries of land clearing, grazing, fertilizing, and cropping, few natural soils are left in the country.

Likewise, in such a long-settled land, only small mammals, such as foxes and hares, make up the country's dominant wildlife, although over 400 varieties of birds, 25 types of amphibians, and 27 kinds of reptiles are found. Large animals such as bears, chamois, and deer that were once plentiful now survive only in the more remote forest and mountain regions. Small herds of wild horses are a distinctive feature of the Camargue.

The People

The population of France stands at 65,073,482 (2009 est.), including 62,448,977 who live in metropolitan France and 2,624,505 who live in the French overseas departments and territories. In 2001, approximately 77 percent of the population lived in urban areas (Population Reference Bureau). However, there are few large cities. Outside of Paris (9.6 million), which, as the nation's largest and the world's 20th biggest city (2007 est.) has always dominated national life, the next most populous cities of Lyon (1.38 million) and Marseille (1.24 million) are far smaller.

The French trace their origins to tribes of Celtic peoples who migrated west and south from the Rhine River valley at the end of the fifth century B.C.E. Their descendants still maintain a dominant presence today in Brittany. Roman rule brought an influx of arrivals from both Italy and elsewhere in the far-flung empire. The wave of invasions of Germanic tribes from central and eastern Europe in the fifth century C.E. led to the settlement of Visigoths in Aquitaine, Burgundians in Burgundy, and Franks in what is now northern France, the last named conquering, in the sixth century, all of formerly Roman Gaul save for the Mediterranean coastlands. Vikings from Scandinavia arrived in Normandy in the 10th century.

Although demographics have been high by European standards throughout much of France's history—the country claimed one-fourth of Europe's population during the Middle Ages—growth was slow, checked for centuries by high infant mortality, poor diet, wars, and epidemics. Beginning in the 16th century, coupled with ongoing territorial expansion, steady growth set in, which made France, at 28 million people, Europe's most populous country at the start of the French Revolution in 1789. Low birthrates led to stagnation as the 19th century progressed—the annual rate of growth stood at .01 percent in 1900. Rates remained low—in part occasioned most tragically in the massive loss of young men in World War I—through the mid-20th century until broken by the baby boom in the post–World War II years. The average number of children per married couple rose from a prewar figure of 1.9 to 2.4 by 1960, contributing to overall growth of 1 percent per year during the 1950s and 1960s, the highest in the country's modern history. Adding to the increase, for 30 years after World War II, France became a nation of mass immigration, welcoming, on average, 50,000 newcomers a year until the mid-1970s in continuing a tradition that, in the 19th and 20th centuries, made the nation a leader in Europe in incorporating immigrants into its society. Postwar recovery and a burgeoning economy produced a demand for cheap labor, supplied most especially by workers from Italy, Spain, Portugal, and Greece. Laws eased entry for the *colons*, French citizens born or naturalized in former colonies in North and West Africa, India, and Indochina, most prominently 1.6 million European *pieds noirs* (black feet), who migrated from Algeria, Morocco, and Tunisia. Non-Europeans from North Africa also arrived.

Restrictions on immigration were enacted beginning in the late 1970s. Tighter limits mean that immigration is now largely confined to family reunion cases and political asylum seekers, while the geographic spread has widened with roughly half of new arrivals now coming from former French colonies in sub-Saharan Africa and Asia. It is estimated that 4.9 million immigrants live in France (2009), who account for 8 percent of the population. The number of illegal immigrants has grown, estimated at approximately 300,000 at the end of the 20th century (Hargreaves 1995, 21).

More diverse than ever before, French society in the 21st century confronts the issue of cultural assimilation that has provoked tensions and turmoil. In conjunction with wider Western trends, the past 30 years have seen smaller families. At the end of the century, couples living together outside of marriage amounted to 15.5 percent, the percent of children born outside of marriage climbed to 37.6 percent, and divorce rose to 45.6 percent (Girling 1998, 67–78). The national birthrate dropped in the 1980s only to rebound in the 1990s. The country's fertility rate in 2008, at 2.02 children, constituted the highest in the European Union (EU), and both birth- and fertility rates have continued to rise in the first decade of the third millennium.

The official language of the country, and the mother tongue of approximately 86 percent of the population, is French, which is based on Latin with many Celtic and Germanic elements. Before the 20th century, French served as the preeminent language of diplomacy as well as the common tongue among the rulers and the educated classes of Europe. The nation's former status as a major colonial power has left a linguistic legacy around the world, where French is the official language in 29 countries, as well as in the United Nations and other international bodies. Created in 1970, the Francophonie is an international organization of 56 countries promoting special ties among French-speaking peoples. A number of regional languages are spoken, most prominently in border areas adjacent to non-French-speaking countries. They include Alsatian, a German dialect; West Flemish, a variant of Dutch; Breton, a Celtic tongue; Corsican (Corsu) and Catalan, with strong affinities to Italian and Spanish, respectively; Occitan and its dialect, Provençal, in southern France; and Basque, spoken by a people in the Pyrenees with an ancient lineage unrelated to any other in France. In 2008, regional languages were granted recognition as belonging to the heritage of France. Immigrant groups speak the language of their origin, most prominently in recent years that of Arabic.

The existence of regional dialects attests to the important role played by the French provinces in the country's history. Although

Bretons in traditional costume, ca. 1875. Distinctive regional customs continue in France today. (Adoc-photos/Art Resource, NY)

shorn of their political power during the Revolution, they retain distinct cultural identities, and particularities in social customs, dress, and cuisine, among others, are actively maintained. In Corsica a movement that has employed violent tactics in recent years seeks outright independence.

Since its early history, France has remained predominantly Roman Catholic in religion. Some 83 to 88 percent of inhabitants profess, even if for many only nominally, the faith whose roots in the country date to antiquity. Today freedom of thought and religion are guaranteed, and church and state are fully separate. Given Catholicism's long-standing status as the religion of the majority—it was the official state religion before the Revolution and under royalist regimes in the 19th century—and the close links maintained historically between the monarchy and the papacy, France has earned the designation "eldest daughter of the church," despite a pronounced streak of institutional autonomy (*gallicisme*) in existence since the 14th century. In conjunction with trends toward secularization in modern Western society, the French today are much less faithful followers than heretofore. Rates of baptism, church attendance, and recruitment of clergy and religious have plummeted since the 1950s. Polls show substantial minorities—up to a third in some cases—who profess agnosticism or atheism. Protestants and Jews have long histories in the country despite their low numbers at just more than 2 percent and 1 percent, respectively. The approximately 700,000 Jews in France today make up the largest Jewish community in Europe outside of Russia. Incidents of anti-Semitism occur, but religious prejudice is targeted more especially today at Muslims, who, in the wake of substantial immigration, now account for the second-largest religious sect in the country, totaling from 5 to 6 million (2009 est.), or between 8 and 10 percent of the population. France is home to western Europe's largest Islamic population.

The French share fully with their western European neighbors the advanced social welfare systems characteristic of modern European societies. Beginning incrementally in the early 20th century, the nation put in place rapid and comprehensive social security programs in the immediate post–World War II years. Unemployment, retirement, family allowance, and paid vacation schemes are generous. The health system is universal, financed by a complex mix of public and private monies. Government spending (approximately 54 percent of gross domestic product [GDP] in 2009) and taxes (approximately 44 percent of GDP in 2007) are high by world standards. Education is free and mandatory between the ages of 6 and 16. Literacy is nearly universal (99 percent). The public education system is highly centralized, while private education is largely Roman Catholic. By the end of the 20th century, fully 80 percent of secondary school students had earned the *baccalauréat*, the ticket to a university education. There are 91 public universities and 175 professional schools, including the prestigious postgraduate *grandes écoles*.

Government

France is a republic (Fr., République française) with a semipresidential system of government that features considerable centralization of administration. The constitution proclaims the nation's attachment to the democratic principles enshrined in the Declaration of the Rights of Man and of the Citizen (1789), which include equality of all citizens before the law, government accountability to the citizenry, guarantee of property against arbitrary seizure, and freedoms of speech and creed. Founded in 1958, the current republic is the fifth in the political history of the country.

The Fifth Republic is a unique synthesis of the American presidential system and the British parliamentary system of government. Power is divided among executive, legislative, and judicial branches. The chief executive is the president, who is the preeminent figure in national politics. He or she is directly elected by popular vote and serves a five-year term. There are no term limits. The president presides over the government (*gouvernement*), that is, the prime minister and the cabinet of ministers whom he or she appoints; commands the armed forces; and concludes treaties.

The president must choose a prime minister and cabinet who reflect the majority in parliament and who will carry out the program of the parliamentary majority. When the president's political party or supporters control parliament, he emerges as the dominant player in policymaking, overseeing enactment of his political agenda. When an opposition party (or parties) controls parliament, however, he or she must share power in an arrangement known as cohabitation.

The government is headed by the prime minister, who, with the ministers, directs the civil service, the government agencies, and the armed forces. The government drafts the national budget. Each ministry has a central administration divided into directorates, which are subdivided into subdirectorates. Staff remain largely the same across political elections. Legislative powers of the executive are limited, although parliament may authorize the executive to issue ordinances (*ordonnances*) in certain specifically defined areas, and individual ministers may issue subordinate orders (*arrêtés*) in their field of responsibility. Except in the case of presidential emergency powers, neither the president nor the prime minister may rule by decree. Cabinets, chaired by the president, usually meet weekly at the Élysée Palace, the presidential residence in Paris.

Parliament consists of two houses that possess approximately coequal powers centering most essentially on consideration of legislation and

Regions of France

GREAT BRITAIN

North Sea

THE NETHERLANDS

Nord-Pas-de-Calais

GERMANY

Strait of Dover

BELGIUM

Lille

LUXEMBOURG

English Channel (La Manche)

Haute-Normandie

Amiens

Picardie

Rouen

Caen

Paris

Metz

Lorraine

Strasbourg

Basse-Normandie

Île de France

Châlons-en-Champagne

Brittany (Bretagne)

Rennes

Champagne-Ardenne

Alsace

Orléans

Pays-de-la-Loire

Nantes

Centre

Dijon

Burgundy (Bourgogne)

Franche-Comté

Besançon

ATLANTIC OCEAN

Poitiers

SWITZER-LAND

Poitou-Charentes

Limoges

Lyon

Bay of Biscay

Limousin

Clermont-Ferrand

Rhône-Alpes

Auvergne

ITALY

N

Bordeaux

Aquitaine

Gulf of Gascogne

Midi-Pyrénées

Toulouse

Montpellier

Provence-Alpes-Côte-d'Azur

Marseille

MONACO

Languedoc-Roussillon

Gulf of Lion

P Y R E N E E S

■ Regional capital
---- Regional boundary

0   100 miles
0   100 km

ANDORRA

SPAIN

Corsica

Mediterranean Sea

© Infobase Publishing

adoption of the national budget. The lower house is the National Assembly (Assemblée Nationale). Its 577 deputies (*députés*) are elected for five-year terms in single-seat constituencies. The chamber may force the resignation of the executive cabinet if an absolute majority votes a motion of censure. The deputies, presided over by the president of the National Assembly, meet in the Palais Bourbon. In a tradition dating from the first National Assembly (1789–91), deputies from left-wing parties sit to the left as seen from the president's seat and those from right-wing parties sit to the right.

The upper house, the Senate (Sénat), is composed of 346 members, all but 12 of whom (chosen by citizens abroad) are elected indirectly by a college of locally elected officials, including department councilors, regional councilors, mayors, and National Assembly deputies. Senators are elected for six-year terms, and one-half of their numbers are elected every three years. Presided over by a president, the Senate meets at the Palais du Luxembourg. Its powers are very limited and, in the event of a disagreement between the two houses, the National Assembly prevails. Some members of parliament customarily hold a second local office, such as city mayor, in a practice dubbed the *cumul* of electoral offices.

Legislative bills proposed by members of parliament (*propositions de loi*) start in the house where they originate. Bills proposed by the government (*projets de loi*) start in the house of the government's choice. All laws must be signed by the president.

Certain advisory bodies also exist. The Council of State (Conseil d'État) must review all bills introduced by the government before submission to parliament, and it protects basic rights as an institution to which individual citizens may appeal who have claims against the administration. A Constitutional Court reviews proposed laws referred to it by either the legislative or the executive branches to determine whether they conform to the constitution. An Economic and Social Council proffers advice on questions pertaining to social and economic policies.

The judiciary is independent of the other two branches. Ordinary courts, intermediate appellate courts, and the Supreme Court (Cour de cassation) adjudicate civil and criminal cases. The Conseil d'État is the supreme court of appeal for matters dealt with by administrative courts. Ordinary courts, including correctional tribunals and police, criminal, commercial, and industrial courts, settle disputes that arise between citizens, as well as those between citizens and corporate entities. Judges are government employees, for the most part appointed, and they are granted special statutory protection from the executive. Trial by jury does not exist except for severe criminal cases, which fall under the jurisdiction of the Courts of Assize. A civil law system is in place in which written statutes form the basis of legal rulings. Basic principles stem from the Napoleonic Code.

Local government centered traditionally on the prefect (*préfet*), the chief official appointed by the national government, which he or she represents at the local level in each of the country's 100 departments (*départements*), in addition to the General Council, a local elected body. Departments are subdivided into districts (*arrondissements*). Decentralization, however, which began in the 1980s, led to the creation of 26 regions, each headed by a regional council directly elected, and a president. The councils have been given a wide range of administrative and fiscal powers. At the lowest level, there are about 36,000 communes (*communes*), each headed by a municipal council (*conseil municipal*) and a mayor (*maire*). Paris, Lyon, and Marseille have popularly elected mayors and are divided into districts, each having its district council.

There are five overseas departments—Guadeloupe, Martinique, French Guiana, Réunion, and Mayotte (as of 2011)—and all are subject to French and European Union (EU) law. So-called overseas collectivities, including French Polynesia, New Caledonia, Saint-Martin, Saint-Barthélemy, and Saint-Pierre and Miquelon, have their own statutory laws and different levels of autonomy. All overseas jurisdictions are represented in both chambers of the national parliament.

Everyone over the age of 18 is eligible to vote. Voting is not compulsory. In general elections, France uses a two-round, first-past-the-post polling method by which an absolute majority of the votes cast is required to be elected in the first round. Otherwise, there is a runoff, and the top-scoring candidate (or list of candidates) is elected, whatever the percentage of votes obtained in a second round. Hybrid systems employing both first-past-the-post and proportional voting are used in regional elections and those in the larger communes. Elections in France always take place on Sundays. Referendums are also held to register citizens' opinions on certain issues, especially those concerning amendments to the constitution and adoption of EU legislation.

Political parties have traditionally been numerous, and rule by coalitions, which often entailed complex political negotiations, characterized previous republican regimes. Under the Fifth Republic, a gradual coalescence into two strong parties on the left and the right has emerged. Current major parties, on the left, include the Socialist Party and, on the right, the Union for a Popular Movement. The Greens, the Communists, and the right-wing National Front are also active.

A prominent player in international affairs for centuries and an acknowledged great power from the 17th through the mid-20th centuries, France continues to play an active global role, with a sizable military and a substantial humanitarian presence. A nuclear power, it holds one of the five permanent seats on the UN Security Council and is a member of many international organizations and agencies. Its influence in many of its former colonies in Africa remains strong.

The Economy

The French economy is large, modern, robust, and diverse. Consistently ranked among the top tier of advanced nations, France stood as the world's fifth-largest economy in 2009 measured by nominal gross domestic product (GDP).

The economy today traces its roots to the ambitious and highly successful program of modernization launched by the state after World War II (*dirigisme*). Thirty years of unprecedented growth ensued, and an affluent society characterized by a standard of living equal to those of other advanced nations emerged. *Dirigisme* peaked in the 1980s, when, under a left-wing government, many industries and banks were nationalized. Governments have since steadily retreated from direct economic intervention, giving corporate capital greater freedom to operate in partially or fully privatizing many large companies and banks, including Air France, Renault, and France Telecom. Nevertheless, the state continues to play a major role in the economy, owning shares in an array of industries, most especially those in power, public transport, and defense. Government spending, at 52.7 percent of GDP (2008 est.), is among the highest in the Group of Eight (G-8) industrial nations. A dynamic services sector accounts for a growing share of economic activity. Luxury and high-technology industries in Paris are joined by large-scale manufacturing in the suburbs, making the capital region France's biggest industrial producer.

Leading economic sectors include machinery, chemicals, pharmaceuticals, electronics, textiles, and shipbuilding. Developments in telecommunications, aerospace, and transportation set world standards for quality and innovation. The consortium Airbus, headquartered in Toulouse, is a global competitor in aircraft manufacturing, the Arianne rocket rivals those of NASA, and Renault and Peugeot automobiles—the two biggest car models—travel the world's roads. France's high-speed train, the TGV (*train à grande vitesse*), has won global plaudits. Banking and financial services play prominent roles. The country is also a major manufacturer of military equipment. The government is the chief customer for guns, warships, aircraft, and nuclear arms, but great quantities of French weaponry are also sold worldwide. France's global prominence attests to the important role that research and development play in the economy, spending for which equals approximately 2.3 percent of GDP.

Membership in labor unions accounts for about 5 percent of the private-sector workforce and is concentrated in the manufacturing, transportation, and heavy-industry fields. Most unions are affiliated

France's renowned high-speed train—the TGV—on the Ventabren Viaduct near Aix-en-Provence, 2001 (Claude Paris/Associated Press)

with one among three competing national federations, including the Communist-dominated General Labor Confederation (CGT), the largest and most powerful; the Workers' Force (FO); and the French Democratic Confederation of Labor (CFDT).

France played a central role in the work of postwar European integration, without which, given the size of its economy, efforts would not have succeeded such that the European Union (EU) has become one of the world's most powerful economic blocs; its currency, the euro, which replaced the franc in 2002, rivals the U.S. dollar in monetary might. France is western Europe's third-leading trading nation, after Germany and the United Kingdom. French trade with EU countries accounts for 60 percent of the total. The United States is France's ninth-largest trading partner.

France's luxury industries occupy important economic niches and have made the nation synonymous with high fashion, perfumes, and cosmetics. L'Oréal Group is the world's largest cosmetics company, and some 20 fashion houses, most now owned by conglomerates, help to set world trends. Tourism is centrally important. France welcomed more than 81 million visitors in 2007, accounting for more than 8 percent of GDP and making it the world's number-one tourist destination in rankings by the World Tourism Organization.

France has been an overwhelmingly agrarian country for most of its history—rural inhabitants made up about 85 percent of the total population in the 18th century. Agriculture has been historically the mainstay of the French economy, and it remains important today, contributing about 2.5 percent of GDP. The modern agricultural population is small, having shrunk considerably since postwar modernization, but it remains prominent in comparison with other advanced nations (about 4 percent of the labor force), a continuing legacy of the widespread existence of the traditional small family farm characteristic of the French countryside in the wake of the Revolution.

French farmers are vigorous lobbyists on behalf of their interests before both national and European authorities, and the government provides considerable subsidies to the sector. The country is self-sufficient in basic food production, is the largest exporter of agricultural products among EU members, and produces about 25 percent of EU agricultural products. It is one of the Continent's leaders in the value of agricultural exports, which include chiefly wheat, sugar beets, beef, wine, and cheese.

About a third of the national territory consists of arable land, and of the total productive area, about 63 percent is under cultivation, 33 percent in pasture, and 4 percent in vineyard. Viticulture has been practiced since antiquity, and the great commercial vineyards of Burgundy, Bordeaux, Alsace, and the Loire and Rhône valleys are world renowned. Champagne is synonymous with the province of its origin. Historically, the most productive farms have been those of northern France. Cereals (wheat, barley, oats, corn, and sorghum), industrial crops (sugar beets, flax), and root crops (potatoes) predominate. Dairy and vegetable farms in Brittany as well as flower gardens, olive gardens, and orchards in Provence are also important. Fruits produced on a large scale include apples (most especially in Normandy), pears, peaches, and cherries. The long coastline, dotted with small harbors, has supported an active fishing industry for centuries. Cod, herring, skate, whiting, sole, tuna, sardines, and lobsters compose the principal catch. Aquaculture consists chiefly of oyster and mussel production. Mountain and upland areas support a timber industry, as well as sheep and goat raising. France is considered one of the world's cheese "capitals"—more than 1,000 different types exist.

Important natural minerals include coal, iron ore, bauxite, zinc, uranium, antimony, potash, feldspar, and gypsum. Intent on reducing dependence on fossil fuels and, with no indigenous supplies of oil, acutely conscious of its vulnerability to a cutoff of foreign sources in the wake of the oil crisis of 1973, the country embarked in the mid-1970s on an ambitious investment program in nuclear energy. By the early 21st century, some 59 nuclear power stations, mostly along the Loire and Rhône Rivers, were supplying 87 percent of the country's electricity, which makes France the largest user of this energy source among developed countries. Much of it is also exported. Disposal of nuclear wastes remains contentious among a small group of activists. Common environmental concerns include forest damage from acid rain, air pollution from industrial and vehicle emissions, and water pollution from urban wastes and agricultural runoff.

1

BEGINNINGS TO THE
LAND OF THE GAULS
(PREHISTORY–52 B.C.E.)

The land that would become France emerged out of the subcontinental landmasses that, shifting over immense periods of time, formed the continent of Europe. Warmer and colder periods alternated until climatic conditions proved propitious enough to permit the growth of vegetation to support animal and, in time, human life.

The first humans appeared probably from Africa. They evolved as they did elsewhere in the world to emerge as modern humans, namely, *Homo sapiens sapiens,* and their level of technical know-how advanced accordingly. Life was everywhere mobile. Small bands of hunter-gatherers lived off the land, dwelling in caves or in hovels and huts made of animal skins. Slowly they began to acquire attributes of a culture, devising belief systems that gave evidence of a spiritual awareness and creating artistic works, spectacularly on display in cave wall paintings, expressive of an urge to record their world.

Acquisition of greater skills proceeded, propelled by advances in knowledge of metals. The Stone Age passed from the use of flaked flint implements to those worked in copper, and progressed in turn to Bronze and Iron Ages, changes made manifest by the tools and weapons left in burial sites. Hunting and gathering gave way to settled farming. Populations continued to move, and peoples identified as Celts appeared who would come to create societies sufficiently sophisticated to carry out agriculture, crafts, and trade on a wide scale. Strong tribes emerged, ruled by aristocrats, in which druidic priests and warriors were the most respected members.

Within the dense forests, the inhabitants lived scattered about the countryside in isolated small villages or farmsteads, using hill forts as refuges and defensive centers since fighting was endemic in this society. Only along the Mediterranean coast did conditions differ. City-states modeled on those of ancient Greece clung to the shoreline here, and for hundreds of years thriving urban residents busily traded with their Celtic neighbors near and far. But their links to the classical world to the East from which they had sprung took pride of place. They would look here, where civilizations had advanced farthest, when dangers lurked, and it was from here a power would come whose armies proved so successful in repelling enemy threats that it would come to rule not only along the coast but also in all the lands, which the conqueror would call Gaul, to the north and west.

The Land Takes Shape

Geologists theorize that through Earth's 4.5-billion-year history, super-continents periodically formed and broke apart in a cyclical configuration until, about 250 million years ago, a single large land area—Pangaea (Greek for "entire Earth")—emerged, surrounded by a single enormous ocean. In time, Pangaea, too, split asunder under the effects of shifting tectonics. About 32 million years, ago the lands that would become Europe formed an island continent, separated from Asia by a shallow sea but possessing land bridge connections, which appeared and disappeared, to North America via Greenland. Sea levels rose and fell and sediments accumulated. The sea that divided Europe and Asia gradually dried up, and Europe emerged as the western appendage of Earth's largest landmass.

Intensely cold climates—far colder than temperatures today—helped shape the geography of Europe's westernmost reaches. Ice sheets spread from Arctic regions to northern Europe, inducing permanently frozen ground—permafrost conditions. The buildup of moisture in the form of ice on land led to a lowering of the sea level, extending the coastline seaward and repeatedly joining what would become Britain to France and the Low Countries. A small ice cap spread radially from the Alps, and very small mountain glaciers occurred in the Pyrenees and the Massif Central. During the last Ice Age some 20,000 years ago, northern France exhibited tundralike conditions. Great blankets of wind-blown dust were deposited over the land. Steppe conditions prevailed in central regions. Recurrent melting of the ice during interglacial periods raised sea levels. Substantial topographical changes took place as coastlines, river valleys, and estuaries took shape. Only the far south escaped the cold. Here in the Mediterranean area, where warmer and drier conditions prevailed, more lush vegetation and more abundant animal life could be found. It was here that human beings made their first appearance.

The First Humans Arrive
The Paleolithic Era

The Paleolithic, or Old Stone Age, era extends over a vest period, roughly from 2.6 or 2.5 million years ago to around 10,000 B.C.E. Over this long span, warmer and cooler climates fluctuated periodically, the ice sheets correspondingly advancing and retreating. The first human beings to reach Europe were probably contemporaries of the later Australopithecines of East Africa, and the most likely point of entry for prehistoric immigrants lay across the Strait of Gibraltar. Though it appears that at no time were the two continents actually linked by a land bridge, the width of the strait, at probably no more than three or four miles (4.8 to 6.4 km), would not have precluded the ability of primitive humans, in common with other nonaquatic mammals, to swim the distance.

The earliest evidence of the genus *Homo*, namely, *Homo habilis* or *Homo erectus*, comes from a group of carved quartz fragments unearthed at Cilhac in the Massif Central, which have been dated at 1.8 million years B.C.E. Standardized multipurpose tools first appeared in France some 500,000 to 300,000 years ago. Finds at Saint-Acheul and Abbeville in the Somme basin and in the Massif Central and the Pyrenees have uncovered implements ranging from simple, small, delicately trimmed stone flakes to large, finished hand axes.

During the Middle Paleolithic era (ca. 300,000 to ca. 30,000 B.C.E.), evidence of cooking and burial of the dead appeared with discovery of the remains of five hearths and reddened earth uncovered at Saint-Estève-Janson in Provence, which date to about 200,000 B.C.E. By 100,000 B.C.E., *Homo habilis* had been succeeded by Neanderthal man, whose brains, while fully equivalent to a modern human's in size, linked them structurally and functionally to their predecessors. Over a period of about 5,000 years, beginning around 40,000 B.C.E., biologically modern human beings (*Homo sapiens sapiens*) supplanted this short, stocky primitive, the exact cause of whose disappearance remains a mystery.

The earliest record of modern humans in Europe was uncovered in 1868 at a cave at Cro-Magnon, in the village of Les Eyzies in the Dordogne Department, where five skeletons (three adult males, one adult female, and a child) were found, along with carved reindeer antlers, ivory pendants, and shells. The site is dated to between 34,000 and 36,000 years ago.

These years mark the start of the Upper Paleolithic era, which lasted for some 20,000 years, during which prehistoric humans reached their highest level of achievement, and for which abundant evidence exists in France. The population expanded, technology advanced, and the first glimmerings of social organization and culture appeared. Small bands of hunter-gatherers, perhaps 25 to 100 individuals, emerged, tracking game and collecting nuts, leafy vegetables, insects, and fruits such as berries, which they used for food and medicine. Women played an active role in gathering food. These groups lived in caves or in temporary huts and hovels made of animal skins, mostly alongside rivers and lakes. Life was hard. The teeth of unearthed skeletons, though not decayed, are often extremely worn, right down to the roots, no doubt because they were used as tools, to soften skins and draw threads. Life was perforce short and dangerous. Humans shared the land with animals, some of which they hunted—mammoth, reindeer, bison, and horse—and some of which hunted them—saber-toothed tigers, lions, and hyenas.

The Upper Paleolithic can be traced through a succession of archaeological periods, proceeding from the Aurignacian culture (ca. 40,000

So-called unicorn, from the Large Hall in the caves at Lascaux (Bildarchiv Preussischer Kulturbesitz/Art Resource, NY)

LASCAUX

On September 12, 1940, four teenage boys discovered a series of caves near the village of Montignac in the Dordogne Department. They found painted on the walls nearly 2,000 figures, many still vividly colored. Estimated to have been created some 16,000 years ago, they consist primarily of images of large animals, many in realistic poses showing motion. Felines, horses, stags, and bison are depicted. Most impressive are four large, black bulls, one of which at 17 feet (5.2 m) is the largest animal yet found in cave art. The level of skill astounds. The ability to employ perspective, apparent in the crossed hind legs of the bison in a painting called *The Crossed Bison,* would not be repeated until the Renaissance.

Lascaux is one among a number of sites in the Vézère valley of southwestern France that have been discovered, providing evidence that this region was probably a major population center during the Upper Paleolithic era. The buildup of excessive carbon dioxide from crowds of visitors visibly damaged the paintings and compelled closure of the caves in 1963. Reproductions are on display.

to 28,000 B.C.E.) to the Gravettian (ca. 28,000 to 22,000 B.C.E.) to the Solutrean (ca. 22,000 to 18,000 B.C.E.), each distinguished by the quality—more precise as each period progresses—of the implements produced. The Magdalenian culture (ca. 18,000 to 10,000 B.C.E.), discovered in a rock shelter in the Vézère valley in the Dordogne, is identified by its flint tools and elaborately worked bone antlers and ivory implements. Life revolved around hunting, mostly reindeer but also red deer and horse, and the culture of the period is evident most magnificently in the display of artistic ability left on the walls of caves and rock shelters, such as those at Lascaux.

The preponderance of finds at sites in southwestern France testifies to this area's status as the region of modern France to be most consistently occupied. Upper Paleolithic France was subject to glacial conditions more rigorous than those during the preceding era, and although the ice sheets across northern Europe did not reach the country, they produced violent winds, which deposited fine dust that turned northern France into a desert. When more temperate phases ensued, shrub vegetation replaced arid steppe, facilitating the return of large animals and, with them, human beings.

Finds associated with that of the Azillan culture (ca. 10,000 to 8,500 B.C.E.) feature tools of the same form as those immediately preceding, but now they are smaller and cruder, giving evidence that their makers were less well nourished than their forebears, a possible consequence of an inability to adapt to changes brought by the melting ice.

The Mesolithic Era

The last of the great glaciers that had waxed and waned for millennia retreated between 10,000 and 9,000 years ago. The onset of rising temperatures led to decreased precipitation, which reduced available water supplies, leading, in turn, to a less nomadic lifestyle.

During the Mesolithic, or Middle Stone Age, era (ca.10,000 to 4,000 B.C.E.), humans in the area that would become France shifted gradually from hunting and gathering to trapping wild game, including deer and boar, in the vast forests that now began to appear, and to fishing in the warming waters of the ocean and rivers. Animal bones but also the remains of fish and crustaceans, including snails—the first evidence of what would become a famed French delicacy—tell us what Mesolithic humans ate. Their diets, too, included more vegetables, grains, nuts, berries, and herbs. Tools and weapons featured sharper points, and crude pottery began to be made.

The temperatures warmed further, and the forests, widespread by 8,500 B.C.E., began to retreat—except in alluvial valleys and fertile basins—in southeastern France in the wake of the progressive spread of a Mediterranean climate. It was here that evidence of primitive farming first appeared. By 8,000 B.C.E., various grasses as well as legumes, such as lentils and peas, began to be gathered. Dogs were domesticated, joined later, around 6,000 B.C.E., by goats and sheep. Sheepherding arrived in southern France, having spread there from the Middle East, and so, too, the earliest efforts at soil cultivation came from western Asia, where new techniques for producing food had been devised three or four thousand years before. Mesolithic culture lingered longest in central and northern France. By the time tillage appeared here, introduced in another 1,500 years by way of the Danube River valley, a new era had begun.

The Neolithic Era

During the Neolithic, or New Stone Age, era (ca. 4,000 to 1,800 B.C.E.), in what amounted to a veritable revolution, reliance on foods produced by crop cultivation no longer supplemented nomadic hunting and gathering, as before, but now replaced them entirely. Farming meant staying in one place, so the growth of agriculture made permanent dwellings possible. Mud brick houses coated with plaster began to appear. Floors were covered with mats and skins.

Planting proliferated and regional variations emerged. In southern areas, corn, millet, and barley were grown combined with herding sheep, which were seasonally migrated between uplands in summer and lowlands in winter. This Mediterranean type of farming spread northward into the Massif Central and the Alps, evidence for which exists in the distinctive forms and decoration of the pottery called "Cardial" or "Cardium" found in the regions. In northern France, agriculture developed through displacement of local inhabitants by newcomers from central Europe, who brought their farming techniques with them. They were distinguished by the large houses they built, which sheltered big families. Villages of several hundred residents appeared. Forests were burned to clear land for planting wheat and barley, and cattle and pigs, now also domesticated, were bred, though rarely sheep, which thrived better in more arid regions. Their settlements, like those of southerners, can be traced from their pottery, a type known as "Ribbon" or "Linear" for its scrolled patterns that first appeared in the Rhine River valley, including Alsace, in the last centuries of the fifth millennium and in the Paris and Loire basins in the first half of the fourth.

Agricultural techniques evolved and expanded, culminating in the appearance, between 4,500 and 3,500 B.C.E., of a culture called Chasséan, named for the type of site discovered near Chassey-le-Camp in Burgundy. Chasséan farmers both cultivated rye and millet and maintained orchards of apples and pears, as well as herds of oxen, sheep, and goats. They lived in individual huts grouped into small villages of several hundred people. Undecorated pottery, stone tools, and wooden canoes have been unearthed. An abundance of statues honoring a fertility goddess provides evidence of both the development of religious beliefs and the relatively high status enjoyed by women. Chasséan culture spread widely to encompass most of present-day France.

By approximately 2,500 B.C.E., Chasséan gave way to what has been labeled the Seine-Oise-Marne culture (2,500 to 1,700 B.C.E.), named for the region in which it was centered. Known most famously for its megalithic tombs, these edifices have been discovered especially in Brittany and in north and west-central France. Large upright standing stones called menhirs (from Breton *men* [stone] and *hir* [long]) dot the countryside from the Cévennes to northwest France, where about

7

1,200 exist. Most famous are those of Brittany, which include the largest at Locmariaquer (65 feet [20 m] high) and the most intriguing, namely, the stones at Carnac, where more than 3,000 individual menhirs are arranged in four groups in rows stretching across 2.5 miles (4 km). Their function remains a mystery. The common megalithic type is the dolmen, a chamber consisting of large upright stones with one or more flat capstones forming the roof. There also exist gallery graves—parallel walls of stone slabs erected to form a corridor covered with a line of capstones and incorporating a port-hole slab—as well as rock tombs dug to a similar design in the chalk valleys of the Marne River. Distinctive pottery—smooth and undecorated—has been found within them, and some include art images carved on walls, notably highly stylized femalelike figures usually interpreted as deities or fertility symbols. The large size and structured layout of these tombs required a lengthy collective effort, which presupposes a fairly well-organized society. And because these tomb forms show strong links with those found in other areas in northern and western Europe, they bear witness to the first systematic development of coastal navigation in the North Sea, English Channel, and Atlantic Ocean.

The great stone tombs mark the end of a period of population increase and cultural differentiation from which a new age—the age of

Interior of a large dolmen under the Merchant's Table in Locmariaquer, Brittany (Library of Congress)

metal—emerged about the turn of the third millennium B.C.E., when for the first time evidence appears of humankind's ability to work these harder substances. Copper came first, introduced between about 2,500 and 1,800 B.C.E. An extensive copper industry has been identified in the Cévennes. The culture that marked the change from Neolithic to the Copper (or Chalcolithic) Age is called the Beaker culture. Though its origins remain uncertain, perhaps deriving from trading contacts with the eastern Mediterranean, it is represented throughout France. Certainly the metal-using culture that arose in Brittany was established as a result of contacts along the Channel coast. Intense commercial activity occurred here in the second millennium B.C.E., in which Nordic, British, and even Aegean peoples searched for new sources of metal—copper in Cornwall; tin in Cornwall, Brittany, and the lower Loire region; and gold in Ireland. In addition to their copper metallurgy, the Beaker people are distinguished by the pottery that gives their culture its name; it consists of a bell-shaped vase of bright red or black with a flat or rounded base. Since their culture is found everywhere in western Europe, the Beaker folk must have been highly mobile. The search for new sources of metal would spawn new societies.

The Bronze Age

Just as copper replaced flint, so bronze, an alloy of copper and tin, came to be highly sought as a superior, tougher metal. Its use spread, though at first it was a luxury reserved for those fortunate enough to possess knowledge of mineral deposits. Introduced by a people who produced distinctive burial urns and weapons, a society of metallurgists, merchants, and stock raisers emerged in Brittany, for which evidence exists in grave goods that include massive weapons, rich and varied amber objects, and even gold. Bronze Age cultures peaked between approximately 1,500 and 1,200 B.C.E. Hoards of bronze items have been found in Atlantic coastal areas, Alsace, and the Rhône River valley. The products of Atlantic workshops—flanged axes, bracelets, spears—were widely exported, giving rise to secondary work sites in central France. Use of metals lagged, however, in southern France, which remained largely a pastoral society. The sporadic finds here are more often imports than local products.

The Urnfield culture appeared about 1,100 B.C.E. and, by 800 B.C.E., had spread throughout France except for Atlantic areas. Practitioners of a unique burial ritual in which the dead were individually cremated and their ashes, burned on a funeral pyre, were placed in an urn and interred in a cemetery, they are identified by the shape and decoration of the urns and other types of grave goods deposited in them. The finest Urnfield bronzes were produced in higher alpine locales. Bronze-hilted swords, pins, pendants, belts, and harness pieces have been found. Helmets and body armor were produced for warriors. The quantity of axes and sickles unearthed testify to the important role that agriculture must have played in this society. Then about 800 B.C.E., newcomers began to arrive gradually, bringing with them knowledge of yet another new metal.

The Iron Age

Between about 1,000 B.C.E. and 700 B.C.E., herdsmen and warriors from north of the Alps introduced into France a knowledge of ironworking. Equipped with a superior military technology in the swords made of iron—the hardest metal yet—that they wielded, they swept all before them, bringing what prehistorians have called the Halstatt culture—named after its type site in Austria—to areas that encompass about two-thirds of France today. Only Urnfield peoples in the southwest and the bronze workers of Brittany resisted their advance. The first iron swords mixed with those of bronze appeared about 800 B.C.E. By now, plows, carts, and horses were in use, permitting expansion of cultivation into upland areas.

Late Iron Age (500 to 100 B.C.E.) peoples identified with Halstatt culture formed a group of migrants of Indo-European origin defined as Celts, from Greek *keltoi*, who, though they possessed diverse characteristics, held in common similarities in material artifacts, social organization, mythological beliefs, and, above all, language. Though evidence is inconclusive, they appear to have developed skills such as metalworking and certain cultural traits from peoples inhabiting the Balkan Peninsula of southeastern Europe. Celts began to settle about 450 B.C.E., and by about 100 B.C.E., they had spread throughout present-day France.

Profound changes took place. Completely new arrays of pottery, jewelry, and weaponry appeared. Known as the La Tène culture, named for an archaeological site in Switzerland, it emerged gradually out of the earlier Halstatt culture without any definitive break. Rather, its rise reflected the by now considerable influences brought by trading links with Greek and, later, Etruscan civilizations flourishing in the Mediterranean peninsulas. Metalwork in bronze, iron, and gold—vessels, helmets, shields, and jewelry, especially torcs (neck rings) and elaborate clasps (fibulae)—identify this culture, together with the elegant, curvilinear animal and vegetal forms characteristic of decoration.

La Tène culture developed most especially in northeastern regions, areas with rich iron-ore deposits and dense forests, which provided timber for houses and cleared land for farming. In the vicinity of the Marne River, a distinctive local variant appeared, distinguished above all by its burial practices, in which the frequency of chariot burials is most striking. They provide vivid evidence of the emergence of a class of warrior elites. Over time, powerful local chieftains came to rule over clusters of people, and the tribes that took shape could be found scattered across the countryside. Forts made of timbered palisades appeared on hills. Towns (Latin, *oppidá;* sing. *oppidum*), some of them outgrowths of the hill forts, began to form about 250 B.C.E. Dwellings were no longer made of masonry but wood, which had been worked into shape once craftsmen acquired carpentry skills. Ritual shafts were dug in which votive offerings were made, and the discovery of carvings with representations of severed heads and elaborate burial goods points to a belief in an afterlife.

Foreign objects found in burial deposits also testify to extensive trade contacts. Because advanced civilization arose early in Mediterranean lands, the southern coastlands of France were the earliest to be touched by their cultures. Phoenicians came first, stepping ashore to trade at present-day Monaco and Port Vendres. Prospering in their homeland since early in the first millennium B.C.E., Greeks fanned out across the Mediterranean world, stopping not just to trade but also to found permanent settlements. Sailing from the Greek city-state of Phocaea, in modern-day Turkey, they established a colony at Massilia in about 600 B.C.E., which, as Marseille today, is France's oldest city. Depredations induced by Greek city-states at war among themselves and with Persians invading Greece from Asia drove the arrival of newcomers. Coastal sub-colonies of Massilia were settled at Olbia (Hyère), Antipolis (Antibes), Nicaea (Nice), and Agatha Tyche (Agde). The conquest of Phocaea by Persia in about 545 B.C.E. brought a mass influx into Massilia.

These Greek communities made trading contacts gradually with nearby interior areas, including up the Rhône River valley, with the peoples of the La Tène culture. Writing later in the fifth century C.E., Roman authors would give a name to the inhabitants living here, *galli*, a Latin term that probably originated as the name of a minor tribe. An entire region came to be called Gallia (Gaul)—the name the Romans would give to continental Europe's western heartland and the territory that today comprises most of France.

The Gauls

By 400 B.C.E., Celtic groups—the Gauls—had spread across much of western Europe. Various tribes, which the Romans later called *pagi*, emerged that ruled over assorted bits of territory. The Romans would define these areas as "nations" (Latin, *civitates;* sing. *civitas*). According to Julius Caesar (100–44 B.C.E.), the Gauls proper lived in Celtica, between the Garonne River and the line of the Seine and Marne Rivers. Constituting essentially an extension of La Tène culture, their societies were far from primitive, though far less advanced than those found at the time in Greece and Italy. They excelled in mining and metalworking, but above all, they were highly skilled farmers and stock raisers. They introduced heavy iron plows, pulled by horses, and they used sickles and reapers to facilitate harvesting. Some farmers used lime to enrich the soil.

Specialization in skills led to distinct occupational groupings—farmers, miners, artisans, and traders—while a social hierarchy developed that, at its apex, found great aristocrats in possession of much wealth acquired, in this overwhelmingly agricultural society, by their control of extensive property. Scattered at intervals in clearings in the vast forests, farmsteads dotted the landscape, together with unfortified artisanal and commercial centers (*vici*) and, for protection in time of need, hill forts, some of which dated back hundreds of years, that were sited generally on riverbanks in the major river valleys. The hill forts were the power centers from which chieftains ruled. Chiefs had their bands of personal partisans bound to their leader by ties of service in return for his protection. Below them were the artisans, peasants, and herdsmen.

Warrior-kings and their followers prized valor in battle but also wisdom, embodied in the person of the religious leader, the druid. Although divided into tribes, the Gauls practiced a set of common beliefs that testifies to a cultural unity. Druid priests played important roles as an aristocratic caste recruited from among the ruling classes. They presided over rituals, including human sacrifices to their gods and goddesses—there were more than 400—and together with the poet-musicians (bards), they kept alive old Celtic myths and traditions. Well-educated elites, the druids comprised the teachers and judges of tribal life, and they were exempt from military service.

Such service constituted the central focus of Celtic society. Across the landscape, warfare was endemic. Groups of warriors, brandishing often finely decorated shields and weapons, would face off, raising a mighty din of war cries and sounding their famous trumpets before joining battle. Tribes fought tribes, ready to make and break alliances to suit the needs of individual chiefs. The lack of political organization made it easier for a power of sufficient strength to impose its will. At the same time, the developing social and economic infrastructure that existed in Gaul provided ready-made support for any invader intent on conquering these lands. And once conquered, such an infrastructure would facilitate holding them. Such an invader appeared in the years just before 100 B.C.E. The newcomer arrived from the south—from Italy—where the thriving city-state of Rome had been expanding its power at an ever-growing rate.

2

ROMAN GAUL
(52 B.C.E.–481 C.E.)

In the waning decades of the pre-Christian era, rule by Rome was already well entrenched in areas that would become southern France, the republic's legions having conquered vast tracts from the Pyrenees to the lower Rhône River region. The pervasive presence of Rome across all the lands that today make up France would quickly ensue, following the conquest of the remainder of ancient Gaul by legions under Julius Caesar, completed by 52 B.C.E. The Romans granted the defeated Celtic peoples a significant degree of autonomy, but their armed might now fully on display in their military campsites and marching columns, they left no doubt that they had come intending to stay. The conquered Celtic nations—hitherto a fractious, violent lot—settled down, exchanging political and military subordination for peace and order. Romanization proceeded gradually and struck deep roots. Administrative cities and countryside villas flourished, knit together by a sturdy system of roads. In the south—in areas closest to Italy—a Roman, and elsewhere, a mixed Gallo-Roman, culture emerged. Latin was spoken by a majority of the Gauls by the first century C.E. By then, too, Christianity had been introduced. In Roman Gaul lay the foundations of all continental Western Europe's future history.

The general peace of the early Roman Empire, disturbed only by occasional minor rebellions and brief civil wars, grew increasingly troubled by the late third century, when in conjunction with a slow diminution of Rome's power, incursions increased in frequency and intensity across the Rhine and Danube frontiers made by marauding Germanic tribes—barbarians to the Romans. The empire coped as best it could. It battled back, and various administrative redivisions were decreed. For a time, Gaul was governed by a separate line of emperors. Sometimes pushed themselves by pressures from enemies behind them, tribes were allowed asylum. They settled in frontier areas and became military allies of Rome. Sicambri, Chamari, and others took service and land under Roman rule on the far northern fringes of Gaul. The Goths appeared in eastern Europe in the late fourth century, and a western branch—the Visigoths—occupied areas along the Danube.

Both Germanic power within the empire and pressure from tribes outside its borders increased, and a general unease persisted. Roman power in the West collapsed utterly in the early fifth century, and Rome itself was sacked in 410 by the Visigoths. The subsequent settlement of the entire tribe, estimated to have totaled some 200,000 people, in southwest Gaul served as a model for absorption of Germanic peoples. Alamans arrived in Alsace, and Burgundians occupied the borderlands of today's eastern France. On the northern frontier, the Salians advanced south and west. Pushing progressively farther and farther, they and allied groups eventually emerged supreme over all of modern France, save for the extreme south, where the Visigoths held sway, and the Brittany Peninsula, where Celtic peoples clung to control. They coalesced under the leadership of a sole, powerful ruler—Clovis—and under a name—Franks—that they bequeathed to a country whose origins they would lay.

Roman Conquest and Pacification

When Julius Caesar, proconsul of the Roman Republic, halted on the banks of the middle Rhône River in 58 B.C.E. to engage the Helvetii tribe, he stood on familiar territory. In this area, called Gallia Transalpine (Gaul across the Alps) in what is today Provence in southern France, Romans had been governing for 75 years. The Greek city-state of Massilia had long been an ally of Rome, though it had suffered from a siege by Caesar for having supported his rival Pompey (106–48 B.C.E.) in their civil war (49–44 B.C.E.) for rulership of the late republic. The city called for help in controlling Celto-Ligurian peoples, who were its immediate neighbors, and Rome responded, dispatching its legions, who arrived, first in 154 B.C.E., when they quickly departed, and again in 125 B.C.E., when they stayed. They secured their presence in August 121 B.C.E., when they defeated the Allobroges, a warlike Gallic tribe living between the Rhône and the Lake of Geneva.

Although Rome's motives are still debated, probable reasons for the occupation include an awareness of the geographic utility of holding an area that could serve as an outpost to defend Italy from incursions from the north, as well as to facilitate communication between Italy and possessions in Spain that Rome had acquired following the

Second Punic War (218–201 B.C.E.) with its inveterate opponent, the city-state of Carthage. The Romans settled in, founding a colony at Narbo Martius (Narbonne) in 118 B.C.E. and building a road—the Via Domitia—linking Italy to the Iberian Peninsula. So securely did Roman might take hold that at some still uncertain date the judicial status of the area changed from that of a war zone to a permanent possession of the empire. Romans came to refer to this land across the mountains as Provincia Nostra (Our Province), or simply Provincia (the Province), a name that endures as Provence.

Unrest and revolt plagued the Province for 50 years, but by the time the new governor, Julius Caesar, turned his attention to lands lying beyond, the area was reliably loyal. To Roman minds the regions to the north and west—territory that now lies in France, Belgium, and parts of Switzerland—seemed wild and forbidding, full of rushing rivers and thick, dark forests, a place that they somewhat disparagingly referred to as Gallia Comata, that is, "Long-haired Gaul," a land peopled by mustachioed barbarians sporting massive tousles of hair and wearing trousers. Their reputation for ferocity was founded in Roman consciousness when Rome's forces were beaten and the city plundered by Brennus (or Brennos) and his Celtic hordes around 390 B.C.E., the shock of that defeat instilling fear of the *terror Gallicus* forever after.

Julius Caesar identified three overall tribal regions:

> *All Gaul is divided into three parts, one of which the Belgae inhabit, the Aquitani another, those who in their own language are called Celts, in our Gauls, the third. All these differ from each other in language, customs, and laws. The river Garonne separates the Gauls from the Aquitani; the Marne and the Seine separate them from the Belgae. (Caesar, Commentaries, 1872, vol. I, 1)*

Various individual tribes made up these general groupings, and their names, too, come to us from Roman accounts: among others, the Veneti in Brittany, the Sequani in Burgundy, the Arverni in Auvergne, the Aedui in the upper Seine region, the Lingones at the headwaters of the Seine and Marne, and, among the Belgic tribes in the far north, the Eburones and the fierce Nervii. Although they were far from backward—those nearest the Roman armies had long engaged in commercial contacts, wine from Italy being in especially great demand—the Gauls fought continuously, within, between, and among tribes. Lacking order and discipline in their political and military dealings, leaders strove to win power over internal rivals and looked for aid from whomever they

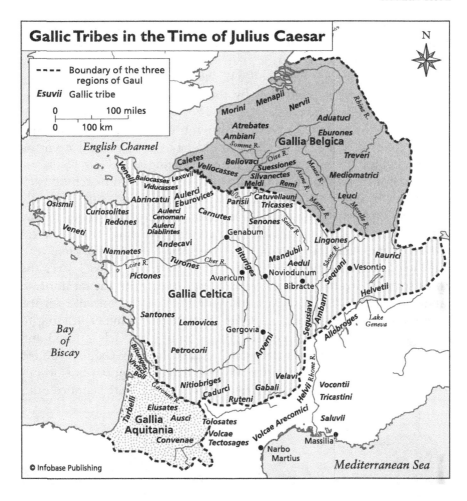

Gallic Tribes in the Time of Julius Caesar

N

- - - - Boundary of the three
regions of Gaul

Esuvii Gallic tribe

0   100 miles
0   100 km

English Channel

Morini Menapii Nervii
Atrebates   Aduatuci
Ambiani   Eburones
Somme R.   **Gallia Belgica**
Treveri
Caletes Bellovaci *Oise R.*
Veliocasses Suessiones Mediomatrici
Balocasses Lexovii Silvanectes
Viducasses Meldi Remi
Abrincatui Aulerci Catuvellauni Leuci
Osismii Eburovices Parisii Tricasses
Curiosolites Aulerci Carnutes Senones
Redones Cenomani
Veneti Aulerci
Diablintes Genabum
Namnetes Andecavi Lingones
Mandubii Raurici
Turones *Cher R.* Aedui Vesontio
Pictones Noviodunum Sequani
Avaricum Bibracte Helvetii

Gallia Celtica

Santones Segusiavi *Lake Geneva*
Lemovices Gergovia Ambarri
Allobroges

Bay
of
Biscay Petrocorii Arverni

Velavi Vocontii
Nitiobriges Gabali Tricastini
Cadurci Ruteni
Elusates
Gallia Ausci Tolosates Saluvii
Aquitania Volcae
Convenae Tectosages Volcae Arecomici
Massilia
Narbo
Martius *Mediterranean Sea*

© Infobase Publishing

could secure it. The powerful empire beckoned for some. Itself not averse to intervening when it perceived it was in its interest to do so, chiefly to advance military and political careers for victorious generals, by the 60s of the first century B.C.E., Rome stepped in regularly, even entering into a formal alliance with the Aedui, who were honored with the titles of "brother" and "friend" of the Roman people.

Tensions in Gaul were further exacerbated by pressures from Germanic tribes, whose existence in northern Europe can be detected from about the mid-fifth century B.C.E. From the third century B.C.E., Germanic groups began to move into Gaul to settle and fuse with the native Celts. In about 109 B.C.E., the Cimbri, moving down from Denmark, together with the Teutones, Aduatuci, and other allies, entered northern Gaul seeking booty and land. Such movements brought pressure on the resident peoples, threatening to displace, in particular, the Helvetii, a tribe that had originally lived beyond the Rhine River in today's Germany who had moved to areas on today's French-Swiss border, and who, by the late 70s B.C.E., began to feel embattled in their territories.

Determined to migrate westward through Gaul, they met resistance from the Aedui, whose lands they would have to cross, and from the Romans, allies of the Aedui. Diplomacy having failed, in 58 B.C.E., Caesar defeated the immigrants in battle and sent them marching back to their own region. His martial might ready to hand, other friendly Gallic nations asked for help. The Suebi, a Germanic tribe, having settled in large numbers in Alsace after coming to the aid of the Arverni and Sequani to defeat the Aedui, were beaten by Caesar in the same year, and they and their allies, under Ariovistus, were driven back over the Rhine frontier. In the following year, Caesar traveled to the far north to vanquish the Belgic tribes and to the Atlantic coast to prevail over the Veneti and their neighbors. Tensions continued to simmer, leading to a savage campaign against certain groups among the Belgae in 53 and culminating, in 52, with the defeat at Alésia of the great Gallic revolt led by Vercingétorix, the leader of the Arverni. After two more years of sporadic fighting, the last lingering sparks of resistance were stamped out.

Vercingétorix surrenders to Julius Caesar. (Art Media/HIP/Art Resource, NY)

VERCINGÉTORIX

Vercingétorix (ca. 82–46 B.C.E.) was born into a noble family of the Gallic tribe of the Arverni in the town of Gergovia in modern Auvergne. His father, Celtillus, had been killed by his own countrymen in a rebellion against his efforts to rule all of Gaul. Vercingétorix succeeded where his father had failed. Although rejected by his fellow nobles and expelled from Gergovia for attempting to rally resistance to Rome, he gathered an army of poor peasants and retook the town. Hailed now as king, he formed alliances with other tribes. Made commander in chief of a large army, he imposed strict military discipline and welded his warriors into an effective fighting force.

Rome was the hated enemy and Julius Caesar the feared commander, who, in pursuing a divide-and-rule strategy, kept the Gallic tribes in disunion to the benefit of Roman power. Launched by the Carnutes tribe, war against Rome commenced in 52 B.C.E.

Adopting an innovative strategy using scorched-earth tactics, Vercingétorix burned towns to deny the Roman legions local provisions. His armies won a few initial engagements, but they failed to stop Caesar's forward progress. Romans occupied the capital of the Bituriges, Avaricum (Bourges), killing the entire population of many thousands. Vercingétorix defeated Caesar at Gergovia, but the battle proved so costly that Gallic forces retreated to Alésia, near present-day Dijon, a major hill fort of the Mandubii tribe, surrounded by river valleys with strong defensive works. Caesar built a fortified ring around the town and set siege. To protect against Gallic forces attempting to relieve the defenders, he constructed another outer defensive ring. Despite these formidable barriers, arriving relief troops, though fewer than expected, almost succeeded, in combination with Vercingétorix's forces fighting inside Alésia, in breaking through. It took Caesar's personal intervention at the head of his troops to turn the tide. The battle remains a classic example of siege warfare, and it marked a major turning point, effectively opening up all of Gaul to Roman conquest.

Facing starvation and low morale, Vercingétorix surrendered without a fight and was imprisoned for five years in the Tulianum, the state prison of Rome. Paraded in triumph before Roman crowds in 46 B.C.E., he was put to death afterward, probably by strangulation, the customary manner of death for captured enemy leaders. Invariably depicted with long, flowing locks and endowed with a fierce, glaring stare, he is remembered for his intense pride in the independence of the Gauls and for his staunch resistance to Roman rule. Vercingétorix is honored in France as the country's first national hero.

Having conquered all of Gallia Comata, Rome had no need for so many legions. Troops were demobilized and settled in full-scale colonies (*coloniae*) of veterans at Narbo Martius, Arelate (Arles), Forum Julii (Fréjus), Baeterrae (Béziers), and Arausio (Orange). Except possibly for Forum Julii, they were set up in, or alongside, existing towns. The administration of some native centers was transformed to conform to Roman municipal arrangements as lesser colonies and their ruling aristocrats made into Roman citizens, chief among them Vienna (Vienne) of the Allobroges and Valentia (Valence) of the Segovellauni. In the south, now more tightly bound to Rome than ever, the colonies would serve as magnets advertising the attractions of Greco-Roman civilization. Roman culture and commerce struck deep roots here.

The Caesarian settlement of Gallia Comata differed dramatically from that in the far southeast. Direct Romanization was neither sought nor encouraged. Only three colonies were founded—at Noviodunum (Nyon), Raurica (Augst), and Lugdunum (Lyon), the last two after Caesar's death—all on the periphery of the newly conquered lands and all geographically located to cover a likely invasion route from the Rhine into the Province and Italy. Military occupation continued, and the power of local aristocratic leaders was strengthened by granting them gifts and concessions.

Caesar's successor after a prolonged civil war, Octavian (r. 27 B.C.E.–C.E. 14), who, in changing his name to Augustus ("revered one") and adopting the title of *princeps* (emperor), launched imperial Rome, brought administrative refinements to the region. Additional colonies of veterans and grants of privileges to local communities advanced the process of Romanization in the Province, which was renamed Gallia Narbonensis in 27 B.C.E. In recognition of its close connections with Rome, it was placed directly under the control of the Roman Senate. The rest of Gaul was formally divided into the provinces of Aquitania (Aquitaine), Lugdunensis (Celtic or Lyonnaise Gaul), and Belgica (Belgic Gaul), a tripartite division based loosely on Caesar's classification. To strengthen the Roman hold on the Three Gauls (Tres Galliae), Augustus decreed the construction of a system of military roads and laid the foundation of a regular imperial administration in following Caesar's policy of using the tribe as the basic unit in defining administration districts. Groups of *civitates* were incorporated into the new provinces, although Caesar's threefold definition of their relationship with Rome as either allied states (nominally sovereign communities), free states (subject to Rome with certain privileges), or tributary states (subject to Rome with no privileges) meant less and less. By the early first century C.E., these distinctions remained simply as badges of rank.

Each province received a governor, who, as the emperor's deputy (his legate *[legatus]*), was appointed by him and answered directly to him. The governor was commissioned as the military commander in chief to protect his province from outside aggression, to maintain internal peace, and to uphold Roman law. Each maintained their main residence at Lugdunum for Lugdunensis, Durocorturun Remorum (Reims) for Belgica, and, after a period at modern-day Saintes and Poitiers, at Burdigala (Bordeaux) for Aquitania.

Sensitive to Gallic self-pride, Augustus founded no further colonies in the Three Gauls. The Roman political presence was concentrated at Lugdunum (or Lugudunum), which, due to its strategic location at the central intersection of the road network, emerged as the virtual capital of Gaul. Founded in 43 B.C.E. by Lucius Munatius Plancus (ca. 87–ca. 15 B.C.E.), a lieutenant of Caesar, the city ranked highest among the three provincial capitals not only as a Roman colony but also as the host and guardian of the worship of Rome and Augustus. The cult was inaugurated on August 1, 12 C.E., at a great altar located just outside the city at Condate, which became a magnificent showplace of Greco-Roman art and architecture.

Gaul remained central to Roman strategic planning so long as vigorous campaigns against the Germanic tribes across the Rhine River continued. Great levies were raised to support imperial armies, which drove east as far as the Elbe River, only to meet disastrous defeat in 9 C.E. in the Teutoberg Forest. Rome retreated, the legions settling down behind earth-and-timber fortresses along the left bank of the Rhine, content to play a purely defensive role. Far behind the frontier districts, in Gaul, freed from the demands of incessant war, both Romans and natives settled down also, to carry on what had become by now a thriving intercultural exchange.

Life in Gaul in the First and Second Centuries

After the suppression of the uprising under Vercingétorix in 52 B.C.E., the Gallic provinces largely acquiesced and, among some tribes, even embraced rule by Rome, which ushered in a period of rapid growth deliberately fostered by Roman authorities. Only very occasional rebellious outbursts disturbed the Pax Romana that reigned in Gaul during the next three centuries. A brief revolt in 21 C.E. under Julius Florus and Julius Sacrovir, from the Treveri and the Aedui, respectively, and

21

more wide-scale insurrections led by Gallic noblemen, Julius Vindex in 68 and Julius Classicus, Julius Tutor, and Julius Sabinus in 69–70, were brutally crushed even as they revived, if only momentarily, the deep-seated dread of the *terror Gallicus*.

Within Gaul, though never forcefully applied, Romanization proceeded steadily, spreading outward from the administrative cities into the surrounding Celtic countryside. Because orderly government stood first in importance to the Romans, the Gallic *civitas* were endowed with a *civitas*-capital, defined as a city-state on the Greco-Roman model that was so familiar to Mediterranean minds. Having one system of administration controlled from a single urban center made for efficient government, eliminated rival centers of local power, and facilitated Rome's ability to oversee its officials and to monitor and promote the Romanization of the leading families in the area. It is impossible to determine to what extent tribal loyalties survived through the centuries of Romanization, but it is known that sentiments of devotion to the *civitas* remained strong. In late Roman Gaul and in the years beyond, the residents of these places continued to think of themselves as, first and foremost, inhabitants of their *civitas*.

Many *civitas*-capitals were based at preexisting Celtic communities, and a number of these Gallic, and then Roman, cities retained their importance into the Middle Ages and beyond. Founded in the third century B.C.E. by the Parisii, a subtribe of the Senones who settled on the Île de la Cité, the Gallic center of Lutetia expanded under the Romans to the Sainte-Geneviève hill on the left bank of the Seine River. Their town of Lutetia Parisorium grew progressively over the Roman centuries to become a prosperous city. Likewise, Burdigala (Bordeaux) had long been a trading port at the mouth of the Garonne.

Roman urban planners invariably strove to lay out a regular street plan for their Gallo-Roman settlements, based on the intersection of two major axial routes, one running north to south (*kardo*) and the other east to west (*decumanus*). At their point of crossing, they would site the forum, the defining public space of Roman urban life where social and commercial intercourse took place. Here, too, would usually be found the basilica, the seat of government, and a classical temple for worship of Roman deities.

The government of the three Roman colonies in the Three Gauls followed Roman municipal charters. A *colonia* consisted of a citizen body that elected colleges of magistrates whose powers were strictly defined by law. Together, the magistrates and former magistrates formed a local order of senators (*decuriones, curiales*) who met to discuss community matters in the senate house (*curia*). The government of the Gallic *civitas,* places that in the beginning were inhabited entirely by non-Romans, would have likely continued preconquest practices, though imitation of Roman municipal forms would have proceeded from an early stage, given the strong inclination to Romanize.

Municipal governments held few substantive powers, responsible for little more than maintenance of roads and bridges, and magistrates were enjoined, above all, to keep the peace and to assist in collecting the taxes owed to Rome. Local militias, recruited from the male youth of the area, were relied on for the former. For the latter, annual levies were set based on the most recent censuses, and the provinces were informed how much was owed. It was up to them to decide who should pay. The tribute (*tributum*) was the chief direct tax of the Roman Empire, divided between a tax on the yield of agricultural land and a levy on wealth. Land under Roman ownership was not subject to the former, and Roman citizens did not pay the latter, exemptions that were bound to breed resentment as a visible sign of subjection to Rome, no matter the strenuous avowals by officialdom that levies were extracted to benefit the provincials in helping to pay for their defense. In any case, during this pacific period the peasants' tax burden proved relatively light. Besides the tribute, there were a variety of indirect taxes, including customs duties and sales taxes. Provincial procurators, not governors, were responsible for collection and disbursement of imperial monies. An imperial mint was located at Lugdunum.

The revenues to be collected from, and that were needed to run, Roman Gaul depended on the prosperity of agriculture, the sole major economic activity of the ancient world. Each city was closely tied to the surrounding countryside, where the leading citizens owned estates. The characteristic rural institution, the independent farmstead—or villa—appeared everywhere, from the wheatfields of the far north to the rocky western coast, where fishing was the chief occupation. Invariably grouped around cities and important towns and close to roads to facilitate market access, villas featured usually a main dwelling, most often a rectangular farmhouse—only the most substantial were of palatial proportions—and the working outbuildings, including barns and storage sheds where the smelting and working of metals for tools took place.

Agriculture in Gaul grew in scale under Roman rule, connected to the vast trading network of the empire. Although crop-growing areas in most of Gaul during Roman times remained mere islands in a sea of forest and marshland, more land than ever before came under cultivation, and labor became more intensive. Estates worked by hundreds of slaves imported from border areas and by free Celtic peasant tenants (*coloni*) could cover thousands of acres. Wheat was probably the preeminent cash crop, the fields of the northeast producing for sale to the army and the need for fast supplies spawning a rare technological innovation, the Gallic harvest machine (*vallus*). Regions had their specialties—hemp in Auvergne, flax in Berry, poultry in Artois. The major innovative contribution to agriculture in Gaul made by Rome came with the introduction of Mediterranean crops—olive, cherry, and peach orchards, but most especially grape vines. Viticulture spread gradually but at the same time steadily and widely.

Raw materials were worked and traded on a hitherto unprecedented scale. The metalwork of the Gauls, known for its excellent quality for several centuries, continued to be made, and Romans praised the skill of the Gauls as miners. A vast new field of activity opened for the local inhabitants with the arrival of Roman building types and techniques. Quarrying became important. The cutting and transporting of stone used in erecting the new buildings was a major industry by itself, and dressed stone, mortar, tiles, and bricks came into use. Fine stone masonry had already been introduced by the Greeks in Gallia Narbonensis, and skilled artisans were readily at hand to create the great monuments that mark the Augustan era here. During that period, pottery was produced intensely, including the distinctive black- and slate-colored ware—bowls, plates, and jugs—while the familiar red ware (*terra sigillata*) was being made at Ledosus (Lezous) in the valley of the Allier as early as 10 C.E. Work crafted by the Ruteni, living near the port of Narbo, was widely dispersed. Wood, oil, fish products, textiles, and metals were produced, and the red-glazed pottery known as "samian" ware was renowned for its fine, durable quality. Local craftsmen and merchants banded together to form guilds to promote their well-being in Lugdunum, probably Gaul's greatest commercial center, where great river shippers (*nautae*) were important traders.

Population figures can be estimated only roughly, but it is probable that from an initial figure of about 8 million, about 12 million people lived in the Three Gauls during the first three imperial centuries—the early or high period—of the Roman Empire. They inhabited a land of growing economic prosperity brought by that empire, a primary reason for acceptance of Roman rule.

The natives aped the Romans in manners and methods, and Rome's physical presence spread. By the reign of Augustus, aqueducts, amphitheaters, baths, and temples proliferated in Provence, where ruins today at Arles, Nîmes, Glanum, and Nice attest to the depth of the Roman

Roman arch, Arles (Library of Congress, LC-USZ62-103322)

imprint, which spread north and west from here. The road network in Gaul, begun under the statesman and general Agrippa (ca. 63–12 B.C.E.), was largely completed under the rule of the emperor Claudius (r. 41–54), while the largest of the aqueducts at Lugdunum was built under the emperor Hadrian (r. 117–38). Marble and stone replaced wood in Gallic urban spaces. Outer defensive fortifications, no longer needed, were torn down. Travelers approaching a Roman-ruled city were greeted now not by walls but rather by rows of tombs lining the road in customary Roman fashion.

The town was the most typical Roman institution, the instrument by which Roman attitudes and customs (*Romanitas*, "Roman-ness") could be introduced to "civilize" (which, etymologically, means "to give town life") the newly conquered territories. Although they contained fewer than 10 percent of the population of Roman Gaul, the cities housed the ruling elites of Roman and Gallo-Roman merchants and administrators, who, together with provincial magnates in the nearby villas, drove adoption of Roman civilization. Latin became universal, and a written culture developed. Values of Roman justice and law, including dedication to family, religion, and duty (*pietas*), were inculcated, and they

25

were never entirely abandoned in the Gallic provinces, even after the fall of the empire here. Gallic warriors were incorporated into Roman legions. The elites copied the manners and modes in vogue in Rome, and Gallic nobles acquired Roman titles and administrative duties, while their sons were educated at schools at Burdigala, Lugdunum, and Augustodunum Aeduorum (Autun). In the first century C.E., Massilia became a renowned center of learning where Gauls were taught literature and philosophy and where Romans were sent in preference to Athens. The aristocracy in a local area consisted of those who had secured wealth and prominence through imperial service, together with local Gauls who had risen through the military or the civil service or who had married into the local Roman elite.

Because religion and government were so intimately tied (Roman emperors were considered to be gods), Rome sought to mold native religions into its own image. In doing so it relied primarily on a strategy by which the new regime co-opted the old. Thus, Roman temples were built on the sites of Celtic shrines. Latin names were given to native deities. Celtic names, usually discarded for gods, were often retained for goddesses, and so divine couples such as Apollo and Sirona appeared. In fact, many mother goddesses survived, and the horse-goddess Epona achieved wide fame throughout the empire. Because Gallo-Roman elites had a growing stake in the Roman order, in time they dropped their old loyalties.

But while the faiths could be adapted, the faith carriers could not. Rome could not countenance a caste system of wise men who constituted a potential source of political unrest and who, as priests presiding over rites of human sacrifice, held a power over life and death that the Roman state alone claimed. Final suppression came under the emperor Claudius. Divided among themselves and with an oral-based faith that limited their ability to communicate across distances, the druids could not compete against the organized might of Rome. They faded from the scene, although religious change proceeded much more slowly among the rural peasantry.

During these centuries, Gaul served essentially as a source for supplies, troops, and manufactured goods, such as clothing and weapons, that could not be produced elsewhere. Even though of relatively marginal importance from the perspective of the vast empire, where the cultural, economic, and political centers were all found in the great cities of the eastern Mediterranean, Gaul ranked among the most peaceful, highly assimilated imperial regions by the time that, in 212, the emperor Caracalla (r. 198–217), who was himself born in

Lugdunum, granted Roman citizenship to all freemen throughout the empire.

Shortly before his reign, the first signs appeared of renewed pressure on the Rhine and Danube frontiers, dormant for 200 years save for sporadic raids by Germanic bands. Pressure proved worrisome in Gaul because legions had to be withdrawn from along the borders to battle the Parthians in Asian areas of the empire. Numbers were small—only three out of 17 and not all were drawn from the same locales—but they were sufficient to weaken the Danube defenses such that, in 166 and again in 170, massive cohorts of Marcomanni and Quadi tribesmen crossed the river and fought their way into Italy itself, plundering cities just north of modern Venice. Emperor Marcus Aurelius (r. 169–80) and his son Commodus (r. 176–92) eventually defeated the raiders, but it was an ominous portent.

Gaul from the Third to the Fifth Centuries

The pressure of the barbarians along the Danube ushered in a period of political and economic unrest from approximately the assassination of Emperor Commodus in 192, which sparked a bloody civil war, to the ascension of Emperor Diocletian in 284. During this so-called crisis of the third century, the military raised and dethroned one emperor after another to find a leader able both to build up the power of the army and to lead it to victory against the renewed threats from enemies to the north and east.

Beginning with the reign of Emperor Septimus Severus (r. 193–211), the old Italian senatorial aristocracy and the wealthy residents of the more settled areas of Italy and southern Gaul saw their power wane as military commanders of frontier areas, especially those in the West, took the lead in making and breaking emperors. From 260 to 274, a Gallic Empire (Imperium Galliarum) emerged in the wake of a power vacuum occasioned by the capture of Emperor Valerian (r. 253–60) by Persians. Comprising territory in Gaul, Britannia, and Hispania (Spain), the regional empire arose not only in response to the general chaos of the third century but also in consequence of the appearance of local power bases and individual legions, even if the degree to which it indicated a growing provincial identification in place of loyalty to Rome remains debatable.

Diocletian (r. 284–305) checked external and internal threats through successful military expeditions, skillful diplomacy, and administrative reorganization, including territorial divisions of the empire into eastern and western halves and of Gaul into two large provinces, with their capitals at Vienne and Trier (in present-day Germany), respectively. Under Diocletian, too, systematic persecution of Christians in Gaul began. Christianity was one among a number of cults originating in eastern parts of the Roman world that began to infiltrate the region in the second century. Small communities existed by the end of the century, their presence confined almost exclusively to large cities where the cosmopolitan commercial populations served as agents in both introducing and spreading the faith. Viewed as potentially seditious for their opposition to emperor worship, Christians were at first only sporadically targeted, but they drew increasing attention as their numbers grew. They often faced a horrific fate. Around the year 177, martyrs at Lugdunum and Vienne were made to endure a mixture of flogging, scorching, and exposure to wild beasts. After public display, their bodies were burnt and the ashes thrown into the Rhône. Emerging leaders of the infant religion—priests and bishops—were not spared. Denis, the bishop of Paris and later the patron saint of the city, was beheaded about the year 250. Christians' radical and exclusive monotheism and their insistence that only members of their own creed could achieve salvation in a blissful, eternal afterlife proved attractive to some and repellant to others. Because its adherents rejected the prescribed religion, belief in which was intimately tied to loyalty to the state, Christianity helped to spread social discord, which intensified as the number of converts multiplied in the wake of the failure of Diocletian's campaigns.

The emperor restored order in the empire but at the price of solidifying the growing role of the military in civic affairs. Under Diocletian and his successors, the civil service was reorganized along military lines, the cultural values of the soldier suffused society, and officers and veterans came to dominate local political offices. By the beginning of the fourth century, these soldiers were no longer Italian peasants; rather, they came from among the very people against whom they were enlisted to fight.

The Roman legions protecting the border districts (limes) in Germany had long proved an effective instrument of Romanization because they were stationed there for long periods, because they comprised largely Roman homegrown natives from among the poorer classes in Italy, and because retiring veterans were usually granted land in the area and often intermarried. From the time of Hadrian, however, inductees began to be assigned to legions in their native provinces, which encouraged the growth of localism in cultural attitudes and, increasingly, in political identity. At the same time, by the third and fourth centuries, demands for military manpower intensified in the wake of increasing pressure on the frontiers and growing internal strife, coupled with a drop in population occasioned by a falling birthrate, plague, and the shortages induced by a labor-intensive economic system based largely on slaves and free tenant farmers. Recruiters turned more and more toward the barbarians next door to fill the ranks.

Beginning with the reign of Marcus Aurelius, the first barbarian elements in the Roman army appeared. After treaties were concluded with tribal leaders, who were plied with gifts, often of gold for the chiefs and grain for the people, members of bordering tribes would serve for a period of years and then return to their homes. Not infrequently, however, such recruitment led to tensions. Barbarians in contact with others farther afield in the wilds of northern Europe could prove obstinate and rebellious, and, so, to counter such problems, during the third century, Romans began settling groups of Germans within the empire. Small bands of either refugees or prisoners of war, called *laeti,* were the first to be allowed into frontier areas. Profoundly different were the free Germans, whole groups called *foederati* (sing. *foederatus*), who with their elite military units were admitted from the end of the fourth century and settled not on the empire's outlying fringes but within or near major provincial cities, where they could be deployed rapidly to meet invaders at any point on the borders or stop their advance should they have breached them. Living in close proximity to Romans, they became "imperial Germans" who added a new ethnic and cultural element to interact with, and at times to compete with, Roman civilization.

Who were these barbarians? The peoples referred to collectively as "Germans" by classical writers included a complex mixture of Iron Age groups that arose in northern regions of central Europe and southern parts of Scandinavia from about the sixth century B.C.E. Some were long resident in the empire, having intermixed with Celtic peoples over many centuries, mostly in the far north in Gallia Belgica. They practiced cereal cultivation, crafted fairly crude ceramic utensils and bronze and iron weapons, and measured wealth in ownership of cattle. They tended to live in self-sufficient small villages, surviving through a combination of animal husbandry and farming, supplemented when possible by fishing. Women wove and spun wool, fashioned into garments that, for women, featured long, sleeveless dresses fastened at the shoulder by brooches and, for men, woolen trousers, smocks, and cloaks. Everyone wore fur wraps to protect against the winter chill.

Societies were organized into tribes—family or family-like units united through common beliefs and social bonds—whose distinguishing feature was the warrior band (*comitatus*), for, just as it had been for the Gauls of centuries past, warfare constituted the primary activity of Germanic men. Chieftains, or kings, were elected by an assembly of the warriors, who carried their chosen man on a raised shield to announce his selection. The nature of this society, structured militarily with loose kindred links and a weak central organization, contributed to constant instability, and conflict, both intra- and intertribal, was the norm. Carried on most intensely in border areas, commercial exchange— German cattle, hides, furs, and amber for Roman grain, jewelry, iron, and gold—exacerbated tensions and helped to destabilize these societies. Some acquired more wealth than others, and this imbalance accentuated social and economic differences. Pro- and anti-Roman factions battled each other. Older tribal confederations such as the Marcomanni splintered and new ones arose. Amid the flux that characterized late antiquity, the Goths emerged as the tribe most respected and feared by both other barbarians and Romans alike.

Infiltrating to the south and east from northeastern Europe in the late second and third centuries, the Goths comprised a large tribal unit that first came into violent conflict with Rome in 278. A western division—the Visigoths—had been alternately serving in or fighting against imperial armies, when, in the late third century, they confronted the terror posed at their backs by the Huns, a tribe of nomadic horse warriors killing and pillaging their way out of central Asia. Petitioning to be allowed entry into the empire in return for military service, they were settled on the south bank of the Danube. They soon rebelled, however, and to the surprise of the Roman world, on August 9, 378, at the Battle of Adrianople, they defeated a Roman army sent against them. Under their king Alaric (r. 395–410) they went on to sack Rome itself in 410.

By that date, wholesale invasion was under way. A series of very cold winters set in after 406, which, in freezing the Rhine, facilitated a mass migration into Gaul. The Alamans (Alamanni, Alemanni) moved into Alsace, the Burgundians occupied central eastern Gaul, and the Visigoths traveled on from northern Italy to settle down in the southwest in Aquitaine. Germanic Saxons settled on the Channel coast, perhaps coming there after a period of residence in southern England. Likewise, Celtic immigrants from Britain arrived in Armorica—Brittany. All of these peoples took up residence in an empire profoundly weakened both in substance and in spirit.

In Gaul, Germanic influences were already well in evidence, the by now heavily Germanized armies serving as the agents of change just as Roman armies had done centuries before. A decline in prosperity had set in starting under Diocletian, who, to pay for his expanded bureaucracy and military, increased taxes, and whose fiscal reforms, which allowed peasants to pay in crops rather than in Roman coins, led to a drop in the use of money and a drop-off in trade and commerce. Rising tax burdens set in motion a vicious circle, leading to a decrease in voluntary civil service—tax gatherers were responsible for paying annual assessments even when they could not collect them—that precipitated further growth in the imperial bureaucracy, which in turn increased the demand for yet more taxes.

By the end of the fourth century, the Roman Empire in the West existed largely in name only. What was left of effective imperial power was now concentrated far to the east, where earlier in the century Emperor Constantine I (r. 306–37) had built a new capital at Constantinople. In western regions of the faltering empire, the long-term military crisis and the dearth of public monies led to a continuous increase in the influence and power of barbarian commanders and their followers. Still, despite the absence of strong central government and the potential for conflict inherent in the ebb and flow of peoples across the land, accommodation rather than confrontation characterized political and administrative conditions in Gaul at this time. The longtime presence of Germanic military muscle here, working to the mutual advantage of both the army and the Roman civil administration, forestalled any dramatic or sudden political transition. Elites in the country adapted readily enough to new rulers, content to let leaders manage military matters while they preserved Roman social and cultural traditions.

By 400, those elites were largely confined to the great landowners, who alone had survived to thrive. By virtue of their vast wealth, their imperial connections, and their private military means, they were immune to taxation. Living far from the frontiers in regions such as Aquitaine, the Rhône valley, and along the Mediterranean coast, great families, such as the Syagrii, Ponti, and Magni, continued the tradition of Roman culture and expanded their holdings through land acquisition, intermarriage, and patronage. Anxious to preserve their privileges, they were willing enough to see political control pass to local rulers, even Germanic kings, who possessed the means to enforce law and order. A growing sense of regionalism began to develop as landlords looked no further than the source of power immediately at hand, and some of them became powerful political players in their own right. The absence of taxes proved their good fortune, but taxes were the instruments of misfortune for everyone else.

In the third and fourth centuries, the status of free tenant farmers grew increasingly indistinguishable from that of slaves. Under Diocletian, peasants who owned no land were registered under their landlord's name on the estates they cultivated, thus tying them to the place where they paid their taxes. The system benefited landlords, who were assured labor services, and the empire found it easier to collect taxes, but the peasants lost their freedom of movement. Free farmers, who owned their own land, were crushed by the tax burdens. In Gaul throughout the fifth century, revolts of the Bagaudae—farmers pushed to rebel by insatiable tax demands—often occurred on a massive scale and required full-blown military operations to quell them. Some freeholders placed themselves under the protection of wealthy aristocrats. Others simply fled. Abandoned lands became common even as many of those who formerly owned land became tenant farmers of great landlords, a status that offered some fiscal relief. By the end of the fifth century, society was well advanced toward becoming a two-tiered world, made up, at the top, of wealthy aristocrats and, at the bottom, of their subordinates, bound to the land and dependent on their patrons. In the midst of the mayhem, cities declined, a drop in the trade that was their lifeblood inevitable in so unsettled conditions. With armies on the march everywhere, urban places adopted once again a feature that so distinguished Gallic communities before Roman rule. Erecting protective walls, residents of Paris and other towns—now much contracted in size—huddled inside fortifications meant to keep others out.

The Visigoths settled down in the early fifth century in southwestern Gaul to disturb the peace no more. Their old enemy the Huns, however, who maintained their marauding ways with a will, advanced farther and farther west, ravaging bands under Attila (406–53), the so-called Scourge of God, penetrating as far as central Gaul. They threatened Paris, when, purportedly through the prayers of Saint Geneviève (ca. 419/22–ca. 502/12), a peasant girl of Frankish and Gallo-Roman birth, they were diverted. Soon afterward, meeting defeat at Chalôns-sur-Marne in 451, Attila and his hordes turned back east.

The Huns were vanquished by an army fighting under the Roman banner, led by the Roman general Flavius Aetius (ca. 396–454). Essential support came, however, from Germanic allies, including Visigoths, Alamans, and another group called Franks. Unlike many other Germanic tribes, the Franks had long been resident in the empire. In a few succeeding decades, they would come to supplant what was left of Roman power in most of the lands that would become France.

3

THE KINGDOM
OF THE FRANKS
(481-987)

Change but also continuity characterized the fifth century in Roman Gaul. Setting in motion 500 years of melding and mixing, the Germanic tribes that swept through the empire's western lands brought new peoples and their cultures. At the same time, much of Roman habits and ways remained undisturbed. Roman political authority gradually gave way as the century progressed, supplanted by new power holders, some long known to the Romans and some newly arrived, but all of them Germanic in origin. The Visigoths in the southwest and the Burgundians in the east carved out their own kingdoms, but none matched the power of the Franks. From their base in northern Gaul under their ruler, Clovis, they created a unified tribe under a single leader. In converting to Christianity—the religion that, since winning official recognition, had become the faith of growing numbers among the Gallo-Roman population—the Franks under Clovis eased their settlement into society, helping to put into motion a process that would end in the merging of the newcomers with those long resident here.

The Franks expanded their territorial base to encompass all the lands of modern France save those on the Mediterranean coast. But the empire they ruled, though large, was loosely structured, the kingdom divided into subkingdoms by descendants of Clovis, who battled externally to expand their holdings and internally to eliminate rivals. A complex, shifting political narrative ensued under two successive dynasties. Royal authority expanded, and then contracted, under the Merovingians in the sixth and seventh centuries, expanded under the great leaders of the early Carolingians—Charles Martel and

Charlemagne—in the seventh century, and contracted again under their successors in the ninth century. New invaders threatened—Arabs from the south and Vikings from the north.

Through all the centuries, life went on as before, based everywhere in agriculture, but the thriving commercial activity once known under the Romans declined and the political unity on which royal power depended fractured. By the 10th century, the kings had largely lost the obedience of those among their subjects who mattered, namely, local lords of substance, who, as dukes, counts, and viscounts, had created virtually independent states on the basis of royal land and revenue grants. At the end of the century, a new royal dynasty, its territory having shrunken to just the lands around Paris, would have to undertake to restore a portion, if not all, of what had been lost.

The Coming of the Franks

The Franks emerged as small separate Germanic tribes—Salians, Sicambri, Ripuari, Chamari, Chattuari, and others—that appeared on the doorstep of the Roman Empire in the early Christian era. While maintaining their own identities, these bands joined together occasionally for common defense or offensive operations. In time, they came to identify themselves by the name *Franks*, which first appeared in Roman sources in the mid-fifth century and meant "the robust," "the brave," and later, by extension, the meaning preferred by the Franks themselves, "the free."

Living in close proximity to the empire, they were a small and divided people who, before the fifth century, either existed as subjugated Roman clients or served as sources of military manpower. At some point the tribe of Salians was allowed to settle in an area south of the Rhine River known as Toxandria, now in the Netherlands, to serve as a buffer between barbarians to the north and east and civilized Gallo-Romans to the south, as a source of recruits for the imperial armies, and as residents who could cultivate the countryside.

During the fourth and early fifth centuries, the Salians provided loyal troops to the armies of the western empire. When the Alans, Sueves, and Vandals swept over the borders in 406 and when the Huns invaded in 451, they proved faithful allies. They were well rewarded for their services in being permitted to spread gradually south into more Romanized areas of today's Belgium and northern France, as well as along the lower Rhine.

In the fifth century, the Salians came to dominate the disparate groups of Franks under their ruling Merovingian dynasty, which took its name from its founder, Merovich, a semilegendary figure. Called by their contemporaries the "long-haired" kings because they favored unshorn hair—in contrast to the Romans and the tonsured clergy—the Salian Franks, under Childeric I (r. ca. 457–81/82), Merovich's son, ruled a kingdom in northwestern Gaul based at Tournai in present-day Belgium, as a *foederatus* of the Romans. Childeric was the last Frankish leader to continue the tradition of service as a German under imperial Roman command. Like barbarian commanders in Roman service before him, he maintained good relations with the Gallo-Roman society within the territories he controlled. Allied with his neighbor to the immediate south, the Domain—or Kingdom—of Soissons, a Roman rump state that emerged out of the chaos of the mid-fifth century, Childeric joined forces with its ruler, Aegidius (?–464 or 465), in helping to defeat the Visigoths at Orléans in 463. The greatest power in continental western Europe at this time, the Visigoths had created virtually an independent kingdom, based at Toulouse, in today's southwestern France and northern Spain. The last refuge of Roman imperial power in Gaul, southern Provence, fell to them in 477. Though his sister was married to a Visigothic king, Childeric remained acutely alive to the threat to his power posed by strong potential rivals. The existence of these battling autonomous realms testified to the by now definitive demise of the military and political might of Rome, its lingering presence in Gaul now confined to the Gallo-Roman aristocracy, the Christian Church hierarchy, and the trappings in titles and riches of the new ruling elites. The formal dissolution of the empire in the West upon the dethronement of the last ruling emperor, Romulus Augustulus (fl. 461/63–76) in 476 merely made official what had long been a fact. It went unnoticed in Gaul, where barbarian rulers were competing for power and where in 481 or 482 in the kingdom of the Franks, Childeric died, to be succeeded by his son Clovis (r. ca. 481–ca. 511).

The Reign of Clovis

When Clovis succeeded his father, he was only one among several kings of the Franks, but he became the ruler under whom real power accrued to the Merovingian dynasty, which held the kingship of Gaul for two and a half centuries. His importance as a central figure in founding modern France has always been recognized. Clovis is the modern French form of Chlodovechus ("praised fighter"); by the eighth century the guttural "ch" would be dropped, giving the Latinized form Ludovicus, which in turn became Louis, the most common of all French royal names.

Clovis inherited the diplomacy of his father, which he continued—but not for long. The death of the powerful Visigothic king Euric (ca. 415–84) left a power vacuum in the southwest that offered too tempting an opportunity to a leader who, after all, was first and foremost a military commander. In 486, allied with other Frankish chieftains, Clovis launched a campaign against Syagrius, ruler of the Kingdom of Soissons to the south, whom he defeated. The conquest sped movement of Frankish groups southward into the heartland of the vanquished ruler's domain in the Seine and Marne region. The triumphant victor established for himself a capital at Paris in 507, which became the center of Frankish power and where he would be buried. Shortly afterward, he issued a written law code for his people, the Lex Salica, the oldest of the Germanic law codes and the basis on which codification in subsequent centuries would proceed.

Clovis moved next to vanquish the Alemanni decisively and to battle the Armoricans in Brittany and the Burgundians. But it was the Visigoths in Spain and southern Gaul who remained the major foe to be faced. The Visigoths were Arians, having converted in 376 to the doctrines of Arius (ca. 250–336), a theologian who had taught a heretical Christian belief that denied the full divinity of Jesus Christ, and Clovis may have calculated that he could gain a valuable ally against his anticipated opponents if he could secure the support of the elite in Gaul. He could do so by joining the faith practiced by the majority of them, namely, Catholic Christianity based on the authority held by the pope at Rome.

Christianity had spread inexorably in the centuries succeeding the emperor Constantine's grant of toleration in the Edict of Milan (313). An end to persecution sped conversion, though practitioners were long largely confined to urban areas. Official recognition facilitated the establishment of a church organization. By the end of the third century, a system of parishes, headed by priests, and dioceses, led by bishops, had been set up. The bishop (episcopus) became the undisputed leader of local religious communities. After appointment by consultation among members of the congregation, he enjoyed autocratic powers. Holding office for life, he ordained priests, admitted new members to the faith, and controlled diocesan finances. Once Christianity became the state religion, bishops were granted imperial subsidies and even civil powers traditionally reserved for Roman provincial governors.

THE CONVERSION OF CLOVIS

The adoption of Christianity by Clovis was an event of supreme importance because, in doing so, his entire people converted also, which sped the integration of the Franks into the Gallo-Roman population, promoting social stability and the unity of the emerging Frankish kingdom. The historian Gregory of Tours (ca. 539–94), has left the following account.

Clovis, king of the Franks (Library of Congress, LC-USZ62-1435)

Queen Clotild continued to pray that her husband might recognize the true god and give up his idol-worship. Nothing could persuade him to accept Christianity. Finally war broke out against the Alamanni and in this conflict he was forced by necessity to accept what he had refused of his own free will. It so turned out that when the two armies met on the battlefield there was great slaughter and the troops of Clovis were rapidly being annihilated. He raised his eyes to heaven when he saw this, felt compunction in his heart and was moved to tears. "Jesus Christ," he said, ". . . if you will give me victory over my enemies . . . then I will believe in you and I will be baptized in your name." . . . Even as he said this the Alamanni turned their backs and began to run away. . . .

. . .

The Queen then ordered Saint Remigius, Bishop of the town of Rheims, to be summoned in secret. . . . The bishop asked Clovis to meet him in private and began to urge him to believe in the true God. . . . The King replied: "I have listened to you willingly, holy father. There remains one obstacle. The people under my command will not agree to forsake their gods. I will go and put to them what you have just said to me." He arranged a meeting with his people, but God in his power had preceded him, and

(continues)

37

CONVERSION OF CLOVIS (continued)

before he could say a word all those present shouted in unison: "We will give up worshipping our mortal gods, pious King, and we are prepared to follow the immortal God about whom Remigius preaches." . . . The public squares were draped with coloured cloths, the churches were adorned with white hangings, the baptistery was prepared. . . . King Clovis asked that he might be baptized first by the bishop. . . . As he advanced for his baptism, the holy man of God addressed him in these pregnant words: "Bow your head in meekness. . . . Worship what you have burnt, burn what you have been wont to worship."

Source: Gregory of Tours, *The History of the Franks* (New York: Penguin Books, 1974), pp. 143–144.

Donations of money and land from the pious, aristocratic women especially prominent among them gave the bishops a power base of enormous significance in the fourth and fifth centuries. By the latter century, these local religious—and often political—leaders were drawn almost exclusively from the aristocracy. They promoted a value system reflective of their class, enjoining the faithful to humble obedience to the church hierarchy.

The conversion of Clovis—at Reims on Christmas Day, 496 or 498, or possibly as late as 506—carried important consequences. Because subjects followed their kings in all things, the religious conversion of the ruler necessarily meant the conversion of his whole people. The Christian faith now made possible a union of the Franks, still very much a minority of the population, with the natives of Gaul—the peasants, artisans, and, most important, the Gallo-Roman aristocracy and its leaders, the bishops. Amalgamation of the two peoples who now shared a common religion proceeded through the sixth century.

Clovis's conversion increased the likelihood that the Christian Gallo-Roman aristocracy in neighboring kingdoms would be inclined to welcome him. In 507, he marched south, and in alliance with the Byzantines who ruled the Eastern Roman Empire, he soundly defeated the Visigoths at Vouillé, northwest of Poitiers, killing Euric's son, King Alaric II (r. 484–507) and taking the capital Toulouse the following year. The Visigoth rulers fled to their lands in Spain. Having emerged as the most successful among all the barbarian chieftains ever to have ruled north of the Alps, Clovis then eliminated others among the Frankish leaders who threatened his hold on power, liquidating them in a campaign of ruthless brutality. Thereafter, for 200 years, the descendants of Clovis were the only Franks eligible to be kings.

The Merovingians: The Sixth and Seventh Centuries

Under Clovis's sons and his grandsons, the expansion of Frankish-ruled regions was largely completed. The Burgundian kingdom was destroyed and absorbed by 534. Southern Provence, which was controlled by Ostrogothic kings next door in Italy, was handed over in 536–37. By 541, campaigns against the Visigoths had reduced their presence north of the Pyrenees to a strip of coast as far east as Narbonne, called Septimania. The Merovingians left the lands south of the Loire largely to their own devices, content to let them live by their own law. Dukes and, in Provence, patricians ruled here subject to the king. The Bretons also retained their own king, though they recognized Frankish authority. South of the Garonne River, a new people with their own distinct traditions emerged in the late sixth and seventh centuries. The Vascones (Basques) invaded the so-called land of the Nine Peoples (Novempopulana) and settled the region between the Garonne and the Pyrenees, which by the seventh century became known as Vasconia (Gascony, or Guienne). Resident in southwestern Europe since ancient times, the Vascones were among the few people who had successfully resisted Romanization, and they retained their own pre-Indo-European language (Euskara) and presumably their own pagan religion because it was not until the 10th century or later that they would become even nominally Christian.

Although the region continued to be conceived as a unified, single kingdom of the Franks, because the Merovingians were a hereditary monarchy, territories were divided up on the death of rulers. Under Clovis's four sons, divisions emerged that would become the bases for power for succeeding generations. Neustria, or Neustrasia (new western land), formed the western part of the kingdom, including most of present-day central and western France. Austrasia (eastern land) made up the regions that today form eastern France, western Germany, and the Low Countries. The imperial fisc, that is, the lands—many of them former Roman imperial holdings—owned by the king and from which taxes to support the royal household were drawn, formed the core of Merovingian wealth. Because these holdings were located largely in the north of Gaul, Clovis's sons ruled from capitals that were located relatively close together, namely, Paris and Metz for Neustria and Austrasia, respectively.

In the sixth century, and especially south of the Loire, the trappings of Roman culture, fiscal systems, and agricultural and commercial structures continued to operate, along with what remained of Roman bureaucracy. The great landowners in the countryside and the bishops in the towns were the authorities on the ground. The Franks had learned much about Roman organization and control, but because it had come through generations of service in and with Roman armies, it was largely limited to military matters. Beginning with Clovis and continuing under his successors, the rulers reunited what the arrival of Germanic tribes two centuries before had splintered, namely, the military traditions of the Franks with the administrative and cultural heritage of the Romans. Following rapidly after the conquest of Gaul, Frankish aristocrats began to intermingle with the Gallo-Romans. North of the Loire, new Frankish settlements appeared and, through intermixture and intermarriage, Frankish identity would replace Roman within a few generations. South of the Loire, the opposite occurred. Only scattered islands of Franks were found here, and they quickly adopted Roman customs.

Thus, the court of Clovis and his successors included not only the traditional officers of a Frankish aristocratic household, headed by the chief manager—his mayor of the palace (*maior domus*, "superior of the house")—but also Roman officials such as secretaries and chancellors, who were secular holdovers of the Roman administration. The kings appointed counts (*comites*) from among the ranks of the nobles to serve as their personal representatives in a particular place, charged with recruiting troops and enforcing the law.

In the countryside, where the overwhelming majority of the population lived, efforts were begun by kings, aristocrats, and churchmen to bring lands that had been abandoned back into production, a process that would continue well into the ninth century. In the north, the kings held vast amounts of territory, which underwent constant transformation as portions were given away to important aristocrats or granted to the Roman Catholic Church. Fairly dense Frankish settlement here led to much deforestation, and from the beginning of the sixth century, a steady abandonment of animal husbandry in favor of crop cultivation began. Although dismemberment of estates was frequent—the aristocrats constantly buying, selling, and exchanging land—the wealthy elites continued to monopolize landholding, with the mass of the population struggling to subsist as tenants or even slaves. Agricultural technology actually regressed—machinery such as the mechanical harvester in use in the first century disappeared, water mills were scarce, and plows, scythes, and hoes were mostly or entirely made of wood, iron having become scarce. Cattle herding, important among Germanic peoples since ancient times, continued and expanded, while cereal production switched increasingly from wheat to barley and rye, darker grains that were hardier and could be easily converted into a strong and nourishing beer, the drink of the common people. The elite drank wine; indeed, because wine was essential for celebration of the Christian mass, grape growing grew.

Cities and towns remained scattered about, though much reduced from their heyday under the Romans. Nearly all had suffered loss of population, and their geographic bounds had shrunk over the centuries of barbarian depredations. The walls still stood that had been constructed around almost all Gallic towns in the third and fourth centuries, the Roman public buildings both inside and outside of them put to new uses or allowed to decay. By the sixth century, the greatest physical change had already taken place, the construction of Christian buildings, including churches, monasteries, and the bishop's house, the proliferation of which mirrored the growing importance of religion in social life.

That cities survived is due largely to their status as places of residence for the bishops, who were joined there in places by kings and counts. Bishops and clergy maintained the public life of urban places, undertaking municipal tasks such as poor relief and maintenance of walls, aqueducts, and other infrastructure. Many bishops controlled huge tracts of land that had passed to the church through inheritance and donation. Because a large population of clerics—the bishop and the priests and deacons who served him—had need of the services of craftsmen, shopkeepers, and small merchants, their places of residence remained centers of economic, social, and cultural significance. And its role as a major religious center ensured that the town or city remained a focus of attraction for inhabitants of the surrounding countryside.

Bishops were traditionally elected by the people and clergy of the diocese, to which was added, under the Frankish kings, approval by the ruler. Invariably members of the educated elite with proven administrative abilities, they could control sees that remained in the same family for generations during these centuries when, because no mechanism existed for an orderly succession, the death of a bishop could bring violence among competing aristocratic families, and when clerical celibacy was more the exception than the rule. At Paris, Orléans, Sens, and elsewhere, it was standard that sons succeeded fathers or nephews would follow uncles. Although various popes demanded sexual abstinence from the fourth century on, the practice was slow to take root. By the sixth century, changing attitudes were reflected such that it was expected that married clerics would refrain from sexual relations and that wives and husbands would live apart, but clerical celibacy would not be confirmed until reforms launched by Pope Gregory VII (r. 1073–85).

Ultimately, the power of a bishop resided in his status as the agent of God's will, and it was under his direction that instruction of the clergy and laity would be carried out and the work of conversion proceed. That task was still very much a work in progress in rural areas. The Christianization of the countryside was not completed until the ninth century, when a network of parishes grouped in dioceses covered every corner of the kingdom. It was achieved not only by bishops, both Gallo-Roman and those educated at Frankish courts, but also by northern Frankish aristocrats, who became actively involved.

The work of rural conversion was also assisted through the establishment of a new form of monasticism. Monasteries could be found in Gaul as early as the fifth century. Martin of Tours (316–97) had inspired a monastic community that combined traditions of primitive living and rigorous self-denial—the first monks had appeared as hermits in the deserts of Egypt—with recognition that ordinary sinners were better advised to live within a community of like-minded companions who could assist one another in providing the spiritual counsel and physical assistance needed in efforts to concentrate the mind on God and conquer earthly passions. Limited largely to southwest Gaul, where he had been active, Martin's monasticism was joined by a parallel variant that developed in the Rhône River valley. The first of the great Rhône monasteries, located on the Mediterranean coastal island of Lérins, was founded between 400 and 410 by Honoratus, a member of a noble Roman family from northern Gaul. Lérins and its offshoots, which appeared in Arles, Lyon, and as far north as Troyes, maintained a strongly aristocratic quality characteristic of communities composed of many well-educated members. Monks practiced silence, prayer, and abstinence while continuing their intellectual pursuits, largely writing and copying manuscripts.

Wandering monks from Ireland, the first of whom—Columbanus (543–615)—arrived in around 590, interjected a new role. Together with his companions—Irish monks traveled in groups of 12 in emulation of Christ and his apostles—Columbanus secured from the ruler of Burgundy the right to establish a community in a ruined fortress at Annegray in the Vosges Mountains. He remained in Burgundy for 20 years, leaving a scattering of monasteries in his wake. Unlike continental monasteries where men and women congregated to escape the world, the Irish foundations constituted the centers of Christian life in their areas, where Irish traditions of learning and cultural preservation were introduced and where instruction of the local populace in the tenets of Christianity took place.

The Irish monks won the active backing of the Frankish aristocracy, who founded many monasteries, endowing them with richly decorated churches. In the seventh century, the precepts introduced by Columbanus began to merge with those of Benedict of Nursia (480–547), an Italian monk whose rule, which combined rigidity with moderation, would become standard by the ninth century thanks in good measure to the vigorous support extended by the emperor Charlemagne and his son.

In the sixth and seventh centuries, the work of religious conversion proceeded at the same time that conflict and confusion characterized political life. Family feuding among the Merovingians was endemic. The years marked by the reigns of Clotaire II (Chlothar, r. 584–629), who consolidated the Frankish subkingdoms under his rule, and his son Dagobert I (r. 623–39) marked the high point as the most peaceful and prosperous period since the rule of Clovis. Dagobert died in 639 and was buried in the basilica of Saint-Denis in Paris—the first in the long line of French kings to be entombed here. For the next 100 years, so-called do-nothing kings (rois fainéants) ruled, many of them so labeled because they were minors under the domination of their mothers or the mayors of the palace. Even strong-willed monarchs such as Dagobert II (r. 676–79) and Chilperic II (r. 715–21) lost their role as the central political player to their mayors. Frankish kings depended entirely for their power on the acquiescence of the aristocracy, and the latter were prepared to respect that monopoly, but when kings proved unwilling or unable to provide the muscle needed to rule, the officials next in line—the mayors of the palace—were prepared to step in. Once having entered the fray, they intended to stay. Conflict between these two power seekers reduced the ability to impose Frankish control, with the result that, by the turn of the eighth century, effective rule by central authorities did not extend very far outside northeastern Gaul.

By the end of the seventh century, mayors were ruling in Neustria and Austrasia. Intent on besting each other, in 687, Austrasian mayor Pippin (Pepin, Pipin, Peppin) of Herstal (r. 680–714) invaded Neustria and defeated its unpopular mayor, Berthar (r. 686–87), at the Battle of Tertry. Pippin declared that the Frankish realm was once more united under one Merovingian king; in political reality, it was united for the first time under one mayor of the palace. For the first time, too, it was united under a new dynasty: the Carolingians.

The Carolingians: The Eighth and Ninth Centuries

The Battle of Tertry signified the long predominance of Austrasia over Neustria and of the effective rule of the Carolingians over the Frankish lands. The Carolingians (known variously as Carlovingians, Carolings, or Karlings) originated in two aristocratic families—the Peppinids and the Arnulfings—dominant in the seventh century. Pippin was the first to be descended from both branches of the family. Although after his great victory at Tertry he began calling himself "duke and prince of the Franks," it was his grandson Charles Martel (r. 715–41) who laid the foundations of the dynasty's power. The most important of the early Carolingians, he did more than any Frankish ruler since Clovis to establish the political dominance of the Franks by reconquering much of the territory that had drifted away from royal control during the years of declining Merovingian authority. Acclaimed mayor by the nobles of Austrasia in 715, Charles won control of Neustria by 717, and the next year, he defeated Chilperic II, the last Merovingian king who attempted to keep a hold on power, at Soissons. A ruler who waged war nonstop, he earned his cognomen "Martel" (Hammer) in a battle that proved decisive for European history. In defeating the Arabs—the new preeminent power in the Mediterranean world—at Tours, or Poitiers, in 732 or 733, he stopped the advance of Islam, marching north from Spain, into the heart of Europe. In campaigns from 734 to 738 on the periphery of Frankish territory—in Burgundy, Provence, and Aquitaine, and against Arabs in the south and Saxons on the northern borders—he remained undefeated. Charles Martel earned legendary status as a brilliant general—he lost only one battle—able to employ innovative techniques such as the feigned retreat to outwit his enemies and so to attack when and where he was least expected.

Proclaiming himself duke of the Franks late in his reign, Charles died on October 22, 741, his territories having been divided among his adult sons the year before. Of these, Pippin III (Pippin the Short or Pippin the Young, r. 741–68) compelled his brother Carloman to retire to a monastery in Rome in 747, thereby adding Carloman's assigned portion, Austrasia, to his own inheritance of Neustria and Burgundy.

The first mayor to secure the consent of the pope—by this date, the long acknowledged titular head of the western, namely, the Roman Catholic, branch of Christendom—he was pronounced king of the Franks at Soissons in 751. Recognition by the pope imparted a sacral element to kingship in signifying the conferral of divine approval on the individual as God's chosen instrument, which the French monarchy would hereafter retain.

Pippin proceeded to subdue the Aquitanians, who, in proving recurrently rebellious, were the most bitter and formidable opponents of the Carolingians. Just as his father had done before him, he prepared the ground for his eldest son, Charlemagne (r. 768–814), who succeeded as king of the Franks in 768, together with his brother Carloman I, with whom he ruled jointly.

Sole ruler of all the Frankish lands that had once been part of Gaul following the death of his brother in 771, Charlemagne moved on to create a Frankish empire that stretched from south of the Pyrenees to northwestern Germany and central Italy, uniting most of western Europe for the first time since the Romans. And with the stability that his rule engendered, Charlemagne oversaw a cultural efflorescence not witnessed since Rome's heyday. Though he was most likely unable to write—he could read some Greek and Latin—he admired learning, and scholarship, the arts, and architecture flourished at his court. From his ruling base at Aix-la-Chapelle (Aachen) in modern Germany, the great king launched monetary, governmental, and ecclesiastical reforms.

The early Carolingians based their power on the support of the aristocrats, without which they would not have been able to reign, and they won the allegiance of these men partly because of the force of their personalities. In Charlemagne, a man of great physical size—he stood 6 feet 3 inches (192 cm)—and unbounded energy, the ability of the Carolingians to both dominate and reward their retainers reached its greatest extent. But they did so also most essentially because of their success in war, which brought for Carolingian backers not only spoils but also offices and lands in the conquered territories.

The basic territorial unit of rule in Charlemagne's Gaul was the county, some of which, especially in the south, had the same boundaries as the ancient *civitates*. In each county, the king gave a portion of the royal lands to his governing agent, the count, as a territorial base from which he could earn the revenue on which to support himself. By the end of the reign, it was common to allow sons to succeed their fathers as counts, so that the office came to be regarded as a hereditary right. Aware that holding land could give rise to ambitions for higher power, to curb any pretensions toward self-rule Charlemagne kept close control of his counts, bringing them frequently to court or on campaign and, in their absence, instituting the office of viscount to act as their deputy in the county. Counts were forbidden to acquire additional counties.

To secure the loyalty of every count more directly, the king tied them personally to himself by an oath of fealty. Subordinates were made to swear to remain true to their ruler in a ceremony that, together with placing the hands inside those of a superior, ensured the bonds of faithfulness. The counts became, in effect, vassals of the king under an innovative superior-to-subordinate relationship. By the late eighth century, under Charlemagne, even the highest aristocrats had been brought into the system. All counts became his vassals, and the system was extended: The count's own officers, from the viscount down, became the count's vassals. The king even created "king's vassals" independent of the counts who could act as royal agents or watchdogs in the provinces. To further ensure loyalty, Charlemagne relied on *missi dominici,* special envoys introduced earlier under Charles Martel sent into the provinces with unique powers to root out corruption, injustice, or disobedience.

In addition to the counts, other vassals were made who promised aid to their lord—especially military aid—in return for which they expected a favor. That favor came to mean a grant of land, commonly called a fief. To confer a parcel of land to a vassal proved to be to the lord's advantage since it provided the basis for the resources—men, horses, and equipment—that he might have to call on in waging future battle. In northern Frankish territories land itself was granted, drawn from royal estates, from enemies, or from ecclesiastical holdings of bishops and abbots. Charlemagne became the effective master of the church in the western Frankish lands, though his ability to control ecclesiastical domains often drew the ire of the clergy, who resented what they saw as exploitation. In the south, the favor granted was often the right to collect a certain revenue. In both cases, the right was for life only, and it could be revoked if a vassal failed to fulfill his obligations. Both these grants and those held by the counts by virtue of their office came, within succeeding generations, to be regarded by their possessors as their legitimate property.

Charlemagne's achievements were of such a magnitude that they won recognition from the highest authority in western Christendom, and his coronation in Rome as Holy Roman Emperor by Pope Leo III (r. 795–816) on Christmas day in 800 acknowledged that he was seen

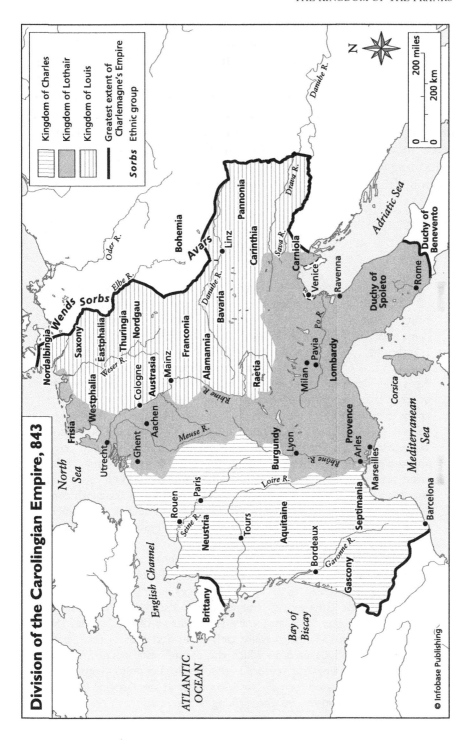

Division of the Carolingian Empire, 843

Legend:
- Kingdom of Charles
- Kingdom of Lothair
- Kingdom of Louis
- Greatest extent of Charlemagne's Empire
- *Sorbs* Ethnic group

N

200 miles
200 km

0
0

Regions and places:

North Sea
Adriatic Sea
Mediterranean Sea
English Channel
ATLANTIC OCEAN
Bay of Biscay

Nordalbingia
Wends
Sorbs
Saxony
Eastphalia
Westphalia
Frisia
Utrecht
Ghent
Aachen
Cologne
Austrasia
Mainz
Thuringia
Nordgau
Franconia
Bohemia
Avars
Linz
Pannonia
Carinthia
Bavaria
Alamannia
Raetia
Carniola
Venice
Ravenna
Caranthia
Milan
Pavia
Lombardy
Duchy of Spoleto
Rome
Duchy of Benevento
Corsica
Provence
Arles
Marseilles
Burgundy
Lyon
Rouen
Paris
Neustria
Seine R.
Tours
Loire R.
Aquitaine
Bordeaux
Gascony
Garonne R.
Septimania
Barcelona
Brittany

Oder R.
Elbe R.
Weser R.
Rhine R.
Meuse R.
Rhône R.
Danube R.
Drava R.
Sava R.
Po R.

© Infobase Publishing

47

as head of both state and church. The emperor bequeathed a vast and varied swath of lands to his sole surviving son, Louis "the Pious" (r. 814–40). But it was an empire hastily built and only loosely united. Faced with opposition from many aristocrats, fearing loss of time-honored privileges, and from his younger sons, fearing disinheritance, Louis agreed to a division of his realm upon his death such that, though the empire remained theoretically intact, subkingdoms were to be parceled out among the heirs. Among the three sons who succeeded him, the youngest, Charles (r. 843–77), known later in life by his distinguishing feature as "the Bald," won for himself, by the Treaty of Verdun

FRANCIA

rancia (or *Frankia*)—the name to which the nation traces its title—is first recorded in the *Panegyrici Latini,* a collection of Roman orations that dates to the third century, in designating the lands ruled by the Frankish kings. The territories labeled *Francia* varied greatly due to the diverse tracts acquired by the Franks and to the predilections of particular authors. Consequently, in the early Middle Ages, the designation meant very different things, though none can be translated as "France." Some writers used the term *Francia* to apply to the whole of the territory controlled by the Frankish kings, namely, Gaul and parts of Germany and the Low Countries. But by the seventh century, it generally came to mean Gaul north of the Loire and the plateau of Langres, although Tours, on the south bank of the river, seems to have been included. Inhabitants of both Neustria and Austrasia would refer to their territory as Francia. In the ninth century, there appeared Francia occidentalis (west Francia) and Francia orientalis (east Francia), a title that survives in Franconia (Franken), the name of the former German province.

In the 10th and 11th centuries, *Francia* continued to carry a general meaning—writers in both eastern and western Europe at the time of the Crusades referred to all Christian forces as Franks—but a narrower focus also emerged as royal power contracted. The Robertians, forerunners of the Capetians, were styled dukes of the Franks. The Capetians began their reign ruling only a small cluster of territories around Paris and Orléans to which the term *Francia* applied. About 1200, the name began to embrace the whole kingdom. From 1254, the king is designated formally in documents as *rex Franciae* (king of France) rather than *rex Francorum* (king of the Franks).

in August 843, both the western portions of the empire, the lands of Francia that stretched from the Atlantic east to the Meuse, Saône, and Rhône Rivers, and the Spanish March, a territory south of the Pyrenees wrested by Charlemagne from the Arabs. A further partition in 855 gave Provence to Charles.

Charles was hard put to hold on to what he had. He faced opposition from a well-entrenched aristocracy. A mere three months after Verdun, he faced a challenge in Aquitaine from his nephew Pippin (838–after 864), a mounting feud among the Neustrian nobility, and a defection by the Bretons. The local notables banded together and forced Charles to accept an agreement at Coulaines by which, in return for their recognition of his authority and a promise to give him aid and counsel, he pledged to protect the church and to judge justly and deal fairly with all. The idea that magnates could commit themselves to specific obligations and that a king's rule could even be made contingent on such a consensual agreement henceforth became a feature that distinguished politics in west Francia. It manifested itself in oaths to govern wisely sworn by all of Charles's successors.

When his brother Louis the German (r. 817–76) invaded in 858, most of the lay aristocracy deserted him, and Charles would have lost his kingdom but for support from the clergy. Counts rebelled and, in turn, made war on each other. His brother and nephew continued to battle him in Aquitaine. Nominoë (?–851), who, because he was created first duke of Brittany by Louis the Pious, had remained staunchly loyal to him, felt no such tie to Louis's son. He rose in revolt, to become by tradition the first non-Carolingian king. And Charles faced added hostility from yet another—this one, an entirely new—quarter.

Fleets of Vikings—marauding warrior bands from Norway and Denmark—appeared off the western coasts beginning between 790 and 800, and they proceeded to raid, burn, and kill. Traveling up the rivers, they returned again and again to attack far inland—Paris, Limoges, Angers, Toulouse, and Tours were ravaged. Towns, castles, and monasteries were plundered, and their residents fled, especially to Burgundy, which was one of few areas to remain largely unscathed. A flourishing monasticism grew up there, brought by refugee monks. Over time, the ruthless raiding of the Vikings gradually intermixed with, and then gave way entirely to, trading activity. Settlements replaced hit-and-run expeditions.

To conduct his defenses better against both Vikings and rebellious nobles, Charles deliberately decreased the number of potentially competing military authorities, in effect reducing the number of counts by giving large blocks of counties to individual aristocrats, such as Baldwin I (r. 862–79), the first count of Flanders, who were loyal to him. But they were loyal to him personally, not necessarily to the Carolingian kingdom. In the Frankish realms, the unity of the kingdom depended on the ability of the ruler to maintain it and on little else. Under the vassalage system of the Carolingians, the power that accrued with the grant of lands and revenues proved intoxicating for many of the magnates, and the urge to preserve—and expand—what they possessed led them to assert their independence when the kings who ruled, as those who did in the 10th century, lacked the means to enforce their will.

The Fragmentation of West Francia: The Tenth Century

The 11 years following the death of Charles the Bald in 877 saw the prestige of the Carolingian dynasty reach its lowest ebb. Charles's grandsons Louis III (r. 879–82) became king of the northern part of West Francia and Carloman II (r. 879—84) that of the southern part on the death of their father, Louis II, "the Stammerer" (r. 877–79), but in reality, it was the territorial lords who ruled. Great local lords, having been given grand estates as loyal vassals, found themselves able to govern because of the political power given them as official agents—counts and viscounts—of royal authority.

In the ninth century, royal power began to crumble away. Among the class of local nobility, a segment emerged that owed its origin to the cavalry that Charles Martel had found it necessary to create in imitation of the mounted Arabs whom he was thereby able to meet and defeat. These "knights"—armored and heavily armed horsemen—became the chief fighting troops as more and more small freemen, who fought on foot, disappeared to be replaced by tenants during the rise of the feudal estates that the knights themselves helped to create. Because only landowners could amass the wealth needed both to support a knight, for whom the head-to-toe armor he wore proved extremely expensive, and to give him the leisure to pursue his calling, knights acquired territory that, with the tenants to work it, became the basis for local feudal arrangements.

In addition, Carolingian kings put more and more power into the hands of royal administrators by delegating to them responsibility for government and defense of various territorially large subkingdoms and provinces. By the early 10th century, these territorial lords were known as dukes (*duces*) or princes (*principes*). By then, these officials ruled as virtual subkings in Aquitaine and Burgundy. The borderlands of the south—Gascony, Septimania (Toulouse), and the Spanish March—split away from west Francia and became semiautonomous. Royal authority became centered in the north of the kingdom in Neustria. Even here, a number of other political entities emerged—Brittany, Anjou, Maine, Blois, and Flanders. Many of these were created by local counts who secured hold of a group of counties and consolidated them into mini-kingdoms.

These local lords became kingmakers in inviting the king of East Francia, Charles III, "the Fat" (r. 884–88), to accept the western throne. On the death of Charles in 888, they reached enough of a consensus that they could settle on the choice of a war hero. They elected Odo (or Eudes) I (r. 888–98), fresh from his success in defending Paris from Viking attacks in 885–86. The eldest son of Robert "the Strong" (820–66), a royal envoy of Charles the Bald who had been made count of Anjou, Odo was the first in the dynastic line known as the Robertians (or Robertines), who, as the Capetians, would rule France for 400 years. The choice of Odo marked a recognition that the dynastic right of the Carolingians was not the only criterion in selecting a king, but that bravery and military ability were also important.

Odo did what he could to preserve what had survived of the Carolingian system, but his real power was narrowly confined. In areas south of the Loire, in the west Frankish part of Burgundy, in territory north of the Seine, and in lands in the far north, he had little direct authority. Great princes were in control here—Baldwin II (ca. 865–918) as count of Flanders from 879, William "the Pious" (875–918) as count of Auvergne from 886 and duke of Aquitaine from 893, Herbert I (ca. 843–907) as count of Vermandois from 907, and Richard, "the Justiciar" (?–921) as count of Autun from 880 and duke of Burgundy from 890, among others. Odo, who had defended a frontier district against the Vikings (and who had been named count of Paris in 882 or 883), thought so much like a local lord that even as king he assumed that dukes and counts had rights and privileges that, because they were necessary for effective defense, were proper in themselves.

Odo's successor, Charles III (r. 893–929) is remembered as "the Simple" in recognition not for any deficiency of intellect but rather for his honesty and good nature. He was evidently of such sweet tempera-ment that he could not help but give away additional territories. Most famously, in 911, he granted a number of counties near Rouen as a fief to Rollo (Hrólfr, ca. 860–ca. 932), a Viking chieftain who would find a dynasty, as dukes of Normandy, that would play a vital role in trad-ing, in seafaring, and in the political affairs of northern France. Most inauspiciously for the Carolingian dynasty, Charles conceded control over much of the area west of the Seine to Robert (866–923), Odo's younger brother, who assumed title as count of Paris.

Believing Charles to be a weak ruler and busily engaged in their own intrigues, lay and ecclesiastical magnates rebelled against him. They secured the election of Robert, who was crowned king at Reims in 922 by the same archbishop who had anointed his older brother. Styled now Robert I (r. 922–23), he secured recognition as duke of the Franks—the title first adopted in the seventh century after Pippin's triumph at Tertry—in tribute to his fighting feats against the Vikings, who had yet to forsake fully their fighting ways. Charles III fought the would-be usurper, and Robert died a year later in battle against him, but the election of the latter had confirmed the Robertians as powerful rivals of the Carolingians. It was a power rooted in the strategic location of their lands. Just as strong, independent-minded regional princes were chipping away at royal territories on the periphery of the kingdom of west Francia, so, too, did Carolingian lands in the heart of Neustria—the Paris and Orléans area—contract as the Robertians built up their power here. Robert's son Hugh, styled "the Great" (898–956), controlled most of these tracts.

Territorial confusion ensued as surrounding territorial power blocs—Burgundy, Flanders, Normandy, Vermandois—fell into disarray themselves or broke apart in a swirl of events in the middle of the 10th century. After Robert I's death in 923, his son-in-law Rudolph (Raoul or Ralph, r. 923–36), the duke of Burgundy, was crowned as his successor, and he managed to retain his throne after the demise of Charles the Simple in 929 until his own death in 936. Hugh the Great's position as the most powerful lord among the lot—by now he was heir to the overlordship of Neustria, count of Paris, and lay abbot of several important monasteries (he would acquire Burgundy to boot in 943)—allowed him to play kingmaker in securing acceptance of the other great magnates to the election of Charles the Simple's son, crowned as Louis IV (r. 936–54), who was called *d-Outremer* or *Transmarinus* (from across the seas) in reference to the years during Rudolph's rule spent in exile in England, where his mother, the daughter of King Edward the Elder (r. 899–924), took him as a child. Hugh and Louis quarreled, but not so much as to prevent Hugh's securing the guardianship of the king's estates, a post from which he watched over Louis's son Lothair (r. 954–86), who succeeded to the kingship at the young age of 13. Carolingian battled Carolingian during his reign; specifically, Lothair clashed with his brother Charles of Lorraine (r. 977–93), whom Holy Roman

Emperor Otto II (r. 967–83) had made duke of Lower Lotharingia, just to the east next door, in a tit-for-tat spate in which each invaded the territory of the other.

When Lothair died and his son Louis V (r. 986–87) met his own demise just a year later, the magnates of west Francia, meeting at Senlis to elect a successor, chose one of their own, Hugh Capet (r. 987–96), over Charles, who, as the ruler of neighboring territories, they suspected, would remain preoccupied with concerns outside the kingdom. In the lands that, under Clovis, had once made up the center of Frankish power, Carolingian rule was definitively dead, supplanted now by a new dynasty in place to meet the challenges ahead.

4

FRANCE IN EMBRYO
(987–1337)

When Hugh Capet won election to the kingship in 987, he was not the first—he was already the fourth—of his family to occupy the throne. But because he was the first in a direct line of descendants who would rule until 1328—and in an indirect line until 1789—his coronation marks the start of a new historical era. To contemporaries, however, the change meant very little. The king's writ held sway within only small bits of the lands over which the imperial might of Charlemagne once lay. Those feudal powers that he retained over certain of the dukes and counts who ruled surrounding territories stemmed more from respect for the spiritually sanctioned, time-honored fealty due to royal princes than from his ability to impose his will.

In the 11th and 12th centuries, northern France was the most thoroughly feudalized region in western Europe, its economy grounded in agriculture and the varying lordships (*seigneuries*) its distinguishing social framework. In theory, society was highly hierarchical, arranged like the rungs of a ladder—the knight did homage to a viscount, who did homage to a count, who did homage to a duke, who did homage to a king. In reality, however, the lines were often blurred. In southern France, this pyramidal structure was much less in evidence, while there were everywhere social bonds—among townsmen and clerics—that cut across, rather than up and down, society's bounds. And at the bottom, peasants toiled in servile or semiservile conditions, living always close to the margin of subsistence.

Feudalism reigned in France under a loose system of lordships in which local rulers fought one another to advance their interests. Such a scenario—in which war was the rule rather than the exception—allowed the monarchy, during the 12th century, to move gradually forward toward advancing its authority over more and more territory.

The economy prospered, towns grew, and cultural life blossomed. By the 13th century, the royal house controlled lands in both northern and southern France. During the reigns of the century's two most powerful rulers—the saintly Louis IX and the enigmatic Philip IV—government grew more effective and efficient. At century's end, even the head of the Roman Catholic Church—the great power of the age—had been brought more closely under French control.

But kings imposed no power over the faith upheld by the pope at Rome. In a world whose rhythms were set by the annual seasons, in an age when life was brief and harsh for all but a favored few, religion ruled society, able to compel God-fearing Christians to set off on crusade and to inspire men and women to build splendid cathedrals of glass and stone.

By 1300, the kingdom had coalesced into a land with a clear sense of a specifically French identity, ruled by a monarch, now empowered with greater clout, who commanded respect. But the threads with which the king's realm had been stitched together were loose indeed. Vast areas retained their own identities and privileges, and those who held great fiefdoms within the royal domain—the English king in Gascony, the duke of Burgundy, and the count of Flanders—remained eager to clip the wings of French rulers. In the 1300s, they would prove so formidable a set of foes as to put the state of the entire kingdom into an uncertain fate.

Royal Power Barely Survives, 987–1108

In 987, Hugh Capet was elected and crowned king by the Gauls, Normans, Aquitanians, Bretons, Goths, and Gascons. But while the king, in theory, might reign over all these peoples, in practice, he did not rule over most of them. The gap that had grown between theory and practice in the 10th century remained wide open at the turn of the first millennium. Hugh's real powers, like those of his immediate predecessors, were much reduced even within his central holdings while in outlying regions they were minimal. The steady shrinking in monarchical might ongoing from the century before would continue through much of the 11th century.

The power that attached to the throne was limited largely to the surviving image of the king as the supreme overlord invested by God with divinely sanctioned authority, the creation of which had been formalized so effectively by Charlemagne. The king stood at the apex of a social hierarchy, the man to whom the great men of his kingdom, as his vassals, were presumed in theory to owe advice and military service. He was the central lawgiver and the keeper of law and order.

The ruler was "chosen" by his people at a solemn assembly, which, in the 11th century, entailed a gathering of nobles, knights, and clerics. But because all the Capetian rulers until the late 12th century designated their eldest surviving son to succeed them, this "election" served merely as a formality before his coronation. In a ceremony filled with pomp and circumstance, the king proceeded to be blessed by the bishops and then to be anointed with the holy chrism, an act that set him apart from his subjects. The anointing of Pippin in 751 is the earliest on record. And because legend said it was chrism brought by a dove from heaven that was used to baptize his predecessor, King Clovis, at Reims, the church here became the traditional coronation site. The anointing of the king was followed by investiture with his regalia—the symbols of his office, including the sword, ring, scepter, and rod, given by the bishops. The crown was then placed on his head, usually by the archbishop of Reims, and he would solemnly ascend the throne.

The king drew what power he had from the rights to enforce justice and to impose tolls and taxes over castles, estates, forests, villages, and towns in the royal domain, namely, the sum total of his lands. He controlled far more bishoprics and key monasteries in his territories than the great regional princes did in theirs, able in some places—Paris, Orléans, Sens—to leave the bishop with little authority beyond the spiritual. The king also frequently regulated prices and levied fees at fairs and markets. At times, the royal court sat as a court of law, although legal developments were not clear-cut and the machinery of government was primitive, based on the monarch's household and, with their educated members, important ecclesiastical establishments, which issued charters in the king's name.

The coronations of the early Capetians were important events in the 11th century, although the sovereign's standing was honored more for its symbolic value than for its substance. Real power lay with those who possessed the resources to give it effect, namely, with the dukes and counts, descendants of the Carolingian nobility, who amassed sufficient wealth in land and revenues to make them territorial princes of note. Furthermore, viscounts and barons as well as chatelains—lords of a castle and plots of lands surrounding it that had been carved out of great noble estates—also competed for power at local levels by the 11th century, each of them, in theory, vassals of those above them. Out of this welter of confusing, ever-changing social arrangements, during the late 11th and 12th centuries, the king and various regional dukes and counts fought their way back to power against such petty lords, reasserting the right to occupy their castles and to impose feudal dominion over them with its demands that they provide military service, aid, and obedience.

During the 11th century, the great principalities that would form the core of France's later provinces took definitive shape. They varied widely, and they all exhibited differing degrees of fragmentation within their bounds. Burgundy had been a subkingdom of the Carolingian Empire but split three ways in the ninth century. One portion became a kingdom in its own right, owing allegiance to the Holy Roman Emperor, and another became the county of Burgundy (Franche-Comté). The section that remained the duchy of Burgundy in West Francia—the lands around Autun, Sens, and Nevers—retained its status, although the power of the dukes diminished such that by the 1070s the nobles ruling surrounding lands—the counts of Troyes, Mâcon, and Chalon-sur-Saône—and major bishops became practically independent players. The dukes lost additional authority to viscounts and other vassals. In the far north, since its founding as an independent principality in 862, Flanders had become, by the 10th century, an important regional power, and the clout of its counts, based on the prosperity engendered by the flourishing cloth trade in its burgeoning cities, would continue to grow.

In the far south (the Midi), a number of territorial powers had evolved—the duchy of Gascony (Guienne), the counties of Toulouse, Carcassonne, Ampurias-Roussillon, and the kingdom of Provence, the last becoming part of the larger kingdom of Burgundy. The south stood in distinct contrast to the north. The feudal arrangements in place in much of the north, based on grants of land or rights as fiefs, did not exist south of the Loire. Holders of land here did so not in exchange for services, as in the north, but for rents, and for a limited period, often a lifetime, rather than on an inheritable basis. There were few great nobles—the counts of Toulouse and Carcassonne were the two leading families. In the 11th century, castles proliferated here, their occupants managing to make hereditary the lands they occupied and battling their immediate neighbors to secure more turf. A new social group, knights, emerged, who like their counterparts in the north were proficient warriors but who, unlike them, remained free to offer their military services whenever and to whomever they chose. The south also witnessed the appearance of urban knights, who would play a vital role in the growth of southern towns.

Among the political groupings in the south, the duchy of Aquitaine was large and diverse. Ducal power peaked under William V, the

Great (r. 990–1030), after which many independent chatelains began to appear. In the mid-11th century, Aquitaine acquired the duchy of Gascony, which remained largely uncultivated and where local lords were left generally undisturbed. The county of Toulouse, formed originally in the 10th century, was not very large, but its counts retained some degree of authority, despite the power of independent ecclesiastical lordships and of nobles who constantly shifted allegiances.

Elsewhere, the duchy of Brittany continued its strong independent bent, with its Celtic-based identity, language, and culture. Heavily impacted by Viking raids, ducal authority declined but revived in the mid-11th century under long and stable reigns. The most centralized and ordered territory was Normandy. In the 10th century, large-scale Scandinavian immigration took place, followed thereafter by an end to links with northern Europe and the gradual adoption of Frankish language, government, social structure, and religious institutions. Dukes here lost considerable control up to the mid-11th century, after which the central ruling authority recovered.

Centered on the Paris and Orléans areas, the king's domain—the Île-de-France—constituted the territory directly under the control of the Crown. It was from this base that the early Capetian kings struggled to hold on to the little that was left to them. In regions that formed a ring around this royal region—Anjou, Blois, Champagne, and Picardy—monarchs tried as much as possible to contain powerful counts, drawing on what resources they could and on the support of allies—clerics and other neighboring princes—to help them do so.

Thus, Hugh Capet, a simple and pious man by all accounts, relied on diplomacy more than war to advance the royal house, making alliances with other territorial princes to counter a powerful rival coalition—the rulers of Anjou, Normandy, Aquitaine, and Flanders—and counting on the allegiance of major bishops and archbishops in his struggles against Charles of Lorraine, the Carolingian ruler to the east who continued to claim the French throne. Hugh's son Robert II, "the Pious" or "the Wise" (r. 996–1031), also leaned heavily on ecclesiastical backing during his long reign, and he returned the favor, granting protection and privileges to many monasteries. During his kingship, the division of the Carolingian Empire into eastern (Holy Roman Empire) and western (Francia) halves, which had remained fluid since its origins in the Treaty of Verdun (843), solidified. Robert's meeting with Emperor Henry II (r. 1014–24) on the border in 1023 symbolized the resolve of each of the rulers to renounce any right to govern the other. King Robert revived a degree of royal influence beyond the Seine and Loire

River valleys, but it did not last long. Focusing closely on their home regions, his successors Henry I (r. 1031–60) and Philip I (r. 1060–1108) struggled to exert their authority, an authority that under Philip was not especially strong even in royal lands.

Philip quarreled with the papacy. His divorce and his determination to keep control of some of the great ecclesiastical estates, whose wealth helped to sustain him, met opposition from a reforming church anxious both to uphold religious scruples and to free itself from the clutches of secular lords. In 1095, a council at Clermont excommunicated him, although to little effect because many French bishops remained his loyal backers.

The rift was later mended, but the clash exemplifies the central role of the church throughout these centuries during which religious players actively participated in politics. In the 11th century, the papacy was more powerful in the south of France than the king. As centralized power broke down, the king's authority over many, though by no means all, bishoprics and abbeys was replaced by that of dukes, counts, and chatelains, who often exploited them for their own enrichment. Under the early Capetians, clerics turned to the episcopate (powerful senior bishops and archbishops) and to the papacy for help to free themselves from lay authority, whether royal or regional.

The abbey at Cluny provides the outstanding example. Established in 909 by Berno of Baume and given its founding charter by William I, "the Pious" (r. 886–918), the duke of Aquitaine and the count of Auvergne, the abbey and its constellation of daughter houses looked to the papacy, which in the early 11th century won for them not only freedom from the exactions of temporal lords but also exemptions from episcopal oversight. The Cluniac monastic rule proved attractive in a time of so much turbulence. Life centered on an orderly routine of liturgical ceremony and prayer in which vows of poverty, chastity, and obedience were practiced in a setting of beautifully decorated cloisters and churches. Major abbeys acquired large estates, and their physical presence and spiritual force combined to make Cluny and its offshoots places of prestige and influence in their own locales and beyond. Cluny itself reigned as the grandest of Europe's monastic houses in the 11th and 12th centuries, when its abbots played prominent roles in statecraft, notably Odilo (ca. 962–ca. 1048), who greatly influenced Robert II.

The church also fought back against the violence consequent to so much political fragmentation. To put in place at least some limitations on the brutality of feudal society, it strove to transform battling warriors into, if not men of peace, at least Christian fighters. First appearing in the late 10th century in Burgundy and Aquitaine, regions especially troubled by unceasing unrest, the peace of God placed under the church's protection priests and ecclesiastical property together with the poor and their belongings. The peace of God was joined by the truce of God, which sought to ban violence at particular times, at first between Saturday evenings and Monday mornings. Both endeavors helped to introduce the notion of law and order into secular society, doing so, in these intensely religious times, in drawing reference to the ultimate harmony in heaven that these movements sought to reflect on an earthly level. These efforts to promote harmonious relations among Christians culminated in a direct bid to redirect internecine belligerency toward a foreign foe made in the call by French-born pope Urban II (r. 1088–99) for a crusade to free the holy places in Jerusalem from control by Muslim infidels, proclaimed at Clermont on November 27, 1095.

That call drew little enthusiasm from King Philip I, whose struggles with an increasingly influential and reforming church left him disinclined to assist actively a religious drive. During his reign, some important chatelains in the king's domain began to hold high office in the royal court. Their presence at the sovereign's side, working on his behalf, marked the first, faint glimmerings of a royal revival.

Royal Power Revives, 1108–1226

Louis VI (r. 1108–37) ascended the throne at the start of the 12th century, the ruler of a principality, centered on Paris and Orléans, still only small and unruly. A born fighter, the king set out to reverse both those facts by waging constant war against the chatelain families in his domain, some of whom wielded considerable power. A king who suffered from poor health and too healthy an appetite—by his mid-40s he was so obese that he could no longer mount a horse—he who was thus dubbed "the Fat" was greatly assisted in his late reign by two able advisers, Suger, abbot of Saint-Denis (ca. 1081–1151), a younger son from a family of minor knights, and Bernard, abbot of Clairvaux (1090–1153), who won fame and influence as the founder of the Cistercian monastic order. Abbot Suger advanced the prestige of the royal house by promoting its ties to Denis, the saint long venerated whose bones were interred, along with those of French kings, in the abbey named for him. Founded by the Merovingians at Paris, the Abbey of Saint Denis was restored by Suger to its ancient splendor.

Suger continued to cultivate the glory of the house of Capet as adviser to Louis's second son. Modest and pious, yet rash and indecisive, Louis VII (r. 1137–80) made the abbot's task difficult. Left behind as regent while Louis went off on the Second Crusade in 1147—a venture that ended in disaster—Suger called on the king to return posthaste to face a mounting threat from a nearby territorial prince. The Angevins—the counts of greater Anjou (Anjou, Maine, Touraine, Vendôme, and Saintonge)—had amassed immense wealth in land, beginning under Geoffrey, "the Fair" (r. 1129–51)—called Geoffrey Plantagenet because he wore a sprig of broom in his hat—and culminating under his son Henry II (r. 1151–89), who added England and Normandy to his already extensive domains. Louis waged war to prevent the transfer of Normandy to the Angevins, but he had to settle instead for only a small slice of territory (Norman Vexin).

A personal catastrophe now compounded this political setback when, in 1152, Louis, who had grown increasingly distant from his wife, Eleanor of Aquitaine (1122–1204), secured a dissolution of his marriage. Eleanor promptly wedded Henry II, adding Aquitaine and Gascony to make Henry's holdings breathtakingly vast. By the 1170s, Henry ruled, or controlled, all of western France, and although he did homage in theory to Louis as his vassal for these lands, his power base here made him, in fact, a rival ruler. Louis fought back as best he could, fomenting discord between Henry and his sons, but he could do no more than contain Angevin power. A combination of political skill, diligence, and luck would win for Louis's son Philip a good deal more.

Though chroniclers present an image of a man little liked by con- temporaries—he is portrayed as cynical, calculating, and greedy with a taste later in life for wine, women, and good fellowship—Philip II "Augustus" (r. 1180–1223) possessed a sharp political acumen and a powerful ambition. His marriage to Isabelle of Hainault (1170–90) brought him Artois as the queen's dowry, which made at least a start in the territorial competition with his Angevin neighbor. Rivalry was inevitable between Philip and Richard I "the Lionheart" (r. 1189–99), Henry II's son. Only a truce between the two, when they agreed to fight the Third Crusade (1189–92) together, separated their warring. Battling resumed in 1198 while Philip proceeded to chip away at Angevin power in Normandy by buying the support of the nobility, towns, and clergy with attractive concessions. When Philip declared that John I (r. 1198–1216), Richard's successor, had forfeited his French fiefdoms for failing to respond to a summons to appear at court, the war went on into the next Angevin reign. Philip overran Normandy by July

1204, when he seized Rouen. Royal influence made headway in Maine, Touraine, Anjou, and Brittany. By 1207, nothing of the once mighty Angevin empire remained north of the Loire. To put the stamp of royal authority on newly acquired territories, Philip built many castles, their characteristic circular stone towers (*donjons*) dotting the land, and he raised a specialist mercenary corps of troops that became an important part of the French army.

Philip was fortunate also in having already instituted experimental means that could now be extended to aid in administering the newly won lands. In 1189, he established the *baillis*, officials charged with preserving royal interests and ensuring that the king's *prévots*—the principal agents of local government—collected the revenues due the Crown. At first, the duties of the *baillis*—called *sénéchaux* in the south—were fluid, but by the late 13th century, they would become the chief financial and legal agents of the Crown within the local areas under their jurisdiction.

Philip won massive territorial gains, but his hold on them remained insecure unless he managed to defeat his rivals definitively in combat. He did so in a spectacular way when he bested the English king together with his allies, the count of Flanders and the Holy Roman Emperor, at the Battle of Bouvines on July 27, 1214. This victory marked a major milestone in the rise of the French monarchy in making it possible for the king to consolidate his conquests and incorporate them into his realm.

The task of building the monarchy's territorial base continued under his son. Louis VIII (r. 1223–26) differed from his father in being allegedly chaste and saintly, but like him, he, too, was an ambitious and able soldier. In his brief three-year reign, he conquered Poitou and captured much of Languedoc from the English. Though some acquisitions—Brittany, Anjou, Maine, and Auvergne—were given in grants (appanages) under Philip and Louis to enrich younger sons and grandsons in the royal family, the two monarchs remained much the most prominent property holders, ruling the royal lands in the Île-de-France and Normandy, as well as castles and counties in the Languedoc and elsewhere. In saving the French throne from the Angevin threat, they made the monarchy the dominant force in the kingdom.

It was a kingdom undergoing economic advancement and social change. Population expanded as the birthrate rose and life expectancy increased. Commercial life stirred and prosperity grew, starting in the 10th century, continuing in the 11th, and blossoming full-blown in the 12th. Agricultural production increased in the wake of meteorological changes that brought both drier and warmer weather and in conjunction with the introduction of technical improvements in working the land. Weightier plows, reinforced with iron, replaced lighter, wholly wooden ones, while the heavier and stronger horse took the place of oxen as draft animals. Cereal cultivation intensified, barley and rye yielding to wheat in many areas. Bread was the staple food, and so plowed land made up 80 to 90 percent of cultivated soils. Even peasants might eat meat—beef, mutton, pork, and poultry, but not game, which was scarce. Fish ponds dotted inland locales to meet the demand required by the numerous meatless days—some 150 a year—prescribed by the church. Wine growing was very important; vineyards spread as far north as Flanders. Population pressure and the promise of higher agricultural yields stimulated land clearance and reclamation, and from the late 11th century, new villages and religious communities began to appear.

Society was stratified into three formal classes, each with its assigned function: the clergy, who cared for souls; the nobles, who fought and helped govern; and the peasants, who labored to provide the food and material needs of everyone. The noble class had won its position in the early age of feudalism—the ninth, 10th, and 11th centuries—largely due to changes in warfare. Many knights had become nobles, and the class reached its peak in the 12th and 13th centuries. During this time, the life of a noble centered around his castle—its walls, towers, and battlements dominating the countryside to symbolize his temporal power. Since each landholder exercised jurisdiction over his tenants, each was very much a "lord" (*dominus*), even though he himself held his land in fief from some higher lord as his vassal.

The noble, mounted on his great warhorse and housed in his stone castle, lived a world apart from the peasants, whose rude huts clustered about the castle gates. The term generally used for peasant was *villein* or *vilain*, derived from Latin *villa*, and by the 13th century, it had acquired a negative tone consequent with the lowly status of those to whom it referred.

Under feudalism, the great rural estates so characteristic of Carolingian times disappeared. In time, too, land arrangements associated with feudalism also changed. Though the lords of the manor still exercised judicial and financial rights over peasants on their lands, by the 13th century in northern France, the heavy labor services of the peasants began to be commuted in return for money rents, sums that paid for lavish lifestyles for the nobility and for new churches and almsgiving for the clergy. Provided they paid rent, tenants practically owned their plots; they were left free to hand them over to heirs or even leave them uncultivated. In the west, farms were leased for a fixed term, tenants paying either a fixed sum of money *(fermage)* or a portion of their crops *(métayage)*. The great church-owned estates were also increasingly hired out to rich peasants. New dues were levied that came to be viewed as customary *(coutumes)*: The lord held monopolies over milling, baking, and wine pressing; he levied tolls and fees at fairs

LIFE IN A THIRTEENTH-CENTURY TOWN

Beginning in the 10th and 11th centuries, towns reemerged as centers of economic activity, which, together with agricultural improvements and increased money in circulation, brought about a revival of commerce that, by the 13th century, swept across western Europe. Villages would often pay rulers to buy their freedom from old feudal dues in order to transform themselves into communes, that is, self-governing towns.

Towns were small by today's standards. All had strong walls. They all contained abbeys and monasteries and many churches, most made of timber and a few made of stone with timbered roofs. Some towns featured the palace of a secular prince. Save for a few built of stone, most houses were tall timber post-and-beam buildings built close together. Neither sunlight nor rain often penetrated to the street because each story of a building jutted out over the one below. In poorer districts, several families lived in one house. The twisting lanes of the town streets were so narrow that pedestrians would bump shoulders in passing one another. There was no paving.

Related crafts—tailors, bakers, blacksmiths, weavers—tended to congregate in the same locales, their names often used to designate a street. Crafts also gave their names to craftsmen—Jean le charpentier (Carpenter), Henri le boulanger (Baker). Surnames were becoming important in an age when tax collectors had to maintain lists to record payments.

Business premises were on the ground floor of residences, fronting directly on the streets, which were filthy. Human wastes and household garbage were often simply thrown out of windows. Ordinances to force residents to keep the streets in front of their houses clean were enacted, but they were usually only partially effective. Toilets consisted generally of a privy in stable yards. A few houses, mostly

and markets; and he could impose taxes or demand military service. The great majority of peasants lived close to subsistence even in the best of times and, though disease wreaked havoc among all classes, the peasantry suffered disproportionately from its ravages. Compounding the precariousness of their life, warring nobles might destroy their crops and kill peasants.

those of the better off, had a closet with a chute to a pit in the cellar, which was occasionally emptied.

Only a few homes featured carpets; rather, floors were covered with rushes. Furniture consisted typically of benches, a long trestle table, which was dismantled after meals, and a long wooden cupboard where spices, because they were extremely expensive, were kept locked. Dining places were set with knives, spoons, and thick slices of day-old bread, which served as plates. Forks were unknown. Fleas, bedbugs, lice, and rodents were constant menaces. Men sported stubbly faces, a clean shave impossible to attain with the instruments available and a thorough grooming by a barber done usually only once a week.

Housewives shopped daily, there being no way to preserve food. Salt was cheap, pepper expensive, and sugar even more so. Many women worked outside the home in a surprising number of crafts and trades—teachers, midwives, laundresses, and even a few in such traditional male professions as weavers, barbers, and carpenters. Unmarried women could own property and inherit wealth in the absence of male heirs. Most women married very young, in their early teens, and arranged marriages were the rule, often to men considerably older.

Most people married within their own class. Very few of either sex could expect to live beyond their 30s and 40s. Fifty was considered a ripe old age. Disease, poor hygiene, tooth decay, wounds from fighting, and ailments ranging from cancer to the common cold caused great suffering. Mental illness and leprosy were widespread, and few availed themselves of hospitals, which were a recent innovation. For women, the greatest hazard was childbirth. Midwives began to deliver by caesarean section in the 13th century, but only if the mother had died in labor in order to baptize the child, whether alive or dead, so as to ensure its salvation. The chances that a baby would survive were even poorer than the mother's. Many died at birth and even more during infancy.

It was an age when one's social rank could easily be discerned by what one wore. Church sumptuary laws allowed dukes several gowns a year, though they invariably exceeded the limit, whereas the poor might wear garments passed down through several generations. Rich ladies sported elaborate headdresses and dressed themselves in gowns of silk and cotton; the wealth of the wearers could be determined by the color of their clothes—bright colors, such as red and yellow, were more expensive than dull ones.

Trade began to intensify and then to spread across wider regions, bringing with it a revival of a vibrant urban life that saw the introduction of a new class—merchants and craftsmen—to medieval society. Towns multiplied in the 11th and 12th centuries under the active encouragement of kings, dukes, and counts, anxious to benefit from the wealth generated by the production and exchange of goods that took place there. Paris, Toulouse, and Lyon prospered on the profits in wine, oil, grain, metalwork, and leather. Troyes and others towns in Champagne were renowned across Europe for their great trade fairs. New ports appeared, such as Harfleur, and new inland towns, such as Caen and Lille. The use of silver currency became widespread.

Because they remained outside the tripartite class division, townsmen were essentially nonfeudal. They were free, and, as such, they could defend themselves and their rights—the walls of a city studded with turrets made it as much a fortress as any castle. If they owed allegiance to the king or to the lord on whose lands their towns stood—and, as these grew, their cities—it was on the basis of free choice, not personal homage. When they organized into groups, they endowed themselves with the clout to win rights to self-governance. Starting sporadically in the late 10th century, rulers granted privileges or franchises, namely, exemptions from tolls and dues in return for a fixed payment and political liberties permitting varying amounts of administrative and judicial freedom. By the 13th century, towns everywhere enjoyed these rights.

Town dwellers were stratified by wealth—at the bottom, unskilled laborers; above them, craftsmen; and, at the top, merchants and those who lived off their properties, rents, or money lending. The well-to-do controlled town government, profiting from their power to set low taxes for themselves and to spend town revenues on their own lavish lifestyles.

By the 12th century, Paris had emerged as the indisputable capital city, surpassing in size and prosperity all other towns in the kingdom's northern lands. The island in the center of the Seine—the Île de la Cité—that had been semirural earlier was built over in the 11th century, and the great cathedral of Notre-Dame located there was completely reconstructed beginning in 1163. Under Philip Augustus, city streets were paved in 1186, and a wall, replete with more than 70 towers, was raised around the town in 1189–90. The king also directed construction of the Louvre castle.

Paris, together with Montpellier, boasted the only two medical colleges in northwestern Europe. In about 1180, the first college—the Dix-Huit—was founded, launching the University of Paris. Pope Innocent III (r. 1198–1216) issued a bull extending recognition as a legal corporation in 1210. In about 1256, Robert de Sorbon established La Sorbonne, a school to permit poor scholars to continue their education. A center of theological studies, as an ecclesiastical tribunal it won prestige in western Europe second only to the papacy as a religious authority. The Sorbonne became just one of several colleges at the by now well-established University of Paris, all of them situated on the left bank of the Seine River in an area that would emerge as the Latin Quarter, the capital city's famed center for scholarly and artistic activities. The masters who taught here gradually formed a tight-knit fraternity, earnestly debating each other over theological and philosophical questions. It was an exercise in intellectual inquiry indicative of the rise of a literate culture.

The Twelfth-Century Renaissance
The Birth of French Literature

During the 12th century, not only profound political, economic, and social changes swept across French lands but also a blossoming of literary, artistic, and scholarly activity took place. Often termed the 12th-century "renaissance" (literally, rebirth), revival might be a more accurate description since the literary motifs and meanings that were discovered at this time traced their origins to classical antiquity. Twelfth-century literature exalted themes such as individual development, adventure, and romance, and it established itself as a secular pursuit, which had largely disappeared with the collapse of the Roman Empire and which continues to characterize literature today.

The south of France led the way. At the end of the 11th century, lyric poems appeared in Aquitaine, written mostly about "courtly love," in which a lady is adored from afar by a lover who seeks to win her favor by displaying gallant, knightly virtues of devotion, patience, and bravery. Composed and disseminated by troubadours (from *trobar,* "to find" or "to invent"), courtly compositions gave rise to a style of life, an ideology, and even an ethical system, and they also spawned a great outpouring of lyric songs. They became hugely popular, carried from court to court by professional minstrels *(jongleurs).* In the 12th century, they spread to northern France, where *trouvères*—the northern equivalent of troubadours—worked, though arrangements produced here featured styles less inventive and substances less sensual than those characteristic of the originals. Poets were drawn to royalty, such as Bernart de Ventadorn (fl. 1147–70), in residence at the court of Eleanor of Aquitaine and Louis VII. By the 14th century, troubadours and *trouvères* gave way to use of the term *poète,* which had formerly referred only to classical writers but now came to be applied, for the first time, to contemporary versifiers.

Lyric poems were written in the vernacular, a testament to the appearance of early variants of French as a vehicle worthy of literary expression despite the universal use of Latin as the language of learning. French evolved gradually from a linguistic foundation based on dialects spoken by the Gauls, to which the Latin of the Romans and the Germanic languages of the Franks and others were introduced. Few traces of the Gaullish idiom remain in the modern language. In the Middle Ages, regional differences were strong, the most striking the divide between the language of the south—the Langue d'oc, which was close to Catalan and was later known as Provençal—and the language of the north—the Langue d'oïl, which displayed strong Celtic and Germanic influences and developed into modern French. Derived from the language *(langue)* that uses *oc* or *oïl* to mean "yes" in the two parts of France, the names "Languedoc" and "Langue d'oïl" later came to designate southern and northern lands, respectively.

Throughout the 12th and 13th centuries, courtly literature was composed together with another much-produced genre: The *chansons de geste* were long narrative songs written in the vernacular by anonymous authors who used fictionalized episodes from history to induce musings on violence and conflict, both political and familial. Such poems include *La chanson de Roland (The Song of Roland),* in which the protagonist, Roland, embodies an affinity for glory and grandeur that would remain an attribute of the French heroic tradition. *La chanson de Guillen* (The song of Guillen) introduced comedy, and *La prise d'Orange* (The taking of Orange) that of melodrama to the genre.

Epic heroes such as Roland constituted ascetic figures not unlike the saints whose virtues writers during this profoundly religious age praised. Indeed, literature had its very beginnings in clerical writings with their moralizing mission to instruct souls, and pious works directed at a broad audience were among the first vernacular tracts to appear in the 12th century.

The history of music in France, as in all of western Europe, began with Christian chant, that is, with musical forms that originated mostly in Hebrew synagogues and that were adapted by early Christian churches. Reforms under Pope Gregory the Great (r. 590–604) led to the creation of Gregorian chant, and subsequent developments sprang from this base. Composition and experimentation took place as early as the first half of the 12th century at the monastery of Saint Martin in Limoges and, later, at Notre-Dame Cathedral, where the works of Pérotin (Perotinus, fl. ca. 1200) made him the most famous composer of the period.

Theater began as religiously inspired drama, though it was often denounced as sinful by some early clergymen. Plays centered on the lives of the Virgin Mary and the saints were especially plentiful. Jean Bodel's (?–1210) *Le jeu de saint* (The game of the saint, 1200–01) is the oldest known example of the miracle play. Vernacular theater emerged from the shadow of the church by the late 1200s, and productions appealed increasingly to the new urban audiences. The earliest surviving secular play is a short farce, *Le garçon et l'aveugle* (The boy and the blind man), composed between 1266 and 1282, in which the performers show how an intelligent young man meets his match.

History centered largely on the glamour of chivalry. Many 12th-century chroniclers, like their predecessors dating back to antiquity, interlaced their works liberally with myth, fable, and fiction. In the 13th century, writing improved markedly in quality, employing a new, critical approach to source materials in contrast to the first French histories, which were written by monks such as Raoul Glaber (ca. 950–1046). *La conquête de Constantinople* (The conquest of Constantinople, ca. 1204) by Geoffroi de Villehardouin (ca. 1150–ca. 1216), one of the first prose works, tells of the Fourth Crusade (1199–1204). The monks of Saint-Denis emerged as the first royal historians. Biographies were also written. The *Histoire de Saint Louis* (History of Saint Louis, 1309) by Jean de Joinville (1225–?) extols the spiritual virtues of the pious king but also conveys an image of Louis as a fully human being.

In the 13th century, prose appears for the first time in wide use in narrative writing, in both history and fiction, although it does not

Feudalism flourished in the Middle Ages. Detail of a castle at Poitiers. Note the peasants tilling the fields outside the walls. Illuminated manuscript from Les très riches heures du duc de Berry, *ca. 1440. Limbourg brothers (15th c.)* (Réunion des Musées Nationaux/Art Resource, NY)

overtake verse until the late 14th century. In the 1200s, a large-scale literature emerged addressed for the first time not to the courtiers at the courts but rather to the wealthy residents of the increasingly prosperous towns. Bawdy, short verses (*fabliaux*, "little fables"), with characteristically tight plots and featuring nonaristocratic characters and settings, appear as the exact opposite of the chivalric epic—courtly emotions of the heart in the latter now replaced by an obsession with the body—and are expressive of growing, urban-based tastes, which preferred satirical humor to edifying sentiment.

All the strands at work come together at the end of the 13th century in the *Roman de la rose* (parts translated as *The Romaunt of the Rose*), arguably the single most important French text of the Middle Ages. Written over the course of 40 years, from about 1230 to 1275, first by the otherwise unknown poet Guillaume de Lorris (fl. 1230) and later by writer and translator Jean de Meun (ca. 1250–ca. 1305), and apparently left unfinished, this sprawling 22,000-line grandiose work, styled as an allegorical dream vision, incorporates the traditions of courtly love, racy humor, social satire, classical literature, and philosophical reflection. For 200 years, along with the Bible, it was the most read book in Europe. It survives in hundreds of illuminated manuscripts.

Royalty emerged as great patrons of art and learning during this period. Four French brothers were among the greatest: Charles V; Philip II; Louis I, duke of Anjou (1339–84); and, the greatest of all, John, duke of Berry (1340–1416). John built a series of castles—paid for by taxing his subjects relentlessly—and filled them with tapestries, jewelry, and paintings. The illustrations in the richly pictorial book of hours *Les très riches heures du duc de Berry* (*The Very Rich Hours of the Duke of Berry,* ca. 1412) give vivid, highly descriptive images of country life in medieval France. The culture of chivalry and romance so cultivated at the courts of French kings and Burgundian dukes were the models for fashion and good manners all across Europe.

A poet who has earned lasting fame, François Villon (ca. 1431–after 1463) was a thief and a vagabond who managed to compose while in prison. In his chief work, Testaments, he reverses the courtly ideal in celebrating society's downcasts destined for the gallows. His question: "Mais où sont les neiges d'antan?" (But where are the snows of yesteryear?) drawn from his "Ballade des dames du temps jadis" (The ballad of yesterday's belles, ca. 1461) has become one of the most celebrated lines of translated secular poetry. Villon is known for his *ballades,* three eight-line stanzas, each with a consistent meter and a particular rhyme scheme, that emerged as one among three "fixed forms" (*formes fixes*) used in poetry and music between the late 13th and 15th centuries. The others include the *rondeau,* characterized by 15 lines written on two rhymes, and the *virelai,* in which each stanza has two rhymes.

In architecture France emerged in the 12th century as the birthplace of an innovative style—the Gothic—and the country continued as a center of monasticism, which thrived under yet another new rule. Bernard of Clairvaux (1090–1153), who arrived at the abbey of

GOTHIC ARCHITECTURE

Originating in the cities of the Île-de-France in the second half of the 12th century, Gothic architecture spread across France in conjunction with the advance of royal power. It went on to be copied throughout western Europe, where it was known as the "French style." Gothic emerged gradually out of the Romanesque ("in the Roman") style, in vogue in the 10th through 12th centuries, in breaking decisively away from the latter's massive masonry, rounded arches, and solid walls through the introduction of a single, outstanding architectural feature, the pointed arch (ogive). Intersecting ribs set

Notre-Dame Cathedral, Paris (Library of Congress)

Cîteaux with a group of companions in 1112 or 1113, oversaw the adoption of the Cistercian ideal and the expansion of the order with an unsurpassed enthusiasm and vigor. Founded in 1098, Cîteaux housed a congregation of monks who practiced a reinvigorated rule

crosswise to form an arched vault constituted the defining structural feature of the style, and this construction technique became the basis for subsequent refinements that produced progressively grander buildings. Early Gothic, which emerged in Abbot Suger's reconstruction of the old Carolingian abbey church of Saint-Denis (begun in 1137 and completed in 1144) and in Louis IX's Sainte-Chapelle (completed in 1248), evolved into High Gothic, when flying buttresses and cross-ribbed vaults were employed fully in great cathedrals built at Bourges, Amiens, and elsewhere, including at Notre-Dame in Paris. Because the building's ribs, piers, and buttresses carried its weight, the walls could be practically eliminated. In their place, brilliant color glitters from the insertion of large, stained-glass windows, which constitute the major pictorial art of the period. The interior brightness marked an unprecedented innovation. Abbot Suger marveled at "the wonderful and uninterrupted light of most sacred windows, pervading the interior beauty" (Suger 1946, 901).

French Gothic cathedrals tend to exhibit standard features. Many are made of limestone, in plentiful supply in France. They are compact. The west fronts display three doors, and intricate, carved figures often adorn the portals—nowhere more beautifully than on the main doorway at Chartres Cathedral. The doors are surmounted by a rose window and two large towers. The east ends sometimes feature side chapels radiating along the outside. Most follow a cross ("cruciform") plan with a long nave, which composes the body of the church, flanked on either side by aisles, a cross arm (transept), and, beyond it, an extension, called the choir, chancel, or presbytery. In southern France, many churches are without transepts and some lack aisles.

Gothic architecture was essentially urban. The growing cities supplied the skilled workers and their money-based economies the funds to pay the laborers and buy the materials. But always the Roman Catholic Church provided the patronage and direction. Built during an age when religious faith framed every facet of life, these soaring edifices were constructed to represent an analogy of the world as God had created it, perfect in proportion, form, and function. Though made of stone, Gothic cathedrals seem weightless, expressing, in their very physicality, humankind's spirituality.

of Saint Bernard, observing poverty and seclusion to the letter. Daily life revolved around manual labor, and contact with laymen was kept to a minimum. By 1300, almost 700 Cistercian communities could be found across France, and monarchs and territorial princes became patrons. Other orders also emerged. The Augustinians worked actively in the world as parish priests and caretakers of the sick, while the Premonstratensions stressed both physical work and preaching and pastoral care. The Carthusians were complete hermits, their worldly needs looked after by lay brothers. Nunneries grew, too, especially in the north and west, none more famous historically than the abbey of the Paraclete, founded for Héloïse (1101–64) by the man with whom she shared an intellectual discourse and a legendary illicit, passionate love, Peter Abelard (1079–1142).

A theologian and philosopher, Abelard encapsulated in his person the revival of learning then taking place. Many ecclesiastical communities busied themselves at this time assembling libraries of books, all copied by hand. In works such *Sic et non* (*Yes and No,* ca. 1120), Abelard made an important contribution in moving theology away from its traditional concentration on interpretation of the Bible and the writings of the early church fathers toward the study and teaching of logic. Interest in ancient Rome also rose sharply in the early 12th century. Classical authors were read and poetry composed in Latin, much of it on Christian themes, while the study of rhetoric, long a staple of scholarly interest, moved away from its origins in the scholarly examination of Latin texts toward a practical application, namely, the composition of letters, for which the school at Orléans was especially renowned. Study of science, medicine, and philosophy received a new stimulus, sparked by the recovery and translation of texts written by classical and Arabic authors, including Euclid, Galen, Aristotle, and Averroës.

While polemicists and clerics taught and argued, isolated groups of heretics began to appear in the early 11th century from among hermits and wandering preachers who championed poverty and decried the wealth of the church and the rich town dwellers. In the 12th century, heresy would emerge full-blown, but it would be restricted largely to southern France, where a more tolerant society aided its growth. Founded by Waldo, a rich merchant of Lyon who renounced his wealth to preach the apostolic power of being poor, the Waldensians were driven from the lands of the archbishop of Lyon to scatter into Languedoc. By 1184, when the pope named them as heretics, they were well established in centers such as Albi, Carcassonne, and Montpellier. Though heavily persecuted, they survived until the Protestant Reformation of the 16th century.

The Cathars proved less fortunate. A sect that had originated in Germany in the early 11th century, the Cathars (Cathar means "pure") spread rapidly in the Midi such that, by midcentury, they could be found

ABELARD AND HÉLÖISE

Philosopher, theologian, and logician Peter Abelard earned renown as a teacher at Paris, where, at the height of his fame, he met Hélöise. As the ward of her uncle, Fulbert, a canon in whose house she lived, Hélöise had become schooled in Latin, Greek, and Hebrew. Abelard persuaded Fulbert to permit him to teach Hélöise, and he moved into the house. The two became lovers. Furious, Fulbert forced them to separate, but they continued to meet in secret. Hélöise became pregnant and bore a son. Hoping to maintain his career prospects by preserving his image as a chaste scholar devoted entirely to philosophical debate, Abelard proposed to marry her in secret. Fulbert assented and, though at first she opposed, Hélöise consented too. After the marriage, she went to stay at a convent at Argenteuil. Believing that she had been abandoned, an incensed Fulbert and his kinsmen brutally attacked Abelard, castrating him while he slept. Hélöise took the habit of a nun, becoming in time an abbess while Abelard became a monk and continued to teach. Parted in life, the two are reputed to lie together in death, their remains reposing in a crypt in the Père-Lachaise cemetery in Paris. Among history's most star-crossed lovers, Hélöise and Abelard corresponded after they entered religious life, and although in the end she accepted his counsel to consider their relationship to be now one of brother to sister, her letters to him remain celebrated examples of human passion and womanly devotion. An excerpt follows:

> You know, dearest, all know, how much I lost in loving you. An infamous and hitherto unheard of crime, in depriving you of my love, tore me from myself. . . . I expect consolation from no other, for you, who alone have caused me to grieve, can alone console me. . . . My love for you rose to such a height of delirium that it sacrificed, without hope of regaining it, the sole object of its desire. At your command I changed my habit as well as my inclination, in order to show you that you were the only master of my heart.
>
> . . .
>
> Although the name of wife seems more holy and more valid, another has always been sweeter to me, that of friend; or, if you will not be shocked, that of concubine or mistress. The more I humbled myself before you, the more, as I thought, should I elevate myself in your favor, and thus injure the less the glory of your excellence.

Source: Orlando Williams Wight, ed., *Lives and Letters of Abelard and Heloise* (New York: M. Doolady, 1861), pp. 150–151.

among both rich and poor. By the 1160s, they had established their own church organization that paralleled that of Catholics. Adherents of a dualist theology that held physical matter to be evil and only the spiritual realm to be sin-free and perfect, they denied that Jesus Christ could exist as a human being and still be the son of God. Believers in a two-person deity, they saw in Rome's opulence proof of its status as a church in service to the evil earthly—not the good heavenly—divinity. Quite evidently, the Cathars posed a threat to both the church and the feudal order. In 1208 Pope Innocent III called for a crusade against them, to which the king and nobility readily responded. Blamed for the spread of heresy in his dominions, Count Raymond VI (r. 1194–1222) of Toulouse speedily submitted in hopes of forestalling military invasion, but to no avail. Led by Simon de Montfort (1208–65), a leading baron of the Île-de-France, the crusade ravaged Languedoc for several years. By the Treaty of Paris of 1229, royal power was established in parts of the region, and Raymond VII (r. 1222–49) agreed to marry his daughter to Alphonse de Poitiers (1220–71), Louis VIII's brother, with succession to rulership of the county of Toulouse to go to the Crown. The diplomatic settlement marked a propitious start for King Louis IX (r. 1226–70), a sovereign whose reign would prove momentous for monarchy in France.

Royal Rule Revives and a New Dynasty Arrives, 1226–1337

Louis IX has entered the annals as France's most revered king because he alone among the monarchs earned so high an acclaim among his contemporaries that they saw fit to attach the title "saint" to his name. Canonized in 1297, Louis enjoyed a reputation that was already the stuff of legend such that his cult spread quickly after his death. Described as "slender, lean, and tall; he had an angelic countenance and a gracious person" (Gwatkin 1932, 7, 331), another chronicler relates:

> In regard to his dress, he would never more wear . . . scarlet robes, nor gilt spurs, nor use stirrups. His dress was of camlet or Persian. . . . He was very sober at his meals, and never ordered anything particular or delicate to be cooked for him, but took patiently whatever was set before him. He mixed his wine with water according to its strength, and drank but one glass. He had commonly at his meals many poor persons behind his chair, whom he fed, and then ordered money to be given to them. He was considered as by far the wisest of any in his council. . . . (Joinville 1963, 528–529)

The king's outstanding trait of piety—he was a regular communicant at mass—has shaped his enduring image. But he was much more besides. A strong ruler and a man of wit, charm, and intelligence, but also one prone to stubbornness, impatience, and sudden anger, he was an innovative lawgiver and a ruler with a powerful command of the workings of the royal bureaucracy.

Louis was only 12 years old when his father died, however, and it was up to his mother, Blanche of Castile (1188–1252), under whose tutelage he was left, to make sure the gains made by Philip II and Louis VIII were kept. Some among the nobility sought to test her strength in an effort to increase their power while Henry III of England (r. 1216–72) itched to regain the lost Angevin lands. A woman of vigor and piety,

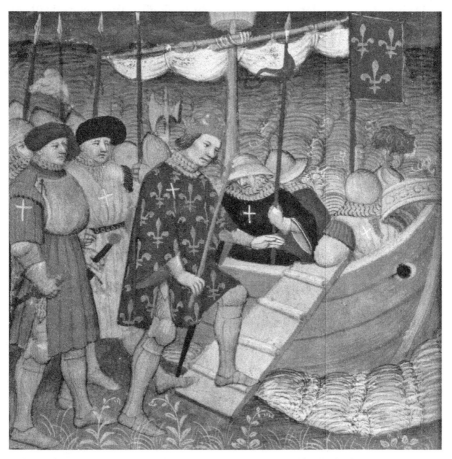

Louis IX departing for the Crusades. 15th century, French manuscript leaf (Bridgeman-Giraudon/Art Resource, NY)

Blanche navigated the ship of state through the dangerous shoals successfully, battling French barons and the English king to safeguard—and even extend—royal rule.

Louis would carry on the task. Defeating King Henry, Count Raymond, and various rebellious lords in Poitou, he established his military and political superiority over all of France save for the southwest, where the duchy of Gascony formed the sole remaining core of the heretofore vast English continental real estate. Now a thoroughly cooperative partner of the French monarchy, Raymond VII proceeded to crush the last resistance of the Cathars, their stronghold at Montségur capitulating to him in 1244. By that date, relations with the regional princes had stabilized, and with the country on strong footing, Louis embarked in 1248 for the Seventh Crusade (1248–54). He returned in 1254, his money depleted, anxious to get back after the recent death of his mother and to leave behind what had turned out to be a disastrous venture—his forces were defeated and captured in 1250.

Louis turned again to the work of territorial acquisition, this time launching a diplomatic drive. He secured a renunciation of the Spanish kingdom of Aragon's claims to Provence and Languedoc, and in 1258 he signed the Treaty of Paris with Henry III, which confirmed the English king in his possession of Gascony and parts of Languedoc in return for his acknowledgment of French sovereignty over Normandy, Anjou, Poitou, Maine, and Touraine. That Louis IX's opponents were gradually brought into line through a mix of diplomacy and war testifies to a shift in the political balance in which feudal relations—the recognition by his vassals of the king's preeminence—became more clearly defined in favor of the monarchy. Viscounts, barons, and chatelains were now slipping into eclipse. In the mid-13th century, many went on crusade, from which they never returned, while others became loyal vassals of the royal power. Their role as a governing force was replaced by a largely ceremonial one.

In 1270, when Louis embarked on another crusade, he left behind a realm in which he was much the most substantial landlord and, perforce, the wealthiest man in the realm. Anxious to advance effective rule, he strove to ensure that financial and judicial administrations were well managed. Royal government came to be fully developed in the king's lands, and its presence more pronounced outside of them as well. A reforming ordinance of 1254 forbade blasphemy, gambling, and usury. Royal officials (*enquêteurs*) were dispatched to seek out and remedy, where possible, injuries and unjust exactions made by the monarchy's administrators.

The central role of faith in the life of the king was mirrored in a religious renewal during his reign that marked a new departure. Unlike the Carthusians and Cistercians, which were now in decline, new mendicant orders no longer preferred the prayer-filled life of the cloister; rather, they embraced an active role in the world, and especially in interacting with the citizens in the expanding towns. No order proved more influential than the Franciscans. Founded by Francis of Assisi (ca. 1180–1226) in Italy, the Franciscans spread through France soon after his death, their appeal in rejecting worldly goods, living by begging and preaching, and ministering to the poor proving so popular that, by 1300, almost 200 monastic houses could be found.

The other main mendicant order sprang from an entirely different source. In 1206, Dominic (1170–1221), a Spanish-born Augustinian canon, began a preaching campaign against the Cathars and Waldensians in Languedoc. Working from their base at Prouille, founded in 1207, the Dominicans were educated men and primarily priests—unlike the Franciscans, who in the beginning were mostly laymen. They, too, spread across France, most especially to Paris, which became a principal center. The Dominicans established a network of schools, which the Franciscans later imitated, and men from both orders emerged as intellectual leaders in theology. Though neither was French born, Albertus Magnus, or Saint Albert the Great (1193/1206–80), and his pupil, Thomas Aquinas (ca. 1275–74), both Dominicans, labored at Paris to reconcile Christian theology with the philosophy of the ancient classical authors. They did so by means of scholasticism (Latin "that which belongs to the school"), a method of learning, already employed by Peter Abelard, that sought by means of dialectic reasoning (examining opposing opinions) to answer questions and resolve contradictions in doctrines and beliefs. Aquinas's masterpiece, the *Summa Theologica* (1265–74), which was left unfinished at his death, constituted an ambitious synthesis of Christian dogma and Greek philosophy, noteworthy for one of its most highly influential assertions, that the existence of God could be known by reason alone.

Louis's son, Philip III (r. 1270–85), as generous an almsgiver and as fervent a servant of the church as was his father, was, unlike him, easily influenced and given to leaving the business of governing to his advisers. He reigned briefly and disastrously. The defeat of a French army, which invaded Aragon in 1276 to support papal policy, left the monarchy heavily encumbered with debt. The lesson was well learned by his son, who would shun expensive expeditions in faraway places to concentrate on the monarchy's immediate interests at home.

Said to be tall and handsome, with golden hair, Philip IV, "the Fair" (r. 1285–1314), was as pious as his predecessors but of such a reserved nature that his character remains enigmatic. Whatever his personal traits, he combined within his person the ability to both delegate authority and maintain effective control of the state.

Until about the middle of the 13th century, the central government was composed of the king and his Curia Regis, a court made up of domestic officers of the royal household and a varying group of lay and ecclesiastical vassals of the king, to whom he delegated judicial and administrative functions at will. After Louis IX's reign, the domestic duties of the household were separated gradually from the governmental business, which was entrusted to groups of ministers (Conseil du Roi) who in time became permanent officials, working with the king as a small coterie of trusted advisers. The number of experts in the two most specialized activities—finance and justice—increased such that they needed a settled location, and by 1300 they had established themselves in Paris, ceasing to follow the court, which throughout the medieval and early-modern periods moved intermittently about the realm. They also required a permanent organization. The judicial branch of the royal court evolved into the Parlement of Paris, which appeared definitively by the 1320s. It served largely as a supreme court of appeal, from which, as it acquired a growing staff and forms of operation, it began slowly to exercise considerable influence over the composition of royal legislation. Its acquisition of the power to register royal edicts before enforcing them, in effect to delay legislation (to "remonstrate" with the king), helped to develop among its members a sense of their own dignity and worth that would deepen over the years. At the same time, during the reign of Philip the Fair officials responsible for governmental income and expenditure formed a financial court, the Chamber of Accounts (Chambre des Comptes). A Court of Aids (Cour des Aides) to handle tax cases and a Court of Monies (Cour des Monnaies) for monetary cases also appeared.

More land accrued to the Crown in 1284 when Philip married Joan I of Navarre (1271–1305), and she brought with her both the kingdom of Navarre and the counties of Champagne, Brie, and Bar, the latter three eventually united with the royal domain. In 1312 he acquired the Lyonnais. Following the failure of the duke of Gascony, King Edward I of England (r. 1272–1307), to appear at the court as a dutiful royal vassal should, Philip initiated war in 1294. Badly beaten at Courtrai in 1302 by the Flemish, England's ally, Philip ended an inconclusive campaign in concluding a treaty at Paris in 1303 under which the marriage of Philip's daughter to the prince of Wales, the future Edward II of England (r. 1307–27), was meant to cap the settlement of the scrap.

By the 14th century, the larger size of armies along with increasing use of more—and more complex—equipment put onerous strains on royal revenues, which, together with the growth in the number of salaried officials and the much larger territorial size of the kingdom, had become burdensome. The king consequently searched relentlessly for added income. He arrested Jews—the money lenders of the Middle Ages in an era when such financial transactions were frowned on as unbecoming actions for nonmaterially minded, good Christians—so as to seize their assets and expelled them altogether in 1306. Italian (Lombard) merchants and rich abbots were compelled to contribute to the royal coffers. The king debased the coinage, and fees and taxes were levied at the great Champagne fairs.

Expecting the revenue of the church to be at his disposal when required, when he demanded from the clergy one-half of their income, Philip fell foul of the pope. In the bull *Clericos laicos* (1296), Pope Boniface VIII (r. 1294–1303) forbade the transfer of any church property to the Crown, and in *Unam sanctum* (1302), he proclaimed the primacy of papal over kingly power. Determined to assert his supremacy, Philip convoked an assembly of French bishops, nobles, and wealthy bourgeois—the first Estates General—who backed their sovereign. Fortified by this display of loyalty, he promptly dispatched his agent William de Nogaret (1260/70–1313) to the papal palace at Agnani, Italy, to arrest Boniface on a charge of heresy. He then seized de facto control of the papacy itself when French cardinals emerged victorious in securing the election of French-born Raymond Bertrand de Got as Pope Clement V (r. 1305–14). Crowned at Lyon with Philip in attendance, the new pope immediately created nine new French cardinals to solidify the royal hold.

In a crowning act indicative of the fact that the pope was now but a tool of the French king, Clement moved the entire papal court in March 1309 to Avignon, an enclave in Provence that, although not a part of France, was surrounded completely by French territory. During the 70-year interregnum (1309–77) of the so-called Babylonian Captivity of the Church (an analogy with the captivity of the ancient Jews at Babylon), the seven French popes and the cardinals—113 out of 134 were also French—would give the church a well-run government but little else, providing scant spiritual leadership and arousing the resentment of others in Europe, especially the English.

Two years before, in October 1307, Philip directed the arrest of hundreds of Knights Templars, a militant order founded early in the 12th century to fight in the Crusades and that had gone on to amass a financial fortune. After many of its members were tortured into giving false confessions and burned at the stake, the order was disbanded by the pope under pressure from Philip in 1312.

The ruthlessness with which the Templars were eradicated testified to the effectiveness of royal bureaucracy during Philip's reign, when the power of the Capetian kings arguably reached its zenith. Philip IV ruled over more land than ever, and government decrees and judicial ordinances were imposed with increasing efficacy throughout the kingdom. Most of the remaining independent principalities had been drawn more closely into the royal orbit; those that continued to resist the king's authority, such as the duchy of Gascony, had to fight to preserve their autonomy.

But the power attained by Philip had been gained at the cost of growing unpopularity. Regional assemblies had come to play an important political role in parts of France in the late 13th century. They acted as courts, endorsed trade regulations, and gave counsel on taxes, military service, and other matters. Assemblies of clergy also met. All grew more restive to assert their rights of self-expression. In 1314, regional assemblies refused outright to endorse a subsidy for monies, and the strength of their opposition compelled the king to cancel the exaction. Driven to exasperation by Philip's seemingly insatiable financial demands, nobles in Champagne and the northeast banded together into armed leagues in 1314–15 to insist on changes. They called for less royal interference in the localities and more deference paid to local privileges. While the leagues disintegrated rapidly, unable to unite around a single set of grievances, they exposed the frailties of a kingdom in which available resources were as yet insufficient to meet overarching royal ambitions. Prolonged wars had been shown to put serious strains on the country.

Philip's three successors, all much weaker than he, were not in a position to defeat the centers of opposition. Dubbed "the Stubborn," though because he was dominated by his uncle and the nobles he might better have been called "the Incompetent," Louis X (r. 1314–16) granted charters to Normandy and Languedoc, promising not to levy revenues beyond those customarily due to the Crown and to limit the power of royal rule. Other charters were bestowed elsewhere, although, like the leagues, the inability of the regions to form a united, broad-based program allowed the king to negotiate separately with each, thus strengthening his hand.

Louis and his brothers, Philip V, "the Tall" (r. 1316–22), and Charles IV (r. 1322–28), failed altogether to subdue foreign threats, all of them troubled by recurrent rebellions in Flanders and in Gascony, ruled by its enduringly recalcitrant English king. In 1324, war broke out once more. French armies invaded Gascony, and because England's new king, Edward III (r. 1327–77), found himself in a much weaker position at home after the murder of his father, Edward II, the new French king, Philip VI (r. 1328–50), kept many of the recent gains.

The grandson of Philip III in the male line, Philip VI was the first of the House of Valois, a junior branch of the royal family that succeeded in conformity with recently established precedents and in keeping with the Salic "Law," cutting women out of the royal running (a ruling demanded by Philip, although up to that time no such prohibition had existed statutorily). The outcome of the wars made for a propitious start for the new Valois ruler. The Treaty of Paris of 1327 left England with a much diminished territorial base in southern France. For the losing side, it was a humiliation that, a decade later, the English would compel the French to remember.

5

THE MAKING OF THE MONARCHY (1337–1598)

Two royal houses, both ambitious for land and power, were bound to collide. For a full 100 years and two decades more—the longest war in Europe's history—the kings of France and England battled for supremacy in France. The conflict launched a hostility between the two countries that would endure periodically for another half millennium, but in clearing the English from French soil, French kings ensured that they would henceforth hold a territorial base, the rule over which they could claim pride of place. And they would govern a people with a markedly more defined sense of what it meant to be French, the war having roused a nascent nationalism that, rallying around the remarkable leadership of Joan of Arc, would grow in conjunction with the rise of an increasingly powerful central government.

For another hundred years after 1453, the monarchy would consolidate its power. The remaining territorial princes were eliminated and their lands incorporated into the national domain, the great nobles stripped of claims to authority in becoming subsidized dependents or ornamental appendages of the royal court, and the Estates General shorn of any representative role in being disallowed from assembling. In the 1500s, population and prosperity slowly recovered from the wars, plagues, and social unrest of the 14th and 15th centuries. For the first time, French kings went on the offensive in setting off in pursuit of European great power pretensions. For the first time, too, exploratory forays across the Atlantic marked the country's early, tentative transoceanic steps.

The kings also placed the French church under the government's—not the pope's—authority. But it proved much less easy to control men's and women's minds. The religious reformation of the early 16th century produced a Protestant revolt breathtaking in scope. Protestant

Calvinists—Huguenots—would wage an all-out effort to win control. Though the religious wars that wracked the country intermittently for three decades in the mid-16th century would end in a settlement that left Catholicism triumphant, the losers could rest reassured, if not altogether contented, under the rule of a tolerant new dynasty.

By 1598, France was close to achieving geopolitical unity, the work of gathering together its large domains—through war, diplomacy, purchase, inheritance, and skillful marriages—largely complete. The borderlands alone remained fluid. The country's religious divide had been decided. The outlines of the modern state had been put in place. The work of solidifying the royal political and social systems, which had been gathering speed, could now proceed under monarchs who would succeed to a degree beyond any yet seen.

The Triumph of the Monarchy: The Hundred Years' War, 1337–1453

The war that began in spring 1337 marked the culmination of a dynastic rivalry that had flared up occasionally—and had simmered constantly—for two centuries. The English king's status as vassal of the king of France for the duchy of Gascony grew increasingly intolerable to French monarchs intent on consolidating their rule. French kings could never rest content while a powerful rival held this continental territory, and the wealth of Gascony made it the more to be coveted. For this reason, the region was highly prized by English monarchs too, who drew much of their revenues in the 14th century from the wine trade with Bordeaux. For their part, the English resented doing homage to their cousins in France. Edward III's mother was Isabel (or Isabella, ca. 1295–1358), a daughter of Philip the Fair, and as his grandson, he inherited a right to the French throne. Because the claim was not pressed vigorously, however, this right was passed peacefully to Philip's nephew, Philip VI of Valois, who was well known to the French court and nobles and was much their preferred choice. But the dynastic claim remained, giving Edward a legal pretext to justify a war, should he seek one.

In the end, however, it was Philip who provoked hostilities. On May 24, 1337, he proclaimed the confiscation of Gascony. The English struck back, securing the support of allies in the wealthy cities in Flanders, whose burghers, anxious not to disrupt the wool trade with England on which their prosperity depended, were recurrently rebel-

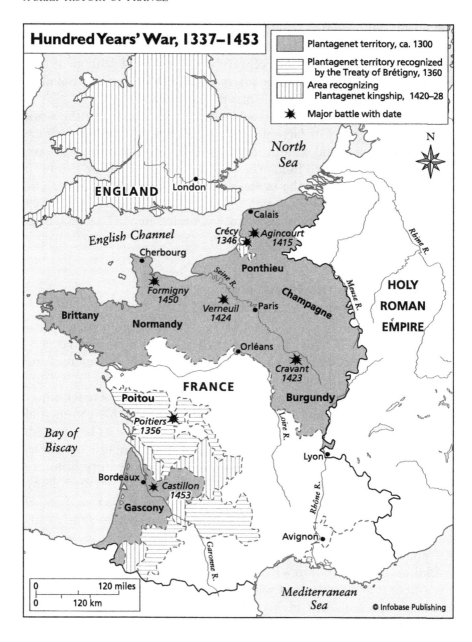

Hundred Years' War, 1337–1453

- Plantagenet territory, ca. 1300
- Plantagenet territory recognized by the Treaty of Brétigny, 1360
- Area recognizing Plantagenet kingship, 1420–28
- ✳ Major battle with date

North Sea

N

ENGLAND
London
English Channel
Calais
Crécy 1346
Agincourt 1415
Cherbourg
Ponthieu
Formigny 1450
Brittany
Normandy
Verneuil 1424
Paris
Champagne
Rhine R.
Meuse R.
HOLY ROMAN EMPIRE
Seine R.
Orléans
Cravant 1423
FRANCE
Poitou
Burgundy
Poitiers 1356
Bay of Biscay
Loire R.
Lyon
Bordeaux
Castillon 1453
Gascony
Rhône R.
Avignon
Garonne R.
Mediterranean Sea

0   120 miles
0   120 km

© Infobase Publishing

lious against the pro-Valois counts. The counts in Flanders remained reliably loyal, but the French court could not be certain that others among the powerful counts and dukes ruling over neighboring territories would follow suit.

During the reigns of the last Capetians, territorial princes in fiefs bordering the royal domain had reasserted their penchant for independence. Though like the English king, they, too, held their lands as vassals of the French monarchy, they ran their fiefdoms largely with a free hand. In 1297, the ruler of Brittany was given formal recognition as a duke. By then, it had its own Parlement and financial institutions, and by the 1330s, the dukes here were claiming a God-given right to rule the Breton "kingdom." In 1341, Edward III intervened actively in a succession crisis, pouring in troops to support the de Montfort faction, one of the rival claimants to the title of duke. Languedoc also retained its own language and laws, maintained a Parlement at Toulouse, and remained largely autonomous under its own government for much of the 14th century. Other provinces—Normandy and Champagne—chafed at royal encroachment of local liberties and privileges.

From 1337 to 1380, despite holding much the greater territory, neither Philip VI nor his successor, John II, "the Fearless" (r. 1350–64), mobilized sufficient military might to prevent invading English armies from ravaging western France at will. At sea, the English navy destroyed the French fleet in June 1340 at the Battle of Sluys, allowing the English to dominate the English Channel for the rest of the war. On two occasions only did the French assemble an army large enough, and keep it in the field long enough, to meet the English in major pitched battles—at Crécy in 1346 and at Poitiers in 1356—and they were defeated disastrously in both encounters. Bearing the brunt of fighting, French nobles suffered appalling losses. Well organized, trained, and paid, the English army employed foot soldiers equipped with the latest in military technology, namely, the deadly long bow, which was greatly superior to the continental cross bow in range and rapidity of fire. Thanks to the long bow, for the first time since the rise of feudalism, the infantry secured a place in battle equal to the heavily armed cavalry.

At Poitiers, King John was taken prisoner. The dauphin (heir), Charles, 18 and without political experience, was left to govern without money or an army. The country he ruled was reeling from the effects not only of war but also of famine, and, most horrendously, of plague. The Black Death arrived in 1348 at Marseille in merchant ships that had originally sailed from the Black Sea region, and the pestilence spread rapidly along trade routes to reach all of France. The plague was of three kinds—a bubonic and a septicemic type carried by fleas, which raged in the summer, and an airborne pulmonary variant, which struck in winter. It is impossible to determine the exact number who perished, but the figures arrived at by modern statisticians, who calculate the population to have fallen from approximately 20.2 million in 1345 to about 16 million after 1350 (INSEE 2009), do not contradict the accounts of contemporary chroniclers, who affirmed that a little less than a third of French men and women died before the pestilence subsided by the end of 1350. In southern France, the plague was preceded by large-scale famine in 1346–47. Royal taxation, stagnant grain prices, increases in feudal dues, and a rise in the cost of agricultural implements added to the deprivations of disease and war to burden the populace, most especially the peasants.

All of these factors combined to produce a wild outburst of fury in the Île-de-France. Beginning in the village of Saint-Leu near Senlis on the Oise River on May 28, 1358, thousands of peasants—mostly small proprietors—went on a rampage, murdering noble men and women. Known as the Jacquerie, the sudden spate of violence was quickly and brutally suppressed—the mob having neither firm leadership nor any clear program—but it was not a unique phenomenon. Local peasant rebellions were rife elsewhere. Plague, too, recurred; there were three or four serious returns before 1400, and outbreaks would periodically reappear in the 15th century.

Paris, too, seethed with unrest. In October 1356, the bourgeoisie, led by Étienne Marcel (?–1358), a rich merchant, secured the support of the Estates General in demanding a complete overhaul of royal administration, with members of the royal council to be elected. Though they failed in their quest, their discontent added to the kingdom's distress. Helpless before the English, in 1360, the dauphin was compelled to agree to the Treaty of Brétigny by the terms of which, in exchange for French payment of a huge sum to ransom King John, Edward III traded his claim to the French throne for possession of a huge swath of southwest France stretching from the Loire to the Pyrenees, together with the port of Calais and a few other bridgeheads on the northern coast.

Though on its surface the treaty seemingly marked a high point of English success, Edward was in reality dangerously overextended. Charles V (r. 1364–80), dubbed "the Wise," took full advantage of that situation. Slim and more bookish than bellicose, and a lover of royal pomp and pageantry, Charles could be petty and devious, but he was a superb organizer. Now in possession of steady income from having instituted an efficient means of tax collection, the French king rebuilt and re-formed the army, enrolling the nobles in companies under royal captains and guaranteeing them regular pay. He gave command to the constable Bernard du Guesclin

(1320–80), a battle-hardened veteran campaigner who, knowing the effectiveness of English fighting practices, switched to guerrilla tactics. By the time that both Charles and the constable died in 1380, the English had been driven from all but Calais and a narrow coastal strip from Bayonne to Bordeaux. Edward III had died three years before, and internal troubles in both kingdoms brought a lull in fighting for a generation.

Misgovernment and factional strife marked the reign of Charles VI (r. 1380–1422). Because the king suffered from recurring fits of insanity that left him incapable of ruling, royal princes fought among themselves to seize control of the kingdom. None proved more powerful than the king's vassal, Duke Philip II, "the Bold" (r. 1363–1404), who had acquired the Duchy of Burgundy as an appanage from his father, John II, in 1363, and had built his territory into a powerful state in adding the Free County (Franche-Comté) of Burgundy as well as Flanders and other fiefs in northern France to his domains. None proved more

The fleur-de-lis banner lies on the ground, marking the French defeat at the Battle of Agincourt (1415). From The Chronicle of Saint-Albans, Flemish, 15th century (Visual Arts Library/Art Resource, NY)

resentful of this new power player than Charles's brother, Louis, duke of Orléans (1372–1407). Louis was assassinated in 1407, and his death paved the way for open civil war in 1411 between rival factions—Burgundians and Armagnacs, who took their name from their leader, Bernard VII, count of Armagnac (1360–1418).

Misrule and civil war left France too tempting a target for England's young new king Henry V (r. 1415–22) to ignore. Proclaiming himself king of France, he renewed the war; on October 25, 1415, he won a great victory at the Battle of Agincourt, where heavily armored French soldiers, bogged down in mud, were slaughtered by the score. Henry aped Edward III's battle tactics, but he proved a much more far-sighted strategist. He strove not solely to battle and raid like his predecessor but also to conquer territory. In alliance with the Burgundians, who as English allies had recently gained possession of Paris and control over Charles VI, in residence there, Henry set out to seize Normandy. Acting together, the two powers secured most of France north of the Loire. In 1420, the Treaty of Troyes stipulated that the French throne would pass to Henry V's son.

Poised for victory, Henry died prematurely in 1422, giving the French the opening they needed. But they were poorly positioned to take advantage of the opportunity. Charles VI died the same year, and though the dauphin claimed the throne, the would-be heir made a poor candidate for leadership. Together with his Armagnac followers, Charles VII (r. 1422–61) remained south of the Loire, where the court had fled. Pessimistic and indecisive, he hesitated to act, even considering flight to Spain.

The nascent patriotism that had emerged among the French people, spawned over time by the long years of plundering and killing at the hands of the foreign invader, needed only a charismatic leader on which it could focus. Such a leader appeared in Joan of Arc, who, although she was later captured by the Burgundians and though Charles did nothing to save her, launched a surge of national sentiment that could not be staunched.

In 1435, the duke of Burgundy abandoned the English. With only one enemy left to fight, Charles's armies drove the English out of one city and castle after another, until in 1453 only Calais remained of their once impressive continental possessions. The Treaty of Étaples (November 3, 1492) effectively settled the outstanding differences between the two countries.

The Hundred Years' War spelled the end of feudal warfare, the need to maintain forces larger than any before and for longer periods

JOAN OF ARC

oan of Arc (Fr., Jeanne d'Arc, ca. 1412–31) was born in Domrémy in Lorraine. Her father was a small farmer who supplemented his work in serving as a village official. One day in 1424, she is said to have experienced visions and heard the voices of several saints who ordered her to go to the king and tell him that she would lead an army to save his realm. It took her four years to secure backing from an army captain in a neighboring town. Arriving in Chinon on March 4,

(continues)

Joan of Arc victorious (Library of Congress)

JOAN OF ARC (continued)

1429, with an armed escort, clad as a man, Joan pointed out the future king who had disguised himself in the crowd. Suspicious of spiritual mystics, Charles had her examined by church authorities, who pronounced her authentic. Given a suit of armor, a horse, and an armed guard, the Maid (la Pucelle) ventured forth, bearing a white banner, she later related, inscribed with the words "Jesus Maria."

She picked up support from additional noblemen, and on April 29, she entered Orléans undetected by the English, who were besieging the town. The siege was successfully lifted, and her fame spread. Other victories followed. Urged to fight to recapture Normandy, she insisted that Charles first be anointed king. At Reims on July 17, 1429, with Joan standing beside the altar, Charles VII was crowned in a ceremony hastily improvised—the crown and royal insignia were in English hands at Saint-Denis. Back on campaign, on May 24, 1430, Joan was captured at Compiègne by the Burgundians, who sold her to the English. Accused of heresy, superstition, schism, and idolatry, she was brought to trial in February 1431. Pronounced guilty and fearing the prospect of death by burning, she abjured. She was sentenced to life imprisonment but soon, on reflection, she retracted her confession. Securing the fate the English had sought all along for her, Joan was burned at the stake in the market square at Rouen on May 31, 1431. Not wishing it to be recorded that he was brought to power with the help of a condemned heretic, Charles secured a revision of the judicial decision by Pope Callixtus III (r. 1455–58), who found her innocent and declared her to be a martyr. She was canonized in 1920.

The story of Joan has acquired legendary status. That an unknown peasant girl could lead an army, secure the coronation of a king, and die an unjust death all under the authority of divine guidance smacks more of fiction than of fact. Yet Joan was, and remains, very real. French politicians invoke her memory, writers and composers from many countries create works about her, and depictions of her in the popular media continue to appear. A national heroine, Joan is one among several patron saints of France.

requiring standing armies. Forms of fighting changed as common-born, well-armed foot soldiers replaced knights, whose equipment costs proved too burdensome, and mercenary troops (companies of soldiers raised on contract by nobles and knights) came increasingly into use.

The end of the war found France depopulated, devastated, and impoverished. Commerce had been crippled. A century of fighting led Venetian and Genoese merchants to bypass France. They traveled now directly to England and Flanders to do business, thus precipitating the end of the great Champagne fairs. The currency became notoriously unstable.

Social unrest was endemic in both town and country. Large areas were so ravaged that they had to be abandoned, adding yet another disruptive factor as displaced people migrated across the land. Only Paris had managed to maintain a modicum of prosperity based on the luxury trade kept active by the demands of the nobility and high clergy, who flocked to the royal court. In 1420, Charles VI completed the construction of new walls around the city, with six gates covered by a series of forts that included the Bastille, built earlier under Charles V as the Bastion de Saint-Antoine between 1370 and 1383.

Landlords suffered not only from labor shortages due to plague and war but also because the need to settle ravaged and abandoned lands forced them to grant perpetual tenancies at fixed rents, to commute payments in kind, and to make other concessions to attract tenants. The feudal manorial system largely disappeared with the freeing of most of the remaining serfs, although many nobles retained many jurisdictional rights over the peasants, including the right to administer justice and to exact dues from tenants beyond the rents due them. These *banalitiés*—payments for the use of the lord's mill, oven, and wine press—and other petty monopolies remained more developed in France than elsewhere in western Europe.

War and disease played havoc with the landholding class in another way. For those who survived—and many did not—some who were faced with declining real income and rising costs to maintain their noble status dropped out of the class entirely. Others lived on in genteel poverty on their country estates. The more fortunate found offices at court or in the army or secured pensions or profitable church benefices. Some married wealthy and socially aspiring bourgeois.

At the same time, rich members of the middle class began moving up the social ladder into the noble class. They might purchase a noble estate and, in time, gain tacit acceptance as an aristocrat, or acquire for a fee letters of ennoblement from the king, an avenue that cash-hungry monarchs were more than happy to open. In addition to the ancient nobility of the sword (*noblesse d'epée*), who had won their status bearing arms in service to the king, there now appeared the new nobility of the robe (*noblesse de la robe*), made up of ennobled wealthy bourgeois, judges in the royal courts, members of the Parlement of Paris, and holders of administrative offices. Their arrival assured the survival of a large noble class at the same time that ennoblement, because it removed wealthy and influential members from the bourgeoisie, checked the rise of the latter class as a political force.

In the last years of the war, Charles VII carried out a thorough reform of the military and financial organs of state. He assembled a formidable army. Annual and permanent taxes were levied, including the salt (*gabelle*) and sales (*aides*) taxes and, most important of all, a direct property tax (*taille*), which replaced the hearth tax of the preceding century and from which the nobility and clergy were exempt.

It was the Estates General that gave the king the green light to impose these taxes, a grant of authority that, because the imposts were permanent, would prove fatal to its efforts to impose restraints on the monarchy. The Estates had been attempting to cultivate that authority in the middle of the 15th century, but because it was divided into the clergy (First Estate), the nobility (Second Estate), and the bourgeoisie (Third Estate) with each sitting and voting separately on behalf of its own interests, the representative assembly was hampered from the start. Now having given away an important controlling power, the Estates General lost the chance that it might develop into an institution that participated, along with the king, in a meaningful way in governing the kingdom. The monarchy no longer needed its services, and after 1440, it receded quietly into disuse, although provincial estates long remained active in local affairs.

France had emerged from the years of turmoil a country conscious of its national identity and loyal to a ruling regime. Equipped with a powerful fighting force and assured of steady income, that regime would now set about deepening and broadening its reach.

Consolidation of the Monarchy, 1453–1515

In 1453, for the first time in 400 years, no part of France except for the city of Calais was ruled by a foreign king. Having expelled the English, the monarchy had earned for itself the respect of a war-weary people who looked to it to restore order and promote recovery. It had built the power to enforce its authority, but the royal government still ruled actually only about half of the kingdom. Even though the king had by now established the right to collect taxes and royal officials exercised a limited, though growing, jurisdiction in most of the country, outside the royal domains great fiefs were held by ancient feudal families, and appanages had been granted to junior branches of the Capetian royal house. In particular, the duchies of Burgundy and Brittany enjoyed the greatest degree of independence.

By the end of the 15th century, these lands were all joined to the territories subject entirely to the central government. The work of doing

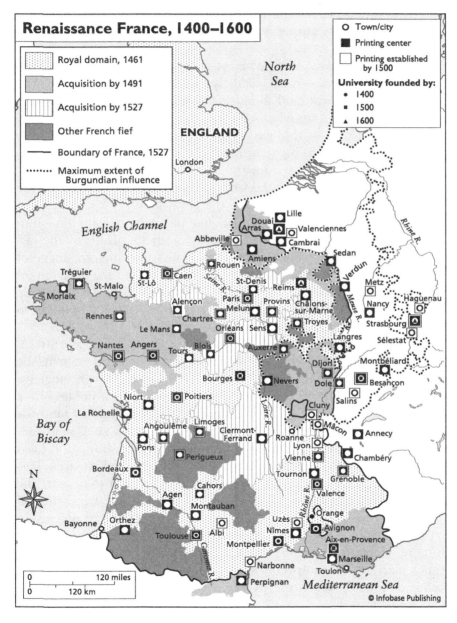

so occupied most of the reign of Louis XI (r. 1461–83). Endowed with a shrewd intellect and boundless energy, Louis could be cruel, and as a monarch, he could be at once both extravagant and miserly. Above all, he could see clearly where he stood geopolitically and where he wished to go. Louis XI's overarching aim to control his realm fully, on which he focused with resolute intensity, spawned in him such a love of deception that at times he would spin a web of intrigue so complex as to defeat its own purposes, earning for him the sobriquet of "the universal spider."

Determined to break the power of the duke of Burgundy, who—a king in all but name—ruled virtually all of the rich lands from the Netherlands to Switzerland along his eastern borders, Louis battled for 15 years using a combination of war and diplomacy that exhausted both sides but that in the end won for him, in the Treaty of Arras (1482), Picardy and, the biggest prize of all, Burgundy itself, which was incorporated into the royal domain.

At the same time, Louis subdued rebellious nobles and reduced the princes of the blood—members of the royal family who were not a brother, son, or grandson in the male line of a king or dauphin—into docile pensioners of the Crown. In 1481, with the death of the last members of the direct line of the House of Anjou, the appanage of Anjou, together with Provence and Angevin claims to the kingdom of Naples in Italy, reverted to the Crown. Only Brittany remained outside the royal ambit. It was left to Louis's son, Charles VIII (r. 1483–98), to fill in this gap in the French royal map.

Or rather it was left to Charles's older sister. Because he was only 13, Anne de Beaujeu (1461–1522) served as regent. A forceful woman, she set to work with a will. The old Celtic duchy with its own language and traditions had never been fully French, and its great nobles broke into open revolt after Louis VIII's death. When its duke, Francis II (1433–88), died in 1488, his daughter Anne (1477–1514), who succeeded him, consented to marry Maximilian of Hapsburg, the head of a powerful house that ruled the Low Countries and Austria. This potential threat proved too much for Anne de Beaujeu to accept. She promptly invaded, forcing Duchess Anne to renounce her betrothal and, instead, marry Charles. In 1532, the Breton Estates tied succession to the duchy to the French Crown rather than to the line of the dukes of Brittany, which, in any case, had merged with that of France following Anne's marriage. With Brittany a fully integrated province, the Atlantic seaboard from Calais to the Pyrenees now flew the flag emblazoned with the fleur-de-lis.

THE FLEUR-DE-LIS

The fleur-de-lis (literally, "lily flower") served in a highly stylized design as the emblem of French royalty. Its adoption is traced to the Christian conversion of King Clovis. Varying legends over the centuries attributed its use as a divine sign bestowed as a blessing, although a story that Clovis had in fact placed a lily in his helmet before the Battle of Vouillé also offered a more mundane explanation. During the reign of Louis IX, the three petals of the flower were purported to represent faith, wisdom, and chivalry. The royal coat of arms featured an azure field scattered with small, golden fleurs-de-lis until, in the late 14th century, Charles V changed the allover pattern to just a single grouping of three. This remained the royal standard, and with the blue background replaced by white—the color of Joan of Arc's banner—it became the national flag under all French monarchical regimes.

The fleur-de-lis on a white field also served as the battle standard of French kings in replacing the oriflamme—a red or orange-red banner flown from a lance used by monarchs from 1124 until the Battle of Agincourt in 1415.

The fleur-de-lis remains an enduring symbol of France. It appears on French postage stamps. Featured on the flag of the Canadian province of Quebec and as the official symbol of the state of Louisiana in the United States, the fleur-de-lis links these two North American places to their French origins.

The acquisition of Brittany left Charles free to indulge his boastful schemes to impose France's power beyond its borders. Dubbed "the Affable" and a grandiose dreamer whose romantic imagination exceeded his intellect—unlike most rulers of the time he was barely literate and, when he did read, allegedly preferred tales of chivalry to state documents—Charles invaded Italy in 1494 to assert his inherited claim to the kingdom of Naples, unleashing a series of wars that would prove disastrous for three French kings. But the Italian wars produced one great benefit: In channeling the energies of the nobles into foreign adventures, it reduced their presence at home, thus promoting domestic peace.

Under Louis XI and Charles VIII, France experienced not only territorial consolidation and the extension of royal rule to every corner of the kingdom but also steady, albeit slow, growth in the organs of government. Progress accelerated under Louis XII (r. 1498–1515) and Francis I (r. 1515–47). Central ruling institutions were expanded and made more efficient, and local government was brought under the control of the increasingly powerful monarchy. Justice and fiscal systems were reformed, and large numbers of royal officers were appointed, who greedily and aggressively set about undermining what remained of feudal privilege and rights of self-rule of the local nobility. One of these officials, Jean Bodin (ca. 1530–96), the lieutenant general and then royal procurator for the district of Laon, argued in his *Les six livres de la République* (*Six Books of the Commonwealth*, 1576) in defense of the unbridled power of kings to rule over their subjects, which became a central tenet of the absolute monarchy that would emerge full-blown in the 17th century.

With the economy now based increasingly on the circulation of money rather than simply the ownership of land, the monarchy had a means ready to hand in taxation to secure needed revenue. And it needed more and more of it in the 1500s. Prices rose steadily throughout the century, and the wars of Francis I required substantial sums. In 1522, the king established a single collection agency, the Treasury, supervised by a forerunner of a finance minister, the comptroller general. The rise in prices cemented the money-based economic system, marking the definitive triumph of a capitalist economy over the feudal order. Under capitalism, the wealthy bourgeoisie improved their ability to move closer socially to the nobility in being able to buy the possessions of those among that class who could not financially compete.

No longer able to rebel successfully and deprived of most of their authority, the great nobles become courtiers and pensioners of the Crown, adding little substance but much surface luster to a royal court that, with their presence, grew in splendor. Lesser nobles, impoverished by agricultural depression and fixed incomes in a time of rising prices, took careers in the army and administration.

The church and the clergy also fell increasingly under the control of the monarchy. Gallicanism, that is, the autonomy of the French church from control by the papacy, fully emerged in the Pragmatic Sanction of Bourges (1438), which denied the fiscal and appointive powers of the pope in favor of the king. By devious ways, taxes paid by the church to Rome were diverted into the royal treasury, and the king exercised de facto power to nominate clerics to all important church benefices. In 1516, the Concordat of Bologna, which replaced the Pragmatic Sanction, gave the pope a steady income from the French faithful while it confirmed the right of the king to choose archbishops, bishops, abbots, and priors, thus allowing the Crown to direct the church in France by controlling the selection of its personnel. The French hierarchy had hoped for rather more freedom from both, but they grudgingly acquiesced. The church provided an annual *don gratuit* (free gift) to the state, which proved essential to royal revenue and made kings, anxious not to upset the lucrative financial inflow, wary of challenging the clergy too directly.

Though towns, too, saw their liberties clipped by a triumphant kingship, urban life and the economy in general gradually recovered in the aftermath of the Hundred Years' War. After bottoming out about 1400, the population grew steadily, especially in the south, reaching the high of 20 million attained before the Black Death around 1600. Paris became one of Europe's largest cities with a population in 1500 of about 150,000.

Blessed with a large territory, a temperate climate, fertile soil, and natural riches, France depended for its economic well-being on agriculture, interregional trade, and small craft and manufacturing activities rather than on long-distance commerce and large-scale industry. Though a nascent free-market system under which prices, production, and distribution of goods were determined by competition was fully operating by the 1500s, capitalism was slow to take root here. No one who came after him matched Jacques Coeur (ca. 1395–1456), the merchant who made such a fortune through trading, provisioning, and minting that he became Charles VIII's finance minister. Rather, banking and finance remained dominated by Italian firms, a consequence of the early appearance of capitalist means and methods on the Italian peninsula.

Under Louis XI, the government labored to build roads, and it abolished some tolls and encouraged native industry. The king introduced the silk industry to France, which prospered most especially in Lyon. Royal regulation of the economy remained minimal, however, the rapid prosperity experienced during the last years of the 15th century and the opening decades of the 16th owing more to the reestablishment of order and security. In a switch of major significance, shifting currents of trade spawned a slow decline of Mediterranean ports, while western seaports began to hum with new activity as opportunities opened with the growth in Atlantic commerce occasioned by the dawning age of exploration. While seeking a northwest passage to India, navigator Jacques Cartier (1491–ca. 1557), from Saint-Malo, sighted Prince Edward Island at the end of June 1534. Sailing into the estuary of the Saint Lawrence River at Gaspé on July 25, he took possession of Canada in the name of Francis I and then proceeded up the river to explore the interior.

Jacques Cartier meeting Native Americans at Hochelaga (present-day Montreal) in 1535
(Library of Congress)

But the attention of the king in whose name a new land had been claimed remained fixed on Europe, where he aimed to ensure his realm's security and extend its power. In 1519, Francis became a candidate for Holy Roman Emperor. Carrying with it the potential to implant a French presence in Germany, the bid launched a bitter rivalry with the Hapsburgs, then western Europe's dominant ruling house. Passed over for the title, which went to Charles of Hapsburg (r. 1519–56), Francis strove to best him in battle on the field—in Italy—where the French had been active since 1494. Even after he was defeated and captured at Pavia (1525), ransomed, and married to the emperor's sister Eleanor (1498–1558), he could not restrain himself from trying again. Throughout the 1530s and 1540s, Francis waged a constant struggle to vanquish his Hapsburg competitor, who as Charles V had emerged as Europe's premier ruler in holding territories in Spain, Germany, and the Low Countries that almost completely surrounded France, together with a growing empire, in South America and the Philippines, of globe-girdling dimensions. Francis's son and successor, Henry II (r. 1547–59), continued his father's foreign policy, adding war with England, which won for him Calais in 1558, the last English possession in France.

But father and son failed to best their great continental opponent, and by the Treaty of Cateau-Cambrésis in 1559, France gave up all claims to Italian territory, conceding a European supremacy to Hapsburg Spain that would endure for another century. The end of the wars brought the onset of an economic downturn. Recurrent harvest failures in the wake of colder climatic conditions helped to fuel inflation further. Unable to bear the burden of taxation, peasants intermittently revolted, especially in Normandy, Brittany, and the southwest. The Italian ventures left the country economically depleted, but they also opened up sources of enrichment. Returning from Italy, the warrior nobility brought back not only luxury goods from the peninsula's wealthy city-states but also an awareness of new cultural and artistic currents fully flowering there.

Cultural Stirrings from 1300 to 1600

When Francis I—France's first Renaissance monarch—invited the renowned Italian artist and inventor Leonardo da Vinci (1452–1519) to the French court in 1516 (he would die in France three years later at Amboise), the act stunningly demonstrated the impact humanism then exerted in France. The outpouring of superlative artistic creation based on study of the heritage of the classical world of ancient Greece and Rome that had emerged in the Italian city-states in the 14th century and blossomed there in the 15th century began to strike roots north of the Alps at the turn of the 16th century. Wealthy urban elites spawned by the rise of capitalism created demand for new literary and pictorial works, as did newly powerful state governments, which, in requiring literate and professionally trained personnel, at the same time stimulated lay education.

Changing thoughts had already begun to percolate at the turn of the 15th century when the scholasticism that so dominated medieval philosophical discourse met an eloquent challenge from the chancellor of the University of Paris. Jean Gerson (1363–1429) sought to simplify and clarify theology by founding it in nominalism, a philosophical viewpoint affirming that only universal and abstract terms—but not objects—exist. He asserted that theological principles should be clearly explained when possible, but also that a healthy respect for mystery—an essential element of Christian faith—must be retained when such explanation is not possible.

Literature produced by and for feudal society suffered during the troubled period of the Hundred Years' War when that system slowly died, the chivalry that it had so extolled surviving only in the empty splendor of tournaments and court ceremonial. Many lyricists and chroniclers began to appear from the ranks of the upper middle classes, members of the well-to-do town bourgeoisie who were drawn to the courts of the king and the great princes as secretaries and administrators and worked for the aristocratic audiences found there. Music, too, declined during a period of such instability, musicians moving to Burgundy, whose glittering court offered a more conducive environment in which to work. The Renaissance would see the flowering of the motet as a distinguishing musical composition. Although originating in the medieval era, it evolved after the mid-15th century into short choral works that, though still written as sacred texts for several voices, became more versatile, suitable, not as before for only a specific liturgy, but now for any religious service.

Expert versifiers include Guillaume de Machaut (ca. 1300–71), who is known for producing *virelai*—in both poetic and musical forms—but is remembered more as a court composer. He is the first important composer of *chansons,* secular songs encompassing a wide array of forms and styles that would evolve over several hundred years to be characterized by simpler, more homophonic styles than those of the medieval *formes fixes.* Eustache Deschamps (ca. 1346–ca. 1406) wrote verses to rouse patriotic sentiments after the reverses following the death of Charles V. Alain Chartier (ca. 1395–ca. 1433), a secretary to Charles VI and Charles VII, clearly saw the decline of chivalry as a military force but still wrote graceful verses on courtly love, no doubt to please his patrons, including his best-known poem, "La belle dame sans merci" (after 1415). An Italian-born widow of one of Charles VI's secretaries, Christine de Pisan (ca. 1364–ca. 1433) wrote love poems for the lords and ladies of the court, though their quality merits less recognition than the fact the she is possibly the first professional woman writer in France. A court poet also, Jean Froissart (ca. 1337–ca. 1404) earned a lasting reputation instead for his prose *Chronicles,* a recounting of the century-long war that opened in the year of his probable birth. Courtly lyrics obtained a final flowering in the work of Charles, duke of Orléans (ca. 1391–1465), who composed perfectly arranged verse tinged with gentle melancholy. Such lyrics faded by the end of the 15th century, works churned out now by nondescript *grands rhétoriqueurs* (formulaic poets).

In the 14th and 15th centuries, French literature centered no longer in the south, where literary life had never fully recovered from the ravages of the Albigensian Crusade, but rather in the north, where the royal court and the great princely courts were clustered close to each other. Due to the centralizing influence of these courts, the variant of the French language in use here served as the vehicle in which epics, romances, and lyric poetry were written. Many although by no means all of the wide variety of dialects that had characterized medieval France gradually disappeared by the 16th century, again, most especially, in the north.

In the 1500s, no monarch championed the promotion of the language more avidly than Francis I. The king issued the decree of Villers-Cotterêts (1539), stipulating that government business be undertaken and recorded solely in French, and he ordered that births, deaths, and marriages throughout the kingdom be systematically registered. The quintessential French Renaissance monarch, Francis was a great patron of learning. He employed the scholar Guillaume Budé (1467–1540), also known by his Latin name Guilielmus Budaeus, to create a royal library at Fontainebleau; it later became one of the bases for the National Library (Bibliothèque Nationale). And at Budé's suggestion, he established the Collegium Trilingue, a learned society to promote study of subjects such as Greek and Hebrew that served as a foundational nucleus of the Institut de France. In 1546, the king began building the Louvre, which is today one of the world's great museums. Francis engaged not only artists from Italy but also architects, who were put to work in converting rustic hunting lodges into sumptuous châteaux. Italian influences were especially pronounced in architectural decoration. In the 1530s, several Florentine artists were hired to decorate the palace at Fontainebleau, giving rise to the First School of Fontainebleau, which generated a native style—Northern Mannerism—that featured a synthesis of Gothic, long dominant in northern Europe, with the highly decorative ornamentation and nude human figures that distinguished Italian High Renaissance. The Mannerist style was promoted, except in portraiture by Catherine de' Medici (1519–89), Henry II's consort, who, like her father-in-law, imported Italian artists and whose court was the only one in northern Europe to rival her ruling Medici family in Florence for patronage of the visual arts.

The appeal of the ancient writers that humanism had awakened found no more prominent a French representative than Michel de Montaigne (1533–92), who demonstrated the variety and vitality of the classical thinkers and the meaningfulness of their legacy to the 16th century. Born into a merchant family and rising to own property, hold office, and acquire noble status, Montaigne introduced the essay as a literary form (*Essais* [Essays], 1580). He literally invented the art of introspection, innovatively using himself as his laboratory. When he looked inward, he did not, like seekers of knowledge in centuries past, pray or seek to understand God's mysteries; rather, he concentrated his

THE LOUVRE

The Louvre, or Musée du Louvre, is the national art museum of France. It is located in Paris on the right bank of the Seine River in the former palace of the Louvre, which, until 1682, was a royal residence built on the site of a 13th-century fortress. In 1546, Francis I began construction of the museum under plans drafted by architect Pierre Lescot (ca. 1510). Subsequent additions were added over the centuries, the entire complex completed by the mid-19th century. In 1793, it opened as a museum, and it became the property of the state in 1848. The vast collection housed today is built around a core grouping of Italian Renaissance paintings owned by Francis I. The collection has been enriched ever since through acquisition of paintings, sculptures, drawings, prints, and objets d'art. Great works by many celebrated artists are on display, including the renowned *Venus de Milo* and *Winged Victory of Samothrace,* which date from ancient Greece, and Leonardo da Vinci's hauntingly evocative *Mona Lisa (La jaconde).* In 1993, the Richelieu gallery opened and, in 1996, the Rohan Wing, which features the fashion collection. The glass-and-metal pyramid entrance designed by U.S. architect I. M. Pei (1917–), and completed in 1989, has become one of the city's many famed landmarks. Covering 48 acres (19 hectares), the Louvre is the world's largest museum. Among its superlative departments, the Department of Painting is considered by many to be the most important worldwide.

The Louvre in the mid-19th century (Library of Congress)

attentions on himself alone, intent on recording his own feelings candidly and clearly. Schooled in the writings of the ancient pagan authors, he is known as a skeptic, though in his later years, always eschewing fanaticism, he turned his thoughts to humane reflection, and he died, as he had been born, a Catholic.

An inventive drive prevailed in the mid-16th century under a group of poets dubbed the Pléiade, drawn from a name in a poem of one of its founding members, Pierre de Ronsard (1524–85). Ronsard and his fellow poets, including Joachim du Bellay (ca. 1522–60), Jean de Baïf

Henry II and his wife Catherine de' Medici. Anonymous, 16th century (Scala/White Images/ Art Resource, NY)

LOIRE CHÂTEAUX

Castle building began in the central valley of the Loire River in the 10th century. The lush, fertile, and scenic region drew the attention of French kings at the turn of the 16th century, and they in turn attracted members of the French nobility, not wishing—or daring—to be far from the seat of power. Under Francis I, the locus of royal rule, for a time, centered here. Large splendid châteaux (Fr., "castle seat" or "country mansion") were constructed here, renovations of castles and fortified manors that had been built in earlier years. Architects borrowed from Italian building designs in blending them with French medieval forms to create a French Renaissance style, which came to dominate under Francis I, that featured both native Gothic and Italian interpretations of classical forms and features. Some 300 were built.

One of the earliest, Azay-le-Rideau, was constructed between 1515 and 1527 on an island in the Indre River. Chambord was also begun early in 1519. With its four immense corner bastions framing a miniature cityscape of towers and chimneys, it is the largest of the châteaux. Built on a promontory overlooking the Loire, Amboise features early Renaissance decorative motifs. It is the site of the first formal French garden, which, centering on the facade of the building, exhibits radiating paths, lawns, flower beds, and pools, some with fountains and decorative sculpture. Straddling the Cher River on pillars of stone, Chenonceaux began as a fortified manor and was completely rebuilt in the early 16th century. King Henry II gave it to his mistress, Diane de Poitiers (1499–1566), who commissioned ornamental gardens and became passionately attached to it. Forced

(1532–89), and others who had studied together in Paris in the 1540s, experimented with many genres ranging from short lyrics to odes, sonnets, and tragedies. Their verse breaks free from religious constraints in featuring a distinctive luxuriant style infused with an intense romantic fervor, and much of their material is gleaned from Greek, Latin, and Italian models.

The mid-15th century that marked such a turning point for France with the end of 100 years of warfare also witnessed the birth of a central event that would transform both the country and the Continent. The introduction of printing with movable type perfected by Johannes Gutenberg (ca. 1400–68) of Mainz, Germany, in the years around 1450 quickened the pace of change—without printing, humanism would not

out by Henry's widow Catherine de' Medici, Diane had to settle for the château at Chaumont.

Built for luxury and comfort, not defense, the châteaux attest to the definitive decline of feudalism in France. Until the French Revolution, they remained favored residences of the kings and nobility. During the Revolution, a number were destroyed and ransacked, their treasures stolen. Later, some were demolished. Those that have survived have become either state-operated properties or privately owned homes. In 2000, the United Nations Educational, Scientific and Cultural Organization designated the central Loire Valley region as a World Heritage Site.

Facade of Château de Chambord (Vanni/Art Resource, NY)

have spread so rapidly—as it accelerated the production of books, pamphlets, and tracts. A press appeared in Paris as early as 1470, and others in regional centers soon followed. Because books became available in quantity, they could be sold at a reasonable price, and the reading public increased rapidly even as literacy rates varied—high among the clergy, nobility, and professional classes and abysmally low for peasants and urban laborers—and despite the fact that many who could read knew only the vernacular in an age when Latin remained the dominant language of intellectual discourse.

And the subject that had long dominated scholarly discourse—religion—remained the topic of most printed works. The Bible was the most popular book from the start. In the 14th century, an advocate of religious reform, Englishman John Wycliffe (ca. 1324–84), had asserted that the Bible alone, not the pope and his assemblage of clerics, had divine authority. His contention typified a criticism of the precepts and discontent over the practices of the Roman Catholic Church that had been brewing for more than a century. A church that had grown ostentatiously wealthy, led by popes many of whom, to observers, were more concerned to advance their temporal ambitions than to care for the spiritual needs of their flock, disturbed the sensibilities of some. Abuses such as simony (buying and selling church offices), indulgences (remission of eternal punishment through payment of a monetary sum), greed for material gain, and violations of vows of priestly celibacy were viewed as scandalous or unjust. When the rebellious German monk Martin Luther (1483–1546) broke into open revolt against Catholicism in October 1517, the shock waves unleashed sent powerful currents, fueled by the mass availability of the printed word, swirling across Europe.

The Wars of Religion, 1562–1598

Lutheranism won many converts in France in the 1520s and 1530s, but it would soon be supplanted as the dominant Protestant sect by the doctrines of a French-born reformer. Born in Noyon, in Picardy, John Calvin (Jean Cauvin; 1509–64) trained extensively in legal and philological studies and became a Protestant probably in 1533. Because he was therefore considered a heretic by the Roman Catholic Church, he settled in Switzerland, where Protestants in various places had secured a dominant hold. There in 1536, he published *The Institutes of the Christian Religion*, destined to become a Protestant classic. Calvin's God was an awesome, remote paternal figure who had decreed from all eternity to elect some chosen souls to salvation and others to eternal damnation. Believing that they made up God's favored company, for whom Christ had died, Calvin's followers strove to confirm their membership among the saints by leading a sober Christian life, working hard, and abstaining from frivolous and sensuous pleasures. With all the rigor of both the lawyer and the theologian that he was, Calvin set up a church in Geneva, which, by the date of his death, had become the headquarters for spreading the faith.

In 1541, Calvin translated his *Institutes* into French. An impressive doctrine able both to persuade scholars and to move the common people, the faith drew followers from among wide circles. Disgust with a Catholic Church grown corrupt and scandal-ridden was widespread.

The power conceded to the king in the concordat of 1516 gave the monarch a splendid instrument of patronage, but the appointment of courtiers, dependents, influential nobles, friends of the king's mistresses, and even foreigners as bishops and abbots put theologically ignorant and indifferent individuals into clerical offices. Turning to Calvin's tenets, learned priests, professors, lawyers, merchants, and growing numbers of the lesser nobility converted to a faith whose practitioners became known as Huguenots, a word of uncertain origin that was first applied in 1562.

Huguenots enjoyed official indulgence at first, but unconcern gradually gave way to mistrust and finally, in the 1550s, to persecution. Grouped into tightly knit congregations led by pastors, elders, and deacons, who made up a consistory, and well organized in local congregations and provincial and national synods, the Huguenots posed a real danger to the central authorities in an age when religious and political uniformity were deemed essential to the security of the state. In the Edict of Chateaubriand (June 27, 1551), civil and ecclesiastical courts were empowered to find and punish Protestants, who were liable to loss of property, including the grant of up to a third of it as a reward to informers. Restrictions on the sale, importation, or printing of unapproved books were imposed. The tongues of Huguenot ministers might be cut out to prevent their speaking heresies, or they might meet death by burning at the stake.

In an atmosphere of fear, secrecy, and intimidation, Huguenots convened their first national synod in Paris in 1559. In June of that year, France lost the steady hand of its vigorous king when Henry II, who, next to war, was fond of nothing more than staged tournaments, died the victim of a grotesque accident after his eye was pierced at a jousting competition. His eldest son, Francis II (r. 1559–60), a sickly boy of 15, took the throne, but it was Henry's wife, Catherine, who, as regent, took the reins of government. Born in Florence into the wealthy and powerful Medici family, Catherine proved a dutiful and docile wife—she bore nine children and tolerated her husband's mistresses. Left on her own after his death, she proved to be a crafty and ruthless agent of state, a first-rate schemer and manipulator. It is doubtful that in her absence her sons could have remained on their thrones. When Francis died the next year, his younger brother, at age 10, succeeded him. Charles IX (r. 1560–74), like his brother before him, also did not rule; rather, his mother governed.

Catherine de' Medici faced a daunting challenge. Bankrupted by foreign wars and still building the rudiments of a national government,

France was now fully divided religiously. By the early 1560s, 2,000 Huguenot congregations existed. While always a minority, they made up for their fewer numbers in possessing an energy, intelligence, and spiritual fervor that they used to forge a powerful political force. And they counted among their adherents many nobles, who, armed and simmering with resentment against the royal officialdom that had deprived them of their prerogatives, were spoiling for a fight.

Religious hatreds were exacerbated by family rivalries and dynastic pretensions. Three great aristocratic families, each controlling considerable territory, struggled for preeminence. The extensive Guise clan, from Lorraine, enormously rich and solidly entrenched in high positions in church and state, vied with both the Montmorency family, its members linked to the Crown through distinguished public service, and the Bourbons, titularly headed by Anthony (Antoine), king of Navarre (r. 1555–62), but, in fact, led by his younger brother, Louis I, the prince de Condé (1530–69).

The Bourbons could claim royal blood, giving them the most authentic claim to the kingship, which, along with religious motives, drove the major players. The feebleness of Catherine's sons made the Crown of France itself, or at least control over its wearer, appear within reach. At the same time, religious differences within families complicated conditions. The head of his family, Anne de Montmorency (1493–1567), constable of France, remained a devout Roman Catholic, but his three nephews, including Gaspard de Coligny (1519–72), admiral of France, became sincere Protestant converts. This stew of intra- and interfamily rivalries guaranteed that the court of Catherine became a snake pit of intrigue, but lesser families and, indeed, residents in cities and regions around the country were torn apart in much the same way.

After the accession of Charles IX, the Huguenots came into the open. Calvinist preachers, protected by armed bodyguards, expelled Catholic priests and taught their own beliefs, this time in French instead of the traditional Latin. The younger Montmorencys and the Bourbons backed them. What became a smoldering tinderbox exploded in March 1562. Infuriated by a massacre of Protestants by forces of the duke of Guise at Vassy, in Normandy, and, emboldened by Catherine's conciliatory policies, the Huguenots responded with a general call to arms. Separated by truces, a series of intermittent, occasionally large-scale but always brutal clashes—nine in all—roiled France for the next three decades.

For several years, Catherine veered among the parties. She offered a degree of toleration to the Huguenots—not enough to please them, but too much to please the Catholics. She held out dynastic marital arrangements with her royal progeny, including with Protestant ruling houses, and even for a time considered war with Spain to end the domestic discord by using a foreign foe to unite the country. Throughout the protracted struggle, Catholics remained strong. And they were unified; as early as 1561, the Guise and Montmorency clans had joined forces to form what would become the Catholic League.

Her central aim to perpetuate the monarchy, Catherine would make overtures to one party when threatened by another. To burnish the image of kingship, she strove to uphold a glittering court, launching construction of the Tuileries palace in 1564, patronizing artists and writers, and assembling a personal library renowned for its rare manuscripts. Her efforts at statesmanship won support from a small but articulate group of *politiques,* Catholic moderates who, in championing reason and tolerance, preferred peace to religious rightness.

The influence of the *politiques* was short-lived. In 1572, Catherine abruptly abandoned conciliation and switched to a new policy: murder. In 1572, having stood their ground, the Huguenots, led by Admiral de Coligny, forthrightly called for war with Spain, the power that surrounded France on almost all sides and that was then locked in a struggle with increasingly successful rebels in the territories it ruled in the Netherlands. Without consulting his mother, young king Charles supported Coligny. Alarmed by Coligny's influence over her son and by the control he exerted as well over the duke of Navarre's young son, Henry (1553–1610), a favorite among the Huguenot party, Catherine moved to sabotage Coligny's ambitions.

To carry out her plans, she chose the occasion of the marriage of her daughter Margaret (1553–1615) to Henry of Navarre, an event set for August 1572 that would draw the admiral and many among the Huguenot nobles to Paris to celebrate the nuptials of one of their own, who had become king of Navarre just two months before following the unexpected death of his mother, Jeanne (1528–72). A Protestant who opposed the match, Jeanne died under suspicious circumstances, some conjecturing the cause to have been a pair of poisoned gloves sent as a wedding gift by Catherine.

The marriage duly took place on August 18, but Catherine's intended victim escaped when, on August 22, an agent of the duke of Guise tried to kill Coligny and failed. Faced with exposure, Catherine decided to mask her guilt by employing wholesale slaughter as a substitute for a single killing. She won over her weak-willed son, and by early on the morning of August 24, the killing had begun. During the infamous St. Bartholomew's Day massacre, perhaps as many as 4,000 perished in Paris alone—men, women, and children cut down in homes and

The St. Bartholomew's Day Massacre, August 23, 1572. Detail, François Dubois (1529–84)
(Erich Lessing/Art Resource, NY)

on streets—and many more were dispatched several days later when the provinces followed the capital's example. Coligny was among the victims, while Henry of Navarre numbered among the few Huguenot leaders to escape.

The massacre solved nothing and aggravated everything. The war went on into the reign of Henry III (r. 1574–89), growing more vicious while the king, though more intelligent than his brother, proved no less incompetent. A profligate who eschewed hunting and the vigorous outdoor activities characteristic of Valois ruling monarchs in favor of fencing and the fine arts, Henry pursued extravagant court pleasures in the company of his young male favorites (*mignons*) in between bouts of pious penitence while his country continued to self-destruct. In 1588, the current duke of Guise took control of Paris in defiance of the king. The Catholic League appeared to have triumphed. Anxious for revenge and contrary to the wishes of his aging, ailing mother, Henry had the duke murdered in December 1588, along with his powerful brother, Louis II, the cardinal of Lorraine (1555–88). Again, royal resort to killing came to nothing—the victory proved short. On January 5, 1589, Catherine died, and in August, King Henry himself was murdered. On August 1, a fanatical Dominican friar, Jacques Clément (1567–89), carrying false papers, was granted admittance to the king, who was lodged with the army at Saint-Cloud. Stating that he had a secret message to deliver, he leaned in closely to whisper into the monarch's ear while plunging a knife into his abdomen.

Clément was killed on the spot. Henry died the next morning but not before recognizing Henry of Navarre as his rightful heir, provided that he fulfill one very important requirement. The throne could be his

Entry of Henry IV into Paris (Library of Congress)

only on condition that he convert to Catholicism. Born a Catholic but taught the tenets of Calvinism in his youth by his mother, Navarre had shifted between the two faiths when it proved expedient. Other claimants could point to their unswerving adherence to the old faith, and a change now would confirm skeptics in their belief that opportunism alone ruled him.

Ambitious for the throne—he is reputed to have said: "Paris is well worth a mass"—Henry possessed sufficient prudence—and patience—to bide his time, waiting until July 1593 to convert. In doing so, he bowed to the reality that Catholicism remained the faith of the majority of the country. Most especially, Paris was devoutly Catholic and in the hands of Catholic League troops. In February 1594, he was crowned king at Chartres Cathedral, and in 1595, Pope Clement VIII (r. 1592–1605) gave the king absolution. The Catholic League dissolved and, with it, all serious resistance.

Henry proved as realistic a ruler as he had a factional leader. Eager to restore unity, he treated former enemies with clemency, a policy that most of his Huguenot followers approved. Agreement was general that enough blood had been shed. Though greeted less than enthusiastically by Protestants, who feared for their future in a country officially, overwhelmingly, and—among some remaining diehard fanatics—intolerantly Catholic, Henry's edict of toleration emerged as a judicious compromise. Issued on April 13, 1598, the Edict of Nantes, while it prohibited the Huguenots from Paris and episcopal sees, granted them the right to worship in the households of Protestant nobles and in designated towns. Because they were a minority, having shrunk to perhaps a tenth of the population, and scattered across the land, in need of some protection, they were guaranteed their own fortified towns—perhaps 100 or more—and granted the right to hold office, to attend university, and to have access to their own courts of justice staffed by both Huguenots and Catholics to safeguard their interests.

Catholics grumbled about the edict, but after a period of protest, especially by the *parlements,* they, too, acquiesced. It was a testament to the measure's evenhandedness that both parties should have disliked the decree, but both accepted it. As such, in an era when religious self-righteousness made compromise a quality rarely to be found, it stands as a tribute to the sound judgment and statesmanlike skill of a king who could now get on with the work of rebuilding his country.

6

THE MONARCHY MADE
MAJESTIC (1598-1789)

In 1598, France lay prostrate, devastated and demoralized after 30 years of religious civil war. A decade later, the country had been transformed, effectively administered and increasingly prosperous under the reign of Henry IV, a ruler of good sense and judicious governance.

His assassination in 1610 left the country suddenly leaderless, the gap filled for half a century by two great statesmen—Richelieu and Mazarin—who strove to secure the monarchy against its internal and external rivals. But however much they tried to assert royal control, they could not prevent peasant uprisings, political divisions, religious troubles, and civil war from rending France.

Stability was restored in mid-century, providing the base from which Louis XIV created a monarchical regime of unparalleled splendor in the last quarter of the 17th century. The reign of the great "sun king" is synonymous with glitter and glory. Although the golden gleams touched few beyond his court, where wealth and power centered, Louis built a state of sufficiently strong means that France became the dominant country in Europe, princes across the Continent, whether following or fighting him, acknowledging his preeminence.

Louis left a legacy of cultural excellence and architectural magnificence, but little survived of his ruling style. The two of his name who followed him—Louis XV and Louis XVI—inherited a kingdom that featured a resurgent nobility, an archaic tax system, a still partially feudal social structure, and an economy that, while vibrant throughout much of the 18th century, left millions of peasants ekeing out a precarious existence. What Louis XIV did bequeath and what his successors were prone to repeat—a penchant for continual war—helped further to deplete the political, the financial, and even—with the loss of France's North American continental empire—the territorial capital of the monarchy.

The regime lost the respect of large segments of the intellectual elite, who, as writers and readers of Enlightenment ideas, ensured the spread of notions of reason, tolerance, and liberty among the thinking classes. By the late 1780s, a host of ministers had tried in vain to devise an effective scheme to address the regime's ever larger revenue shortfalls. Finally compelled to convoke the Estates General, a body that had not met in 175 years, King Louis XVI hoped that its members could develop a workable solution. Called to patch up an ailing monarchy, the representatives proceeded instead to set in motion a series of events, breathtaking in their speed and scope, on a scale and to a degree beyond any yet seen.

The Age of Henry IV, 1598–1610

In the same year that Henry IV issued his edict of toleration (1598), he concluded a successful three-year war against the greatest power of the age. With English and Dutch help, he eliminated the Spanish threat to his kingdom. The Peace of Vervins guaranteed France possession of Brittany, Calais, and strips of northern territory that Spain had occupied. It was Cateau-Cambrésis in reverse, this time marking not France's but rather Spain's defeat and the end of its French adventures.

A compulsive womanizer and an impressively personable man who could charm anyone from proud nobles to poor peasants, Henry, the first of France's Bourbon kings, was above all a consummate politician and statesman. He knew what his country needed. The settlement of religious discord and the victory over Spain allowed him to concentrate on domestic reconstruction. France stood in ruin after more than 30 years of slaughter, royal indifference, and administrative incompetence. Pillaged cities, broken bridges and roads, and a poverty-ridden economy were the legacy of conflict, hatred, and neglect. The ship of state was rudderless. Peasant uprisings were endemic, and the *parlements* were actively opposing the Crown.

Working feverishly to advance *l'utilité publicq* (the public good), Henry relied on no one but himself—he did not convene the Estates General—and, through himself, his ministers and emissaries to set in place an effective government that could put the country back into working order. Capable of arousing strong loyalties, he was fortunate in finding dedicated and intelligent public servants, some of whom, significantly enough, were Huguenots.

Maximilien de Béthune, the duke of Sully (1560–1641), a soldier and statesman, became superintendent of finances in 1598 and carried through an impressive program of fiscal reform. Able not only to collect taxes but also to ensure that the monies made their way into the royal coffers—and not into the hands of greedy minor officials—Sully was also an enthusiastic supporter of agriculture. The state sponsored efforts to encourage farmers by clearing land, draining marshes, and securing property from grasping creditors. Roads, waterways, and bridges were rebuilt. Sully was ably assisted by his associate, Barthélemy de Laffemas (1545–ca. 1612), an ennobled Protestant and economist schooled in the mercantilist doctrines of the age, which advocated vigorous trade rivalry among states in pursuit of national economic self-sufficiency. As such, he worked to secure a surplus of exports over imports, encouraged domestic luxury industries that would make importation of items such as silk unnecessary, and sponsored French expansion in North America. In 1608, the city of Quebec was founded by Samuel de Champlain (ca. 1567–1635), an intrepid navigator, soldier, explorer, and diplomat who became in all but name the governor who put the fledgling colony of New France on a firm footing.

Henry's efforts were crowned with rapid and remarkable success. The public debt was converted into a surplus, and France became for the first time a first-rate economic power. After decades of stagnation, the population grew and prosperity was widespread.

But progress under Henry met an untimely end. While preparing for a war, together with German Protestants, against Catholic Spain and Austria, the king was stabbed to death on May 14, 1610, in Paris by François Ravaillac (1578–1610), a sometime tutor and pious paranoiac who claimed to hear voices and was convinced Henry intended to make war on the pope. Though Ravaillac was brutally tortured before he was drawn and quartered—the punishment for regicides—revenge brought little solace to a country left bewildered and bereft, led now by a boy not yet nine.

Louis XIII: The Rule of Richelieu, 1610–1643

Because Louis was only a child, the Parlement of Paris declared his mother, Marie de' Medici (1573–1642), regent, and she proceeded to rule during the next four years with stunning ineptitude. Compelling the valued Sully to submit his resignation early in 1611, she switched from trusting Henry's able ministers to surrounding herself with court favorites, the most conspicuous of whom were Léonora Galigaï (ca. 1568–1617), her lady-in-waiting, and Galigaï's husband, Concino Concini (1575–1617). Both came from Florence, Italy, and both were ambitious and ostentatious, if intelligent, adventurers who thought nothing of snubbing even the adolescent king.

Troubles resurfaced rapidly. Without the great Henry to rein them in, ambitious princes revived their quarreling. Ever jealous to maintain their independence from the pope, the Gallican clergy grew angry over rumors that Henry's murderer had been in the pay of the Jesuits—the order that had been founded in the mid-16th century by Ignatius of Loyola (1491–1556), a Spanish priest and former knight from a Basque noble family, to advance the cause of the papacy in the struggle to drive back Protestantism. Huguenots braced to resist expected repression.

In 1614, Marie convoked the Estates General. For six months it wrangled, and then dissolved, accomplishing nothing except to update its reputation for incompetence. Fed up with the irksome court confidants, 16-year-old Louis induced some of his entourage to murder Concini in 1617. The queen mother went into exile while Louis proclaimed himself officially of age. Though sharp-minded and hardworking, the young king was moody and spiteful, and in constant need of advice, which he first demonstrated in setting out to rule in league with one of his hunting companions, Charles, the duc de Luynes (1578–1621), a proponent of a rabid Catholic policy. Luynes's death in 1621 gave the queen mother an opening to renew her influence. She had already made peace with her son in 1619 with the help of a superbly skillful negotiator named Richelieu. As a principal minister to Louis, Richelieu would in effect rule France.

Armand Jean du Plessis, Cardinal Richelieu (1585–1642), is an intriguing figure. A study in contrasts, he combined within his person a determination to advance both his personal well-being and the state's welfare. A cleric whose real vocation was politics, he awed others by his very presence. His overarching ambition drove him to seek power, while a shrewd intellect and a toughness of will gave him the means to do so. Born in Paris into a family of ancient noble lineage, Richelieu was a bishop by 1607. He won the cardinal's hat in 1622 in recognition of his role in reconciling royal son and mother. Fighting off jealous courtiers, he held the reins of power firmly in his grasp by 1624. And despite intrigues against both his post and his life, he would keep them until his death in 1642.

Richelieu's path to power made him the characteristic product and, in the policies that he would pursue, the preeminent promoter of the early-modern state. He directed all his energies to a single purpose—

raison d'état (reason of state), namely, securing the monarchy against its rivals, both internal and external.

First to test the cardinal's mettle were the Huguenots. Protestant nobles staged an uprising in 1625, which they repeated in 1627 in a rebellion centered on the western port of La Rochelle. Richelieu took personal charge of the expedition sent against them. After a year's siege in which the Huguenots were encouraged and misled by occasional help from England, the government secured the surrender of the by now starving inhabitants in late October 1628. Other Huguenot strongholds capitulated soon after. By the Peace of Alais in June 1629, the Protestants retained the right to practice their religion, but they lost their special towns, their ports and fortresses, and their legal privileges.

With his characteristic mixture of ruthlessness and mildness—with the former always in the ascendant—Richelieu had broken the political and military power of the Huguenots and rendered them docile. He would set out to do the same with the nobility. There were still far too many members of this privileged caste who, with their vast estates, small private armies, and ceaseless intriguing, stood in the way of the king's absolute power to rule. Although he did not balk at executing rebellious nobles and razing their castles to the ground, the wily cardinal strove above all to transform, once and for all, the nobility into decorative court appendages and dutiful servants of the state. He found the means to do so by increasing the administrative authority of the central government. Provincial *intendants* (commissioners) were appointed to superintend royal policy and enforce royal orders. They took precedence in conflicts both with local aristocrats, who had hitherto exercised so much unchecked power, and with provincial *parlements,* who found their old power much reduced as courts of final instance and fiscal purveyors.

Richelieu imposed a tax on the clergy's properties, which brought him into conflict with the papacy, and other financial exactions were levied at the same time that he encouraged the creation of a navy, improved communications, built canals, supervised the lucrative silk industry, and launched overseas trading and colonial companies. Not unexpectedly, new taxes between 1620 and 1640 incited rebellions. Riots broke out in 1630 at Dijon; in 1631, at Paris; and in 1632, at Lyon. Sporadic but extremely violent outbursts occurred in the countryside as well, where imposts proved especially onerous on the peasantry, much of the old seigneurial burden now replaced by fiscal exactions.

The taxes were needed most essentially to fund an ambitious foreign policy that aimed to advance France in Europe. The House of Hapsburg was the greatest power; consequently, it was against the Hapsburgs, who ruled in Spain, Austria, the southern Netherlands (present-day Belgium), and parts of Italy, that Richelieu directed his most sustained efforts. The Thirty Years' War (1618–48) offered an opportunity. In that vast, complicated, partly religious, partly political conflict that tore apart Germany, Richelieu did not scruple to ally himself with Protestant Sweden, then one of the preeminent powers in northern Europe, if by doing so he could wrest European hegemony from Spain, the power that had so dominated both the continental and the international map for a century and a half. In 1635, when peace overtures threatened to subvert his plans, he intervened actively in the conflict, which was still raging when he died in 1642.

The Reign of Louis XIV
The Rule of Cardinal Mazarin, 1643–1661

Only five months later, Louis XIII followed his chief minister and master, dying in Paris. The pattern by which he had succeeded to the throne was repeated in that of his son. Like Louis XIII before him, Louis XIV was a child—not yet five. Consequently, his reign also began under a regency. Like his father, too, the young Louis found his widowed mother in charge, and both she and he would go on, also, to govern with the aid of a cunning cardinal-statesman.

Jules, Cardinal Mazarin (1602–61) pursued policies very similar to those of his predecessor, but the two men were much less alike in character. Where Richelieu was ruthless, Mazarin was tactful; where Richelieu resorted readily to force, Mazarin relied more on diplomacy. He would retain his influence without opposition until his death in 1661.

The regent, Anne of Austria (1601–66), and the boy king, for whom Mazarin also served as tutor, found him lovable, but not so the country. Suspect in being a foreigner—Mazarin was born Giulio Mazarini in Italy and naturalized in 1639—he was disliked most particularly because his loyalty to his adopted country took precedence, but only slightly, over his loyalty to his family, an attachment to which he was always careful to include himself and whose defining manifestation was greed—he amassed a vast fortune for both.

Mazarin strove, as Richelieu had, to raise the stature of the monarchy both domestically and internationally. Once again, ambitious goals required money to meet them. Imitating his predecessor, Mazarin raised taxes through the 1640s, had them collected by greedy profiteers, and justified them by the need to keep France in the Thirty Years'

War. Although France and Spain continued to do battle, the Peace of Westphalia, which ended the general fighting in October 1648, left the country triumphant. It loosened the hold of the Hapsburgs over Europe by leaving Austria and Spain much weakened, and it won for France territorial gains in three bishoprics in Lorraine—Metz, Toul, and Verdun. Named along with Sweden as one of the guarantors of the peace, France gained an excuse to meddle willfully for more than a century in a Germany broken up into a checkerboard of ministates.

By the time the treaties ending the war were signed, the cardinal and the court faced a revolt of potentially power-altering import. Since the reign of Louis XI, the feudal social order had been long in retreat, and the drive to reduce the remaining powers of the nobility and the *parlements* had peaked under Richelieu. His death offered the chance to undo his work. In the summer of 1648, rural antitax uprisings launched unrest that, when discontented aristocrats united with rebellious *parlements,* sparked the first Fronde (Fr., "sling," which Parisian mobs used to smash the windows of the cardinal's supporters). Called the Fronde parlementaire, it was led by the Parlement of Paris, which, as the oldest of the 12 *parlements,* was always the most outspoken. In a flurry of demands to the queen mother, it asked for the recall of royal *intendants* and the right to pass on proposed taxes. By March 1649, the *parlements* had won most of their claims, and Mazarin crept quietly away from court into voluntary exile.

But in early 1650, the second Fronde—the Fronde princière—resurrected the insurrection. The Crown gave every evidence that it had no intention of keeping its promises, and the great nobles refused to surrender their pretensions. Royal forces faced rebel troops, led by Louis II, the prince de Condé (1621–86), who was joined by the viscomte de Turenne (1611–75), a brilliant general, and Cardinal de Retz (1613–79), a courtier and archbishop of Paris. The rebels reached an alliance with Spain, even allowing Spanish soldiers to enter the country. The royal family was forced briefly, and uncomfortably, out of a Paris loyal to the rebels. Amid a confusion of conflicting and self-centered ambitions—Turenne and the cardinal switched sides—Mazarin assembled a loyalist coalition and raised an army to defeat both the insurrectionists and the Spaniards. By September 1653, all resistance had been stamped out and rebellious cities restored to royal control. Concessions made under pressure were rescinded, and the Parlement of Paris was cowed into submission.

Mazarin kept his hands firmly on the tiller of the ship of state during his remaining years, capping his career with the Peace of the Pyrenees (1659), which ended hostilities with Spain. France gained the provinces of Roussillon and Artois, and King Louis XIV acquired a Spanish bride. The soon-to-be groom was also soon to rule. As an adolescent during the Frondes, he had witnessed, silent and bewildered, the disloyalty of the nobility, the *parlements,* and the city of Paris. As a grown man, he would never forget royalty's retreat, steadfastly resolving never to allow a repeat.

The Social Scene

On March 9, 1661, Mazarin died; on March 10, Louis XIV summoned his ministers and advisers and told them, one by one, that they would assist him in his counsels, but that they would do so only when he asked for them. He would listen to advice, but he alone would govern.

Louis was a king for whom ruling meant everything. Eager to master the details of government, he loved both its substance—from planning grand strategy to determining points of policy—and its style—from setting fashion trends to regulating court protocol. Louis was short, and so the famous high heels and high wig he wore were the deliberate external supports he chose to show his steely, inner sense of command and need to control. When he was born, he was called Louis Dieudonné (God-given), in gratitude to the Almighty for the grant of an heir to Louis XIII, whose procreative powers had been widely doubted. And the man who became king would consciously strive to become the earthly embodiment of that heavenly provider.

That divine providence itself favored absolute power under royal rule became official doctrine, a rationale for rulership most assiduously advanced by Jacques-Béninge Bossuet (1627–1704), who, as bishop of Meaux and tutor to the dauphin (1661–1711)—Louis XIV's only surviving legitimate son—declared that the rights of the king transcend even those of the pope. Attitudes in opposition to such notions, expressed notably by François Fénelon (1651–1715), a prelate who challenged Bossuet's theological precepts and who declared that, on the contrary, kings exist to serve their subjects (*Les aventures de Télémaque [The Adventures of Telemachus]*, 1699), were rigorously denounced.

When Louis took the sun as his device and vigorously acted the role of the *roi soleil,* (sun king) from whose person all power emanated, the cult of monarchy reached its apogee. The king probably never said: *L'état c'est moi* (I am the state)—the most famous words attributed to him—but they accurately encapsulate his view of himself.

Yet, the golden rays that shined forth from his presence warmed few of his subjects. Louis governed approximately 20 million men and women—the largest country in Europe west of Russia—of whom more than 15 million were peasants, many living near the edge of misery and, in bad harvest years, starvation. The plains and low hills north of the Loire River were densely populated, and peasants here concentrated on grain production. Livestock raising supplemented grain growing in Brittany and western Normandy. The average life expectancy was perhaps 25. A good share of the peasants' crop went every year to the local lord as feudal dues, to the local church as tithes, and to the local royal official as taxes. In the cities, more than a million urban dwellers formed a poor laboring class, conscious only of their destitution and economic insecurity. Slightly more than about a million made up a lower middle class (petit bourgeoisie) of self-employed craftsmen and small shopkeepers. The rest—about 2 million—were well-off bourgeois, nobles, and priests. Few clerics were poor, many were rich, and all enjoyed influence as leaders either spiritually in their parishes or temporally, among politicians in Paris. At the tip of the social and economic pyramid stood the courtiers, who, bedecked in their finest attire, walked a careful line, anxious to lavish flattery on a king who insisted that they be seen at court yet careful to keep their distance from a monarch who believed his splendor depended on maintaining an aura of remoteness.

At the beginning of the reign, the king's court was peripatetic, moving from château to château, assembling and disassembling theaters, fireworks,

Western facade of Versailles (François Mori/Associated Press)

hunts, and gambling casinos as it moved about. Never forgetting the rebelliousness of the Parisians during his youth, Louis disliked Paris and so he set out to convert a simple royal hunting lodge at Versailles, 13 miles (22 km) outside the city, into a showplace to mirror his own magnificence.

THE DAILY ROUTINE OF LOUIS XIV

A soldier and diplomat, Louis de Rouvroy, duc de Saint-Simon (1675–1755), was born to inherit the title of duke granted to his father, who was a favorite of Louis XIII. Intensely interested in the lives and intrigues of those around him at the court of Louis XIV, he engaged informants ranging from courtiers to servants to gather information that offers a glimpse into the private world of the great king.

At eight o'clock the chief valet de chambre on duty, who alone had slept in the royal chamber . . . awoke the King. The chief physician, the chief surgeon, and the nurse . . . entered at the same time. The latter kissed the King; the others rubbed and often changed his shirt, because he was in the habit of sweating a great deal. At the quarter, the grand chamberlain was called . . . and those who had, what was called the grandes entrées. The chamberlain . . . drew back the curtains . . . and presented the holy water from the vase, at the head of the bed. . . . They all passed into the cabinet of the council. A short religious service being over, . . . immediately after, other privileged courtiers entered, and then everybody, in time to find the King putting on his shoes and stockings. . . . Every other day we saw him shave himself; and he had a little short wig in which he always appeared, even in bed. . . . He often spoke of the chase, and sometimes said a word to somebody. . . .

As soon as he was dressed he prayed to God, at the side of the bed, where all the clergy present knelt, the cardinals without cushions, all the laity remaining standing; and the captain of the guards came to the balustrade during the prayer, after which the King passed into his cabinet. . . . He gave orders to each for the day.

. . .

At ten o'clock his supper was served. After supper, the King . . . wishing to retire, went and fed his dogs, then said good night, passed into his chamber; where he said his prayers. He said good night with an indication of the head. . . . Then commenced what was called the petit coucher, at which only the specially privileged remained. . . . They did not leave until he got into bed.

The reigning architectural style was baroque, distinguished by monumental proportions, colonnades, domes, and grand, massive staircases. Begun under architect Salomon de Brosse (1571–1626), who melded elements traditional to French building (Gothic features and

Louis XIV at age 63 (Library of Congress)

Source: Louis de Rouvroy, duc de Saint-Simon, *The Memoirs of the Duke of Saint-Simon on the Reign of Louis XIV and the Regency* (London: Allen & Unwin, 1900), pp. 21–27.

lofty roofs) with Italian designs on display in his Palais du Luxembourg (1615–20), baroque was perfected under François Mansart (1598–1666). It reached its height under Louis le Vau (1612–70) and designer Charles Le Brun (1619–90), whose Vaux-le-Vicomte castle (1656–61) exemplifies the grandiosity of a style that included gardens, laid out by landscape architect André Le Nôtre (1613–1700), integrated so skillfully into the scene as to become an indispensable component of the palatial composition. Louis enlisted France's leading architects, painters, and sculptors, including Le Nôtre, to construct Versailles, arguably Europe's most famous palace, to which the king moved his government in 1682 while it was still under construction.

Louis insisted that the nobility attend him at court, a ruinously expensive policy for them but politically profitable for him, who, in removing them from their local base of power, set them adrift to live by the favor of their royal master. The most trivial detail of the king's daily routine was invested with pomp and solemnity; great lords competed for the privilege of handing the king his shirt or soup spoon.

By the middle of the reign, the old nobility of the sword was thoroughly domesticated. Every element of society, including the world of arts and letters, felt the impact of Louis's imprint.

A Classical Age in Culture

The king proved a generous patron of the arts, and he strove to make them, too, march to the royal beat. In 1672, he became the official protector of the Académie Française, established in 1635 by Richelieu, whose members stood guard over the French language in prescribing what was and was not acceptable. The Académie des Sciences to promote scientific study and the Comédie-Française that of theatrical productions were founded in 1666 and 1680, respectively, and other academies—in painting, sculpture, and music—were active. In music, the *chanson* evolved to include, beginning in the late 16th century, solo songs, and these works, generally accompanied by lute or keyboard, flourished in the 17th century, composed by artists such as Denis Gaultier (1603–72) and Michel Lambert (1610–96). The foundations for French literature of the period were set by François de Malherbe (1555–1628), the court poet to Henry IV and Louis XIII, whose poetry and prose proved instrumental in helping to solidify the French spoken in Paris as the standard language throughout the country.

During the reign of Louis XIV, artists labored under the constraint of the officially approved style of classicism, which taught that art is a science; that it is moral, designed to uplift the public; that it is dignified and never vulgar; and that it is natural, able to capture nature in all its idealized beauty. Arguably the founder and the greatest practitioner of 17th-century classical painting, Nicolas Poussin (1594–1665), with his crowded but orderly scenes filled with calmly posed figures drawn from classical mythology or Christian history, met the standards to perfection.

Many of the great talents of the 17th century treated classicism more as a demand for discipline and less as an impediment to invention, and the king was intelligent enough to encourage them, knowing that masterpieces are not made on command. Born in Rouen, Pierre Corneille (1602–84) was one of the leading dramatic writers. In his trio of great tragedies—*Horace* (1640), *Cinna* (1641), and *Polyeucte* (1642)—he peopled his stage with larger-than-life heroes who defy or seek to remake their world, succeeding or failing but doing so always with great nobility. Corneille's successor and considered the greatest writer of French classical tragedy, Jean Racine (1639–99), also drew themes from classical myths and Old Testament narratives. Noted for his simple plots and sophisticated language, using rhymed Alexandrian verse, all of Racine's dramas (*Iphigénie*, 1674; *Phèdre*, 1677) follow a strict classical formality in which the characters convey intense human passions beneath a formal rational surface of restrained emotions and actions.

Eschewing tragedy for comedy, Molière (1622–73) is the outstanding exemplar of the genre. Born Jean-Baptiste Poquelin in Paris, the son of a well-to-do upholsterer, Molière died young, but not before pouring out a series of productions that have earned for him a lasting reputation as France's greatest comic dramatist. Molière's plays (*L'école des femmes [School of Women]*, 1662; *Le misanthrope [The Misanthropist]*, 1666) are peopled with characters who display universal human failings—miserliness, snobbery, hypocrisy—and they are often drawn from types he found around him. Some of his victims—or who thought they were—were furious, and *Tartuffe* (first version 1664), in which a religious imposter nearly ruins a gullible family, drew the ire of members of both the church and the court, forcing the king himself to defend the playwright against the charge of blasphemy. Molière was a genius not only in understanding human nature but also in his innovative use of language—he became famed for his quick turns of phrase and the repetitions he used to comic effect—and his influence on the French language has been profound.

Much of the music to accompany Molière's comedies was composed by Jean-Baptiste Lully (1632–87), who spent most of his life working at Louis XIV's court, where he also wrote ballets and solemn, dignified operas, called *tragédies-lyriques,* modeled on the tragedies of Corneille and Racine. Lully helped to popularize a new musical style, labeled like that in architecture, baroque, which had been evolving from Renaissance forms since the early 1600s and would come to distinguish the musical period until the mid-18th century. Baroque music was marked by precise instrumental scoring, the use of longer sustained notes (ornamentation) on keyboard instruments such as the harpsichord, and the adoption of basso continuo—an accompaniment that gave harmonic structure to the music. In favoring the use of solo voices it helped to establish opera, invented in the late Renaissance. Accompanying its rise, popular new dances appeared, including the rigaudon, the gavotte, and, perhaps best known, the minuet.

A member of a literary group that included Molière, Jean de La Fontaine (1621–95) wrote his first book of *Fables choisies* (*Selected Fables*) in 1668. Subsequent volumes followed to earn him a reputation as France's most enduringly famous author of these tales. Likewise, François de La Rochefoucauld (1613–80) remains renowned as a writer of epigrammatic maxims (*Maximes,* 1664) whose talent has never been surpassed. Writer Savinien Cyrano de Bergerac (1619–55), made famous in history as a romantic hero by his frequent duels, won recognition, though posthumously, as an author of early works of science fiction (*Des états et empires du soleil* [*States and Empires of the Sun*], 1662).

The urge for precision and order that so marked the era was well under way in the sciences as the result of a new philosophy based on doubtful questioning and a new method of factual inquiry. Impatient with the quibbling of the scholastics and the pretentious claims to certainty of the theologians, René Descartes (1596–1650), born at La Haye in Touraine, spent much of his life abroad, writing widely on philosophical and psychological subjects. He was the first to apply algebra to geometry and, in optics, to discover the law of reflection. In his most celebrated and influential work, *Discours de la méthode* (*Discourse on Method,* 1637), Descartes devised a set of four rules by which to produce dependable knowledge: accept only clear, self-evidently true ideas; analyze; arrange each acceptable idea from the simplest moving up to the most complex; and establish as complete a way of thinking as can be. By following this program and looking within himself, he drew his famous first truth: "Cogito, ergo sum" (I think, therefore I am). Moving forward from this initial first step, he cautiously proved the existence of God, of matter, and of motion. Reasoning in this way—starting from a basic rule or principle and using it to arrive at valid conclusions—

Descartes in his Cartesian system founded the deductive method of inquiry. With powerful conviction, he asserted the autonomy of the rational self, offering the hope that there were no limits to humankind's ability to conquer ignorance. The realities of the times were, however, quite different—realities that France's ruler set out to remedy.

Loius XIV at Home: The Gains and Pains of Glory

While earlier monarchs had welded a unified realm, it remained a far from uniform one. The France over which Louis began his reign constituted a bewildering congeries of overlapping and conflicting jurisdictions. Brittany, Provence, and Normandy had their own *parlements* and local Estates, their own laws and liberties. In addition to the main royal courts, there were hundreds of local jurisdictions specializing in everything from tax cases to those dealing with crimes committed in the woods and on the roads and waterways. Every professional corporation had its own set of laws (*coutumes*), and there were literally hundreds of them. Tariff barriers were everywhere, and no standard system of weights and measures existed. The *intendants* and other royal officials whom Richelieu had dispatched into the provinces and the lawyers enjoined to codify this mass of legislation and customs had made no more than a beginning. Louis determined to act decisively to reduce the disorder.

He started with his own royal council. To establish a system responsible only to himself, he acted as his own prime minister and excluded from his High Council the princes of the blood (relatives), the princes of the church, the great generals and nobles, his younger brother (called Monsieur), and even his mother. Instead, he relied on men who owed their position and power to him alone. The most prominent included Michel Le Tellier (1603–85), secretary of state for war and later chancellor, and Nicolas Fouquet (1615–80), superintendent of finances.

Louis brought everyone and everything into line: Disobedient cities were saddled with garrisons of soldiers, old willful aristocratic army commanders were replaced by compliant professional officers. The *parlements* were stripped of all but their judicial functions—an edict of 1673 commanded that they register all royal decrees without delay, depriving them of their politically important role to delay legislation. Louis enlarged the army, expanded the powers of the *intendants*, and streamlined the bureaucracy. Many specialized local jurisdictions were gradually incorporated into bailiwick courts, which became the central unit of local legal governance.

When Fouquet built up a personal following and became so immensely rich as to threaten the sensitivities of the king, Louis had him arrested and imprisoned, his place taken by Fouquet's enemy. Born into a merchant family, Jean-Baptiste Colbert (1619–83) moved rapidly from post to post. In 1665, he was officially named controller general of finances; in 1668, secretary of state for the navy. The consummate mercantilist, Colbert strove to grow the prosperity of the economy, partly for its own sake, but fundamentally to enhance the political power of the state. He began by saving money. Sums collected by improving the management of royal estates, abolishing sinecures (income-earning offices requiring little or no work), exposing false claims to nobility, and squeezing more money from the provinces and the clergy were prudently husbanded. During the 1660s—a decade of unparalleled economic activity—he founded new luxury industries, such as the tapestry works at Beauvais, and purchased others, notably the Gobelins works at Paris for the production of tapestries and furniture; he developed a merchant marine, built a great canal—the Canal du Midi, completed in May 1681—to link the Mediterranean and the Atlantic, encouraged iron foundries, brought in Flemish and Venetian glassmakers, built docks and shipyards in Brest and Toulon, imposed new high tariffs in 1664 and 1667 directed against Dutch and English competitors, and began a simplification of the complex internal tariff structure and a rationalization of the tax system.

The goal of making the king Europe's most powerful ruler depended on achieving mastery of all spheres of public life, including religion. Louis's own religious convictions are somewhat obscure. The libertinism so evident in the elaborate festivities of his younger years gave way in the 1690s to a more austere, sedate routine and to a measure of piety as he surrounded himself with the religiously inclined, among them his favorite royal mistress of his later years, the widow Scarron (1635–1719), whom he called Madame de Maintenon and whom he probably married in secret after the death of Queen Maria Theresa (Fr., Marie-Thérèse, 1638–83). But his determination to control religious affairs brought him into conflict with Catholics—both Jansenists and the pope—as well as Protestants.

The Jansenists were Augustinians, namely, followers of Saint Augustine, who like him held a pessimistic view of human nature and possibilities in stressing humankind's sinfulness and utter helplessness before God. Called "Calvinists who go to mass" by their enemies, they were vigorously opposed by the Jesuits and other more "forgiving" Catholics, who held that the faithful can play an active part in securing their salvation. Catholic conformists took offense at a highly controversial polemic concerning reception of the Eucharist, published in 1643 by Antoine Arnaud (1612–94), head of a distinguished group of theologians who became leader of the Jansenist faction. The Jesuits had the support of the papacy, and in 1653, Pope Innocent X (r. 1644–55) condemned five propositions of the Jansenists. Firing back, mathematician Blaise Pascal (1623–62) published his *18 lettres provinciales* (*18 Provincial Letters*, 1656) in Arnaud's defense, while in his *Pensées sur la religion et sur quelques autres sujets* (*Thoughts on Religion and Certain Other Subjects*, 1670) he explored in lucid, quotable aphorisms humankind's lost condition after the fall from God's grace.

Louis began his reign harassing the Jansenists, but he soon left them alone, finding them useful allies in his own efforts to assert his independence from Rome. In the 1670s, the king claimed clerical appointive powers and the right to collect the income from vacant sees, which Pope Innocent XI (r. 1676–89) vigorously opposed. Unrepentant, Louis in 1682 issued four articles, which included an assertion of the king's freedom from papal jurisdiction in secular matters and the superiority of a general church council over the pope. Schism seemed a possibility, but in the end, neither king nor pope sought a complete break. Innocent died in 1689, and his successors found ways to settle matters amicably; by 1693, these Gallican articles had been rescinded. The persecution of the Jansenists resumed.

Increasingly inclined to listen to the advice of Madame de Maintenon and to his Jesuit advisers, Louis also launched a drive to eradicate Protestants. Begun in 1679, the campaign gained momentum in the early 1680s. Huguenots were at first paid to convert, but more forceful measures soon ensued. The chief means of pressure were so-called *dragonnades*—the quartering of dragoons on unwilling Huguenot families—that, because they were brutal, procured thousands of quick conversions, most notably in Languedoc and Béarn. Finally, on October 22, 1685, in the Edict of Fontainebleau, the king officially revoked the Edict of Nantes and forbade Huguenots to practice their faith, to educate their children in the religion, or to leave the country. The first two proscriptions succeeded—churches were demolished, Huguenots were expelled from cities, and children even were kidnapped to prevent their inculcation into Protestantism. But the prohibition on emigration failed. Many stayed in France and went underground, but more than 200,000 left to find shelter in welcoming Protestant countries in Europe—mainly England, the Dutch Republic, and Brandenburg—and overseas in English North America. The émigrés took with them valuable skills and also a great deal of anger. The revocation proved to be one of Louis's great mistakes. It strengthened his enemies abroad, against whom he was battling in a struggle to secure in Europe the same dominant place he claimed at home.

Louis XIV Abroad: Two Score Years of War

Under Louis XIV, France flexed its muscle for the first time in a major way on both a continental and an international scale. Colbert's intensive efforts to fortify the monarchy included active intervention in the competition for overseas territories. French East Indies and West Indies Companies were founded, based on reconstructions of earlier bodies established by Richelieu. In India, energetic efforts by the East Indies director-general François Caron (1600–73) led to establishment of trading "factories"—commercial settlements—at Surat in 1663 and, in 1673, at Chandernagore (present-day Chandannagar) and at Pondichéry (present-day Puducherry), the latter in particular transformed from a small fishing village into a flourishing port city. From these and other bases, the French engaged in constant conflict with Dutch and English competitors, battling their European rivals for privileges with local potentates.

In North America, Montreal (Mount Royal) had been founded in 1642 as Ville-Marie, a fur-trading post. The fledgling colony of New France was made a royal province in 1663. Under Jean Talon (1626–94), its first *intendant,* royal rule was firmly imposed. The powers of the bishop of Quebec, the chief authority figure after the death of Champlain, were limited, detachments of soldiers were dispatched, and 700 to 900 women colonists (*filles du roi*) arrived in a bid to promote the growth of the remote territory by boosting a settled farming population and so expand the economic foundation beyond its fishing and fur-trading base. Further strengthening took place under the authoritarian rule of Louis de Frontenac (1622–98), who served as governor-general from 1672 to 1682 and again from 1689 until his death. Extensive French missionary efforts to convert the indigenous population spurred European exploration of the continent. Jacques Marquette (1637–75), a Jesuit, and Louis Jolliet (1645–1700), a French-Canadian trapper, were the first to travel and map the upper Mississippi region. No explorer proved more intrepid than René Robert Cavalier, Sieur de La Salle (1643–87), who explored the Great Lakes and in 1682 claimed the entire Mississippi River basin for France, naming the territory Louisiana (Fr., la Louisiane) in honor of the king. To match the

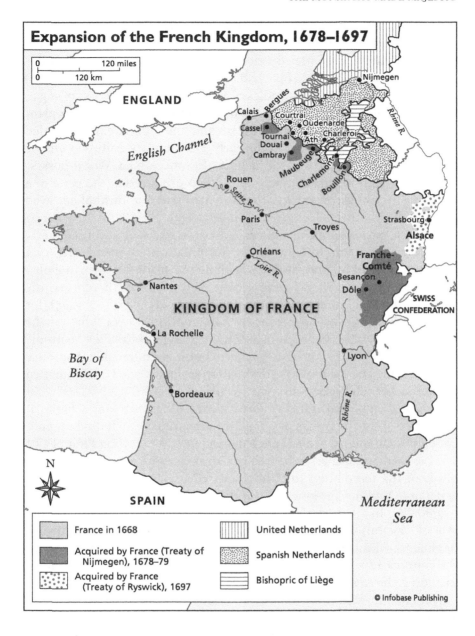

Expansion of the French Kingdom, 1678–1697

Legend:
- France in 1668
- Acquired by France (Treaty of Nijmegen), 1678–79
- Acquired by France (Treaty of Ryswick), 1697
- United Netherlands
- Spanish Netherlands
- Bishopric of Liège

© Infobase Publishing

settlements that anchored France's New World possessions along the St. Lawrence River in the north, on the southwest frontier Mobile was founded as a fort in 1702, followed, on May 7, 1718, by New Orleans (Fr., Nouvelle Orléans), established by the territory's governor, Jean-Baptiste Le Moyne de Bienville (1680–1767).

In the Caribbean, the islands of Martinique and Guadeloupe had been acquired in 1635. In 1648, they were joined by Saint-Barthélémy and Saint-Martin, the latter divided that year with the Dutch. By mid-century, the native Carib people had been either exterminated or exiled, and the colonies in the West Indies began intensive production of sugar, among the most sought-after commodities in Europe. Grown on plantations worked by African slaves, it became the biggest export. Settled by French pirates beginning in the early 17th century, Saint-Domingue (present-day Haiti) became the richest of France's New World possessions, its wealth in sugar, coffee, and indigo produced at the price of a brutally efficient slave system. It is estimated that one-third of enslaved laborers died within a few years of their arrival.

Overseas possessions introduced a division that would subsequently characterize French foreign policy formulation in mandating that attention be paid to, and, at times, a choice be made between, a global and a continental focus. In the second half of the 17th century, the main playing field remained Europe, however, where Louis's search for glory led him to seek hegemony. Debate continues over whether the king and his advisers consciously sought to extend France's "natural" frontiers to the Rhine and the Pyrenees, but it is undeniable that, once in firm control of the nation's administrative apparatus, Louis intended to extend French borders by every available means.

Prospects appeared initially advantageous. England's king Charles II (r. 1660–85) was in Louis's pay. The German princes, including up-and-coming Brandenburg, were French dependents. When King Philip IV (r. 1621–65) of Spain died in September 1665, leaving a sickly four-year-old heir, the temptation to pounce proved irresistible. Led by superb generals—Marshal Turenne and the great Condé—Louis's armies fought formidably. In the peace signed at Aix-la-Chapelle in May 1668, the War of Devolution resulted in a settlement with France's Triple Alliance opponents—England, Sweden, and the Dutch Republic—that won for the country 12 strongholds on the frontier of the Spanish Netherlands, including the town of Lille.

Not content with these mere crumbs and burning with impatience to avenge himself on the Dutch—the architects of the Triple Alliance, and as a small merchant republic the antithesis of Louis's imperial monarchy—he engineered their isolation and returned to war in 1672. But the Dutch refused to surrender. They held out long enough for their ruling stadholder (head of state), William III (r. 1650–1702)—Louis's most implacable foe—to cement a reverse coalition, made up of the Dutch Republic, England, Spain, Brandenburg, and the duchy of Lorraine.

By 1678, the two sides battled to a draw and, in treaties signed at the Dutch city of Nijmegen in 1678–79, Franche-Comté—the Free County of Burgundy long sought by French kings—fell to Louis, and French territory in northern and eastern border districts was strengthened by the addition of several fortified towns.

Anxious to extend his control eastward, Louis built on the foothold won by the Treaty of Westphalia in setting up four *chambres de réunion* (special courts) in 1679 to examine French claims in Alsace and Lorraine, two regions honeycombed with complex feudal territorial arrangements in which Louis's jurisdictional assertions competed with those of the Holy Roman Emperor and various other monarchs. Not unexpectedly, in case after case the courts found in favor of France, and for the next several years, troops arrived to annex the two provinces peacefully. Their efforts culminated in 1681, when they reached the Rhine to occupy the free city of Strasbourg.

Louis crossed the river, and in October 1688, he laid waste the Palatinate. He declared war on the Dutch, but he faced far more than one opponent, William III having put in place in 1686 the League of Augsburg, a Dutch-engineered coalition that included Spain, Sweden, the Holy Roman Emperor, the Palatinate, Bavaria, and Saxony. England joined too after William took the English throne on the invitation of Parliament in the Glorious Revolution of 1688. Though the opposition appeared daunting, France was well prepared. Its armies were superbly trained and arranged, largely the work of François-Michel Le Tellier, marquis de Louvois (1641–91)—the sole master of the military after the death of Turenne—who instituted major reforms, including opening command positions to commoners, creating provincial militias, and establishing military schools. For eight years the War of the League of Augsburg raged, bringing devastation to the invaded lands and depression, unemployment, and famine to France. When general peace was made in late 1697 at Ryswick, in the Netherlands, few were happy with the terms, Louis least of all. Compelled to recognize William III as king of England, he had to give up most of the conquests obtained from the "reunions," save for Strasbourg, Saarlouis, and bits of territory in Alsace.

One major prize still to be claimed kept his bellicose ambitions alive. Spain's Hapsburg king, Charles II (r. 1665–1700), childless and in seemingly perpetual poor health, stirred the greedy hopes of several European rulers. At last, on November 1, 1700, he died. His will, insisting the Spanish dominions be left undivided, made Philip of Anjou (1683–1746), Louis's second grandson, sole heir on condition that he renounce his claim to the throne of France. Louis accepted in his adolescent grandson's name. But neighboring powers remained wary, not trusting Louis to keep his word and fearing the potential power inherent in a France and Spain united under the same Bourbon ruling house. Determined to prevent the destruction of the European balance of power that such a union would produce, most of Louis's old foes—England, the Dutch Republic, Prussia, Austria—formed a Grand Alliance. Their suspicions were proved right when Louis violated his own pledges in 1701 by declaring that Spain's new king, Philip V (r. 1700–January 1724 and September 1724–46) had a right to both countries' thrones, a right the French intended to secure by launching attacks in the Spanish Netherlands (present-day Belgium). In the War of the Spanish Succession, Spain, together with Bavaria—a reliable puppet of France as an inveterate adversary of Hapsburg Austria—were France's only allies. Led by brilliant generals, the Englishman John Churchill, duke of Marlborough (1650–1722), and Prince Eugene of Savoy (1663–1736), in the service of Austria, most prominent among them, the allies repeatedly defeated Louis's forces, driving them from the Spanish Netherlands, Germany, and Italy. But the victories proved costly—bloodbaths for both sides—and, mutually exhausted after over a decade of war, the belligerents concluded peace in a series of treaties in 1713 at Utrecht, the Netherlands, and in 1714 at Rastatt and Baden, Germany. A settlement of decisive importance, Utrecht marked the triumph of England (Great Britain after 1707), launching it on a path to mastery of the seas, and, conversely, the defeat of France. While the Bourbon king of Spain kept his throne, the two crowns were separated permanently.

France remained a great power, but Louis's dream of supremacy was frustrated. The Peace of Utrecht stands as a final judgment on the reign of Louis XIV. The old king died on September 1, 1715, after a lengthy illness, his children and most of his grandchildren dead before him, the power of his country reduced, many of his promises left unfulfilled, and, at the end, his lifelong pursuit of splendor and glory a source of bitter regret and self-blame.

Autocratic Interlude, 1715–1743

The authority of the king who claimed unlimited ruling powers lasted but a day after his death. On September 2, 1715, the Parlement of Paris, which had the royal will in its care, declared portions of the document invalid. In doing so, the magistrates bowed to the wishes of the regent, Louis XIV's nephew, Philippe II, duc d'Orléans (1674–1723), who, distrusted by the late king, balked at being saddled by him with a regency council and who resented the designation of Louis-Auguste de Bourbon, duc du Maine (1670–1736), one of Louis's legitimized bastards, as guardian of young king Louis XV (r. 1715–74), the five-year-old great grandson of the great king. In return for the favor, the Parlement resumed its power to remonstrate, in effect to obstruct, legislation. The nobility of the robe thus reasserted itself. The nobility of the sword resurfaced as well in a series of six councils called the Polysynodie, which for a time pushed aside the secretaries of state. The experiment failed—the old ministries were back in place by 1718—but the nobility never returned to its former docile state. Until 1789, nobles of all stripes continued to claim the right to a voice in making legislation.

The regent's most urgent need was for money. Decades of war had burdened the country with a mountain of public debt. Tax rolls were out of date, and many towns and their wealthy residents found ways to join the nobles and clerics in securing exemptions from imposts. Tax collecting was "farmed" to private entrepreneurs who contracted to supply the state with a fixed sum, but often too much remained in the pockets of the farmer. Orléans allowed a portion of the public debt to be repudiated, but this partial bankruptcy proved insufficient.

Orléans's desperate search for financial remedies led him to John Law (1671–1729), a Scottish adventurer, a reputed genius with money, and, like himself, an avid gambler whom he had met earlier at the betting tables. In 1716, Law secured from the regent a royal edict to found the Banque générale, the first bank in France, which worked well and swelled public confidence in his abilities. In 1717, Law established a Compagnie de la Louisiane ou d'Occident, which came to control huge tracts of land around the mouth of the Mississippi River, recently claimed by France and where the company had been given a 25-year exclusive right to trade. In 1719, the Banque générale became the state bank of France. Now appointed comptroller-general of finances and councillor of state, Law invited the public to invest in the Mississippi venture, which, together with the bank's issuance of paper money, set off a frenzy of speculation. Speculation brought inflation. Investors hungry to make quick profits caused the company's share prices to skyrocket. A wise few recognized that no amount of overseas trade could sustain such prices, and financial gambling gradually declined. During 1720, the whole so-called Mississippi Bubble burst. Thousands who had borrowed or mortgaged heavily lost everything. Law fled into exile, leaving behind not only shaken confidence in the state and an increased suspicion of credit but also a few lasting benefits. Some road and canal projects planned by Law were not abandoned.

In international affairs, the regent fared much better. After decades of war, he managed to put in place a fragile alliance with Britain in pursuing a pacific foreign policy that would endure for two decades. Orléans died in December 1723, to be succeeded by the duke of Bourbon, who proved so completely incompetent that in 1726 Cardinal Fleury (1653–1743), Louis XV's aged tutor, found it easy to secure his dismissal and to become, in effect, first minister. Louis was content to let him run the government. Married in 1725 to Marie Leszczyńska (1703–68), daughter of the deposed king of Poland, the king busied himself with hunting and in highly public love affairs.

Both flexible and firm, Fleury pursued a plan of peace at all costs, his foreign policy based on an alliance with Spain. Only the War of the Polish Succession (1733–38), which Fleury entered very reluctantly, disturbed the pacific picture. Awarded to Louis's father-in-law Stanisław Leszczyński (1677–1766) under terms of the settlement, the Duchy of Lorraine was stipulated to revert to France on his death. The currency was stabilized, and with it France experienced economic prosperity. A few ripples riled the religious scene. A revived Jansenism spawned controversy, the lower clergy were restive against the bishops, and some among the public were caught up in a wave of spiritual fervor sparked by supposed miracles. At the same time, a new wave of intellectual trendsetters scoffed at conventional theology altogether.

Reason Rules an Enlightened Age

Whether deists (believers in a remote, disinterested God), skeptics, or atheists, the intellectuals who formulated the new ideas that swept across educated 18th-century Europe—identified by their French-language name *philosophes*—were most definitely not enthusiasts for organized religion, which in their view thrived on the promotion of superstitious bigotry. And many educated Christians also agreed with them in abhorring blind faith, instead idolizing rational inquiry and seeking sober intelligence and tolerance as guides to human action. Because they professed to have discovered a new formula by which humankind could advance, believing that society could be transformed by trusting in reason and relying on science, the era during which they thought and wrote is called the Enlightenment (Fr., *siècle des lumières*).

The philosophes were progressives who looked optimistically to a better tomorrow, but they were well aware of their debt to yesterday, declaring their admiration for the ancient pagan philosophers, the critical thinkers of the Renaissance, and the innovative religious, political, and scientific scholars of the 17th century. Even priests had prepared the way for them. In 1681, the Benedictine monk Jean Mabillon (1632–1707) published in Paris a Latin treatise *De re diplomatica* (Concerning charters), which, as an exercise in validating the authenticity of documents, founded diplomatics, that is, the science of reading historical records with a critical eye to discovering forgeries and false additions. And the philosophes never tired of quoting Pierre Bayle (1647–1706). Born the son of a Huguenot minister, Bayle fled to the Netherlands, where he published his four-volume masterpiece *Dictionnaire historique et critique* (*Historical and Critical Dictionary*, 1695–97). A sounding board for everything Bayle abhorred—intolerance, superstition, unquestioning religion, persecution—and adored—freedom of thought and expression—the *Dictionnaire* presents a vision of a world in which humankind, acknowledging its ignorance and imperfections, lives in peace and forbearance, and it serves as a forerunner of modern historical criticism.

The Enlightenment was an international movement, but the French representatives were the most celebrated and conspicuous. French was the language of intellectual discourse, diplomacy, and commercial intercourse all across Europe, and so Paris was the headquarters and French the favored idiom of these thinkers who lived scattered across the Western world.

The French philosophes initiated and shaped much of the dialog. Arguably the greatest, Voltaire, claimed as his motto *au fait!* (to the facts!), which served as the rallying cry of the age, and in his career he epitomizes the ideas dear to the era. Professing a deism based on reason and social utility, he championed tolerance, skepticism, and rigorous objectivity.

As much the student as the teacher, Voltaire learned a great deal from the writings of others, notably Charles-Louis de Secondat, baron de la Brède et de Montesquieu (1689–1755). The son of a magistrate, Montesquieu became president of the Parlement of Bordeaux and earned a reputation as a writer with his *Lettres persanes* (*Persian Letters*, 1721). Interested above all in history and political philosophy, he traveled and studied throughout Europe. In his famous *De l'esprit des lois* (*Spirit of the Laws*, 1750), he argued that "physical causes," such as climate, soil, and territorial size, interact with "moral causes," such as religion, to shape a country's society. Each form of government is based on a principle: democratic republics, that of public spirit; aristocratic republics, that of the ruling nobility's self-restraint;

VOLTAIRE

Born François-Marie Arouet in Paris, the son of prosperous bourgeois parents, Voltaire (November 21, 1694–May 30, 1778) was intended for the law but chose literature instead. In his fashionable Jesuit school and equally upscale salons, he soon became famous for his brilliant literary gifts and unmatched wit. He was incarcerated briefly in the Bastille for writing scurrilous verses against the regent, then released on a promise to leave for England. He emerged from prison with a new name, "Voltaire" (an anagram of the Latinized spelling of Arouet, the younger), and he spent three years (1726–29) across the Channel, where he acquired a lifelong admiration for English liberties and where he strengthened his political and philosophical convictions.

Back in official good grace (1744), he traveled to Paris and Versailles, where he became a court favorite and won election to the Académie Française before accepting a long-standing invitation from King Frederick II of Prussia (r. 1740–86) to visit his court. In Berlin, he completed his great historical work *Le siècle de Louis XIV* (*The Age of Louis XIV,* 1751) and a major philosophical work *Micromégas* (1752). His acid-tongued wit clashing with Frederick's autocratic nature, Voltaire moved on, buying a large estate at Ferney, just inside the French border near Geneva, Switzerland, where he set up workshops, composed for—and acted in—his theater, carried on a voluminous correspondence, and welcomed so many visitors that he earned a reputation as the "innkeeper of Europe." He wrote in defense of tolerance and against bigotry and superstition in works of social, literary, and religious criticism such as his famous *Candide, ou l'optimisme* (*Candide: Or Optimism,* 1759), one among his *Contes philosophiques* (*The Fables of Reason*) written over a period of years. He intervened courageously on behalf of religious persecution and unjust judicial practices. At his death in Paris, where he returned after a 20-year absence, Voltaire stood at the summit of great popularity.

He is remembered for his defense of civil rights, but most of all for his philosophical stories, which illustrate his great themes. In repudiating what he viewed as the cruel and vengeful God of the

monarchies, that of hierarchy; and despotisms (which to Montesquieu were always bad), that of fear. Montesquieu's celebrated insistence on separation of powers—the division of authority among discrete branches of government to prevent any one person or group from

Old Testament in favor of the divine watchmaker, who stands aloof after having made the world perfectly by giving it unchangeable physical and moral laws, he personifies the 18th-century deist. Voltaire believed that if they followed a path based on reason and moral altruism, human beings had within themselves the power to build a better world.

Voltaire (Library of Congress)

accruing too much control, which American revolutionaries would wholeheartedly embrace—was actually made as an argument, in the great French debate then raging, in favor of a strong nobility to serve as a counterweight to a despotic king. Montesquieu affirmed that liberty could not exist when the same individual held the power both to make and to break the law.

Younger men joined the ranks of the philosophes as the 18th century progressed, including the gifted mathematician the marquis de Condorcet (1743–94) and the rich, German-born philosopher Paul-Henri, baron d'Holbach (1723–89), who challenged Christianity in advocating a radical materialism based on rationalism. In the later 1700s, a materialist poet, though no philosophe, Donatien-Alphonse-François, marquis de Sade (1740–1814)—the marquis de Sade—is better remembered for his erotic tales (*Justine ou les malheurs de la vertu [Justine, or the Misfortunes of Virtue]*, 1791). An aristocratic libertine and a willful opponent of authority, Sade spent an event-filled life entering and escaping prisons. The term *sadism* endures as a testament to an author for whom violence took pride of place over pleasure in carnal pursuits.

An effort to assemble all the strands of the new thinking into a single compendium drove Denis Diderot (1713–84) to embark on his great project. The son of a prosperous craftsman from Langres, Diderot thought of entering the priesthood but lost his faith and drifted to Paris, where he made a precarious living in occasionally writing and where, in 1747, he was contracted to write his *Encyclopédie (Encyclopedia)*, the first volume of which appeared in 1751. Joined by his chief associate, the mathematician Jean Le Rond d'Alembert (1717–83), Diderot wrote many of the articles himself, while Voltaire, Montesquieu, and others also penned pieces. A ponderous, multivolume work filled with much drudgery, the *Encyclopédie* also contained useful information on crafts and science, interspersed throughout with entries explaining the principles and extolling the virtues of the new thinking. Diderot also wrote essays in art theory and experimental dialogue such as *Le neveu de Rameau (Rameau's Nephew*, ca. 1761), as well as philosophical novels such as *Jacques le fataliste (Jacques, the Fatalist*, 1765–80).

Among the contributors to the *Encyclopédie*, Diderot's friend Jean-Jacques Rousseau (1712–78) stands with Voltaire as another of the Enlightenment's towering personalities. He, too, championed deism throughout his life, but his variant was tinged with greater emotion and sentiment than Voltaire's more coldly rational interpretation. Born in Geneva, Switzerland, the son of a watchmaker of French origin who abandoned him, Rousseau never overcame his Protestant Calvinist background, which marked all of his thinking, sparked his criticism of luxuries, and in the end led to his alienation from all of his friends, including Diderot. But in a troubled life, much of its spent wandering, he produced profoundly influential works of social theory and cultural criticism.

In 1720, he earned fame fast with his prize-winning essay *Discours sur les sciences et les arts (Discourse on the Arts and Sciences)*, which argued that humans, born good, have been corrupted by a so-called civilized society that has perverted reason and promoted artificial passions, such as snobbery, to the detriment of elemental ones, such as feeling for family. This central principle informed all his writing. In the 1760s, now increasingly at odds with the other philosophes, Rousseau produced in rapid succession his three great masterpieces, *Julie, ou la nouvelle Heloïse* (1761), a sentimental epistolary novel; *Émile* (1762), a tract on education; and *Le contrat social (The Social Contract,* 1762). In the *Contrat,* Rousseau attempts to answer the age-old political question: Why should individuals obey authority? In Rousseau's realm the residents obey the laws willingly because they themselves have made them. The good society is ruled by the "general will," namely, the good of all, arrived at by a community of rational, public-minded citizens who, meeting in frequent assemblies, control their agent, the government.

Rousseau's writings introduced a new style of extreme emotional expression that would flower fully in the romanticism of the next century but that had already appeared in the pictorial arts. Painter Antoine Watteau (1684–1721) brought a deep, dreamlike quality to his canvases of country life. His work much influenced a new sensitivity that emerged in the rococo style, a trend in art, architecture, and decoration that spread all over Europe characterized by elegant, ornate furniture, ornamental art objects, and sensuous paintings. The sentimental pastorals and amorous scenes of François Boucher (1703–70) became synonymous with the style, as did the work of Jean-Honoré Fragonard (1732–1806).

Rococo scenery and historical subjects were the main themes in mid-18th century art, but they were not universal. Jean-Baptiste Chardin (1699–1779), largely self-taught, interpreted the life of the Parisian bourgeoisie in his genre paintings and still lifes by means of an exquisite mastery of color and design.

Chardin did not depict the upper classes, still less the royal court, but Boucher became director of the Gobelins tapestry works, the favorite painter of Louis XV, and the protégé of the king's mistress, Madame de Pompadour (1721–64). The king's entourage also included a devoted band of followers of François Quesnay (1694–1774), the court physician. Grouped around Quesnay, the Physiocrats propounded a theory of political economy that held agriculture to be the sole source of wealth and that decreed manufacturing, commerce, and industry, because they derive from it, to be essentially nonproductive. By taxing the owners of the land—those who earned income from it—the state would aid those who work on it and, through them, the country as a whole. Advocates of free trade, they appealed to the government to reject and repeal the many constraints—regulations, taxes, tariffs, and monopolies—that, because they crippled investment and enterprise, stifled economic growth. In keeping with the spirit of the times, their ideas were rational and sensible, but they would face formidable resistance from the powers in place in a mid-18th-century world far from the idealized Enlightenment vision.

Louis XV: Privilege Persists and Resists, 1743–1774

In January 1743, Cardinal Fleury died, and like his great-grandfather before him, Louis XV, at age 33, announced that he would govern without a first minister. But as Louis XIV had shown, intentions must be matched by aptitude. Handsome, affable, and intelligent, Louis XV was too uncertain, too indolent, and too intent on pursuing pleasure, occupied with hunting and an ever-changing galaxy of mistresses, to lead effectively. The most famous of his paramours, Jeanne Poisson, he made Madame (Marquise) de Pompadour. She became the king's official mistress in 1745 and remained friends with her royal lover until her death, long after Louis's libido had led him elsewhere. Beautiful, witty, and bright, and a generous patron of the decorative arts, she exerted such a powerful influence that she could appoint and dismiss ministers and military commanders.

Her presence symbolized the rule of favorites and the rapid shift of personnel that characterized Louis's rule, which stood in marked contrast to Fleury's sensible appointment policies. The long and slow inflation that had begun after the cardinal's accession continued through the reign. It acted as a stimulus to the economy and brought widespread prosperity and economic expansion. The upper middle classes in the cities—financiers, lawyers, cotton and silk manufacturers—flourished, though investment slowed in the wake of the collapse of Law's schemes, internal tariffs and guild regulations remained stubbornly in place, and the poor, as always, remained poor.

Unlike domestic affairs, in foreign policy Fleury's prescriptions were not pursued, his pacific efforts ending in a series of wars that marked the mid-1700s. The War of the Austrian Succession (1740–48) found France fighting against its traditional enemies Austria and Britain in support of Prussia's attempt to wrest the wealthy province of Silesia from Hapsburg hands. The Peace of Aix-la-Chapelle in 1748 marked less a settlement than it did a truce, but the switch engineered by Austrian state chancellor Prince Wenzel von Kaunitz (1711–94), who secured an alliance with France in the First Treaty of Versailles (1756), constituted no less than a diplomatic revolution.

The high-stakes game in Europe played out in conjunction with an ongoing, equally significant struggle with Britain overseas; whether in peace or war, it amounted to virtual nonstop competition between the two powers. Colonial possessions were prized as strategic outposts and commercial centers. They provided the mother country with materials impossible to procure in Europe—furs from Canada, sugar from the West Indies, spices from India—and, in return, they served as protected markets for European-produced finished goods. Since the late 17th century, the French and British—Dutch, Spanish, and Portuguese competitors had declined in power—had been waging a seesaw struggle, surrendering and restoring assorted bits of territory across the globe. When the Seven Years' War (1756–63) broke out in Europe, skirmishing had already begun in North America. The war began brightly for France overseas, but it ended disastrously. In India, all the ambitious plans assiduously pursued by Joseph-François, marquis Dupleix (1697–1763), commandant general of the French East Indies Company, to build a French empire in Asia were ruined when the British took the fort at Chandernagore and routed the French and their Indian allies at the decisive Battle of Plassey (June 23, 1757). Early in 1759, the British captured Guadeloupe. In September, they climbed the heights at Quebec, French Canada's capital, and after a pitched battle on the Plains of Abraham in which French general Louis-Joseph, marquis de Montcalm (1712–59), and British general James Wolfe (1727–59) were both killed, they took the fortress itself. In September 1760, Montreal fell and, with it, all of Canada. In Europe, too, France faced defeat—the army at Minden (August 1, 1759) and the navy at Quiberon Bay (November 20, 1759). At Paris on February 10, 1763, the British and French made peace. Though they surrendered their entire North American holdings to the British in Canada—save for the tiny islands of Saint-Pierre and Miquelon used by the fishing fleets off of Newfoundland—and to the Spanish in the Mississippi Delta, the French regarded the settlement as a diplomatic coup because they won back the valuable sugar islands the British had taken in the Caribbean.

But the country was exhausted. The war proved ruinously expensive for a regime that, since the 1740s, had been searching for a way to clip the power of privilege, which deprived the state of sources of revenue that it desperately needed. Many checks on the king's power were built into the system. Most official positions—judgeships, places in the army, and all but the highest government posts—were the private property of their holders. Under this so-called venality of office, they could be bought, traded, or sold with little interference from the monarchy. Hence, bureaucrats and judges operated with considerable independence, loyal more often to their corporate profession than to their sovereign. Exemptions from one tax or another were endemic, granted to nobles, towns, and corporations at varying times over the past. The clergy paid no levies, contributing instead a *don gratuit* (voluntary gift), voted every five years at general assemblies. Provincial estates battled constantly with royal officials, while the *parlements* had their obstructive power newly restored by the regent at the century's start.

In May 1759, urged by his comptroller general of finance, Jean-Baptiste de Machaut d'Arnouville (1701–94), Louis XV boldly—and uncharacteristically—confronted the entire system of privilege. He issued a decree imposing a 5 percent income tax (*vingtième*) on all his subjects, regardless of class. The king stood firm for awhile, until, battered by opposition from the clerics and even from his own family, he softened and withdrew all his demands.

In the 1750s and 1760s, the *parlements* took the lead in defending privilege against a wavering king. They trumpeted disobedience to royal authority in the name of the "French constitution," an unwritten set of precepts enshrining their traditional rights that, in fact, held little, if any, legal standing. Louis's powerful secretary of state for foreign affairs since 1758, Étienne-François, the duc de Choiseul (1719–85), succumbed to the *parlements'* demands, needing peace at home to win a settlement with Britain. But when in 1764 the Breton Parlement at Rennes, backed by the others, suspended the administration of justice in protest at the royal *corvée*—the service due the king for construction and maintenance of roads—Louis took action. In March 1766, he claimed sole sovereign authority in lecturing the Parlement of Paris on its duties. He went further in September 1768 in appointing as his chancellor René Nicolas de Maupeou (1714–92), a former member of the Parlement who had grown to detest his colleagues' obduracy. Securing Choiseul's dismissal, Maupeou forged resolutely ahead. In January 1771, he disbanded the *parlements*, including that of Paris, replacing the latter's members, who were exiled from the city, with six judicial courts. He reimposed the 5 percent tax, abolished venality of office, and improved revenue collection. Louis held firm in his support until, in May 1774, death intervened to remove him from the scene. Dubbed by his subjects at his birth the *bien-aimé* (well-loved), the king retained little goodwill at his passing. But well wishes abounded for his grandson, who succeeded as Louis XVI (r. 1774–92). Much hope was placed in the new young king, who was himself anxious to receive his peoples' approval. "What I should like most," he is reputed to have said on his accession, "is to be loved" (Wright 1960, 42). To secure that end, before the year 1774 was out, he dismissed Maupeou and recalled the *parlements*.

Louis XVI: The Search for Financial Security, 1774–1789

Only an accident of birth qualified Louis XVI to mount the throne in 1774 at age 20. Well meaning but lazy, he spent as much time as he could hunting, tinkering with locks, and working at carpentry, lacking interest in anything that would distract him from these pleasures, even including his beautiful and vivacious Austrian princess, Marie-Antoinette (1755–93), whom he married at 16 and whose delayed conception of an heir—a son was not born until 1785—had raised anxious worries scurrying through the court.

Louis inherited a realm that, in the 1770s and 1780s, retained the prosperity and economic progress of the previous half-century. Industrial production, foreign trade, and commerce all expanded, despite the persistence of costly internal tolls and customs duties and change-resisting guilds. Prices rose and the population grew, which benefited the middle classes but hurt urban wage earners, whose expenses far outstripped their earnings. France remained overwhelmingly agricultural, and the higher prices for foodstuffs benefited the nobility, clergy, and upper bourgeoisie, who together owned about 60 percent of the land, much of whose crop went on the market. For the peasants, who owned the rest or who rented or sharecropped portions of the land held by others, life was truly precarious. Only a few had anything left to sell after allowing for family consumption, purchases of next year's seed, and payment of seigneurial dues, church tithes, and national taxes. Demographic growth brought added pressure, given that neither the amount of land in cultivation nor productivity per acre grew very much.

The years of sustained growth produced an overall income distribution effect that led the rich to get richer and the poor to become poorer, with the exception of a very few hardworking and inventive peasants and artisans able to take advantage of opportunities for advancement. For the vast majority of the members of the Third Estate, frustration

Louis XVI (Library of Congress)

and hostility toward the country's semifeudal social order and inept bureaucratic monarchy were mounting.

The chaotic and antiquated system of raising revenue proved wholly insufficient in facing a financial burden that included payment on a large national debt, expenditures for the military forces, and spending for wars. Financed by loans, these wars included French support of the American Revolution (1776–83), a struggle in which the French intervened less out of love for liberty than out of a wish to avenge themselves on the British. The venture proved especially costly. Since nothing could be done without the funds to run it, the first 15 years of Louis XVI's reign entailed essentially a search for a finance minister who could extricate the country from its money woes.

The king's first appointment was his boldest. Anne-Robert Turgot (1727–81) was made comptroller general of finances only three months after Louis's accession. The son of a trade supervisor, and educated at the Sorbonne, Parisian-born Turgot was an intellectual and a friend of the philosophes, who, as *intendant* at Limoges, he had vigorously attacked old abuses. Turgot drafted a radical plan of reform in six edicts that aimed to abolish useless sinecures, internal customs barriers, guilds, and most important, the *corvée,* which he proposed to replace with a new land tax. But criticism was immediate, outraged members of the Parlement of Paris insisting that all public financial exactions must, as always, be drawn from the lower classes. Lacking the courage to back his minister, Louis demurred, dismissing Turgot in May 1776. The king temporized. He turned next to a Swiss Protestant banker who had settled in Paris and made a fortune in speculation. The king hoped that a man with a dazzling reputation as a financial wizard could make economic magic for him. Jacques Necker (1732–1804) did indeed prove an able conjuror, but the numbers he produced did nothing more than hide the truth. To carry the strain of supporting the American Revolution and other costs, the government had been borrowing funds for capital outlays, followed in turn by more borrowing to pay interest on the earlier loans. Aware of the financial nightmare posed by this mountain of public debt, Necker published a report in 1781 that juggled the figures to reverse the reality, showing an excess of income rather than expenditure, thus hiding the desperate need for tax reform. His last act of magic was to resign before he could be dismissed.

Necker's ablest successor was Charles-Alexandre de Calonne (1734–1802), an energetic and tactful administrator who had served as *intendant* at Lille. Appointed comptroller general in 1783, he, like Turgot, boldly attacked privilege, proposing to abolish the *corvée,* reduce the salt tax, raise the stamp tax, and, most impressively, replace the unfair *taille* with a land levy that would tax rich as well as poor. Diplomat that he was, Calonne knew that such measures could succeed only with the approval of the prospective victims. To bypass the stubbornly recalcitrant *parlements,* he won Louis's consent to convene an Assembly of Notables. It met in February 1787. Expecting the members to be reliably compliant, once assembled they proved surprisingly defiant, refusing to ratify Calonne's proposals. The comptroller general's foes—Necker and the queen's entourage prominent among them—now pounced, convincing the king to let Calonne go.

The leader of the opposition to Calonne in the assembly, Étienne-Charles Loménie de Brienne (1727–94), the archbishop of Toulouse, stepped to the fore. A consummate courtier who owed his appointment to the faction around the queen, Brienne was strictly a financial amateur, unable to come up with any viable alternative other than to adopt his fallen foe's central idea: a new land tax to be paid by all the classes. The *parlements* once again refused to register the edict, shifting this time to the argument that only the Estates General—the advisory body made up of representatives of the three Estates of the realm—had the power to approve such a tax. Having yielded to the privileged in recalling the *parlements* at the beginning of his reign, Louis now found himself saddled with a virtual revolt of these same aristocrats. Reluctantly, he capitulated. In July 1788, he issued an edict convoking the Estates General for the following spring, and he recalled Necker in a desperate effort to stave off bankruptcy until then.

The Parlement of Paris registered the decree but stipulated that the Estates General should meet on the same basis as the last one called 175 years before. The 1614 assembly had been dominated by the First and Second Estates, the privileged orders of clergy and nobility, respectively; these representatives had sat as separate houses and the agreement of both, together with that of the Third Estate, which represented all the other classes, had been needed to take any action. The Parlement's ruling outraged bourgeois intellectuals, who, fully aware of the uncooperative attitudes of their social superiors, now saw clearly the reality behind the magistrates' pose as defenders of liberty—they were in fact simply defenders of aristocratic privilege.

Reformers would look for new spokesmen to challenge privilege, the cancer at the core of the system. By 1789, the French monarchy confronted resistance and disaffection from the top through the middle to the bottom of society. The *parlements* resisted any attempt to wrest from them their cherished prerogatives, weakening the loyalty of the nobility to the regime. The middle classes resented aristocratic advantages, rebuked the government for its lack of financial responsibility, opposed the state's interference in the economy, and reproached the church for its unwillingness to help fight national bankruptcy by relinquishing its wealth. The peasants balked at paying dues to the nobility, tithes to the church, and taxes to the government. Urban laborers grumbled at economic shortages, high prices, and intimidating military garrisons.

Many among the intellectual elites, imbued with Enlightenment ideas, repudiated a regime that held democratic precepts in disdain.

The first evidence of political organization emerged in the winter of 1788–89. Writings circulated broadly, most notably a pamphlet by a priest—the vicar general of Chartres—and an avid reader of 18th-century ideas, Emmanuel-Joseph, or Abbé, Sieyès (1748–1836) titled *Qu'est-ce que le tiers état? (What Is the Third Estate?)* in which he answered his own question: "1st. What is the third estate? Everything. 2nd. What has it been up to now in the political order? Nothing. 3rd. What does it demand? To become something in it." Across the country, groups of electors chose their representatives who would attend the Estates General, and then they drafted *cahiers de doléances* (grievance petitions) outlining their positions and requests. The *cahiers* of the nobility and clergy were defensive, the nobility concerned chiefly with preserving their traditional rights and the clergy with continuing their control over the extensive properties of the church and of its customary authority over education. Though written in language as respectful as those of the others, the *cahiers* of the Third Estate were filled with statements that spoke of natural rights and social equality, forthrightly registering expectations for change.

The winter of 1788–89 proved unusually harsh. Colder than normal temperatures prevailed. Food became scarce, prices rose, and the numbers of unemployed in the cities mounted. Still, spirits ran high. With hope and enthusiasm, the French awaited the coming of spring, when the great representative body that was set to convene offered the prospect of a better future in dealing, at last, with the failings and frustrations that had been gathering for so long.

7

THE GREAT REVOLUTION
AND THE GRAND EMPIRE
(1789–1815)

In the high summer of 1789, preoccupied as he so often was with hunting, Louis XVI penned a single entry in his diary at Versailles: "July 14. Nothing." But not far away, in Paris, the fall of the ancient fortress of the Bastille made that day forever memorable as the signature deed signaling the onset of a revolution no one—least of all France's weak-willed, incurious king—expected. The pent-up resentment at privilege and ineffective royal rule—the distinguishing characteristics of the political and social system that would later be called the ancien régime—snowballed swiftly to unleash a cascading sequence of momentous incidents and measures that changed the country—and the rest of the world—in ways that only a revolution of epoch-making proportions could. The French Revolution fully deserves that description. A fundamental event of modern history, its legacy remains the fact of its enduring impact.

In ringing pledges to enshrine liberty, equality, and fraternity, revolutionaries made a nation where before only a state had existed. They moved France forward on a path from autocracy toward democracy, only to plunge the country back into a dictatorship that, in launching a reign of terror, became so brutal as to pervert the principles the rulers purported to defend and make enemies of many of their own compatriots.

Exhausted from years of turmoil and settling of scores, from civil and foreign wars, the French paused in 1795. They looked back to the start of the Revolution to try once again an experiment in balanced constitutional government. But extremes of left and right, of radical republicans and recalcitrant royalists, destroyed any hope of building an effective ruling consensus.

The brilliant military exploits of a rising young general seemed to give proof of the potential inherent in the Revolution's championing of ability and initiative. In Napoléon Bonaparte, ambition showed itself boundless and talent proved prodigious. Eager to rule, once he attained absolute power, he called a definitive halt to the Revolution, putting in place law and order. By 1804, he had earned for himself an imperial throne and an admiring, awestruck public willing to exchange democracy for stability under a regime that won for the country—which just a decade before had been shunned by all of Europe's rulers—the control of the entire Continent. After a decade as emperor, the proud Napoléon, ever zealous for power, overreached his pretensions, though to the end his appeal remained real—even in defeat. His final fall at Waterloo proved so momentous a clash that it would help to keep alive a legendary stature that would never entirely die.

In 1815, a quarter century of great drama ended. France would never be the same. New political systems—constitutional monarchy, republic, empire—had been put in place. But which among the several governing systems spawned by the great revolution would work best? During the next half-century the country would attempt to find the solution.

From Absolutism to Constitutionalism, 1789–1792

After months of preparations, the Estates General of France convened at Versailles on May 5, 1789, with all the pomp and pageantry the monarchy could muster. The atmosphere was cordial and the mood optimistic, but the symbolism on display in the opening ritual dramatically showed the stratified society that the deputies represented. The 610 delegates of the Third Estate—half of them lawyers, the rest merchants and career bureaucrats, and all of them men of education and standing—filed into the hall dressed in plain black, compelled by ancient ceremonial custom to enter by a side door and to remove their hats, whereas the nobility and clergy, resplendent in their colorful silk breeches and scarlet robes, entered through the front with their head coverings intact. While such gratuitous indignities might have been accepted in an earlier age, they were not to be borne in a world where the ideas of the philosophes freely circulated and where a revolution—in America—had already set an example in putting those ideas in practice.

But rather than noisily complain, and well aware by now that the privileged orders would block any reform, the commoners quietly announced that, until the king would agree to fuse the three orders into a single chamber, they would do nothing. The war of nerves lasted six

Opening of the Estates General, May 5, 1789 (Library of Congress)

weeks, the delegates of the Third Estate meeting daily, which gave them an opportunity to hone their arguments and find leaders. In June, three parish priests deserted the meeting hall of the First Estate and moved to the Third. To encourage the perception that it represented the interests of the entire country, on June 17, the Third Estate voted to call itself the National Assembly, and it urged the privileged delegates to join it.

Louis XVI relented and agreed to call a second convocation of the Estates General for June 23. Not having received the announcement in time to forestall their next meeting set for June 20, the Third Estate members duly arrived on that date in a driving rainstorm to find the hall closed. They milled about angrily until their president, Jean-Sylvain Bailly (1736–93), a distinguished astronomer, led them to a nearby indoor tennis court. In an emotional meeting here, they swore, in the Tennis Court Oath, that they would continue to meet until their goals had been met and that they would do so as representatives not solely of one estate but rather of the entire nation. A new consolidated power had now emerged as a counterweight to privilege.

On June 23, in a famous reply to a royal messenger, Honoré-Gabriel Riqueti, comte de Mirabeau (1749–91), a brilliant orator acclaimed for his denunciations of absolutism and aristocratic privilege acting as a spokesman for the Third Estate, replied: "If you have orders to remove us from this hall, you must also get the authority to use force, for we shall yield to nothing but bayonets" (Roberts 2004, 433). On that day, two archbishops and 150 other clerics crossed over to the Third Estate,

154

and, two days later, 50 liberal nobles did the same. Blind to what was already a fact, that the separation of orders was now a dead letter, Louis stupidly dismissed the joint assembly, ordering the deputies to deliberate by the three individual estates. Protesting, the Third Estate refused to budge. Finally yielding to their defiance, Louis agreed on June 27 to the joint meeting of the three orders. The representatives set to work immediately, appointing a committee to draft a constitution and so adopting the appropriate title National Constituent Assembly. But the king was not done. He called up troops to shore up his authority. On July 12, he dismissed Necker, by now thoroughly despised by royalists as untrustworthy and a publicity seeker, and replaced him with Louis-Auguste Le Tonnelier, baron de Breteuil (1730–1807), one of the queen's favorites.

While the king plotted and the parliamentarians planned in the grand setting of Versailles, the people of Paris were taking matters into their own hands. The harsh winter had seen bread prices rise sharply, and economic hardship led hungry refugees from the countryside flocking to the city to find food and work. Beginning in April, rioters had raided food shops and bakeries. By mid-July, the cost of bread had jumped to nearly twice its normal price, and tempers soared as high as the midsummer heat. Inflammatory orators, such as Camille Desmoulins (1760–94), a newly minted lawyer and a committed critic of the ancien régime, harangued onlookers every night at the Palais Royale. Eagar to take action, craftsmen, day laborers, and domestic servants rushed to secure weapons.

By the morning of July 13, the electors of Paris, who had chosen the deputies who represented the city in the Estates General, formed a committee to govern the city. Crowds gathered at the Hôtel de Ville—the city hall—demanding and getting arms, and in the early morning of July 14, they plundered the Invalides, a military hospital for aged and sick soldiers built by Louis XIV whose governor had promptly surrendered. They then marched to the fortress prison of the Bastille on the rue Saint-Antoine, where a multitude of by now some 800—mostly artisans, small merchants, and workers—sought to bargain for the gunpowder stored there. The governor of the antique bastion, Bernard René de Launay (1740–89), grew nervous after the impatient crowd had begun to enter the outer courtyard, and he ordered his men to fire their cannon. Ninety-eight persons were killed and some 70 wounded. The enraged throng fought its way into the inner courtyard, and the governor surrendered. Freeing the meager seven captives held there, the rampaging mob took the troops prisoner and lynched de Launay, stabbing him to death and then cutting off his head and placing it on a pike as they marched triumphantly back to city hall.

Citizens with guns and pikes outside the Bastille with the heads of "traitors" carried on pikes (Library of Congress)

The storming of the Bastille carried far more political and mythological than military consequences. Honored as an annual national holiday in symbolizing the birth of the modern French nation, the act produced as an immediate result a new council to rule the city, which included

Bailly as mayor and Marie-Joseph-Paul, the marquis de La Fayette (or Lafayette) (1757–1834), a supporter of democratic change and a popular figure since his participation in the American Revolution, as commander of a citizens' militia, the National Guard. And bowing to the show of force, the king himself proceeded to Paris, where on July 17, he received the new national cockade with its colors of red, white, and blue.

Meanwhile, the scarcity of grain had spawned rioting in rural areas as well. Destitute men and women wandered the countryside in search of bread. Small property-owning peasants, frightened that hungry bands were in fact part of an aristocratic plot to seize their holdings, armed themselves, and in actions known as "the Great Fear" *(la grande peur)* broke into the châteaux of the wealthy in many areas, less to pillage than to destroy the ancient feudal records that documented their servile obligations.

By late July 1789, well aware of so much open defiance of authority, the aristocrats in the National Assembly at Versailles grew increasingly

THE FRENCH FLAG

The national flag of France (Fr., *le drapeau français*) consists of three vertical bands of blue at the hoist, white, and red. Known as the tricolor (Fr., *le tricolore*), the colors date from the Revolution when, in July 1789, Louis XVI sported a cockade to which had been added blue and red—the colors that had been those of the city of Paris since 1358 when they were used by the followers of rebel Étienne Marcel—to the white of the House of Bourbon as a symbol of royal solidarity with the revolutionary changes. The color combination was widely acclaimed, although at first it was seen more frequently on cockades than on flags. In flags flown during the following few years, the order and the position of the stripes varied. Following the proclamation of the republic in 1792, the National Convention authorized painter Jacques-Louis David to design a definitive configuration, which first appeared in 1794. But as late as 1848, for a short period, the order of the colors was blue, red, and white. Except for restored monarchist regimes in 1814–15 and 1815–30, when the royal white returned, the flag has been the national banner. The colors and pattern have inspired, directly and indirectly, a number of other flags, especially those of former French territories such as Haiti and countries in Africa.

discomfited. On July 27, the constitutional committee presented to the assembly its draft of the Declaration of the Rights of Man and of the Citizen, and opened the floor to debate. On August 4, when one deputy rose to introduce a resolution to compel the payment of dues and taxes, a number of the nobility, who had been planning a bold move, made a counterproposal. One after another of the noble deputies, and with them propertied commoners, stood up to renounce their privileges and prerogatives. In a drama that went on until August 11, the remnants of feudal rights came crashing down: serfdom, all personal obligations, tax exemptions, church tithes, financial dues, and restrictions on hunting and fishing on noble-owned property were decreed to be dead. A social order based on birth and rank was no more. All offices of state were heretofore to be open to free competition based solely on talent. Later, in July 1790, hereditary nobility was abolished altogether. Duly passed, the Declaration of the Rights of Man and of the Citizen proclaimed liberty, equality, and fraternity. In declaring that law is the expression not of God's, but of the

THE DECLARATION OF THE RIGHTS OF MAN AND OF THE CITIZEN

Approved on August 26, 1789, by the National Assembly, the Declaration of the Rights of Man and of the Citizen summarizes the principles that those who launched the French Revolution sought to proclaim. A stellar statement of the faith in unalianable rights and reason that moved 18th-century thinkers, the document enshrines human liberties, and it has served ever since as both an inspiration and a guide for freedom-seeking peoples worldwide. Its 17 articles include the following:

1. *Men are born and remain free and equal in rights. Social distinctions may be founded only upon the general good.*
2. *The aim of all political association is the preservation of the natural and imprescriptible rights of man. These rights are liberty, property, security, and resistance to oppression.*
3. *The principle of all sovereignty resides essentially in the nation. No body or individual may exercise any authority which does not proceed directly from the nation.*
4. *Liberty consists in the freedom to do everything which injures no one else; hence the exercise of the natural rights of each man has*

people's will, and in affirming that the source of all sovereignty "resides essentially" in the nation, it defined for the first time "the nation" to be in fact "the citizens," without whose consent it could not exist.

While France was transformed during these months from an absolute into a constitutional monarchy, those with a stake in opposing change were fleeing the country. Aristocratic émigrés—one of the king's brothers, Charles, comte d'Artois (1757–1836) among the first—were joined by craftsmen in the luxury trades and others who served their bewigged patrons in crossing the borders, where they agitated relentlessly to win the sympathy of Europe's rulers for the French king.

The monarch was by now a prisoner of events, which some 7,000 armed Parisian women and assorted agitators made manifest when they proceeded to Versailles on October 5 in a march to demand bread. Early the next morning, the tired, angry crowd poured through a chance opening in the courtyard of the palace. After the queen's bedchamber had been invaded and several of the royal bodyguard slain, Louis

---

no limits except those which assure to the other members of the society the enjoyment of the same rights. These limits can only be determined by law.

5. Law can only prohibit such actions as are hurtful to society. Nothing may be prevented which is not forbidden by law, and no one may be forced to do anything not provided for by the law.

6. Law is the expression of the general will. Every citizen has a right to participate personally, or through his representative, in its foundation. . . .

7. No person shall be accused, arrested, or imprisoned except in the cases and according to the forms prescribed by law. . . .

10. No one shall be disquieted on account of his opinions, including his religious views, provided their manifestation does not disturb the public order established by law.

11. The free communication of ideas and opinions is one of the most precious of the rights of man. Every citizen may, accordingly, speak, write, and print with freedom, but shall be responsible for such abuses of this freedom as shall be defined by law.

Source: "Declaration of the Rights of Man and of the Citizen." Available online. URL: http://www.constitution.org/fr/fr_drm.htm. Accessed August 11, 2009.

yielded to the women's entreaties. Capping their triumph in declaring that they would bring "the baker, the baker's wife, and the baker's little apprentice [the dauphin]" (Padover 1939, 184) back to the capital, the throng escorted the royal family back to Paris, the women and men perched on cannon and holding aloft on pikes the severed heads of the slain palace guards. The National Assembly followed 10 days later. Until now stubbornly refusing to approve the Declaration of Rights and the abolition of privilege, Louis promptly ratified all the decrees of the assembly, while at the same time he stealthily sent secret dispatches to his brother monarchs in Austria and Spain, telling them that he did not profess what the new policies expressed.

In bringing the king to Paris, the people announced that they intended to participate actively in politics. Formerly the preserve of the deputies at Versailles, once in Paris, affairs of state became truly matters for the general public. Parisians attended meetings of the National Assembly as spectators and members. The chief instruments of popular politics outside the assembly were the new political clubs, such as the Cordeliers, which drew workers and shopkeepers, and the more exclusive Jacobins, the name by which the Dominicans were known in Paris in whose former monastery they met, and who, to widen their appeal, lowered their dues and established branches around the country.

Keeping a wary eye on the king, the National Assembly completed its draft constituent work in crafting a document that provided for a balance of power between the king, who was limited to a suspensive veto (he could delay but not annul legislation), and the legislature, which emerged as a single-chamber parliament. Voters were divided between "active" and "passive" citizens. Everyone enjoyed equal protection of the law, but only active citizens—males at least 25 years of age who paid direct taxes equivalent to three days' wages every year—could vote. Radical critics such as Parisian journalist Jean-Paul Marat (1743–93) and Maximilian Robespierre (1758–94), a young lawyer, a deputy from Arras, and a member of the Jacobins, fumed that democracy had given way to plutocracy (rule by the wealthy), but the compromise formula corresponded to the concerns of most, who, while eager to promote equality, were determined to preserve the sanctity of property. Anxious as well to foster national unity, in a deliberate effort to break up historical divisions and, within them, their local loyalties and cultural differences, the National Assembly issued a decree on March 4, 1790, replacing the provinces with 83 *départements* (departments), which were given names derived largely from physical features.

Because taxes were virtually uncollectible and the daily business of running a government required money, the assembly eyed with relish the rich and extensive properties of the church. In October 1789, the bishop of Autun, Charles-Maurice de Talleyrand-Périgord (1754–1838), proposed the nationalization of church lands. The proposition became law in November, and sales began in December. Most of the real estate went to well-to-do peasants or middle-class speculators, which accelerated the growth of the small, property-holding peasantry and committed it strongly as a class to the revolutionary cause. In expectation of new revenues forthcoming from the sales, the assembly, at the same time, issued an *assignat* (mortgage bond) designed to pay the state's clamoring creditors. Its value held firm for a time. In July 1790, it still stood where it had seven months before—at 95 percent of face value.

In that same month, the assembly passed its most controversial measure. The Civil Constitution of the Clergy transformed the church into a branch of the government. Church buildings became the property of the state, and priests and bishops were now to be selected by the qualified electors. Clergy were placed on fixed salaries and under strict government supervision.

A church made so utterly dependent on the state exceeded by far the goal sought by even the most independent-minded Gallican clergy, and the legislation aroused fierce opposition. Louis very reluctantly approved the act, but resistance was soon widespread and open. Striking back, the National Assembly decreed in November 1790 that all clerics would have to swear an oath of loyalty to the constitution. Only seven bishops and fewer than half of priests complied. The assembly retaliated in branding the holdouts "refractory," or nonjuring, clergy. By the time Pope Pius VI (r. 1775–99) formally denounced the Civil Constitution and, with it, the Declaration of the Rights of Man and of the Citizen in March 1791, every practicing Catholic was compelled to choose sides. Conservative elements—women, peasants, and, most especially, the devout in areas of western France—sheltered refractory priests. The church ruling produced deeply divisive effects, turning many against the Revolution.

The splits opened by it renewed royalist anxieties. Many more fled, including in June 1791 the king's other brother, Louis-Stanislas, the count of Provence (1755–1824). In the same month, the queen's party—the stiffest opponents of change from the start—convinced the king, by now increasingly paralyzed emotionally by events, that it was time that he, too, should leave. They departed Paris on the evening of June 20, disguised as servants of a Russian baroness. After a 24-hour nerve-wracking journey in a coach across France, the royal party was recognized at Varennes, arrested, and ignominiously brought back in a slow procession to the city. The deed showed the true sentiments of the king—the notion that he was a willing accomplice of the Revolution had been shown to be false.

Reaction was swift. On July 15, 1791, the Cordeliers, headed by lawyer Georges-Jacques Danton (1753–94), presented a petition to the National Assembly demanding that Louis be deposed and that he stand trial. When on July 17 some 7,000 Parisians assembled on the Champs de Mars to sign the petition, the National Guard, hearing a gunshot, fired into the crowd, killing at least 13 and wounding another 30. The incident opened up divisions among the advocates of change. Moderates now grew frightened, believing it was wise to shore up the king and so put a stop to the drift toward further instability. Supporters of a constitutional monarchy, such as the marquis de La Fayette and the Abbé Sieyès, withdrew from the Jacobins to form a new club, the Feuillants, where they were joined by more than 200 legislators. Bailly resigned as mayor of Paris. Radicals grew emboldened, thinking the time might have arrived to strive for a republic.

News from abroad now intervened. In August 1791, the emperor of Austria, Leopold II (r. 1790–92), brother of Queen Marie-Antoinette, and King Frederick William II of Prussia (r. 1786–97) issued the Declaration of Pillnitz, declaring that they would be willing to take action to restore monarchical rule in France. Because they quickly added that they would act only in concert with the other European powers, the declaration dashed the hopes of the queen and those around her—and of the émigrés—that help would be forthcoming, but it succeeded, nevertheless, in arousing rage among the members of the assembly.

The task that the National Assembly had assigned itself two years before was finished in September with the adoption of the constitution and the taking of an oath of loyalty to it by Louis, whose title "king of the French by the grace of God and the will of the French people" conveyed the degree to which the doctrine of popular sovereignty underpinned the new governing system. The king kept his throne, but one with only very limited authority and dependent on annual appropriations from the legislature.

On September 30, 1791, the National Constituent Assembly dissolved, to be succeeded on October 1 by the Legislative Assembly, elected on the basis of the new suffrage. In its brief one year of existence, the assembly came to be dominated by its most outspoken members, the Girondins, a faction of the Jacobins who originated as an informal gathering of deputies from Bordeaux led by a gifted orator, the attorney Pierre-Victurnien Vergniaud (1753–93). Foreign affairs came to the fore. Bold unilateral acts that had been taken earlier—the papal enclave at Avignon had been annexed and the ancient feudal dues owed to German princes in Alsace had been abolished—were followed now by calls for outright war from the most bellicose of the Girondins, the Brissotins, followers of Jacques-Pierre Brissot (1754–93), a sometime political journalist ambitious for leadership. A moderate Feuillant ministry was forced out of office in March 1792 by the Girondins, who, now that they held power, promptly declared war on Austria on April 20. The martial mood was matched in Vienna, where Emperor Leopold had been succeeded by his son Francis II (r. 1792–1806), a young firebrand itching for battle. Soon Prussia joined Austria, and on July 25, 1792, the two powers issued the Brunswick Manifesto, stating that the allies aimed at nothing less than to reestablish royal rule under Louis XVI. They warned the Paris populace that if any harm should befall the royal couple, death and destruction would be swiftly forthcoming.

The manifesto redoubled revolutionary fervor. Partisans of the Revolution rallied together, the declaration having strengthened those it was supposed to frighten and embarrassed those—the royal party—it was intended to protect. With foreign armies now poised to invade, tensions in Paris mounted. People hoarded necessities, making items such as firewood scarce and expensive. Circulating now as paper money, the *assignats* rapidly depreciated, hurting most especially city workers, who possessed no other bills of exchange in bartering for essentials and who were unable, like rural peasants, to stockpile food. Agitators flourished. Troops from the provinces marched into the city, among them recruits from Marseille, who arrived singing a catchy new song—the "Marseillaise."

Local sansculottes (literally, "without knee breeches"), a social term referring to urban residents of modest means that now took on a political meaning in referring to passionate, politically active, revolutionary democrats, took to the streets to demand the deposition of a treacherous, treasonable king. On August 4, representatives of the working-class *section* (ward)—the Faubourg Saint-Antoine—threatened to use force if the Legislative Assembly did not remove the king by August 9.

THE "MARSEILLAISE"

The announcement that war had been declared on April 20, 1792, reached troops stationed at Strasbourg on April 24. Posted on the easternmost border of a country brimming with revolutionary fervor and bracing for battle, soldiers celebrated that night in the home of the city's mayor. Among the revelers, Claude-Joseph Rouget de Lisle (1760–1836), a captain of engineers from the Jura, drafted extemporaneously the words and melody of what was originally called "Le chant de guerre pour l'armée du Rhin" (The Battle Song for the Army of the Rhine). Later dubbed "La Strasbourgeoise" (The Song of Strasbourg), the song spread, reaching the south of France by early summer. On the evening of June 22 at a banquet in Marseille, a medical student from Montpellier, François Miroir, sang the ballad, which proved so popular it accompanied a battalion of volunteers marching to Paris. They reached the capital on July 30, singing the tune that Parisians identified with the new arrivals in calling it the "Hymn of the Massilians" or simply "La Marseillaise" (The Song of Marseille).

French armies sang its rousing verses wherever they went, spreading the tune across Europe, where it was translated into many languages. Napoléon Bonaparte called it the republic's greatest general. Formally adopted by a decree of July 14, 1795, it became the world's first specifically national, as opposed to royal (such as "God Save the King") anthem. Its opening lines *"Allôns, enfants de la Patrie! Le jour de gloire est arrivé"* (Forward, children of the Fatherland! / The day of glory has arrived) have stirred powerful patriotic sentiments ever since.

Ironically, its author's republican credentials proved less than sterling. A moderate monarchist, Rouget de Lisle was arrested in 1793 for royalist sympathies. He survived the Revolution and died in poverty. On July 14, 1915, his ashes were reinterred with honors in the Invalides in Paris.

The Second Revolution and the Reign of Terror, 1792–1795

In the early morning hours of August 10, 1792, deputies from the city's 48 wards met at the Paris city hall, suspended the municipal government, and declared a new administration, the Commune. A gun was fired, and tocsins (alarm bells) rang throughout the capital, calling the citizens to action. They marched en masse on the Tuileries, the palace that had served as the residence of French royalty before Louis XIV removed the court to Versailles and where the royal family was housed after its forcible return in October 1789. Clashing with the king's elite regiments, they killed some 800 of these Swiss Guards along with a smattering of servants and kitchen staff in a frenzy of violence that left in its wake 300 of their own dead amid pools of blood. The royal family fled in terror to the assembly, throwing themselves on the mercy of the legislators. Once again, as on Bastille Day, the people of Paris had taken the initiative in changing the course of events.

On August 11, the Legislative Assembly recognized the Commune, surrendered the royal family to its custody, and called for elections for a new legislature based on a truly revolutionary franchise—every French male over 21 who was neither a dependent nor a domestic servant was given the vote. Electors went to the polls in an atmosphere electric with tension. In late July, an Austrian army had invaded French soil. Rumors ran rife that the prisons were full of royalists, priests, and traitors to the Revolution waiting until troops left the capital for the front, when they would break out to overthrow the government. Acting on that belief, in early September, mobs attacked prisons in Paris and the provinces, slaughtering more than 1,200, including clerics, Swiss Guards, nobles, and anyone whom they suspected as being enemies of the state.

The duly elected National Convention that first met on September 20, 1792, was more radical than any of its predecessors. There were no professed royalists—constitutional monarchy was now dead—but only different varieties of republicans. On September 21, it abolished the monarchy and declared France a republic. The two most important organized factions were the Girondins, formerly the radicals in the Legislative Assembly but now, fearing mob rule, more moderate, who sat at the right in the lower tiers in a newly renovated hall in the Tuileries, and, to the left, the members of the radical "Mountain" (Montagnards), so-called because they occupied the upper tiers. The "Plain," the majority of the deputies, less dogmatic than these two, sat in the center and held the balance of power. Extreme radicals emerged, notably the Enragés ("Enraged Ones"), who, under their chief spokesman, Jacques Roux (1752–94), demanded not only political and civil but also social and economic equality, including redistribution of wealth to the poor and the expropriation of business profits by the state. For three years, the National Convention would govern the country on an emergency basis, unhindered by constitutional limitations, putting a republican constitution adopted in 1793 on hold until the crisis had passed.

165

On the very day that the legislature first assembled, French armies scored a decisive win over the Prussians at Valmy, in northeastern France. The victory left the military to take the initiative on other fronts. By November, the convention annexed Savoy, and French troops had conquered all Austria's Belgian provinces. These triumphs transformed the war from one of defense to a crusade on behalf of freedom from monarchical oppression for other Europeans, even if practices did not always match principles. French soldiers might have proclaimed liberty to newly conquered peoples, but they often brought misery instead, following up their occupation by systematic looting. And victories threatened to make new enemies. In declaring the Scheldt River open to navigation to all—a clear violation of the Treaty of Westphalia of 1648—the French government aroused the animosity of the Dutch, the nation that had long profited commercially from its closure. Whatever potential they held for a wider war, however, conquests abroad did give the government breathing space to deal with an urgent domestic matter—what to do with the king.

The trial of "Louis Capet," as he was now addressed, took place in December, the debate over the fate of the king simultaneously a struggle for power in the Convention. In the end, the Girondins, supporters of a liberal, moderate republic who would have preferred to banish the fallen monarch to the United States, narrowly lost a vote for death pushed by the Mountain. On the morning of January 21, 1793, Louis mounted the scaffold at the renamed Place de la Révolution (today's Place de la Concorde), there to die by means of a new killing machine—the guillotine, much admired because it was deemed to be much more humane.

The victory of French arms together with the execution of the king ensured not only the continuation but also the expansion of foreign war, the fear of French revolutionary ideas and the shock of the act of regicide having now thoroughly aroused France's remaining nonbelligerent neighbors. Hostilities with Britain, Spain, and the Dutch Republic broke out in March 1793. Prosecution of a wider war demanded a larger army, but the Convention's decision to conscript 300,000 men proved difficult to carry out. The call to arms incited massive resistance in places, particularly in western France, a region already inflamed by the Revolution's religious changes.

In the Convention, Girondins battled Montagnards throughout the first half of 1793, the political factions repeatedly shifting. In the end, it was the latter, those who had strongly backed the killing of the king, who along with the Paris Commune moved to the ascendant. They

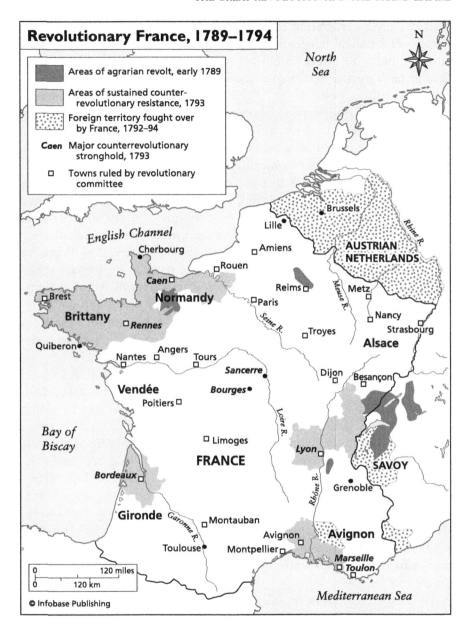

Revolutionary France, 1789–1794

- Areas of agrarian revolt, early 1789
- Areas of sustained counter-revolutionary resistance, 1793
- Foreign territory fought over by France, 1792–94
- *Caen* Major counterrevolutionary stronghold, 1793
- □ Towns ruled by revolutionary committee

N

North Sea

English Channel

Brussels

Lille

Amiens

Cherbourg

Rouen

AUSTRIAN NETHERLANDS

Caen □

Reims □

Metz □

Brest □

Normandy

Paris

Meuse R.

Nancy □

Brittany

Rennes

Troyes

Strasbourg □

Seine R.

Rhine R.

Alsace

Quiberon ●

Angers □

Tours □

Sancerre ●

Dijon □

Besançon □

Nantes □

Bourges ●

Vendée

Poitiers □

Loire R.

Bay of Biscay

□ Limoges

Lyon □

SAVOY

FRANCE

Bordeaux □

Rhône R.

Grenoble ●

Gironde

Garonne R.

□ Montauban

Toulouse ●

Avignon □

Avignon

Montpellier □

Marseille □

Toulon □

0   120 miles
0   120 km

Mediterranean Sea

© Infobase Publishing

were united in favor of war, knowing that, having killed the king, they would be the victims should the Bourbons succeed in remounting their throne. The Girondins, who had split on the vote, were divided. In May, the Girondins arrested Jacques-René Hébert (1757–94), a radical pamphleteer and leader of the Cordeliers Club who opposed their policies. The incarceration infuriated the sansculottes, who secured his release. The radical left had flexed its muscle, and one of its members moved quickly to direct its efforts. Maximilien Robespierre forced the Girondins from the National Convention, and in July 1793, he won election to the Committee of Public Safety, charged with overseeing general policy—one of two committees, together with the Committee of General Security, to deal with police matters—that had been created in April. The Convention gradually abdicated power into their hands, and soon the 12-member Committee of Public Safety became the effective governing authority, with Robespierre the dominant voice. Born in Arras to a bourgeois family, Robespierre was educated in Paris, where he learned the law and took as his guiding principle the theory of the general will of Rousseau, whom he had once met. Cold and calculating, he clawed his way to the top not by charm or oratorical skill but by sheer persistence and a fanatical belief in the truth of his ideas. Backed by his brilliant, utterly ruthless young lieutenant, Louis-Antoine Saint-Just (1767–94), Robespierre launched a policy of repression and regimentation. Seeing threats mounting everywhere, he and his associates were determined to stamp them out, which opened the way to unrestricted authoritarian rule.

By midsummer 1793, insurrection had broken out in half of France. Rebels in the western region of the Vendée were in the ascendant. Austro-Prussian armies took Valenciennes. Belgium was lost in March 1793. General Charles-François Dumouriez (1739–1823), the victor at Valmy, defected to the enemy. Several Girondin leaders escaped after the suppression of their members to launch a Federalist Insurrection in the provinces, and Lyon, Caen, Bordeaux, and Marseille fell to their forces. In the southeast, royalists succeeded in dominating the movement. They turned the port city of Toulon over to the British. In Paris itself, an unknown woman from the provinces, Charlotte Corday (1768–93), a follower of the Girondins, murdered the journalist Marat, stabbing him in his bath with a knife from his own kitchen, declaring that she did so "for liberty."

The new ruling clique mobilized the nation's matériel and manpower. On August 23, 1793, the government proclaimed a *levée en masse* (massed levy), calling on all the citizens—men, women, young, and old—in whatever their station—soldiers, workers, nurses, farmers, veterans—to rally to the defense of the nation in appealing to their love of a country that, they were told, was theirs to defend because it was they who had created it. Modern ideas of patriotism and nationalism were born. A page in the history of modern warfare had also been turned.

War would now become total, involving all elements of the population and all the resources of the state. Strict economic controls were put in place, including price ceilings. A new revolutionary calendar enacted in October 1793 was designed to rationalize the year with months named after the seasons, the old Gregorian calendar not reestablished until 1806. An anti-Christian campaign was launched with a "cult of the Supreme Being" actively promoted in place of traditional faith. The Christian Sunday was replaced with the *décadi,* or decimal day of rest. Churches and cemeteries were desecrated, statues smashed, and crucifixes paraded upside down for citizens to spit upon. The anticlerical campaign was especially violent in Paris and the Midi, and it played an important role in radicalizing the politics of the Revolution, exciting the passion of the revolutionaries at the same that it intensified the opposition of their foes in areas where royalist sentiments were strongest.

Believing that terror was necessary because the virtuous republic could not be secure until its enemies had been found and wiped out, the Committee of Public Safety under Robespierre began a large-scale purge. Death became the order of the day in a reign of terror during which the great and the lowly shared the same fate. A revolutionary tribunal, under its efficient chief prosecutor, Antoine-Quentin Fouquier-Tinville (1746–95), handed down sentences. By September 1793, the governmental machinery hastened its work, judicial scruples now routinely set aside and death sentences, hitherto sparingly decreed, pronounced speedily. The hated former queen and the dead king's rabidly royalist sister, Princess Elisabeth (1764–94), went to the guillotine, dubbed the "National Razor" as the patriotic instrument of execution. Louis-Philippe II, duke of Orléans (1747–93), so fervent a supporter of the Revolution that he took the name Philippe Égalité (equality) and voted for the king's death, was not spared. The great French chemist Antoine Lavoisier (1743–94), famous for having coined the term "oxygen," was condemned for the crime of having been a tax-collecting farmer under the monarchy. The widow and playwright Olympe de Gouges (1755–93), who launched the Western world's first modern drive for women's rights in arguing for their full political and personal emancipation in her *Déclaration des droits de la femme et de la citoyenne* (Declaration of the Rights of Woman and of the Citizenness, 1792), was arrested and guillotined, her other writings in defense of Louis XVI having made her suspect.

Leading Girondins were executed, including Bailly, Vergniaud, Jean-Marie Roland (1734–93), who served as minister of the interior, and his wife, Jeanne-Marie (1754–93). Madame Roland, well educated and

169

THE REIGN OF TERROR

The Reign of Terror lasted from September 5, 1793, to July 27, 1794. Estimates of the number of those killed vary from approximately 16,000 to 40,000. Though executions were carried out across the country, Paris is the place and the guillotine located here the instrument that have became synonymous with the terror. The remains of many hundreds of victims, including the former king and queen, were buried in unmarked graves in the Madeleine cemetery, which was closed in 1794 and is today the site of the Chapelle Expiatoire (Expiatory Chapel). An observer in Paris left the following description:

> Never can I forget the mournful appearance of these funereal processions to the place of execution. The march was opened by a detachment of mounted gendarmes—the carts followed; they were the same carts as those that are used in Paris for carrying wood; four boards were placed across them for seats, and on each board sat two, and sometimes three victims; their hands were tied behind their backs, and the constant jolting of the cart made them nod their heads up and down, to the great amusement of the spectators. On the front of the cart stood Samson, the executioner, or one of his sons or assistants; gendarmes on foot marched by the side; . . . In the middle of the Place de la Révolution was erected a guillotine, in front of a colossal statue of Liberty, represented seated on a rock, a Phrygian cap on her head, a spear in her hand, the other reposing on a shield. On one side of the scaffold were drawn out a sufficient number of carts, with large baskets painted red, to receive the heads and bodies of the victims. Those bearing the condemned moved on slowly to the foot of the guillotine; the culprits were led out in turn, and, if necessary, supported by two of the executioner's valets . . . but their assistance was rarely required. Most of these unfortunates ascended the scaffold with a determined step—many of them looked up firmly on the menacing instrument of death, beholding for the last time the rays of the glorious sun, beaming on the

Paris-born, in whose salon had gathered leading Girondin figures for whom she acted as guide and adviser, is remembered for her parting remarks, allegedly uttered as she mounted the scaffold: "Liberty, oh liberty, what crimes are committed in thy name" (Roberts 2000, 522). Those who were in a position to do so, such as La Fayette serving in the

Une exécution capitale, Place de la Révolution (A capital execution in Revolution Square). *Oil on canvas, Pierre-Antoine Demachy (1723–1807)* (Réunion des Musées Nationaux/Art Resource, NY)

polished axe; and I have seen some young men actually dance a few steps before they went up to be strapped to the perpendicular plane, which was then tilted to a horizontal plane in a moment, and ran on the grooves until the neck was secured and closed in by a moving board, when the head passed through what was called, in derision, la lunette républicaine *[the republican spectacles]; the weighty knife was then dropped with a heavy fall; and, with incredible dexterity and rapidity, two executioners tossed the body into the basket, while another threw the head after it.*

Source: J. G. Millingen, "The Revolutionary Tribunal, Paris, October 1793." In John Carey, ed., *Eyewitness to History* (Cambridge, Mass.: Harvard University Press, 1988), pp. 252–253.

army at the front, fled. In the provinces, the committee's *représentants en mission* (traveling henchmen) were charged with routing out opposition and ensuring revolutionary orthodoxy. The Federalist Insurrection was crushed—Lyon surrendered on October 9, 1793, and Toulon on December 19. *Mitraillades* (firing squads) mowed down victims who were compelled first to dig their own graves. At Nantes, approximately 2,000 were drowned on barges sunk in the Loire. While aristocrats are remembered in history as the terror's primary victims, in fact, most among those who died were sansculottes and peasants, ordinary citizens accused by the revolutionary tribunal of treason and sedition.

Jacobin unity soon cracked under the strain. A faction on the more moderate right under Danton hinted that it was time to put a brake on the instrument of terror, while another on the more radical left led by Hébert demanded an even more vigorous pursuit of would-be enemies. Robespierre struck back ruthlessly at his critics. In March 1794, the committee arrested and guillotined the Hébertist faction; in April, it was the turn of Danton and his followers. But just as he emerged apparently at his triumphal peak, Robespierre himself was forced to contend with internal dissensions among his backers. A decision by the ruling clique in June 1794 to keep the state's machinery moving by adding more courts and all but eliminating the few judicial protections still in existence seemed to confirm the fears among those who were not central members of the power group that an indefinite dictatorship without limits was planned. A plot was hatched within the Convention, led by Joseph Fouché (1759–1820), an utterly unscrupulous ex-terrorist who had crushed the insurrection in Lyon, and in late July, the schemers challenged the man whom they secretly called "the dictator." Attempting to defend himself, Robespierre was howled down on the floor of the Convention, whose members voted his and his associates' arrest. Failing to rally the Paris crowds to their defense, Robespierre and his minions were hustled into tumbrels at dawn on July 28, 1794—10 Thermidor on the republican calendar—to be taken along the same path to the guillotine followed before them by so many whom they had condemned.

Thermidor marked the climax of the terror, and a gradual "Thermidorian reaction" set in. The public had grown weary of the tension and bloodletting. Appeals to fear no longer seemed believable, internal dissension having been suppressed and the threat of foreign invasion turned back. The Committee of Public Safety was reduced in its authority, the Paris Commune stripped of its autonomy, the government decentralized, economic controls dismantled, and judicial tribunals ended. The Jacobin clubs eventually closed down. Thousands were released from the prisons, and many émigrés returned.

Promulgated in August 1795, a new fundamental law—the Constitution of the Year III—marked a return to a structure of government strongly reminiscent of the one drawn up in 1789–90, save that there was no provision for a king. A revulsion against the recent terror spawned a deepening conservative mood among many, some even espousing monarchist sentiments. To protect the republic, the Convention adopted a Law of the Two-Thirds: two-thirds of the new legislature to be elected under the new law was to be made up of themselves. Strengthened by public attitudes now leaning its way, the right had had enough. In October 1795, as the Convention was preparing to adjourn, royalist agitators led a mob into the streets. On October 5 (13 Vendémiaire), they were dispersed quickly with a mere whiff of grapeshot by government forces led by a young, hitherto unemployed general named Napoléon Bonaparte (1769–1821). A new force had entered the French political scene: The army had actively intervened. And it was led by one among a new generation of military leaders raised up by the Revolution.

The Directory: Republic in Retreat, 1795–1799

The Directory marked the second time—the constitutional monarchy under the Legislative Assembly of 1791–92 was the first—that France embarked on an experiment in balanced constitutional government. The constitution of 1795 placed power in the hands of an educated, wealthy minority. The suffrage rolls were reduced by more than a million, voters choosing electors to a two-house legislature (Corps Législatif)—the Council of Five Hundred, empowered to propose and discuss matters, and the Council of the Ancients, made up of married men over 40 authorized to do nothing more than to reject or ratify the measures sent to them by the Five Hundred. The executive branch was labeled the Directoire (Directory), made up of five members at least 40 years of age chosen by the Ancients for a five-year term from 50 names submitted by the Five Hundred. To ensure stability, executive and legislative terms were staggered: One director and one-third of the legislative bodies were to be replaced each year.

The new government confronted a war against the First Coalition of European powers in which it was holding its own, but on the home front unrest in the reliably royalist Vendée region flared again, efforts to stabilize the currency resulted in partial bankruptcy, inflation skyrocketed, and starvation in rural regions was widespread. Facing these challenges, the regime fared quite well, managing to pacify the Vendée, reorganize the tax system, assuage hunger by controlling the price of bread and distributing it to the neediest areas, and bring down prices, which fell partially because of good harvests.

However, the stability that had served as the rationale for the new governing system proved harder to ensure. The group in power faced constant sniping, on the left, from revived Jacobins and, on the right, from revenge-seeking royalists, who were aided by British subsidies. A small band of rabid, leftist radicals led by François-Noël "Gracchus" Babeuf (1760–97) advocated a "conspiracy of the equals" to break the power of the rich over the poor by abolishing private property outright and nationalizing, that is, giving the government ownership of wealth. The chief conspirators were arrested and, early in 1797, two of them, including Babeuf, went to the guillotine.

The threat from the right was larger and more dangerous. Royalists now appeared openly without fear. Catholicism, led by nonjuring priests, experienced a revival. Two of the five directors showed increasing sympathy for the restoration of a constitutional monarchy. Ironically, though, supporters of the Bourbons faced one of their greatest challenges from the former royal family itself. In June 1795, the young dauphin, called "Louis XVII" by the émigrés, died of the maltreatment he had received since 1793. This made Louis, count of Provence, next in line to the throne. Lacking any sense of political reality, from his exile in Italy, the heir issued the Declaration of Verona, which affirmed that, should royalty be restored, he would put back into place the entire old regime, including returning confiscated property and reviving old institutions—provinces and *parlements*—and old privileges, dues, and taxes. By 1797, even most monarchists had acquired a vested interest in a system that had eliminated all of these relics of the past and were not prepared to turn the clock back quite so far.

They were quite prepared, however, to get back into the game of politics, seeking to regain some of the power they had once held in abundance. Their hopes were encouraged when, in elections in spring 1797, moderate royalists scored impressive wins, ousting all but a dozen of the 150 or so members of the legislature. Taken aback by the results, leaders in the government recoiled in fear. Once again a threat to the republic seemed clear. Three of the directors, deciding to forgo even the semblance of legality, took direct action. In a coup d'état on September 4, 1797 (18 Fructidor), a contingent of troops led by the toughened veteran general Pierre-François Augereau (1757–1816) invaded the legislative chambers and arrested 53 deputies. Most of the troublesome election results were promptly annulled, and censorship proclaimed. Opposition leaders were exiled to French Guiana.

Engineered by the ruling power holders to keep them in control, Fructidor benefited, in the end, not the directors but one of their servants. The coup plotters had called on Napoléon Bonaparte, a young general then scoring smashing successes on a campaign in Italy, to send them military aid, and it was he who had dispatched General Augereau. The directors' growing dependence on the army carried ominous overtones for the regime's future, but the government could do little to reverse the direction because it was the military—specifically, the brilliant Bonaparte who outshone all the rest—that gave the rulers something to brag about.

Born in 1769 into the minor, poor nobility of Corsica, only one year after France had annexed the island, Napoléon Bonaparte from an early age set his sights on a career in the army. After attending military schools in Paris and the provinces, he secured a commission in an artillery regiment in 1785. His readings of the writings of the philosophes made him a dedicated advocate of the Revolution, and his Jacobin connections and military talents brought him rapid distinction during Robespierre's rule. Napoléon's moment of recognition came in 1793, when, having distinguished himself in the recapture of Toulon, a thankful government made him a brigadier general. Briefly imprisoned during the Thermidorean reaction that followed and dropped from the army, he spent several years in Paris restoring his fortunes. In 1796, his marriage to Joséphine de Beauharnais (1763–1814), a Caribbean-born widow and the mistress of Paul Barras (1755–1829), one of the five original directors, opened up connections that led to a command. He marched off at the head of the Army of Northern Italy, one of three French armies detailed to defeat Austria's forces and converge on its capital, Vienna.

France had broken up the First Coalition by concluding a treaty with Prussia in March 1795, leaving French forces in possession of the left bank of the Rhine. Defeated and occupied, the Netherlands became a French satellite in May. In June, Spain dropped out and only two enemies remained: Austria and Britain. Fighting the Austrians in northern Italy, Napoléon scored brilliant, lightening victories, gaining Nice and Savoy for France. In October 1795, all of Belgium was annexed. By October 1797, Austria sued for peace and, at Campo Formio, was allowed to retain only Venice in Italy, the rest of the peninsula becoming a French sphere of influence under a string of satellite republics. Switzerland, too, became a French ally with creation of the Helvetian Republic in April 1798, and Geneva was annexed directly to France.

Britain remained the sole challenger. Determined to cut the British lifeline to India and, with it, trade with Asia, Napoléon sailed to Egypt in May 1798 with a fleet of 400 ships, a small army, and a bevy of scientists. Marching triumphantly to Cairo, Bonaparte lost the security provided by his rearguard when, on August 1, British admiral Horatio Nelson (1758–1805) surprised the French fleet anchored at Aboukir Bay, outside Alexandria, and annihilated it at the Battle of the Nile. Believing the French defeated, the Ottoman Empire (modern-day Turkey), the ousted ruler of Egypt, prepared to attack, but Bonaparte, aware he could not beat the combined onslaught of Turkish forces, launched a preemptive strike in leading his Armée d'Orient into Syria. Failing to take the fortress city of Acre, he retreated to Egypt, where he halted an advancing Ottoman army. The situation there now stable if stagnant—his forces were cut off from France by British naval power—he suddenly reappeared in Paris, leaving his army behind to sulk in anger until they surrendered in 1802 and were repatriated on British ships, bringing with them a priceless hoard of Egyptian antiquities that included the Rosetta Stone, whose translation, much of it done by scholar Jean-François Champollion (1790–1832), would aid in the decipherment of hieroglyphic writing.

Recently elected one of the directors, Abbé Sieyès had summoned Bonaparte home to back up a plot to put in place an energetic executive able to meet renewed foreign and domestic threats. Launched in December 1798, a Second Coalition of powers had taken the field against France—Britain, Austria, Russia, and the Ottoman Empire—and had scored quick victories. In the Directory's legislature, ex-Jacobins had won enough seats in 1798–99 to challenge the governing faction. The new majority replaced four of the five directors. The Jacobin club was again legalized, and its members launched a noisy campaign for a return to a Robespierrist system. In the first week of November 1799, a rumor spread through Paris that the Jacobins were planning a popular rebellion.

Bonaparte came back to play his assigned role, but he almost lost his nerve in the ensuing drama. Badly bungling the effort, he took two days to overthrow the government. On the second day—November 9, 1799 (18 Brumaire)—Napoléon's brother Lucien (1775–1840) rallied the troops by inventing a plot that, he declared, had to be stopped. His forces surrounded the formerly royal palace in the suburb of Saint-Cloud, where the government was assembled. Napoléon spoke to the members of the Council of the Ancients. When a deputy protested at the military intimidation in asking, "And the constitution?" Bonaparte angrily replied: "The constitution? You yourselves have destroyed it; you violated it on the eighteenth Fructidor. . . . It no longer holds any man's respect" (Durant 1975, 122). He ordered the drums to sound. The troops under his command invaded the premises. Shouting "Down with the Jacobins!" they scattered the deputies, some of whom jumped from the windows. The Directory came to an end, destroyed by the weight of burdensome war costs, by its choice of leaders—such as Sieyès and Bonaparte—more ambitious to serve themselves than the regime, and, in the end, by its inability to win the support of the French public through its failure to breach the divisions between left and right.

The Consulate: Napoléon Bonaparte Takes Control, 1799–1804

Having gained a foothold on power, Bonaparte had no intention of letting it slip, a possibility that never arose because he showed an uncanny ability to give the country what it wanted and needed—peace at home and abroad. Those who were now in control drafted a governing blueprint that slyly enshrined autocratic rule behind a democratic facade. Confident that he knew better than the citizens what was good for them, Napoléon may have owed his rise to the Revolution, but he never concealed his opinion that the people were poorly equipped to rule themselves, believing them to be far too easily swayed by charm, eloquence, and the opinions of others, including journalists, politicians, and priests. Under the Constitution of the Year VIII, promulgated in December 1799, all Frenchmen 21 and over were given the vote to choose one-tenth of their number to be communal notables, and these in turn were to choose one-tenth of their number in a series of increasingly smaller voter pools leading to national notables. Democracy ended here—the officials who were to govern were all to be appointed from—not elected by—the notables. There were three parliamentary assemblies: A Conseil d'État (Council of State), appointed by the head of state, was empowered to propose new laws to be discussed by a Tribunat (Tribunate) of 100 "tribunes" who would in turn pass along recommendations to a Corps Législatif (Legislature) of 300 members authorized to approve or reject—but not to discuss—the proposals. The members of the Tribunate and the Legislature were appointed by a Sénat Conservateur (Senate Conservative), a body of approximately 60 members over 40 years of age who could also annul laws it judged to be unconstitutional. For an executive, the constitution stipulated creation of a board of three consuls. Authorized to serve 10-year terms and to share rulership, ultimate power rested in reality in the hands of only one of them—the first consul—Napoléon himself.

The war against the Second Coalition continued. By luck and calculation, Bonaparte secured the withdrawal of the Russians. Having rebuilt

French armies, he scored a crushing though bloody victory against the Austrians at Marengo (June 14, 1800) in Italy, and French forces routed the Austrians in Germany as well. The Treaty of Lunéville (February 9, 1801) expanded French control over Italy and western Germany. Once again left alone to fight, Britain decided the moment was right to negotiate, and the Treaty of Amiens (March 25, 1802) brought peace between the two ancient enemies for the first time in a decade.

The French public—all but jealous generals and die-hard Jacobins—were enthralled by Bonaparte's successes. Royal misrule, the terror, civil war, and years of foreign war were gone, replaced by martial glory won under the leadership of this brilliant Corsican. In May 1802, the puppet Senate proposed to lengthen his 10-year term of office to 20. The First Consul let it be known that he would prefer to be made consul for life, and the public, in a plebiscite on August 2, approved with barely a ripple of dissent.

Even before Bonaparte had made peace with the foreign powers, he had moved to make sure his hold at home was secure. He repressed the royalists—who were still a threat in the west—as well as Jacobin radicals and independent newspapers. Having thoroughly pacified the country, he then set out to reform domestic life. Apart from generalship, in which he excelled in having been trained in military matters, Napoléon took an intense interest in the administrative arts. Decrees on local government of 1789–90, under which wide powers had been devolved to the new departments, were reversed when, in the interests of orderly administration, Bonaparte moved in February 1800 to centralize and strengthen government by creating the office of *préfet* (prefect). The prefect headed a department, and he was appointed by, and responsible to, Paris, while subprefects and mayors were responsible to him in a chain of command under a system that, in thoroughly centralizing French public administration, ensured that decisions made in the capital were applied in even the smallest hamlets. The reform would survive the downfall of the regime and remain a distinguishing feature of French government for a century and a half.

Legal reforms proved equally important. Nothing excited his interest as passionately as his project to unify France's myriad, confused collection of existing laws. Eagerly presiding at 35 of the 87 sessions held by the Council of State between 1801 and 1804, Napoléon oversaw enactment of a standardized, clearly written, and accessible civil code that strengthened laws on behalf of property owners and enshrined some of the fundamental legal achievements of the Revolution, including religious toleration and equality before the law. Arguably his greatest achievement, the Code Napoléon, as it was called after 1807, remains the bedrock of French civil law, constitutes Europe's first successful codification, and exerted a profound influence in many other countries. The man who guided its creation saw its enduring value. "My real glory," Bonaparte reflected after his downfall from power, "is not the forty battles I won. . . . What nothing can destroy, what will live forever, is my Civil Code" (Durant 1975, 767).

To settle religious matters that had aroused so much contention since the Civil Constitution of the Clergy in 1790, Bonaparte secured a concordat with Pope Pius VII (r. 1800–23) in September 1801. A man of no strong religious convictions himself, he sought an accommodation with the Vatican both as a realist, who judged that the nonjuring clergy who had remained loyal to Rome remained popular and that most French citizens were professing, if not practicing, Catholics, and as a political strategist. An agreement would lead wary clerics to rally around the Consulate and away from the royalists. Under the concordat, the pope recognized the sale of church lands and the right of the French government to nominate bishops, while permission to hold public services was restored to the church. To reassure those who remained stubbornly opposed, Bonaparte later published a set of Organic Articles that reaffirmed the supremacy of the state over the church and insisted on the legal requirement of civil marriage.

To acknowledge those who deserved but who, with the abolition of privilege, could no longer expect special recognition, he founded the Legion of Honor in May 1802. Created to reward civic and military achievement and headed by the first consul himself, it was meant to enshrine the principle, proclaimed by the Revolution and so aptly embodied in Napoléon's own success, that careers open to talent were deserving of merit.

To stabilize the currency and make it easier for the government to borrow, he founded the Bank of France on January 18, 1800, which was given control over France's credit system. For the next century, the franc would remain one of Europe's most stable monetary units. Taxes were collected more equitably and efficiently, and new educational reforms put in place.

The fragile peace reached in 1802 proved brief indeed, and war with Great Britain resumed in May 1803. Bonaparte prepared troops and ships for an invasion, while an unexpected event gave him an occasion to advance further his position. On the evening of December 24, 1800, a bomb went off while the First Consul was on his way to the opera, killing a number of bystanders but sparing its intended victim.

The perpetrators were royalist extremists, and Bonaparte seized on the opportunity to crush his opponents, one of whom most especially brought him international condemnation. Prince Louis-Antoine, duc d'Enghien (1772–1804), a young royal prince living in exile in Baden, Germany, who was suspected of plotting a royal restoration, was kidnapped by Bonaparte's agents, brought to Paris, tried secretly on false charges, and summarily shot. He moved equally against enemies on the left. Critics of the regime went into exile, none more famous than Madame de Staël (1766–1817), a daughter of Jacques Necker and famed as a salon hostess who supported the Revolution. She left France during the terror and returned only to incur the displeasure of Napoléon for her opposition to his antidemocratic plans. Forced to leave France after 1800, in traveling across Europe, often accompanied by Benjamin Constant (1767–1830), a writer who helped launch romanticism, she wrote works that exerted a great influence on literary women in underscoring the importance of emotion and imagination.

In a country rife with potential enemies, where political currents of every imaginable kind had been swirling for a decade and more, Bonaparte was well aware that only by making his rule hereditary could his hold on power be fully secured. Public opinion, some of it genuine but most of it manipulated, rallied behind him. On May 18, 1804, the Senate craftily joined republican rhetoric with Roman imperial language in a single sentence of a new constitution that proclaimed Napoléon to be "First Consul of the Republic" and "Emperor of the French." The by now standard plebiscite registered the public's overwhelming approval. Bonaparte was duly enthroned on December 2, 1804. The solemnity of the occasion demanded that the pope himself travel all the way from Rome to attend the ceremony. But in the carefully staged drama, Pius VII was called upon to play merely a supporting role. When he held up the imperial headdress, Napoléon immediately grasped it. It was to himself alone that he owed this badge of majesty, and so he himself placed the crown on his head.

The Napoleonic Empire at Home, 1804–1815

Stability seemed at last to have arrived under the empire Napoléon established in France. Many of the émigrés, who had been drifting back since 1795, were given positions of prestige in the new imperial court or ministerial posts. The new emperor created a series of new titles and a new Napoleonic nobility emerged, separate but also mingling awkwardly with the old. Many of the emperor's successful generals—made

Emperor Napoléon Bonaparte (Library of Congress)

marshals—became dukes or princes. To ensure that the empire would have an heir, Bonaparte, after hesitating for years, divorced Josephine in 1809 and married Archduchess Marie-Louise (1791–1847) from the Austrian Hapsburg court, who in 1811 furnished him with a son, Napoléon II, dubbed *l'aiglon* (the eagle) and made king of Rome.

The country hummed with new energy. The government encouraged the growth of industry by providing cheaper credit and better technical education. Business boomed, the need to feed, clothe, and equip Bonaparte's large armies providing a huge market for domestic suppliers. Workers had steady employment at rising wage levels. Though initially unpopular, the metric system, introduced under the Directory in 1799, laid the basis for an efficient measurement scheme. The public secondary schools (*lycées*) and the all-important qualifying examination for higher education—the *baccalauréat*—were educational innovations that have endured. The new national military academy founded at Saint-Cyr, near Versailles, in 1808 survived as well, gaining in stature over time. The public administration ran smoothly, staffed by talented and efficient bureaucrats regardless of political background, and so loyal to the new regime.

Prosperity though came at a price. Liberty largely disappeared. Rigorous censorship ensured that no political opinion appeared, save that which was friendly to the government. A network of police spies unearthed subversives. Bonaparte's increasingly autocratic frame of mind made him seek control of every aspect of policy, turning advisers into nothing more than messengers. And the costs of never-ending war, by increasing social regimentation and fiscal taxation, gradually took their toll, as did the heartbreak brought to thousands of homes left bereft by the departure of men, called away in seemingly never-ending demands to fill the armed ranks, who would never return.

The Napoleonic Empire Abroad, 1804–1815

While Bonaparte was preparing to make himself emperor, Britain, under Prime Minister William Pitt, the younger (1759–1806), the leader who had waged war against France before, forged yet another coalition against its by now decade-old enemy. He found a willing ally in the idealistic young Russian ruler, Czar Alexander I (r. 1801–25), who looked askance at Napoléon's all-controlling efforts in Germany and Italy. In November 1804, the czar signed a defensive treaty with the Austrians, and by spring 1805, when Emperor Napoléon I crowned himself king of Italy and made his stepson Eugène de Beauharnais (1781–1824) viceroy, all three had had enough. By August 1805, the Third Coalition—Britain, Austria, Russia, Portugal, Sweden, and Naples—had formed.

Extricating himself from overseas entanglements from which the renewed war with Britain severed his connections and that, in any case, only distracted from his continental ambitions, Bonaparte withdrew

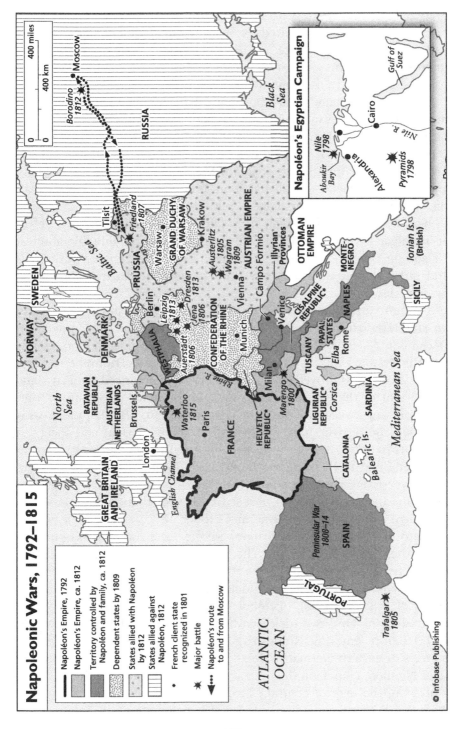

Napoleonic Wars, 1792–1815

Napoléon's Egyptian Campaign

Gulf of Suez

Cairo

Nile R.

Nile 1798

Alexandria

Aboukir Bay

Pyramids 1798

400 miles

400 km

Moscow

Borodino 1812

RUSSIA

Black Sea

Tilsit

Friedland 1807

Warsaw

GRAND DUCHY OF WARSAW

Kraków

AUSTRIAN EMPIRE

Austerlitz 1805

Wagram 1809

Illyrian Provinces

Campo Formio

OTTOMAN EMPIRE

Ionian Is. (British)

MONTE NEGRO

Baltic Sea

PRUSSIA

Berlin

Leipzig 1813

Dresden 1813

Jena 1806

Vienna

Venice

CISALPINE REPUBLIC*

NAPLES

SICILY

NORWAY

SWEDEN

DENMARK

WESTPHALIA

Auerstädt 1806

CONFEDERATION OF THE RHINE

Munich

Milan

TUSCANY

PAPAL STATES

Rome

Elba

Marengo 1800

BATAVIAN REPUBLIC*

AUSTRIAN NETHERLANDS

Brussels

Waterloo 1815

Paris

FRANCE

Rhine R.

HELVETIC REPUBLIC*

LIGURIAN REPUBLIC*

Corsica

SARDINIA

Mediterranean Sea

North Sea

London

English Channel

GREAT BRITAIN AND IRELAND

CATALONIA

Balearic Is.

SPAIN

Peninsular War 1808–14

PORTUGAL

Trafalgar 1805

ATLANTIC OCEAN

Napoléon's Empire, 1792
Napoléon's Empire, ca. 1812
Territory controlled by Napoléon and family, ca. 1812
Dependent states by 1809
States allied with Napoléon by 1812
States allied against Napoléon, 1812
French client state recognized in 1801
Major battle
Napoléon's route to and from Moscow

© Infobase Publishing

French forces from the Caribbean colony of Haiti after a successful revolt there in 1804. Acquired by Spain in the Treaty of Paris of 1763 and ceded back to France in 1800, Louisiana had originally been intended as a granary for French West Indian sugar islands. Napoléon sold the territory to the United States in 1803.

Delaying his plans for an invasion of Britain, Bonaparte prepared his armies for a continental campaign. They were superbly led under a bevy of celebrated marshals—Michel Ney (1769–1815), Louis-Nicolas Davout (1770–1823), Jean Lannes (1769–1809), Nicolas Soult (1769–1851)—who were joined by Joachim Murat (1767–1815) in Germany and André Masséna (1758–1817) in Italy. The legions marched all the way to Vienna. Campaigns at sea faltered, however, when efforts to beat the formidable British navy failed. The French-Spanish defeat at Trafalgar by ships under the command of the redoubtable admiral Nelson on October 21, 1805, guaranteed Britain's command of the seas and put a definitive end to any French plans for an invasion of the British Isles.

Though vanquished on the waters, Napoléon remained unbeatable on land. His triumph over the Austrians at Austerlitz, in Moravia, on December 2—arguably his greatest ever and one that he commemorated in commissioning construction of the Arc de Triomphe in Paris (built 1806–36)—proved so substantial that it convinced the Prussians to stay out of the war and compelled the humbled Austrians to sign a humiliating peace at Pressburg (December 26, 1805). France won full sovereignty over Italy, annexing Piedmont, Parma, and Piacenza outright. In 1806, Bonaparte turned his attention to Germany, putting an official end to the long-moribund Holy Roman Empire in forming the Confederation of the Rhine, a league of minor states under the French emperor's protection. Roused by fear of French domination of Germany, Prussia declared war in October 1806, and soon a Fourth Coalition—Prussia, Russia, Britain, Saxony, and Sweden—assembled, all of these powers intent on checking the seemingly unquenchable French need for conquest.

The Prussians dropped out quickly, routed by French armies at the Battle of Jena-Auerstadt (October 14, 1806). The victors arrived in Berlin and, moving east, defeated the Russians at Friedland (June 14, 1807) before entering Königsberg (present-day Kaliningrad) on the borders of eastern Germany. Meeting the Russian czar on a raft in the river Niemen, Napoléon drew up with Alexander the Treaties of Tilsit, redrawing the map of central Europe most notably in creating a new duchy of Warsaw carved out of Prussian acquisitions in Poland. And to put his stamp on a Europe now fully under his control, the emperor turned to his family as the most reliable source of compliant rulers: Joseph Bonaparte (1768–1844) was made king of Spain; Louis Bonaparte (1778–1846), king of Holland; Jérôme Bonaparte (1784–1860), king of Westphalia. After 1809, when Austria in a rash bid to defeat him joined with Britain in a Fifth Coalition and suffered yet another ignominious crushing at Wagram (July 5–6, 1809), Napoléon Bonaparte stood at the pinnacle of success, the master of all Europe.

Conquering a continent, however, proved easier than controlling one. Napoléon needed to consolidate his hold, but because his policies were directed everywhere at aggrandizement on behalf of France, the rapacity of the emperor's soldiers and administrators bred increasing resentment on the part of the locals. Bonaparte imposed heavy exactions in money and men to help wage his wars. Inaugurating his Continental System, he issued decrees at Berlin (November 21, 1806) and Milan (December 17, 1807) closing all continental ports to British shipping. The British retaliated in kind, and in the end they made out much the better in the commercial dueling. Ongoing industrialization in Britain, where the Industrial Revolution had first bloomed some half-century earlier, led to the production of a large output of goods, making them cheaper and increasing demand for them on the Continent, where no such productive pace had yet taken place. Though the decrees proved a boon to French manufacturers and traders in giving them a protective barrier behind which they could conduct business free from competition, they aroused European resentment, hurting coastal economies not only in conquered territories but also in France and spawning widespread smuggling to evade them. The brush fires from a guerrilla war in Spain, where imported French revolutionary doctrines aroused opposition from devout Catholics and loyalists to the country's monarchy, also helped to keep discontent smoldering. Disquieting flickers appeared even in France, where a business recession in 1810–11 hurt the bourgeoisie, the social group who served as the mainstay of the regime.

Czar Alexander set in motion renewed opposition to Napoléon when, in 1810, he withdrew from the Continental System. By 1812, Russia had become no more than a nominal ally, and Bonaparte was resolved to bring the country to heel. On June 24, he launched an invasion, his Grande Armée of perhaps 600,000, built around a core of veterans, the largest force ever to serve under his command. Defeated after a bloody all-day battle at Borodino in September, the Russians withdrew behind Moscow, leaving the capital to be occupied by the French. Arriving to dictate peace terms, Bonaparte found no one there to greet him—the

Retreat of the Grande Armée from Moscow, 1812 (Library of Congress)

Russian court had fled with the army. Within 24 hours, Napoléon, too, would leave, abandoning a city three-quarters destroyed by fires that had been set either intentionally or accidentally by the Russians. The retreat from Moscow turned into a slow rout. The troops straggled back along the same route, already laid waste, by which they had come, the army's overtaxed supply system having broken down and the soldiers harassed by Russian snipers and felled by the numbing cold of a Russian winter that quickly set in.

Czar Alexander pursued the French into central Europe, a strategy encouraged by the British, who sought to secure a victory once and for all over an enemy who seemed bent on waging never-ending war. The Prussians and the Austrians broke with Bonaparte during a lull in fighting over the winter of 1812–13, and a Sixth Coalition came together in a Grand Alliance against France of all Europe's major nations, plus Sweden, Spain, and Portugal.

Napoléon trounced the allies at Dresden in late August 1813, but on October 16–19, near Leipzig, in the so-called Battle of the Nations, he met decisive defeat by an allied force that had finally learned that close cooperation was the only way to beat their great opponent. His army now much reduced and in full retreat all the way back to France, Bonaparte combed the country in a desperate search for new recruits at the same time that he was compelled to confront failure in Spain, where his armies had been driven back across the French border by an army under the British commander, Arthur Wellesley, duke of Wellington (1769–1852). Too proud to accept an offer of peace if he agreed to stay within France's natural frontiers, the emperor faced no other choice than to surrender, abdicating on April 16, 1814, after allied forces had brushed aside a small French army and entered Paris.

Exiled to Elba, a small, barren island off the Italian coast, Napoléon left the fate of France in the hands of the victors. Disinclined at first to permit the return of a Bourbon king, the allies were convinced to do so both through the fervent urging of a small faction of royalists, who stirred up demonstrations in favor of the old regime that impressed the triumphant statesmen, and through effective lobbying by Talleyrand, a consummate survivor who as a revolutionary enthusiast had left the church, gone into exile during the terror, returned to fill various government posts, and now served as head of a provisional government. Told the good news by an excited aide, who exclaimed: "Sire! You are king of France!" the pretender, in exile in Britain, calmly replied: "And when have I been anything else?" (Sauvigny 1955, 72). Louis XVIII (r. 1814–15; 1815–24) entered Paris on May 3, 1814. Now foreign minister, Talleyrand negotiated the first Peace of Paris at the Congress of Vienna, where, to blunt the harsh demands of Prussia and Russia, he skillfully and successfully divided the Allies to achieve a stunningly lenient settlement. Under the treaty, the diplomats agreed that most of the overseas territories taken by Britain during the war should be returned and France should retain the borders it held as of January 1, 1792, frontiers that included the Rhine River and the towns of Annecy and Chambéry in Savoy.

A mere 10 months later, the diplomats at the Congress of Vienna, just finishing their work of mapping out a postwar world, were dealt a stunning surprise in receiving a message marked "urgent" informing them that Napoléon had escaped from Elba. King Louis fled just before Bonaparte arrived in Paris on March 20, 1815, following a triumphal march north with former soldiers flocking to his side. The delegates at Vienna declared the returning emperor an outlaw whom anyone might kill with impunity. Both sides quickly assembled their armies. Once again, Bonaparte took the field, and beginning on June 18, 1815, near the Belgian village of Waterloo south of Brussels, he was beaten—but just barely—after a monumental three-day battle. The victory of the Allies was a narrow one, Napoléon losing only after last-minute help had arrived from a Prussian army, but this time the defeat proved decisive. The emperor was exiled to the island of St. Helena in the south Atlantic, where he worked on his memoirs, writing that, as the man who both preserved and propagated the achievements of the Revolution, history must treat him well. Depressed, bitter, and racked by ailments, he died on May 5, 1821, murmuring at the last, *Á la tête de l'armée* (At the head of the army) (Durant 1975, 769).

The Hundred Days during which Bonaparte had returned to rule necessitated a new treaty of peace. Much harsher than the first, the second Treaty of Paris reduced France to the frontiers of 1790, installed an occupation army of 150,000 troops for from three to five years, and required payment of an indemnity of 700 million francs. Louis XVIII returned—this time for good. Royalty was back, having seemingly come full circle; but after more than a quarter century of dramatic, precedent-shattering action, the country the royals had known in 1789 was no longer in existence.

What were the effects of years of revolution and prolonged war? In France, the Revolution brought democratic government in place of absolutism, albeit one limited by property qualifications, produced a free peasantry that would acquire increasing amounts of property, replaced feudal with civil courts, and launched the bourgeoisie as the dominant business and administrative class. Across Europe, changes both ideological and institutional followed in the wake of Revolutionary and Napoleonic armies. French officials brought with them the principles, if not always the practice, of representative democracy, including concepts of equality under the law, religious toleration, and an end to hierarchical privilege. Even where they failed to plant lasting roots, these precepts would survive to inspire revolutionaries across the Continent in the century just dawning.

Most fundamentally, the Revolution gave birth to modern political culture. From the French Revolution stems the principle that only governments created by the popular will as expressed in a constitution are legitimate and the notion that sovereignty resides in the nation, that is, in the citizens who possess inalienable rights. The Revolution gave birth to nationalism as a doctrine under which the people join together in community not on grounds of territorial location or governmental subjugation but on the basis of patriotism, namely, devotion to, and pride in, a place that, since it exists to advance their well-being, merits such sentiments.

The language of politics would heretofore reflect the Revolution's impact. The designations of "right"—to mean conservative and more moderate—and "left"—to mean liberal and more radical—derive from the events of 1789–95. The word *revolution* itself was redefined. Before the French Revolution, it had meant sudden, even extreme, change, but change produced independent of human will or action; now it meant change that men and women themselves brought about, implying that they themselves held the power to create a better world. The French Revolution proved that society could be transformed, and transformed drastically. This would be the legacy that would endure most profoundly. It would cast its shadow not only in faraway places well into the future, but also in France, its homeland, in the years just immediately ahead.

8

THE SEARCH FOR STABILITY
(1815–1870)

The period from 1814 to 1848 was both preceded and followed by major revolutions and imperial rule by autocratic leaders. France strove to recover a lost stability and to restore order during this era, while at the same time, the country underwent significant change and experimentation. Intense intellectual and artistic activity characterized a half century when social thinkers propounded an unprecedented number of theories and remedies, many of which were formulated in response to the mass-production industrialism then first being introduced in France. The nation tested an early parliamentary system of government, which it rarely abandoned thereafter, to find a workable compromise that could reconcile the competing claims made by monarchy, aristocracy, and democracy.

The Bourbons brought a return of legitimacy and a bit of the glamour attached to the royal name, while the Orléanist king Louis-Philippe showed a somewhat more progressive attitude toward the emerging 19th-century society, but neither regime prevailed. It proved impossible to put the genie of revolution, once unleashed in 1789, back into the bottle. Each ignited an uprising, the second of which gave republicans in 1848 an opportunity to try once again to create a government in their image. But too many social strains and economic stresses in a country prone to insurrection—with a discontented working class, a rabidly radical press, and leaders who still had little real understanding of the rising industrial world—brought a return to strong-man rule. Recurrent rebellion evoked longings for stability, and the son of Napoléon Bonaparte's brother carried a name that, in conjuring up images of a bygone era now cloaked in wistful memories of imperial order and glory, proved for many too hard to resist. Like his illustrious uncle before him, Louis-Napoléon created an empire that brought order, prosperity, and foreign victories, but in the end it failed to achieve the power and reproduce the splendor attained by the great emperor. While a Bonaparte, Napoléon III was an authoritarian with a difference. Breaking with imperialistic tradition, he proceeded during the second decade of his reign to soften his one-man ruling system. The government relaxed its grip and liberalized its machinery, though the effects would never be fully known because an unnecessary war with Prussia cut short its prospects. Defeated militarily, the Second Empire collapsed completely, with few regrets shed by anyone—for the first time a regime died without domestic bloodletting—but it left the nation to face a new foreign challenge—a united Germany—as a powerful neighbor. The second adventure in empire had outlasted all the other government experiments since 1814. Would a republic hastily established in 1870—the third to be tried since 1792—prove any more, or less, durable?

The Bourbons Bring Monarchy—and Revolution—Back, 1815–1830

When the Bourbons returned in 1814–15 from almost a quarter century of exile, bringing with them the white royal flag of old, they came back to a nation whose population stood at approximately 29 million, still the largest of any other European country, except for Russia. And France remained a peasant nation; three out of four inhabitants lived by farming.

It was a country, however, that had changed profoundly in many ways. In matters of government, the revolutionary era had introduced an instrument that had come to be expected by most French citizens, namely, that some sort of elected assembly was a necessary part of the ruling apparatus. Even under his dictatorship, Napoléon I had retained the principle of a representative body, though deprived of most of its powers. For all his shortcomings, and whatever else he was—historians endlessly debate his motives and character—the new king was shrewd enough to acknowledge that fact.

Nearly 60 and prematurely aging, a genial and courteous widower, gouty and very fat, Louis XVIII possessed a reasonably acute judgment of men. Though inclined to believe the Crown he had gained was his by divine right, he had sufficient sense to recognize that, in the current state, both of Europe and of France, an attempt to restore the old order intact would stir up a great deal of trouble. Under the hastily drafted charter by which he governed, the rights of 1789 were recognized— equality before the law and individual freedoms—and purchasers were allowed to retain the lands once owned by the nobles and the church. Napoleonic-era changes were also maintained—the judiciary, bureaucracy, administrative structure, economic institutions, and Napoleonic Code, as well as titles, pensions, and decorations. There were some limitations. Although religious freedom was guaranteed, Catholicism was made the state religion. Press restrictions were imposed, and the electorate entrusted only to wealthy landlords and bourgeois.

The ruling charter vested executive power in the king; the ministers, who could sit in either chamber, were responsible only to him. Legislative power rested with the king, the upper-house Chamber of Peers, and the lower-house Chamber of Deputies. The king—or his ministers—proposed laws, which they introduced in either chamber, except tax bills, which had to go to the deputies first. The consent of both chambers was needed for taxation, and both bodies met every year.

Elections were held in August 1815, in great hurry, even before a new electoral law was in place. Occupation troops ranged at will, while royalists seeking revenge against revolutionary and Napoleonic supporters launched a spontaneous "white terror" in the south. The Chamber of Deputies that was elected turned out to be more royalist than the king himself, dominated by the Ultras—rabid monarchists who looked for philosophical justification for their position to writers such as the viscomte de Bonald (1754–1840) and François-René, viscomte de Chateaubriand (1768–1848), both renowned counterrevolutionary authors of works justifying rule by a powerful king. The self-styled "liberal" party was a complex amalgam variously loyal to republicanism, constitutional monarchism, or the memory of Napoléon. The marquis de La Fayette was a republican, while Benjamin Constant was a constitutional monarchist. In the middle stood moderate royalists, supporters of the duc de Richelieu (1766–1822), the king's favorite, and Élie, duc Decazes (1780–1860), and who were backed by a group of writers called "doctrinaires," including François Guizot (1787–1874) and the duc de Broglie (1785–1870).

From 1816 to 1820, the Bourbon compromise worked fairly well under the ministries of Richelieu and Decazes, both of whom steered carefully between reactionaries on the right and radicals on the left. The nation grew more accustomed to a true parliamentary system; the title "president of the council of ministers" (premier or prime minister) came into common use, while the roots of political parties appeared in the rise of the three loosely organized factions. Protective tariffs pleased farmers who hoped that they would sustain the high prices ushered in by wartime shortages under Napoléon but that were now threatened, for the first time, by potential competition from Russian grain. France's war indemnity was paid and the allied occupation ended. In international affairs, the country rejoined the other great powers—Britain, Austria, Prussia, and Russia—as a full-fledged member of the postwar Quintuple Alliance, a loose institution by which Europe's major nations sought to bolster legitimacy of rule and curtail radical change across the Continent through the mechanism of several diplomatic congresses.

Richelieu resigned in 1818, succeeded by Decazes, who moved in a more liberal direction, until early in 1820 a fanatical antimonarchist workman assassinated the ultraroyalist duc de Berry (1778–1820), the king's nephew and third in line to the throne. Outraged royalists blamed Decazes and his liberalizing policies. Richelieu returned to office to head a rightward-leaning coalition that imposed stricter controls. In the ascendant, the Ultras secured a government in 1821 under the duc de Villèle (1773–1854), a shrewd, cautious man who strengthened censorship. The government's success in foreign policy—a French army occupied Spain to protect its king from revolutionaries—gave it the confidence to call an election, which returned a chamber made up overwhelmingly of Ultras.

Long ailing, the king died in 1824, succeeded by his brother, the comte d'Artois, as King Charles X (r. 1824–30). Warmly welcomed, the new monarch was crowned at Reims Cathedral in 1825 in a five-hour spectacle of medieval pomp and splendor. Tall and imposing, Charles looked the very image of a king. Generous and eager to please, he possessed many qualities that make for a wise ruler, although good judgment was not one of them. As he was the most prominent among the émigrés, it was expected that Charles would want to do something for the aristocrats who had, like him, returned. The question of lands confiscated during the Revolution still proved vexing, and while it made sense to try to settle the issue, a measure passed by the legislature among a group of laws in 1824–25 intended to indemnify returned exiles for the loss of their property aroused considerable resentment. Most of the beneficiaries got less than they had expected, while opponents charged that average citizens had been forced to pay to benefit a few thousand who had fled their country in a time of crisis. The Ultras replied that these thousands had been forced to leave—by the crime of the guillotine under the terrorist republican regime. Another law to punish perpetrators of sacrilegious acts in church by long imprisonment and even death, though it proved totally unenforceable, outraged secularists, while a restrictive press act frightened defenders of liberty.

The left suspected a move underfoot to restore the pre-1789 regime. The king, who solidly backed Villèle, followed his chief minister's advice to create 76 reliably loyal new peers in the upper house and to call a quick election, hoping thereby to get a favorable Chamber of Deputies by giving the opposition no time to launch an effective campaign. What Villèle got was a chamber in which the opposition—on both right and left—far outnumbered the government's supporters. Unable to survive as prime minister, Villèle submitted his resignation in early 1828, which the king reluctantly accepted. Disliking the new ministry, Charles X intrigued for one more to his taste, appointing a new government in early August 1829 under Prince Jules de Polignac (1780–1847). The choice proved disastrous. An émigré and an Ultra, Polignac stood at the top of a government bound to incense the left, whose members included a vehemently reactionary minister of the interior and a minister of war who was said to have betrayed Napoléon.

With a politically restive populace and faced with a recession that began in 1826, the government launched a venture to give itself some badly needed prestige. In May and June 1830, an expedition was dispatched against the city of Algiers in North Africa in retaliation for supposed insults from its ruler, the Islamic dey. In a mere 20 days, resistance was crushed, and the French resolved thereafter to stay. In 1831, the French Foreign Legion would be established as a regiment trained for service in Algeria. Its mission to keep order in overseas possessions would grow in conjunction with the expansion of France's empire.

Meanwhile, opposition mounted at home. The Chamber of Deputies reminded the king that his ministers did not have the confidence of the country and asked for their dismissal. Charles complied. He dismissed the chamber and called for new elections, which, in late June and early July 1830, were swept by the opposition. Undeterred, the king and his ministers, relying on the power given to them in the charter to enact ordinances required to protect the state, issued four orders, which dissolved the newly elected chamber (it had not yet met), altered the electoral system, sharply limited publication of newspapers and pamphlets, and set new elections for September. Opposition journalists refused to obey the ruling. Workers began to gather in the streets. On July 28, a general uprising began—the Hôtel de Ville and Notre-Dame Cathedral were seized. What began as a revolt turned into a revolution when some government troops mutinied to join the insurgents. The Revolution of 1830 proved breathtakingly brief. By the afternoon of July 29, the rebels controlled Paris, gaining the city at a cost of some 1,800 lost lives among their compatriots as well as approximately 200 soldiers.

Charles X would have to go, but what would replace him: a new king or a republic? Moderate liberals, led by Adolphe Thiers (1797–1877), a lawyer, journalist, and historian, put forward the duke of Orléans—the head of a junior branch of the House of Bourbon whose father, Philippe Égalité, had sympathized with the Revolution and had been executed in the terror—as a likely candidate for a new monarchical regime. Following the lead of their hero La Fayette, who signified his support for the move in shouting his classic phrase: "Here is the best of republics!" (Wright, 142), parliamentarians of all stripes but for die-hard republicans rallied around the choice. On August 2, Charles abdicated and departed to a second exile in Britain. The Bourbon return had ended in failure, brought down not so much by extremists of both left and right who so rankled public affairs throughout the regime's 15-year reign but by Charles and his advisers, who proved unable to work the system in a way that could have saved their positions. If France failed to develop a strong constitutional monarchy, one that might have provided the stability based on legitimacy that has distinguished modern Britain, the fault lies with these men.

The July Monarchy and the February Revolution, 1830–1848

Louis-Philippe I (r. 1830–48) became the "citizen king" whose throne was based on a contract not between God and king but between people and king, a reality made symbolically evident in his title "king of the French"—not "king of France"—and in the simple coronation ceremony held on August 9, 1830, in the chambers of parliament, one that stood in glaring contrast to Charles X's glittering gala. The counterrevolutionary Bourbons gave way to the Orléanists, who ruling now under the red, white, and blue banner of the Revolution were far more willing than their predecessors to accept changes brought by the events of 1789. The governing charter was revised to stress, at least indirectly, the sovereignty of the people. The chambers gained the right to initiate legislation, the franchise was widened, though it remained still highly restricted, and censorship was abolished.

The "citizen king" was also the "bourgeois monarch" in reference partly to the upper middle classes who formed the regime's base of power and partly to a ruler who looked and acted like a typical member of Parisian bourgeois society, a man who put in a long day at the office and was thrifty as well. But the exterior that seemed to reveal a not very extraordinary man concealed an interior marked by a fierce determination to be a king rather than a figurehead. Intelligent and shrewd, Louis-Philippe could be accommodating but only to a point. He intended always to be the one to give—and not to take—orders, and he resolutely opposed democratic reforms such as broadening the suffrage or making the ministry responsible to the Chamber of Deputies.

The decade from 1830 to 1840 was marked by habitual instability both in the government—ministries averaged less than a year—and in society. Memories of 1792 stirred among those who believed they had made the Revolution of 1830 and had been cheated of it. Attempts to assassinate the king took on an almost ritualistic character—there were 10 near misses during the reign, prompting the king to quip: "there seems to be a closed season on all kinds of game except me" (Wright 1960, 152). Violent street demonstrations broke out in the cities among the growing, though still largely forbidden, trade union movement. A

Louis-Philippe going to the Hôtel de Ville, July 31, 1830 (Library of Congress)

law of 1834 outlawing political organizations sparked a major uprising among silk workers in Lyon and an attempt at insurrection in Paris. Both were savagely suppressed by the National Guard and the army. Efforts to clamp down on dissent led to passage of the September Laws of 1835, which imposed sharp restrictions on the press, but sentiment smoldered against a regime deemed to be intolerant, unjust, and incapable of remedying social distress.

Even though the Ultras faded from the political scene and the extreme left was miniscule given the narrow suffrage, chronic conflict between right-center and left-center became a hallmark of politics in the Chamber of Deputies, a confrontation that was sharpened by the rise of intense personal rivalries and ambitions. Legitimists planned and schemed for a return of the Bourbons, while republicans formed a series of underground organizations in Paris with branches in other major cities.

Alongside the Legitimist and republican threats to the regime, a third challenge appeared. Die-hard Bonapartists remained numerous in the country, their devotion still strong to an imperial era, whose glories they remembered glowingly. After Napoléon's son, the duke of Reichstadt (Napoléon II to his followers), died of pulmonary tuberculosis in 1832, the Bonapartist pretender became Louis-Napoléon Bonaparte (1808–73), son of the emperor's brother Louis. Banned from France, he had grown up in exile. He fought briefly for Italian freedom and made a ludicrous attempt to incite an uprising in the garrison at Strasbourg in 1836, when he was arrested and shipped off to the United States. He tried again in 1840 and was again arrested. This time, sentenced to life imprisonment, he entered the fortress of Ham on the very day his uncle's ashes were interred in a magnificent tomb in the Hôtel des Invalides in Paris in a ceremony staged by the government as part of its effort to win the patriotic sentiment of Napoleonic enthusiasts.

None of the failed insurrections of the 1830s seriously shook the regime. By 1840, stability had set in. The nation was prosperous and at peace. Under the leadership of François Guizot, the de facto head of a ministry formed in October 1840, the country entered one of the longest periods of stable government yet seen. A talented historian and a Protestant—one of the first to rise high in government—Guizot was propelled into politics by the Revolution of 1830. A cold and self-righteous man, he maintained himself there by his administrative skills and his brilliant oratory. His crowning achievement to date had been an educational law in 1833 that obligated every commune in the country of more than 500 inhabitants to establish a public elementary school for boys and provide expanded teacher training facilities, actions that did much to promote unity in a country still marked by many language dialects and regional differences. One among the circle of so-called doctrinaires, Guizot held to attitudes perfectly in line with sentiments professed by the middle classes now in the ascendant. He sincerely believed opportunity was available to all to use their talents to succeed. In government, the *juste milieu* (middle way) was best—the golden mean of a constitutional monarchy, run by those who, because they possessed sufficient property and education, would ensure that moderation was maintained and would move ahead cautiously, and only after careful preparation, toward opening up civic affairs to wider public participation.

During his ministry, Guizot backed up his previous educational reforms with further changes. Under Victor Cousin (1792–1867), appointed minister of public instruction in 1840, the system of primary education was reorganized. A founder of the philosophical school of eclecticism, which held that no single belief theory was entirely correct, Cousin promoted philosophical freedom in the universities and introduced study of the history of philosophy into academic curricula.

The regime made a start in bringing France into the industrial age by pursuing policies that included high tariffs, low taxes, government noninterference in business and commerce, and generous aid to private enterprise. State monies went toward building the army, schools, agricultural development, and, most especially, public works, including roads, canals, and, the most important of all, railways.

Steady, though not spectacular, growth in trade and production took place, while at the same time, despite these signs of progress, resistance to change and a lack of dynamism remained in evidence, a characteristic of French economic affairs that persisted throughout much of the modern era. The causes are much debated. France had abundant cheap labor, thus its need for machinery was less pressing. The banking system developed late, and so liquid capital remained limited, unable to generate the funds required for investment. Entrepreneurs maintained a cautious stance based on keeping their income rather than creating wealth, while the social ethos inherited from the ancien régime—that business was a less than noble profession—inhibited confident, competitive attitudes. Whatever the reasons, France was gradually surpassed in economic prowess during the 19th century by major rivals—Britain, Germany, and the United States.

An agrarian crisis and a rapid rise in food prices spawned by bad weather throughout western Europe in 1845–47 led to the most severe depression in a generation at the same time that the leaders on the political left, hitherto deeply divided both by personal rivalry and by principle—some calling for moderate change and others for a radical overthrow of the government—came together to launch a new assault on a regime seen as dreary and unrepresentative led by a king grown increasingly ineffective. By the 1840s, Louis-Philippe was aging and tired, touched by tragedy—his eldest son and heir was killed in a carriage accident in 1842—and constantly vilified by his opponents, which made him more resolved than ever to resist change.

Defeated in an election, reformers began to agitate for an expansion of the franchise and to raise charges of government corruption. Reviving a tactic first tried in 1840, opposition leaders held a banquet in Paris in July 1847 as a venue at which they could utilize their speaking skills to inspire their supporters, inform other listeners, and perhaps persuade the government to make a start at parliamentary reform. Other banquets followed. But when the government learned that 100 opposition deputies appeared on the list of invitees to a banquet scheduled for February 22, 1848, it grew alarmed and forbade the gathering, reversing its previous permission. The leaders of the opposition voted to accept the cancellation, but on the morning of the 22nd, a crowd of students and workers gathered on the Place de la Madeleine in which participants called for Guizot's dismissal. Street agitation spread, and by February 23, the crowds had grown larger and more aggressive. Believing that what was rapidly growing into full-scale riots was a minor affair and confident that his army—large, well equipped, and with plans already in hand to meet a potential insurrection—could handle matters, Louis-Philippe exuded confidence. But rioting intensified. The National Guard deserted the government, its loyalty having been weakened by many among its members drawn from a lesser bourgeoisie anxious for a share of political power, while the army, commanded by incompetent generals, performed much more poorly than expected. Although toward the close of the second day of fighting the armed forces rallied and were poised to put the rebels to flight, the king held back, reluctant to give his consent to what would have been a bloodbath. Acceding to the opposition's demands, he dismissed Guizot and scrambled to assemble a government, but events moved too quickly for him. In working-class quarters, barricades appeared—some of them built of paving stones torn from the streets—overseen by citizens armed with stolen weaponry. Urged to flee and organize an army with which to besiege the city, the king demurred, abdicating in favor of his 10-year-old grandson. Ever the proper bourgeois to the end, he left for the suburbs in a cab and from there to eventual exile in Britain. Angry rioters ransacked the Tuileries palace and moved on to the Chamber of Deputies, where they broke in on the proceedings. Shouting for a republic, they secured their aim with the support of Alphonse de Lamartine (1790–1869), a poet and statesman renowned for his eloquent oratory. The deputies joined the public in gathering at the Hôtel de Ville, the traditional site at which republics were proclaimed, while the young, would-be Orléanist heir left quickly with his family to join his grandfather across the Channel.

The Revolution of 1848 marked the third time since 1792 that constitutional monarchy had gone down to defeat. A provisional government was formed while the crowds clamored for work, a demand that officials appeased by creating "national workshops" around the city where the unemployed were paid to labor at make-work tasks such as excavation and road repair. New forces of public order were raised and trained, while the government's minister of foreign affairs, Lamartine, quietly hastened to arrange an understanding with Britain to calm international concerns that France, perceived as the Continent's prime potential troublemaker since 1789, was set to embark yet again on a revolutionary path.

The Revolution of 1848 could not be halted at France's borders—it sparked uprisings all across Europe—but French leaders themselves pulled back, terrified that their inflammatory rhetoric so long directed at Louis-Philippe's regime might have raised the specter of social revolution. Lamartine called for a republic without anarchy and without socialism. Socialism began to rise to prominence as a doctrine now being formulated by thinkers and activists intent on advancing the interests of the new class of industrial workers who were rapidly appearing. They included Louis Blanc (1811–82), a radical bourgeois journalist and one of the leaders of the provisional government, who, in a successful essay titled "L'Organisation du travail" (Organization of Labor, 1839) called for the right to work for all and for state intervention in organizing labor in a formula met by the national workshops.

On April 23, 1848, elections for a constituent assembly held under universal male suffrage returned a moderate republican majority. Voters in 10 departments elected Lamartine a deputy, grateful to him for having delivered them from socialism. But socialism would not disappear. It was one among a number of social theories then coming to the fore.

Social Science Arrives and Natural Science Thrives

From the 1820s until the 1870s, the basic premises of social organization came under continuous debate launched by a series of French thinkers whose theories opened issues that have concerned Western society ever since. Both the Enlightenment, with its professions attesting to the perfectibility of humankind, and the French Revolution, with its demonstration that society could be purposefully changed, provided a powerful stimulus to speculation. Though late and slow to arrive in France, the new industrialism and with it the rise of a factory-based laboring class induced deep, innovative currents of thought. In the years after 1830, theorists made France the central source of socialist ideas about how to reorder private ownership of property for the betterment of all.

The two great precursors in the field were labeled "utopian" socialists because, coming from backgrounds far removed from the workaday world, they proposed idyllic solutions to society's ills to be achieved by peaceful means. A liberal aristocrat, the duc de Saint-Simon (1760–1825) supported the Revolution, narrowly escaped the terror, and acquired—and then lost—a wife and two fortunes. Through it all he proclaimed a belief in progress through the application of science and technology to social problems. Saint-Simon formulated a hierarchical society of unequals, guided by an elite of engineers and businessmen, in which the classes would collaborate for the good of all. A forerunner of modern concepts of technocracy, Saint-Simon's ideas, carried on by a school of disciples, proved highly influential among later 19th-century industrialists and economists.

Like Saint-Simon, Charles Fourier (1772–1837) stressed class collaboration but without a presiding managerial elite. Rejecting religion, marriage, and family, he sought salvation in a new society created by voluntary associations of capital, labor, and talent. Reacting against the growth of large cities and mass production, he proposed building a scattering of small communities he called phalansteries, where modern techniques would be combined with free human instinct to produce perfect harmony.

Fourier and Saint-Simon drew followers, but it was Étienne Cabet (1788–1856) who aroused the most enthusiasm among the utopians. An attorney from Dijon and a participant in the 1830 insurrection, he won many thousands of enthusiasts in preaching the ideal of a classless society and complete communal ownership, to be achieved not by force of arms but by example and persuasion. Disheartened by the turbulence of the February revolution, Cabet led supporters to the United States to found an unsuccessful utopia.

Mild-mannered socialism failed to produce results such as those brought by revolutionary violence, and a new mood, already building before 1848, began to make itself felt. Conflict between labor and capital was growing more obvious and physical force more appealing. Louis Blanc's workshops offered a practical mechanism by which workers might take ownership of a factory. Other thinkers reflected the new, tougher outlook. A student of the law and medicine who turned to organizing secret republican and socialist societies, political activist Louis-Auguste Blanqui (1805–81) was the chief heir to François-Noël Babeuf's legacy of direct revolutionary action in espousing the idea of the dictatorship of the proletariat, that is, the forcible overthrow of the rich and powerful on behalf of the poor and dispossessed until a new, more perfect society could be crafted. A revolutionary with a will never to quit, Blanqui spent 40 of his 79 years in prison because of his attempts to seize violent control of the state.

Unlike Saint-Simon, Fourier, and Blanqui, Pierre-Joseph Proudhon (1809–65) was a real workingman, a self-educated printer from Besançon. Gifted with the ability to coin memorable phrases, evidenced in the answer he gave in his first and best-known work *Qu'est-ce que c'est la propriété?* (*What Is Property?* 1840): "It is theft!" Proudhon was a paradoxical apostle for the emerging creed of socialism. He called himself an anarchist, though in fact he believed in private property in principle, rejecting only bourgeois property, which he believed was acquired by exploitation of workers. He founded an organized group, and the French labor movement arguably drew as much inspiration from him as from Karl Marx (1818–83), the German political philosopher then formulating his history-changing doctrine of communism. Proudhon rejected Marx's notion of a political revolution led by professional agitators. Rather, he affirmed that workers themselves must bring about change using economic, not political, methods. His was a purely theoretical ideal: The state would be replaced by a society based on free contracts in which power and property would be scattered so that no one class or elite could dominate. Though unschooled in economics and the author of several impossibly dense tracts, Proudhon formulated doctrines that proved strongly attractive to later leaders of French trade unionism.

Not all theories of social reform came from the left. Moderate and conservative views were also propounded, inspired partly by the urge to uphold Christian principles and partly by a genuine concern to redress the abuses produced by economic activity that was then largely unrestricted by government regulation (laissez-faire). The foundations of Christian socialism were laid by Catholics, including Philippe Buchez (1796–1865), who proclaimed that the principles of popular sovereignty and equality paralleled the message of the Gospel, and Félicité-Robert de Lamennais (1782–1854), who in his celebrated journal *L'Avenir* ("the future") advocated a liberal Christianity and the separation of church and state and who eventually broke with Rome. More truly conservative, Frédéric Le Play (1806–82) emerged as the main representative of traditional Catholicism who sought to reform society by restoring the authority of landowners and employers. A writer and one of the founders of the Society of St. Vincent de Paul (1833), Frédéric Ozanam (1813–53) sought to reform society, not through theorizing, but by aiding the poor.

Catholics—both theorists and activists—worked in a reinvigorated spiritual climate. The decline in religious belief and practice that so characterized the tumultuous years of the Revolution was followed by a resurgence of spiritual fervor. Forms of popular devotion increased, notably the cult of the Virgin Mary, which since the 16th century had played a growing role in Roman Catholic theology. The doctrine of the Immaculate Conception, that the mother of Jesus Christ was born free of original sin, was declared dogma by the Vatican in 1854, and the vision of the Virgin that allegedly came to the peasant girl Bernadette Soubirous (1844–79) in Lourdes, in southwestern France, in February 1858, in which Mary confirmed that belief, led to the founding of the shrine whose fame endures.

Unlike social science, natural science could draw on support from public authorities. Beginning with the Revolution and continuing through the Napoleonic era, the state encouraged scientific research and

Lourdes, ca. 1890s. Crutches left by those who claimed to have been cured hang to the left of the grotto. (Library of Congress, LC-DIG-ppmsc, 05305)

its practical applications. French scientists, many of them based at the Institut de France, the Collège de France, and the École Polytechnique, led the world in the early 19th century, although a lack of funds caused a decline in investigative efforts by the 1830s. Illustrious mathematicians Joseph-Louis, comte de La Grange (1736–1813) and Gaspard Monge (1746–1818) were joined by physicists Nicolas-Léonard Sadi Carnot (1796–1832) and André-Marie Ampère (1775–1836). Zoologist Georges Cuvier (1769–1832) formulated anatomic principles and laid the foundations for the study of paleontology. Naturalist Jean-Baptiste Lamarck (1744–1829) is known for his studies in invertebrate zoology and his theoretical work on evolution, which, with his belief that complex forms in nature derive from simpler ones, later strongly influenced Charles Darwin (1809–82). Experiments in utilizing light processes led Joseph-Nicéphore Niépce (1765–1833) and Jacques Daguerre (1789–1851) to develop the earliest type of photography. Teacher Louis Braille (1809–52), himself blind as a result of an accident as a child, devised a raised-dot system for reading and writing adopted, after his death, by the blind and visually impaired throughout the world.

Natural science and social science merged in the theories of Auguste Comte (1798–1857), who gave birth to the science of society, which he called sociology. Born in Montpellier, Comte broke with his Catholic and monarchist family and moved to Paris, where he married and divorced and began to study and write. He completed his four-volume masterpiece, *Système de politique positive (The System of Positive Polity)*, over three years (1851–54). One of the first theorists of social evolution, he formulated a "law of three phases" in arguing that society could be classified in sequences, starting with the theological—the period before the Enlightenment when humans were moved by blind faith in God—and moving through the metaphysical—the period just before the Revolution when humans began to reason and question authority and religion—to end in the scientific, which he called the positive—the current period when humans began to utilize science to provide solutions to social problems. A positive science, he affirmed, deals only with careful observation of the facts, a stage that his society was far from attaining, and it was the central mission of that society to move toward that goal. Comte gave positivism its motto: "Love as a principle and order as the basis; progress as the goal." The doctrine exerted an enormous impact in France, grounding theory in the real world of facts, just as socialism sought to achieve concrete results, either through trade unionism—achieving a redress of grievances working within the current system—or through revolution—overthrowing existing social, political, and economic conditions. Social theory thus moved away from idealistic utopianism toward realistic activism. This trend was mirrored by similar gradual changes in French arts and culture.

Neoclassicism to Romanticism to Realism

The years of the Revolution and the Napoleonic era were not conducive to intellectual pursuits owing to the strains and stresses of political upheaval and war. Rationalism in thought and neoclassicism in the decorative and visual arts remained preeminent. Drawing on Western classical art, in essence that of ancient Greece and Rome, neoclassicism emerged in the mid-18th century and received a powerful stimulus in the years that Napoléon strove to create an imperial domain for France to rival that of its Roman predecessor. In painting, the movement can be encapsulated in the career of one man. Jacques-Louis David (1748–1825) was strongly influenced by the classical work of Nicolas Poussin in adopting themes from Greek and Roman sources and employing the forms and gestures of ancient sculpture. His *Oath of the Horatii* (1784–85), which he painted in Rome and which won rave reviews at the Paris Salon of 1785, exemplifies the style. An ardent revolutionary, he adopted a realistic tone to depict contemporary scenes (*Death of Marat*, 1795), and he served as the official painter to Napoléon I, whose reign he recorded in prolific portraits and depictions of major events. David strongly influenced pupils such as Antoine Gros (1771–1835) (*Bonaparte at the Bridge of Arcole*, 1796) and Jean-Auguste-Dominique Ingres (1780–1867), whose *Vow of Louis XIII* won acclaim at the Paris Salon of 1824 and whose works would also, in turn, inspire many later painters.

At the same time as these artists worked, new modes of thinking and designing gradually took shape. A movement defined as romanticism came to dominate, though by no means fully rule, the cultural scene, it being impossible to confine creative periods in precise time frames, there being too many contradictions and variants within romanticism itself for it to be strictly defined. Nevertheless, the years of tension and turmoil had undermined the solid foundation of certainty on which the 18th-century age of reason had rested. For many, pessimism replaced optimism. A deeper interest in, and speculation about, spiritual issues, including questionings about death and eternity, rose to the fore.

Romantics revolted against rigid rules and formulas and affirmed that humankind is—or should be—guided by warm-hearted emotion rather than cold-blooded reason. The universe did not operate, as Enlightenment thinkers had so confidently affirmed, according to unvarying mechanical laws; rather, it was constantly changing and evolving. Romantics searched for beauty and found it, not in what they saw as the ugly reality of an emerging industrial world, but in the glories of nature that could be found all around them and in the cultures and customs of mysterious, faraway places—the exotic East—and heroic, myth-filled, long-ago times—the Middle Ages.

Romanticism was an international movement that could look to Jean-Jacques Rousseau among others for its inspirational predecessors. It was from Rousseau in particular that George Sand (1804–76), the pen name of Aurore Dupin, drew guidance in writing her novels (*Leila*, 1833), which she used to advocate social reforms and humanitarianism, as well as to confront social prejudices and conventions in the same way that she did—in a succession of celebrated love affairs—in her own life.

Romanticism rose steadily in popularity in the 1820s and 1830s. The emotion-charged play *Hernani* by Victor Hugo (1802–85), which opened in February 1830, created a sensation, despite being panned by critics, who, wedded to the past, complained that it violated one classical rule after another. Born in Besançon, poet, novelist, and playwright Hugo provided the greatest literary impetus to romanticism in France. He sought to emulate Chateaubriand, whose works emphasized introspection and pessimism, and who in the early 19th century exerted a profound impact on religious and literary culture with his assertion that Christianity was morally and aesthetically superior to other creeds (*Génie du christianisme [Genius of Christianity]*, 1802). Like Chateaubriand, who served as foreign minister (1823–24), Hugo, too, became active in politics, turning away from writing after a period, from 1829 to 1843, during which he produced his great historical novel, *Notre-Dame de Paris* (*The Hunchback of Notre Dame*, 1831) and several volumes of lyric poetry. Raised a Bonapartist, he became a royalist and then a republican. A firm critic of Louis-Napoléon, he spent 15 years in exile on the British island of Guernsey, where he completed his longest and most famous work, *Les misérables* (1862).

The writer who most fulfilled the romantics' penchant for a legendary past filled with gallant heroes was Alexandre Dumas (1802–70). With little formal education, Dumas became a prolific writer remembered for his historical novels *Les trois mousquetaires* (*The Three Musketeers*, 1844) and *Le comte de Monte-Cristo* (*The Count of Monte Cristo*, 1844). François Guizot earned a reputation as an eloquent writer of nonfiction history, but France's premier historian of this and later periods was Jules Michelet (1798–1874), whose multivolume *Histoire de France* (*History of France*, 1833–67) and *Histoire de la révolution française* (*History of the French*

Revolution, 1847–53) were meticulously researched and written in an eloquent, lyrical style interlaced with humanistic, democratic ideas.

The election of Alphonse Lamartine to the Académie Française in 1830 marked the triumph of romanticism in poetry. With a gift for composing short poems whose lyrics are known for their strong sentiments tinged with a gentle melancholy, Lamartine also wrote history, biography, and fiction, and he returned to writing after the assumption to power of Napoléon III, whose regime he opposed.

Romanticism in painting emerged full-blown in the work of Théodore Géricault (1791–1824), whose renowned *Raft of the Medusa* (1819), drawn on an actual shipwreck, constitutes a moving paean against inhumanity. Géricault imparted a profound influence to Eugène Delacroix (1798–1863), the greatest of the romantic painters, whose *Massacre at Chios* (1824) depicts a similar horrific incident during the war for Greek independence and is considered a veritable manifesto of the romantic school. Noted for his expanded range of color, Delacroix has

In Liberty Leading the People, *Eugène Delacroix depicts Marianne as a warrior armed with a rifle and raising the republican tricolor in rallying the charge during the Revolution of 1830.* (Scala/Art Resource, NY)

MARIANNE AND THE GALLIC ROOSTER

F rance has two unofficial symbols, each of which evokes a particular element of the national heritage. The image of a woman named Marianne represents France as a republic and the principles of liberty and equality under the law for which it stands. The name and its origins are uncertain, although an image of a female figure, accompanied by accessories such as the cockerel, the tricolor cockade, and the revolutionary Phrygian cap, date to the Revolution of 1789. Two Mariannes were authorized by the Second Republic: a bellicose and a pacific version. Her image on postage stamps first appeared in 1849. Statues were erected under the Third Republic, and during World War II, she represented liberty against Nazi tyranny and the Free French against the Vichy regime. The cult has declined in recent times, the need to call attention to republican virtues no longer essential now that the republic is firmly established. But an image of Marianne is featured on the official logo of the French Republic and on French euro coins.

The Gallic rooster (Fr., *le coq gaullois*) claims a much older history that dates to the Middle Ages, given that it symbolizes France as a national territory and the broad history and culture with which it is associated. Its connection to France stems from a play on Latin words, *Gallus*, meaning an inhabitant of Gaul, and *gallus*, meaning rooster, or cockerel. The Gallic rooster won widespread popularity during the French Revolution, and it is frequently used today as a national mascot at sporting events and as an advertising logo.

left an evocative glorification of the striving for human freedom in his *Liberty Leading the People* (1830), a tribute to the Revolution of 1830, with its depiction of Marianne, an allegorical female figure denoting deliverance from oppression.

Even at the height of the romantic movement, a few forerunners of new moods emerged. Stendhal (pseudonym of Henri-Marie Beyle, 1783–1842) wrote masterpieces of romantic fiction, including his famous *Le rouge et le noir* (*The Red and the Black*, 1830), that point the way to the psychological novels of the late 19th century. A transition away from romanticism toward realism and materialism is best seen in the novels, plays, essays, and short stories of Honoré de Balzac (1799–1850), whose work *La comédie humaine* (*The Human Comedy*, 1842–48) consists of a cycle of approximately 90 novels, among them *Les chouans* (*The Chouans*, 1829), *Sarrasine* (1830), and *Père Goriot* (*Father Goriot*, 1834), that combine romantic sentimentality with historical accuracy and factual descriptions.

The Revolution of 1848 marked not only a political but also a cultural turning point for the nation. Part the product and part the culmination of romanticism, the revolution in its artistic manifestations was followed, in the 1850s, by a dramatic change of tone and temper in literature and the arts. A new mood of realism, which strove to depict subjects as they appear in everyday life, is especially evident in literature in the works of Gustave Flaubert (1821–80). Born in Rouen, the son of a well-to-do physician, Flaubert applied his trademark skill at dissecting characters and society in almost clinical fashion, which, in his most famous novel, *Madame Bovary* (1857), produced an objective if somewhat sordid—he was tried but acquitted for offenses to public morals—portrayal of ordinary individuals whom he makes unforgettable together with an accurate depiction of the historical period. Poet Charles Baudelaire (1821–67) shared Flaubert's contempt for the bourgeoisie. An unhappy child and adolescent, he early adopted a bohemian lifestyle that scandalized his family. When he resolved to devote himself to writing, he was determined to convey the exploration of his inner states. Like Flaubert, he earned the ire of the government. Though fined for violating public sensibilities in his *Les fleurs du mal* (*Flowers of Evil*, 1857), a work now acknowledged as a classic, literary circles came to his support, appreciating his great skill in choosing exquisitely appropriate poetic verse to convey the never-ending conflict between the ideal and the sensual.

If Flaubert can be considered the father of realistic fiction, Gustave Courbet (1819–77) fills that role in painting. Proudly adopting the label of "realist" pinned to him by his rivals, he led the charge in the visual arts away from the flights of fancy depicted so preeminently in the works of Delacroix toward portrayals of virtually photographic precision (*A Burial at Ornans*, 1850). A superb landscape artist, Jean-François Millet (1814–75), himself the son of peasants, painted detailed portraits and scenes drawn from nature (*The Winnower*, 1848).

Honoré Daumier (1808–79) was acclaimed the greatest political caricaturist of the age. A more rigorous, science-based approach to history was taken by leading philologist and historian of religion Ernest Renan (1823–92), whose *Vie de Jésus* (*Life of Jesus*, 1863) attempts to reconcile religion and science in offering a more rationally based—and less theologically centered—interpretation of Christ.

In architecture, though neoclassicism continued to inspire building forms down to the Second Empire, a more eclectic style based on elements drawn from both the classical and the baroque emerged in the works of planners trained at the École des Beaux-Arts, on view notably in the Paris Opera, built from 1861 to 1875 to a design by Jean-Louis-Charles Garnier (1825–98). Among sculptural artists, the works of François Rude (1784–1855) displayed classical precision, romantic expression, and realistic appearance, while the flowing draperies and graceful figures of his pupil Jean-Baptiste Carpeaux (1827–75) make him a leading exponent of the romantic school.

Trends evolved throughout the world of arts, except in music, in which romantic strands remained dominant throughout the 19th century. Hector Berlioz (1803–69) earned renown for his *Symphonie fantastique* (1830). Paris-born Georges Bizet (1838–75) is best known for his opera *Carmen* (1875), a masterpiece of lyrical drama, while Charles Gounod (1818–93), also Paris-born, wrote not only operas but also religious music, symphonies, and melodies. His style and lyrics influenced Belgian-born César Franck (1822–90), whose symphonies and sonatas were imbued with mystical and brooding qualities. No one has surpassed Polish-born Frédéric Chopin (1810–49) for works for solo piano that earned for him a reputation as the poet of that instrument. Writing in the classical tradition of French composition, Paris-born composer, pianist, and organist Camille Saint-Saëns (1835–1921) combined elegant and exact forms with a lyrical style in piano and violin concertos, melodies, symphonic poems, and the opera *Samson et Dalila* (1877), his most famous work. German-born Jacques Offenbach (1819–80) is the quintessential composer of comic opera, or "opera bouffe," romantic operettas reflecting the lively Parisian spirit that his works have forever identified with the Second Empire. His career climaxed only after his death with the premiere of *Contes d'Hoffmann* (*Tales of Hoffmann*, 1881), which contains his memorable "Barcarolle." Opera dominated vocal music in France during the 18th century, but the popular chanson underwent a rebirth in the 1800s, first with salon melodies followed at mid-century by highly sophisticated works featuring romantic songs composed to a poem, often with piano or orchestral accompaniment.

The salons that had played so prominent a role as gathering places for intellectuals in the 18th century remained popular, but exposure to literary tastes began to broaden among the public as improved technology increased the speed and quantity of printing. Predecessors of the modern library, *cabinets de lecture* (reading rooms), introduced in major cities in the 18th century, spread rapidly in the early decades of the 19th century. Accompanying the growth of newspapers, the *roman-feuilleton* (serial novel) flourished in the 1840s. In these fictional stories set in fanciful worlds, readers could escape the very real troubles that afflicted the country at the end of that decade.

The Second Republic, 1848–1852

The provisional government cobbled together in February 1848 contained competent men—all solidly bourgeois save for one solitary laborer, Alexandre Martin (1815–95), known as workman Albert—but only the poet Lamartine possessed sufficient name recognition to emerge as spokesman for the government. Elections in April for a constituent assembly produced a moderate majority, which Lamartine proved incapable of dominating. No one appeared with the leadership skills needed to deal with crisis, which pervaded public life. The peasantry in less prosperous central and southern France rose spontaneously in rural risings reminiscent of the Great Fear of 1789. They quickly turned against the regime after the government imposed a surtax on landowners to pay for the national workshops. The workshops themselves became the focus of fear and hostility. The projects proved exorbitantly expensive and a scandal to those among the better-off who viewed them as a reward for idleness. They had failed to lower the high level of unemployment, while the hopes of radicals to use them as a revolutionary base frightened moderates and conservatives. Plans were drawn up to close them down along with a far more drastic measure—to offer either enlistment in the army to younger enrolled men or work in the provinces to those who were older. The program was duly enacted, leaving working-class leaders, who learned of the scheme on June 21, bitterly resentful. They organized a protest for June 22. Demonstrations that day rapidly turned into open clashes, and for five days, a short, violent civil war—the so-called June Days—raged in the streets of Paris. The forces of order—the army, the Mobile Guard, and the National Guard—led by General Eugène Cavaignac (1802–57), a conservative republican, savagely slaughtered perhaps as many as 3,000 rioters after they had surrendered, adding to the approximately 1,500 killed in the fighting. Thousands who were arrested were deported to labor camps in Algeria.

A five-man civilian executive council was replaced temporarily by a military dictatorship under Cavaignac. Lamartine disappeared into the political wilderness, while the Parisian radicals were obliterated as a political force, their leaders either killed, imprisoned, or exiled. Class divisions hardened in the wake of the insurrection—the middle classes and aristocrats further confirmed in their fear of the lower orders and the workers sullen and embittered at a regime that had betrayed their interests.

The enthusiasm that had marked the early days of the republic dissipated. Cavaignac was named temporary president of the council of ministers, which he recast in a more conservative mold. Many reforms enacted in February and March, including a reduction of the working day in Paris factories to 10 hours, were repealed. A constituent assembly elected in June drew up a final draft of a constitution for the republic. Completed in November, the constitution of 1848 enshrined two central principles: the sovereignty of the people and the separation of powers. It provided for a single-chamber Corps Législatif (Legislative Assembly) to be elected for three years, assured civil rights, and retained universal male suffrage. Voters chose a president, responsible to the assembly, to serve a four-year nonrenewable term.

Hovering in the wings all the while, Louis-Napoléon followed events keenly. Having escaped from prison in 1846, he returned from exile in Britain at the outbreak of the February revolution, and he quickly announced his intention to run for the presidency in the elections that were set for December. Despite having little money and no clear platform except to promise something for everyone, Louis waged a superbly skillful campaign, winning in a landslide in securing the support most especially of Orléanists, legitimists, and Catholics. Five months, later elections to the Legislative Assembly produced a triumph for monarchists, divided though they were between legitimist and Orléanist factions. Moderate republicans were almost annihilated, but radical republicans made some gains.

Drawing on this modest upsurge, the radicals on the left retained their itch for power. Attempting an uprising in June 1849, they drew little popular support and were easily suppressed, but their failed gamble gave Louis-Napoléon an opportunity to exile many of the leaders and in so doing to free himself from any serious threats from the left. At the end of October, he felt sufficiently secure to dismiss his cabinet and appoint one wholly to his liking.

Education remained the outstanding domestic issue. Catholics had waged a 10-year campaign to obtain greater influence, and now, with an assembly filled with friendly conservatives and with moderates who, in the wake of the June Days, were inclined to fortify clerical influence and the respect for law and order that would presumably be taught in church-run schools, their efforts paid off. On March 15, 1850, the Falloux Law, named for its architect, minister of public instruction

Frédéric-Albert, count of Falloux (1811–86), gave the church the right to operate *collèges* (elementary and secondary schools) alongside those of the state, increased sectarian influence in the supervision of public elementary schools, and added schools for girls to those for boys in communes whose population exceeded 500. Local officials could appoint a priest to teach in a state school and could even provide no school at all, if a church school already existed. The clericals had won their victory but at the expense of arousing anticlericals anew, who grew more convinced than ever that the church sought a complete lock on education as part of a campaign to tighten its control on the state.

Louis-Napoléon never intended to content himself with serving just one term as president, as the constitution prescribed. The stage was set to further his ambitions as early as May 1849, when, to curb the voting strength of radicals, who were winning by-elections, a new suffrage law, in raising the voting age and requiring three years' residence, deprived 3 million citizens of the right to vote. His efforts to revise the constitution to lift the four-year term limit, however, failed in the assembly in July 1851. Blocked by the legal path, he schemed to overthrow the system entirely.

To do so he needed the backing of the army. Since 1799, the military had remained aloof from politics, but it had seen its morale and prestige decline steadily since the heady days of the Napoleonic Empire. Most of the officers disliked the republic, viewing it as a government of bickering lawyers, and they leaned toward a return to monarchy. Accordingly, they cooperated fully in Louis's plan. The assembly reconvened, and Louis introduced a proposal to restore universal suffrage, a clever move that, knowing full well the legislators would reject the measure, would allow him to pose before the public as the champion of democracy.

On the morning of December 2, 1851, the leading legislators were roused from their beds and arrested. The assembly was dissolved and martial law declared. Monarchists raised cries of protest—some of their assembly members tried to depose the president but were arrested. On the night of December 3, barricades went up in the working-class quarters of Paris. Anti-Bonapartist rioters were dispersed with considerable loss of life, and government forces met with even heavier resistance in the provinces. Louis ordered a referendum, which returned the expected approval for the move, though the figure of 92 percent is highly suspect, given the level of opposition. Voters ratified a revision of the constitution providing for a 10-year presidential term and a reduction in the legislature's powers.

An authoritarian republic was now in place, but it was obvious that it existed only as a way station on the road to dictatorship. On December

2, 1852, Louis-Napoléon announced his intention to promote himself from president to emperor. No murmurs of protest were raised. Docile voters registered their approval, once again in a plebiscite, this time by a vote of 97 percent. Only one year after the coup d'état, France became an empire for the second time under a third Napoléon.

The Second Empire, 1852–1870

Under Napoléon III's authoritarian constitution, in the two-house legislature the Senate was given some important constitutional powers, but, because all of its members were appointed, it could be reliably counted on to give the emperor no problems. The Legislative Assembly, while elected, met no more than three months a year under appointed officers and was allowed to debate only what was put before it. A muzzled press, an omnipresent police, and an efficient administration ensured that no one and nothing might surface to trouble the imperial will.

Emperor Napoléon III, Empress Eugénie, and their son, the Prince Imperial (1856–79), ca. 1860 (Adoc-photos/Art Resource, NY)

That will remained elusive. Louis-Napoléon held few if any sincere convictions. A charming and well-meaning man, he was intensely secretive, making few pronouncements and relying only on a few trusted supporters and on his relatives, including the new empress, the Spanish countess Eugénie de Montijo (1826–1920), who was beautiful and devoutly religious, and who exerted an increasingly conservative influence on him. Having seized power with the backing of only a handful of followers, the emperor needed a wider base of support, which he found in rounding up candidates for the Legislative Assembly from different political persuasions, together with men grown newly wealthy in commerce and industry.

214

Supported by the business class, the church hierarchy, and the peasantry, Louis-Napoléon's authoritarian grip held firm throughout most of the 1850s, the calm ruffled only by a few ripples. Opposition sentiment appeared in the elections of 1857, when five republican members of the assembly were elected, and in 1858, when Italian conspirator Felice Orsini (1819–58) came close to assassinating the emperor and empress with a bomb.

The country still remained very rural, although a drift to the cities set in during mid-century. Large landowners coexisted with small peasant farmers, who remained stubbornly resistant to change, inclined to invest their meager savings in more land than in improved agricultural implements. Tenants and sharecroppers could be found in addition to a large population of landless laborers. Regional variations were marked—northern and eastern areas, especially along the Belgian border, were the most technologically advanced.

By mid-century, the harnessing of steam to produce power—the defining achievement of the Industrial Revolution—was well advanced. Steam in conjunction with iron produced the railway age. By 1870, the major lines were completed, and by the 1880s, the secondary lines, which brought connecting links to places that had remained isolated for centuries. The business slump of the late 1840s was followed by a major boom. Industrial production doubled between 1852 and 1870, and foreign trade grew more than in any other European country. New forms of business organization based on limited liability and favoring large-scale enterprise emerged with adoption of a law to allow the formation of corporations in 1867. The stock exchange flourished with the resulting growth in capital formation. In the cities, department stores appeared. The government encouraged private investment. Both deposit and investment banks were formed, and iron and textile industries were modernized. In 1860, the regime undertook an about-face from France's traditional high-tariff policy when it concluded the Chevalier-Cobden Treaty with Britain, followed by similar agreements with other nations that introduced widespread free trade, the only such interlude during the century.

Under the emperor's prefect of the Seine, Georges-Eugène, Baron Haussmann (1809–91), Paris was literally rebuilt. Much of the medieval city disappeared, replaced by wide boulevards interspersed by circular plazas, the designs motivated as much by the need for urban renovation as by the desire to facilitate military maneuvers and forestall the characteristic street barricades of the capital's 19th-century insurrections. Haussmann's rebuilding destroyed large areas where workers and middle-class residents had resided in the same buildings. These structures were replaced by new apartment houses far too expensive for poorer tenants, and this launched a general move by them to the suburbs. Henceforth, the heart of the city would be thoroughly bourgeois, ringed all around by a "red" proletarian belt.

Placidity at home gave the regime the chance to pursue a rather aggressive, if erratic, foreign policy. In alliance with Britain, France waged the Crimean War (1854–56) against Russia, and the peace conference, held in Paris, signified the country's status as a central player in European diplomacy. The Suez Canal was begun in 1859 and opened in 1869, built largely with French capital under the direction of admin-

THE FRENCH RIVIERA

The French Riviera (Fr., *la Côte d'Azur* [azure coast]) extends along France's southeastern Mediterranean coast from the Italian border west to approximately the town of Hyères. The sunny, hot, and dry summers and mild winters made it one of the world's earliest resort locales. It first emerged as a fashionable destination for upper-class British travelers seeking good health in the late 18th century, before then having been a remote, poor region known largely for fishing, olive groves, and cultivation of flowers with which to make perfume. A warm climate was prescribed to cure a variety of diseases and illnesses, and British resident enclaves were founded at Cannes and elsewhere. The incorporation of Nice and its environs into France in 1860 and the arrival of the first railroad in 1864 made the Riviera accessible to large numbers of visitors, who arrived from all over Europe. The region welcomed aristocrats from distant Russia as well as royalty, including Napoléon III and Britain's queen Victoria (r. 1837–1901). Gambling appeared in mid-century when the prince of Monaco built a resort and casino in his tiny principality adjacent to France, where gaming was then illegal.

At the turn of the 20th century, painters such as Auguste Renoir and Pablo Picasso began to join the titled rich in frequenting coastal communities. They were followed after World War I by American writers, including Edith Wharton (1862–1937) and F. Scott Fitzgerald (1896–1940). The launching of the Cannes Film Festival in September 1946 marked not only the return of French films to world cinema but also the return of the Riviera as a resort destination after the ravages

istrator Ferdinand de Lesseps (1805–94). The emperor's decision to help Camillo Benso, count of Cavour (1810–61), the prime minister of Piedmont, drive the Austrians out of northern Italy in 1859 led to war with Vienna and to a settlement in which Italy emerged as a united nation and France won territories—Nice and Savoy—that extended its Mediterranean coastline to include what would become the fabled French Riviera.

The Italian war marked a turning point for the regime. The victory won the emperor prestige, but not from all quarters. His support of Italian nationalism alienated French Catholics because it endangered the pope's temporal rule of the Papal States. The trade treaty with

of World War II. The rich and famous came back, now joined for the first time by many thousands from among the less well-to-do. Trade fairs and business conventions also make the Riviera a prime venue.

Promenade des Anglais, Nice, ca. 1909 (Library of Congress)

Britain aroused concern among manufacturers, fearful that without tariff protection the boom of the 1850s would be threatened.

The policy turn toward domestic liberalization launched late in 1859 and that continued spottily throughout the 1860s may have been inspired by a wish to find a new base of support to replace those lost, or it may have been spawned by a concern to reconcile conflicting past political traditions by giving liberals a more active voice to balance the authoritarian character of the regime. In any case, more moderate press laws were enacted in 1860–61. The Legislative Assembly was given some real power to debate and granted greater control over finances. In great secrecy in 1869, Louis contacted Émile Ollivier (1825–1913), a leading opposition figure elected to the legislature in 1857. A dedicated moderate republican, Ollivier was, however, not averse to subordinating political principles to duty to country. In early January 1870, an Ollivier cabinet appeared, and in May, a plebiscite ratified a new, liberal constitution, which put in place a working parliamentary system while preserving important powers for the emperor.

But the scheme was given no time to proceed. The 1860s proved ruinous for Louis-Napoléon's foreign policy. His Mexican venture—an attempt to put in place a French puppet empire under Archduke Maximilian of Austria (1832–67)—drained manpower and funds and ended in disaster. Through the course of several wars—with Denmark (1864) and Austria (1866)—Prussia emerged, under the competent statesmanship of its chancellor, Otto von Bismarck (1815–98), as a potent and aggressive continental power. France backed the loser in the Austro-Prussian War, and the emperor's wounded pride demanded that he secure a victory somewhere. A bid to buy the Grand Duchy of Luxembourg was nixed by Bismarck.

Conscious of the new power on the rise to the east, when news broke in July 1870 that a prince from the Prussian royal House of Hohenzollern would accept the vacant Spanish throne, French public opinion voiced alarm at the potential menace posed by a Prussian presence on two of the country's borders. The candidacy was withdrawn. France appeared to have won the diplomatic round when, the emperor ill and distracted, the empress and Louis's new foreign minister, the duc de Gramont (1819–80), insisted that the French ambassador in Berlin demand an assurance from King William I of Prussia (r. 1861–88) that the Hohenzollern candidacy would not be renewed, an impertinent demand to a reigning sovereign made worse by the ambassador importuning the king in a public park at Ems, a spa where William was taking the waters. The ambassador and the king exchanged cordial remarks, but Bismarck, ever ready to advance Prussia's position, shortened the conversation to make it sound as if the king had abruptly dismissed the French envoy. He released the edited "Ems dispatch" to the press, which published the news. Reacting to the apparent snub of their diplomat, crowds gathered in the streets of Paris, clamoring for a march on Berlin to avenge French honor. Government officials hesitated when the truth about Ems became known, but by then events had overtaken them. The nationalist hysteria now at fever pitch, France declared war on July 19, 1870.

Brimming with confidence, the French counted on their weaponry, the *chassepot* rifle—believed better than the Prussian needle gun—and the *mitrailleuse*—an early machine gun. But superior military technology could not make up for poor advance planning and faulty generalship. A French army was surrounded in the fortress of Metz while an attempt to relieve the besieged forces, led by General Edme de Mac-Mahon (1808–98) and the emperor himself, met with defeat at Sedan on September 1. Prussian armies advanced on Paris, and with their approach, the Second Empire collapsed.

With the emperor now a Prussian captive, republicans saw their chance. On September 4, crowds burst into the Legislative Assembly and turned for leadership to Léon Gambetta (1838–82), a lawyer, eloquent orator, and opponent of Napoléon III who had been elected to the assembly in 1869. Louis-Napoléon was deposed—the imperial family departing for Britain, the perennial destination for 19th-century French royal exiles—while the Bonapartist caretaker government was replaced by one of national defense, with Gambetta in the key post of minister of the interior, which he believed he could use to consolidate a republican victory. The war went on, the capital of a broken France moving first to Tours and then to Bordeaux. Although initially opposed to war, once it had been declared Gambetta rallied to his nation's cause, and with Paris now surrounded by Prussian troops, he made a dramatic escape in a hot-air balloon to direct the struggle. The capital braced for a siege that, in the end, would prove more devastating for the defenders than for the invaders.

9

REPUBLICAN RULE TAKES ROOT (1870–1914)

France emerged from the defeat of 1870–71 on profoundly unsteady feet. Its political direction remained unsure. A republic was declared, which the voters in the countryside promptly decided would be led by monarchists. Urban dwellers fought back, creating in Paris a "Commune" more radical than any governing experiment yet, which the government quelled but only at the price of unparalleled savagery.

It took a decade for the republic to find its way, helped by the moderation of its supporters and by the divisions and mistakes of its opponents. The regime's survival assured by 1880, the nation settled into a governing routine that, with its powerless presidents and its premiers presiding over unstable ruling coalitions, often made for sterile politics but that, by the 1890s, had become familiarly comfortable and sufficiently strong to withstand the turmoil unleashed by the Dreyfus affair, the one crisis that carried the potential to wreck the system. Republican consolidation was completed in 1905 when the recurrently vexatious religious issue was settled definitively with the separation of church and state.

With politics now following a regular routine, the country embarked on a prosperity drive, every economic indicator on the rise save for population growth. At the turn of the 20th century, France's standard of living ranked among the highest on the Continent. Paris became the internationally acknowledged trendsetting capital of the arts, high fashion, and entertainment. A new age beckoned with a host of marvelous inventions—automobiles, airplanes, the cinema—many of them pioneered in France.

In the years after 1900, new social strains arose in what was by now a mature industrial society. Socialists battled for workers' rights. Anarchists sought the destruction of the state. Right-wing activists glorified order and authority.

220

Disagreements ran rife. Only in foreign affairs were French citizens of every social stripe able to unite, and only around one central issue—Alsace-Lorraine—that for 30 years had never disappeared. The loss of the two provinces in the Franco-Prussian War burned deep, the statues in Paris of Strasbourg and Metz kept draped in black crêpe as a symbolic statement of the national resolve not to forget. Between 1871 and 1914, Franco-German relations evolved from vague mistrust into hardened hostility. A system of alliances gradually took shape with Europe's great powers formed up on two sides, each probing for advantage while building up formidable military machines that turned the Continent into a powder keg set to explode. Statesmen long expected that a crisis would arise to light the match; and yet, when at last it arrived—in the early summer of 1914—it appeared quite by surprise.

Making the Third Republic Secure, 1870–1899

In January 1871, Paris fell to the Prussians. In early February, Gambetta was out of office, and at Chancellor Bismarck's insistence a National Assembly was chosen in a hasty, impromptu election to put a government in place that could make both peace and a constitution for the country. In a dramatic repudiation of Gambetta and his supporters, who staunchly advocated that the war continue, peace-seeking rural voters elected more than 400 monarchists to the assembly. Only some 200 republicans and a handful of Bonapartists were selected. The new German Empire, proclaimed at Versailles in January, dictated terms in the peace signed at Frankfurt on May 10, 1871. France was saddled with a huge indemnity, an occupation army, and the loss of all of Alsace and half of Lorraine, rich in iron ore, coal, and textile manufacturing, and largely French-speaking. It was a bitter settlement with which to begin a new government, headed by Adolphe Thiers, a lifelong Orléanist and by now very elderly.

A bitter civil war in Paris and several other major cities added to the strain. A city already seething with tension in the wake of the prolonged siege, Paris erupted in fury when the government suspended hostilities and the provinces voted for peace. Republican Paris rejected the monarchist character of the new assembly, and its decision to move the government to Versailles inflamed Parisians' sensitivities. On March 18, 1871, when Thiers's government attempted to haul 20 cannons away from the city, angry mobs dragged the arms to the heights of Montmartre and drove off the troops. Thiers refused either to hit back or to negotiate; instead, he withdrew all officials and armed forces from

Paris Commune, barricade in the rue Royale, May 1871 (Adoc-photos/Art Resource, NY)

the city and prepared for a siege. Left to themselves, socialists, follow-ers both of Blanqui—then a prisoner at Versailles—and of Proudhon, joined with anarchists, anticlericals, proud republicans, anti-German patriots, and assorted agitators to organize the city as a self-govern-ing Commune, calling for the entire country to be converted into a decentralized federation of similarly organized cities. For nine weeks a standoff ensued. The Commune drafted measures favored by the workers, but before they could be implemented, having assembled a force sufficiently strong to strike, Thiers mounted an attack on May 21. Communards dug in and fought back, battling street by street. After a week of bloodletting, and facing imminent defeat, the Communards set fire to most of the public buildings—the Hôtel de Ville and the Tuileries palace were burned, Notre-Dame and the Louvre barely saved. Neither side showed mercy. Government forces shot anyone caught with a weapon; the Communards executed a host of hostages, includ-ing members of the old police force and the archbishop of Paris. In the most murderous civil clash in modern French history, an estimated 20,000 died in the suppression of the Commune during Bloody Week. Thousands more were deported to penal colonies, while others man-aged to escape into exile. The Commune left a lasting imprint, and the myths it engendered inspired generations of left-wing radicals and communists, who, following Karl Marx, affirmed that it was the first clear-cut case of the proletariat fighting back against its oppressors.

With a government run by now triumphant monarchists, the republic appeared doomed. Yet, the civil war itself may have helped it to survive. Republicanism was purged of its most radical leaders and, for the next several decades, fell under the control of moderates whose more temperate policies calmed the fears of the conservative countryside, while at the same time the victory of a republican form of government, never mind that it was dominated by the right, showed that it could be tough even against republicans when they threatened the public order.

The new republic was helped by the disunity—they were split three ways—and the stupidity of the monarchists. The Bonapartists hoped to bring Napoléon III back to power. Divided into roughly equal factions, the Legitimists and the Orléanists could not unite around a candidate for a revived French throne. Henry, the comte de Chambord (1820–83), grandson of Charles X, scuttled any chance when, returning to France in 1871 for the first time since 1830, he set out terms that implied a return to the arbitrary, paternalistic pre-1830 conditions, including restoration of the Bourbons' fleur-de-lis flag.

Most monarchist politicians wanted a British-type king, subject to a parliament's control. While the supporters of the pretenders bickered, the candidates on the right began to lose to republicans in one by-election after another. Right-wing leaders grew nervous. Seeking to repress the left and move toward some type of monarchical restoration, they were given no help from Thiers, who, though a constitutional monarchist, was happy enough with the existing political arrangement. Under his tutelage, the nation restored some of its self-confidence while it learned that a republic could be sane and responsible. An army composed largely of professionals having performed so poorly, general conscription was introduced in 1872, and within four years of the 1870–71 defeat, the country raised an army on a par with that of Germany; by 1873, the war indemnity was paid and German troops departed 18 months ahead of schedule. In May 1873, Thiers, too, was gone, replaced by Edme-Patrice-Maurice, comte de Mac-Mahon, a distinguished royalist general made a marshal who commanded the defeated army at Sedan and under whose leadership the Commune had been repressed, but, as a military man, a figure who lacked political skills. Legislative affairs were managed by the duc Albert de Broglie (1821–1901), a monarchist who was realist enough to seek compromise.

Since 1870, though a government was operating, no permanent political structure was in place. In 1875, a provisional state of affairs was finally put to right in a series of laws passed by the assembly that together composed a constitution. Made possible by the cooperation of moderates on both left and right, the compromise document was republican in name but monarchist in form. The nation would be governed by a two-house legislature consisting of a Senate and a Chamber of Deputies, a cabinet led by a premier responsible to that legislature, and a president of the republic elected by an absolute majority of both.

It was a patchwork arrangement that would last for 65 years, and at the outset it proved sufficiently workable to confirm the republicanism of the republic when, on May 16, 1877 (seize mai), President Mac-Mahon precipitated a crisis. Acting within his constitutional power, he dismissed the premier, dissolved the chamber, and appealed to the country to give him a legislature to his liking. Instead, the nation returned a significant republican majority to the Chamber of Deputies, and elections in 1879 produced a Senate with a similar makeup. Unable to govern, Mac-Mahon resigned. Jules Grévy (1807–91), a die-hard republican, followed him in the presidency. The monarchists had shot their bolt and lost. The presidency emerged from the Mac-Mahon debacle as an impotent position; real power would henceforth lie with the premier, who, because he was responsible to the Chamber of Deputies, needed a majority of support there to govern. Since no single party ever succeeded in winning a majority at the polls, a working government had to be constructed.

Every four years, the country elected a Chamber of Deputies by universal male suffrage, and the premier, usually the head of the party that won the most seats, negotiated with that body to create, after often laborious wheeling and dealing, a coalition cabinet to govern the nation. Since at any time deputies could vote no confidence in the government, cabinets could rise and fall between election cycles, which they often did, giving the country an unsettled parliamentary regime that demanded skillful politicians to run it. But enough of them existed to keep the system in place, and it would take a world war, in 1940, to cause it to break.

From 1879 to 1899, political power remained largely in the hands of the moderate wing of republicans—the so-called Opportunists. The monarchists no longer possessed the strength to threaten the regime. On the far left, the Radicals constituted an emerging republican faction that, though growing as a force, were too weak to hope for anything more than a share in power. Formally organized political parties on the modern model did not exist; rather, groups coalesced and factions formed based on shared principles and goals.

Though the republic grew more and more assured, challenges still lurked. Monarchists acknowledged defeat, but they remained unreconciled. Autocratic bureaucrats and army officers, many of them conservative Catholics, secretly harbored royalist sentiments. Industrialization aggravated the split between the countryside, where the peasantry accepted the republic, and the city, where urban workers felt hobbled by antilabor laws. Though tolerated since the 1860s, trade unionism was not legalized until 1884.

Catholics emerged reinvigorated under the influence of both journalist Louis Veuillot (1813–83), a zealot who crusaded with all the fervor of a convert in demanding unrestricted control of education by the church, and a new religious order. Founded in 1845, the Assumptionist Fathers drew massive crowds, resuscitating the practice of pilgrimages that had been moribund since the Middle Ages on behalf of an emotional, fanatical appeal to faith. Through their low-cost journal La Croix ("the cross"), their millions of readers were told to return to devotion to make amends for 75 years of error and sin that had culminated in the defeat of 1871. With funds they collected, the Sacré-Coeur Basilica was built in Paris as a sign to the divine of the country's penitence.

The contempt professed by many Catholics for the republic was returned in kind. The Third Republic avidly embraced freedom of conscience. Viewing with disdain the insistence of religious authorities on molding the beliefs of citizens in the principles of the faith, the government moved cautiously but always in the direction of curbing the church's power. Laws were passed outlawing a number of monastic orders. Many devout Catholics could only recoil in horror at a series of school laws sponsored by minister of education and then premier Jules Ferry (1832–93) that, from 1879 to 1886, replaced religious with civic education and forced priests out of teaching positions in primary public instruction. Installation of lay elementary educators marked a deliberate new drive to inculcate republicanism as the creed of patriotic citizens, but the new corps of instructors also fueled old quarrels in pitting the local teacher against the local priest in a symbolic, but also very real, duel.

Scandals and affairs kept divisions alive, stoked by sensationalist newspapers and journals, at liberty to publish largely at will following legislation enshrining freedom of the press in 1881. Enough discontent existed in 1887 that it could coalesce around a single agent. A newcomer to politics, General Georges Boulanger (1837–91) was regarded as one of the true republicans in the officers' corps, and the Radicals secured his appointment as minister of war in early 1886. As war minister, he made himself a national hero virtually overnight. Reforming the army won him the support of the troops; sending soldiers to put down a strike won him the backing of businessmen; restoring the custom of military parades and issuing a public challenge to German chancellor Bismarck won him the adulation of all patriots. With a political war chest filled with abundant financial means from enthusiasts of both left and right, Boulanger scored resounding victories at the polls. He was poised to seize power when good republicans were shocked to learn of his secret dealings with monarchists. Once made public, his prestige rapidly diminished, and he fled the country, committing suicide in September 1891 at the grave of his mistress across the border in Brussels.

The Radicals, whose darling Boulanger had been, emerged from the episode divided and discredited, leaving their rivals the moderates (Opportunists) to govern another decade. Having survived a near brush with a possible dictatorship, republicans sighed with relief, their traditional distrust of strong men in politics deepened. On the right, some monarchists gave up the fight altogether, becoming conservative republicans. Catholics were encouraged to accept the republic as a fact and participate in its politics in a policy called *ralliement* from no less a source than the Vatican when Pope Leo XIII (r. 1878–1903) issued a statement in 1892 recommending that course. Bitter opposition now reposed largely with elements on the far right, who remained unreconciled. They took on a new militant spirit, proclaiming their fervent patriotism and putting blind trust in the army in adopting attitudes that heretofore had been associated with the Jacobin left.

The Boulanger affair fizzled out as a fiasco. The Dreyfus affair was a far more serious matter—it came close to destroying the republic. In 1880, a French company was formed to build a canal in Panama. To win support for their scheme, company officers paid bribes to politicians and newspapermen. But the company went bankrupt, and a public scandal erupted. Among the Panama Canal Company agents were several Jews who had allegedly bought off the politicians. Seizing on fear of a Jewish stranglehold over the country's finances, anti-Semites raised a hue and cry.

Racism had experienced a resurgence in France in the mid-19th century. Joseph-Arthur, comte de Gobineau (1816–82), launched modern theories of racial superiority with his most famous work, *Essai sur l'inégalité des races humaines* (*Essay on the Inequality of the Human Races*, 1853–55), in which he extolled the preeminence of the Aryan, or Nordic, race. Most prominent of all, Catholic journalist Édouard Drumont (1844–1913) founded an Anti-Semitic League in 1889 and a

Captain Alfred Dreyfus, second from right, with three other military officers, ca. 1900–16
(Library of Congress)

nationalist, anti-Semitic newspaper *La Libre Parole* ("the free word") in 1892. In fall 1894, the journal published sensational news that Alfred Dreyfus (1859–1935), a captain and the first Jew to join the French General Staff, had been arrested and charged with spying for the Germans after French counterintelligence had found an unsigned letter in a German embassy mailbox.

Yet the arrest raised more questions than it provided answers. Dreyfus's motives remained a mystery: He had no need of the money, the Germans paying what amounted to small change for Dreyfus, who came from a rich family from Alsace; furthermore, he had every reason to hate the Germans, forced as he was to leave his home province when it was ceded after the Franco-Prussian War. The only evidence against

227

him was a torn-up memorandum that some experts declared was in Dreyfus's handwriting. But what swayed the deliberators at his court-martial was information that Major Hubert-Joseph Henry (1846–98) of Military Intelligence hinted was so top secret that he could not even reveal it to the judges. In 1894, Dreyfus was convicted and sent to Devil's Island, the pestilential penal colony in French Guiana in South America, while much of public opinion congratulated the army for its superb efficiency.

Nevertheless, military secrets continued to flow to the German embassy. New evidence in 1896 cast suspicion on Major Ferdinand Esterhazy (1847–1923), a staff officer and the real culprit. The new chief of counterintelligence, Colonel Marie-Georges Picquart (1854–1914) reluctantly reopened the Dreyfus file and concluded that Dreyfus was innocent. Convinced Picquart was wrong, army authorities exiled him to the Tunisian desert, but the press learned of the goings-on and a few newspapers launched a crusade for a new trial. Henry took the precaution of forging some new documents to strengthen the case against Dreyfus, and the army accepted their validity, stubbornly refusing to reconsider the matter.

In what the French call simply *l'Affaire* (the Affair), by 1898, virtually the entire educated population had taken sides over the issue. Families were split; fights broke out in cafés and in the streets. In August 1898, faced with exposure, Henry confessed to his forgeries and committed suicide. A new trial was inevitable and the verdict, in September 1899, stunned those who believed Dreyfus to be innocent. He was found guilty but with extenuating circumstances. The president pardoned him, and his family, worried about his health after so much time in the tropics, accepted it.

But the affair had by now acquired a life of its own. Most republicans, as Dreyfusards, viewed the case as a battle between the forces of righteousness and of justice against those of bigotry and blind patriotism. Beyond those driven by pure religious hatred, the anti-Dreyfusards—religious and military leaders, their backers, and others on the far right—stuck to the principle that loyalty to the state should supersede the rights of individual citizens. Converted into a towering symbol, Dreyfus himself was almost forgotten. In 1904, he won a retrial, was acquitted, and, in 1906, was reinstated and decorated with the Legion of Honor.

The immediate political impact of the Dreyfus affair was to bring the Radicals into power in 1899, the turmoil having badly split the moderates. Suspicions across the entire left against the army and the church were aroused anew. The controversy had stirred emotions on every side in a nation now moving ahead under an unprecedented prosperity drive.

Economic Expansion and Social and Technological Change

During the half-century after the Franco-Prussian War, France experienced a remarkable spurt of economic growth. Industrial output tripled between 1870 and 1914; indexes of national income and investments abroad registered large gains. The currency remained stable, and the national budget balanced. Most of the progress occurred from about 1895 to 1914, the 1870s and 1880s experiencing not so much a decline as a slowdown in the significant expansion that had taken place during the Second Empire. Agriculture suffered in mid-century due to competition from overseas imports, while viticulture suffered major losses from the disastrous effects of a disease called *phylloxera,* which destroyed a third of the country's vineyards. Production of champagne, however, which had begun on a large scale in the first half of the century, brought a new and increasingly important addition to the wine industry.

After 1895, industrial development expanded. The discovery of the vast Briey iron-ore fields in French Lorraine proved especially significant. The Germans drew the 1871 boundary to give themselves most of the known iron deposits in the area, but the bulk of a huge subterranean field was found to lie just inside the French frontier. A new smelting process perfected in 1878 made the find exploitable, and by 1914, there were 20 iron- and steelworks in the region, producing two-thirds of the country's total pig iron (crude iron) and steel and supplying enough raw ore to make France the world's largest exporter of the mineral.

The new laboring masses created by the development of large industry became thoroughly imbued, as they did everywhere in Europe, with a distinct class consciousness in confronting working conditions that included long hours and dangerous and unhealthy environments. As a result, they began to clamor for greater rights to organize and for redress of grievances. Louis Napoléon had pursued a conciliatory approach, legalizing strikes (1864) and workers' cooperatives (1867) and encouraging mutual aid societies and credit institutions. Moves toward international cooperation led to formation of the First International in 1864, bringing together advocates for workers' rights from across Europe. A new militancy emerged when moderates were replaced by extremists—

229

CHAMPAGNE

The sparkling wine that takes its name from the northeastern French region where it is exclusively produced, champagne was perfected over a period of years in the 17th century. Vineyards cultivated here since at least the fifth century yielded wines traditionally used in anointing French kings during coronation festivities at Reims. At the far northern extreme of sustainable viticulture, the region of Champagne featured wines that were lighter-bodied and thinner, and vintners strove to produce a beverage to compete with the acclaimed vintages from Burgundy just to the south.

To counter the high-acidic and low-sugar levels, experimenters added sugar to a finished wine to create a second fermentation. Though he did not invent champagne, Benedictine monk Dom Perignon (1638–1715) discovered many advances in its production at his abbey at Hautvilliers, including holding the cork in place with a wire collar to withstand the fermentation process, a technique perfected only after so many bottles exploded, or the cork jolted away, that the beverage earned the label the "devil's wine."

In the traditional method of production, first developed in the 19th century, after initial fermentation and bottling, a second alcoholic fermentation occurs in the bottle, induced by adding sugar and yeast. Aging takes a minimum of 1.5 years. After aging, each bottle is turned, either mechanically or manually *(remuage)*, so that the dregs settle in the neck of the bottle. The bottles are chilled and, after the neck is frozen, the cap is removed. The pressure in the bottle forces out the ice containing the dregs, and the bottle is quickly corked to keep the carbon dioxide in solution.

Champagne experienced explosive growth in the first half of the 19th century, with production of approximately 300,000 bottles in 1800 expanding to 20 million by 1850 (Phillips 2000, 241). A series of disturbances known as the champagne wars erupted in 1910–11 spawned by years of crop losses from disease and the resulting lost income and by suspicions that merchants were importing grapes from outside the region. Following the outbursts, the government mandated that the label *Appellation d'Origine contrôlée* be used, signifying that wines produced only from grapes grown in designated geographical boundaries could be entitled to bear the name champagne. By the early 20th century, the reputation of champagne as a beverage with which to mark a celebratory occasion was well established.

determined republicans—in the French section of the International, indicative of the appearance of a revolutionary socialism espoused by bourgeois critics such as Blanqui and Marx, demanding that workers actively endeavor to overthrow existing institutions. When strikes that erupted near Saint-Étienne in 1869 produced bloodshed in having to be forcibly repressed, the regime withdrew its support.

The bureaucracy rather than parliament took the lead in regulating employment conditions in the workplace. Because social gains remained minimal—women and children were restricted to a 10-hour working day in 1900, Sunday was made an obligatory rest day in 1906, and an optional social insurance plan was authorized in 1910—labor remained restive. Trade unions were legalized in 1884, and the largest, the Confédération Général du Travail (General Confederation of Labor, CGT), was formed at Limoges in 1895. Although labor councils to mediate disputes were set up in 1899 and a ministry of labor established in 1906, efforts to win substantial concessions largely failed. Most French workers remained largely outside unions during these years—out of a total labor force of about 7 million at the turn of the 20th century, only about 1 million were organized—while labor itself was divided both organizationally into several rivals and tactically—some calling for gradual reforms by constitutional means and others, the CGT among them, advocating radical change through strikes, boycotts, and sabotage under a doctrine of revolutionary syndicalism. Discontent was blunted somewhat by slowly improving living standards, although real wages rose little in the 20 years before 1914 due to increasing prices.

At the same time, growth of industry in cities and suburbs led to increasing numbers of urban workers, while in the countryside the peasantry was in steady though slow decline. Farmers included landowners, tenants (*fermiers*), and sharecroppers (*métayers*) whose holdings ranged from several hundred acres to tiny plots. Peasants in some regions lived in villages or sizable towns, working the fields outside, while in other places, they lived in farmhouses dispersed across the countryside. Until about 1899, the 19th-century trend of land subdivision increased the number of farms, but these numbers began to fall afterward, a decline that continued well into the 20th century with consolidation of minuscule holdings into middle-sized farms.

The nation returned to its traditional policy of high tariffs with enactment of the Méline Tariff in 1892, which, with an added hike in rates in 1910, made France one of the most protectionist countries in the world. Napoléon III's turn toward freer trade had never been widely popular with business interests, even as it had forced much of industry in the 1860s to modernize in order to compete. Though their impact on economic growth remains debatable, high tariffs did not stifle the boom at the turn of the 20th century; by making imports prohibitively expensive, they enabled French farms to keep the country self-sufficient in food production.

The active role assumed by French bankers, engineers, and technicians in the industrial development of the rest of the Continent marked a uniquely new business endeavor. By 1914, French investments in Europe, with Russia the recipient of fully 25 percent of the approximately 45 billion francs expended, far outstripped sums directed to the French Empire. Most funds were channeled abroad through major new investment banks—the Banque de Paris et des Pays-Bas, founded in 1872, became the most famous. Along with capital flows, French technical experts supplied the know-how to build railroads, canals, and other infrastructural projects elsewhere in Europe and also in Asia.

The golden glow given to the era in its being called, when observers later looked back, the Belle Époque, translated literally as "the beautiful era" and roughly as "the good old days," was in reality less rosy for many; nevertheless, the 20 years before 1914 were indeed sufficiently fortunate that the French could take smug satisfaction in quoting a German epigram defining an idyllic existence as "to live like God in France." The country was prosperous at home and at peace abroad. During these years Paris earned its reputation as the world capital of romance, fine dining and entertainment, and high fashion.

The capital participated fully in the international vogue for lavish exhibitions in holding major world's fairs in 1889, when the Eiffel Tower was inaugurated, and in 1900. In the latter year, too, the Paris subway (La Métropolitaine) opened. The 1890s saw the dawn of the cabaret, or music hall, its rise epitomized by the fame of the Folies Bergère. Founded in 1863, it became the archtype, remaining highly successful through the 1920s and 1930s as the venue where shows featured exotic costumes and often a good deal of nudity among the women dancers. Opening its doors in 1889, the Moulin Rouge (Red Windmill) gained special notoriety in staging performances of the highly dramatic apache (gang) dance, associated with Parisian street culture, and of the cancan, which emerged out of working-class dancehalls in Montparnasse about 1830 to assume its modern-day incarnation here. Born in the Montmartre district in the 1880s, *chanson réaliste* (realist song) was a musical style influenced by literary realism that dealt with themes

THE EIFFEL TOWER

The Eiffel Tower (Fr., *Tour eiffel*) sits astride the Seine River in Paris on the Champs de Mars. Named after its designer, civil engineer Gustave Eiffel (1832–1923), the 7,000-ton tower is the tallest structure in Paris, rising to a height of 1,063 feet (300 m) without its modern broadcasting antenna, the equivalent of an 81-story building.

Designed to serve as the entrance arch for the world's fair marking the 100th anniversary of the French Revolution, the tower was begun in 1887, inaugurated in March 1889, and opened to the public two months later on May 6. Some among the public greeted its completion with widespread criticism, the column of riveted iron plates considered an eyesore on the cityscape. Leaders in the arts penned denunciatory letters to Paris newspapers, but the general populace took a liking to the tower, which has never diminished.

Eiffel Tower (Library of Congress)

The tower was intended to last for 20 years, when ownership would revert to the city. Municipal officials planned to dismantle it—the rules of the architectural competition to choose a designer had specified that the structure must be easily demolished. By 1909, however, the Eiffel Tower proved valuable for communication purposes. Radio transmission from the tower began in the early 20th century, and it served as a military communication center during World War I. Today it features a meteorological station and television transmission antennas.

Made up of four immense arched legs, set on masonry piers, that curve inward to join in a single, tapered tower, the structure is today considered to be a unique, striking work of art. The Eiffel Tower is recognized universally as a landmark symbol of both Paris and France.

Moulin Rouge, ca. 1900 (Library of Congress, LC-USZ62-133253)

drawn from the poor and working classes of Paris. Many artists were women, among the most famous, Yvette Guilbert (1865–1944), whose bawdy songs of tragedy and lost love drew throngs to the Moulin Rouge. Performing in cabarets and *café-concerts* (or *café-chantants*), singers such as Mistinguett (1875–1956), and, later, American-born Josephine Baker (1906–75), Maurice Chevalier (1888–1972), and Tino Rossi (1907–83) earned acclaim. While they shocked the sensibilities of some late Victorian-era moralists, cabarets proved popular, and the large crowds they drew promoted the image of the city as a free-spirited place. At the same time, Paris remained a prominent showcase for traditional music, including performances of opera, symphonic music, and ballet. The Ballets Russes, an itinerant ballet troupe under the distinguished directorship of Sergey Diaghilev (1872–1929), performed from 1909 to 1929 at the Théâtre Mogador and Théâtre du Châtelet. By century's end, railways densely covered Europe—the Orient Express, soon to earn fame for readers of travelogues, spy stories, and mystery thrillers, began service between Paris and Constantinople in 1888—making the city, with its museums, cafés, and popular attractions, a prime destination for visitors, both domestic and foreign.

The era featured startlingly new technological innovations. France pioneered synthetic fiber production in setting up the world's first rayon mill. Inventor Gustave Trouvé (1839–1902) launched a working three-wheeled automobile in 1881, while the foundations for the modern industry were laid in the early 1890s by Émile Levassor (1843–97) and Armand Peugeot (1849–1915). Louis Renault (1877–1944) followed with the establishment of the family firm in 1899. The new mode of transport gained a popular boost from the new sport of auto racing, the first in the world held in 1887 on a 3.2-mile (2-km) course in Paris and the first long-distance race in 1895 in a Paris-to-Bordeaux and back run. In aviation, Clément Ader (1841–1925) launched his steam-powered craft, *Éole*, for a short 164-feet (50-m) flight near Paris in 1890, making it the first self-propelled flight in history, though his subsequent designs proved incapable of sustaining elevation. Pioneers of modern heavier-than-air craft include Louis Blériot (1872–1936), the first to cross the English Channel, on July 25, 1909. From August 22 to

Louis Blériot flying his airplane, July 21, 1909 (Library of Congress)

235

CAFÉS OF PARIS

The cafés of Paris have served as social and culinary centers since at least the 17th century. The word café is French for "coffee," and the custom of drinking the beverage was introduced to Parisian society in 1669 by the ambassador of the Ottoman sultan Mehmed IV (r. 1648–87), who, arriving in the city with an entourage, brought with him a large quantity of coffee beans, which proved immediately popular. The oldest café still in existence is Café Procope on rue Baci, which opened in 1686.

Cafés became much more than places serving only coffee, however. They soon emerged as popular meeting sites. Originating in the 18th century as an outdoor café where small groups of entertainers performed popular music—usually lighthearted and occasionally risqué—the café-concert, or café-chantant (singing café), gained wide popularity in the late 19th and early 20th centuries. Many cafés have earned fame as favored sites of the city's artistic and literary lights. Intellectuals such as Jean-Paul Sartre and Simone de Beauvoir, along with writers, including American author Ernest Hemingway (1899–1961), and painters such as Pablo Picasso (1881–1973), frequented Les Deux Magots and Café de Flore in the Saint-Germain-des-Prés neighborhood. The Café de la Paix attained the height of its popularity at the turn of the 20th century when artists were joined there by social and political luminaries, including Edward, prince of Wales, the future Edward VII, king of Great Britain (r. 1901–10).

During the Belle Époque, cafés were important to avant-garde artists not only as venues for the exchange of ideas but also as places

29, 1909, aircraft builders and their pilots assembled from around the world at Reims to exhibit and compare their flying machines. At this first international aviation meet, new world records were set, notably for speed when U.S. aviator and designer Glenn Hammond Curtiss (1878–1930) won the first Gordon Bennett Cup in flying his plane 47 miles (75.6 km) per hour. On October 22, 1909, Raymonde de Laroche (1886–1919) became the first woman to fly solo, and she was the first woman in the world to receive a pilot's license. She set women's altitude records before dying in a crash during an experimental test.

Two inventive brothers launched cinema when Auguste (1862–1954) and Louis (1864–1948) Lumière exhibited short sequences of moving pictures in a Paris café on December 28, 1895. Louis devised visual and

that served a renowned, stimulating libation. Henri de Toulouse-Lautrec, Vincent van Gogh, and other artists and thinkers drank absinthe, the so-called green fairy, a chartreuse-colored, anise- or liquorice-flavored potion believed to elevate creative powers. Absinthe was widely popular until the early 1900s when it was banned for its alleged hallucinatory effects.

Cafés are the city's traditional meeting places, serving as neighborhood social centers and networking sources for social and political purposes. Dining is generally offered at most cafés, which feature complete restaurant menus and a full bar. Some cafés serve also as tobacco shops *(bureaux de tabac),* selling everything from newspapers to train tickets. To sit and relax for several hours at a café and observe the passing urban scene is to partake of the quintessential Parisian ambiance.

Poster of a woman sampling her companion's glass of absinthe at a Paris café, ca. 1900–05 (Library of Congress)

narrative techniques that would become standard. The films he made, however, were created to advertise the equipment he manufactured; Georges Méliès (1861–1938), a professional entertainer, first realized the commercial potential of film as entertainment. He reconstructed news stories in his studio (*L'affaire Dreyfus,* 1899) and crafted innovative narrative films using trick photography, which is especially remembered in his *Voyage dans la lune (Trip to the Moon,* 1902). In 1902, Charles Pathé (1863–1957) bought the Lumière patents, built a new camera, and with it launched a production company, which churned out 300 films in the early years of the new century. Competition soon came from Léon Gaumont (1864–1946). By 1905, moving picture theaters had sprung up all over France. By 1914, French producers had cornered 90 percent of the world market, and France's Max Linder (1883–1925) emerged as the world's first major movie star.

Despite its notable advances, France failed to capitalize fully on its trendsetting start. New industries never supplanted textiles, which in 1914 remained the chief product, as it was at the beginning of the 1800s, in employing the largest number of workers and comprising France's biggest export. Just as it had throughout the 19th century, the structure of industry stayed the same in the early years of the 20th, the family firm still the predominant form of business organization. Corporate structures and investment levels lagged behind competitor nations, notably Germany, Britain, and the United States. By 1914, the country had lost its prominent position in the production of rayon, aluminum, automobiles, and electronic goods.

During the 1870s, the economic elite of the Third Republic were drawn from the same wealthy upper middle class (*haute bourgeoisie*) that provided the political leaders. Most were Orléanist by tradition, but most converted to republicanism during the decade. Though skeptics on religion, many were no longer anticlerical as were their forebears in the late 18th and early 19th centuries. They viewed the church as a necessary bulwark in helping to ensure an orderly and law-abiding society. A powerful minority were Protestant. They played a major role in industry, banking, politics, and media. The middle bourgeoisie (*moyenne bourgeoisie*)—average business and professional men—emerged to dominate parliament and the cabinet from the 1880s to about 1900, after which men of lower social origin gradually took precedence. The lower bourgeoisie (*petite bourgeoisie*)—small shopkeepers, clerks, white-collar employees, school teachers, and lower civil servants— were distinguished by their patriotic republicanism and social beliefs that tended toward egalitarianism and positivism. The power of such attitudes reflected the pervasive influence and rich variety of French intellectual, artistic, and scientific life.

Intellectual, Artistic, and Scientific Currents

By 1870, the positivism so identified with the worldview of Auguste Comte with its faith in science and inevitable progress had become the favored philosophic system of all good republicans at the same time that the skepticism toward accepted belief and demand for fact-backed inquiry that marked the outlook of Ernest Renan continued to be powerfully influential as well. Carrying on the dominant mood, Hippolyte Taine (1828–93), a literary critic, philosopher, and historian, stressed order, clarity, and logic—the rationalist legacy of Descartes's Cartesian mode of thought—in applying scientific methodology to the study of history and human nature. Proclaiming that the study of facts alone sufficed, he sought to reduce ideas to their essentials, to uncover a set formula to explain, for example, in his *Les origines de la France contemporaine* (*The Origins of Contemporary France,* 1876–93), the cause of recent events.

In literature, two chief currents flowed from Renan's skepticism and Taine's rationalism. The works of Anatole France (1844–1924) reflect the former. Paris-born, mostly self-educated, and a voracious reader, France penned a great volume of dramas, novels (*Thaïs,* 1890; *Le lys rouge,* 1894), and historical works written with an eloquent grace and filled with compassion, which won him the Nobel Prize in literature in 1921. He fought for the exoneration of Dreyfus, as did Émile Zola (1840–1902), whose moving diatribe *J'accuse* (*I accuse,* 1898), published in the newspaper *L'Aurore,* reflected his humanitarian concerns and his politics. Zola was the greatest French representative of realism—or naturalism—whose novels embody his belief that fiction should be written with the objectivity of a scientist, based like history on rigorous research from documents. In *Germinal* (1885), the story of a miners' strike that proved highly successful, Zola's concentration on the gritty side of human existence exemplifies the brutal power of his work at the same time that it reflects his preoccupation with social issues for which redress of wrongs he considered essential.

Zola championed a new style of art then emerging in the pictorial work of his friend Édouard Manet (1832–83), which sought to move beyond Courbet's realism toward a more accurate visual representation. Artists acquired a better understanding of the nature of light through recent advances in optics, which they sought to express in an innovative technique called impressionism. Manet pointed the way. In 1863, he painted *Olympia* and *Déjeuner sur l'herbe,* two canvases scandalously innovative in displaying a bold treatment of both light and the nude—a traditional subject he used in a new way. In *Déjeuner,* a nude woman lunching casually with two fully dressed men shocked the proprieties of the time. Refused entry to the annual official salon, Manet displayed his *Déjeuner* along with the works of other rebellious artists at a counter exhibition (Salon des Refusés). In 1874, these impressionist artists held their first collective showing. Characterized by an emphasis on the depiction of light in all its changing qualities and on an effort to portray movement as a central part of human perception by employing primary colors, drawing objects from unusual angles, and using ordinary subject matter, impressionism predominated among pictorial trends in the mid-19th century. Manet's works were dismissed by academic critics, but an

Paul Cézanne, Still Life with Curtain, Jug, and Bowl of Fruit *(1893–94). Sold at auction in 1999 for US$60.5 million, this painting fetched one of the highest prices ever paid for an artwork during the 20th century.* (Erich Lessing/Art Resource, NY)

entire school of impressionist painters inspired by him took shape to include an array of talent on display in works by such artists as Pierre-Auguste Renoir (1841–1919), Camille Pissarro (1830–1903), Edgar Degas (1834–1917), and Claude Monet (1840–1926). Paul Cézanne (1839–1906) distanced himself gradually from the impressionists to combine their techniques with conventional rules of representation in creating compositions in which color and design are closely joined and forms are reduced to the simplest shapes—spheres, cones, cubes, and cylinders. Cézanne used distortion to convey his conception of reality. In doing so, he laid the foundation for radical departures in pictorial art, and his works form a bridge between those of 19th-century impressionists and those of 20th-century artists. Innovative departures also mark the work of Paul Signac (1863–1935) and Georges Seurat (1859–91), who, in an effort to formulate principles for painting similar to those for music, devised the technique of pointillism—applying small, closely packed dots of paint of unmixed color to create a solid form.

Sweeping Europe beginning in the mid-1890s until about 1910, art nouveau (new art) profoundly influenced the decorative arts and architecture. Featuring organic, plant-inspired motifs and highly intricate, curvaceous shapes, art nouveau won lasting fame in the glass designs of René Lalique (1860–1945) and Émile Gallé (1846–1904) and in the rooftop edifices for the Paris Métro stations designed by architect Hector Guimard (1867–1942), the most prominent representative of the style in France.

In sculpture, the romanticism predominant earlier in the century gave way to a revitalized art based on direct study of the human form. The physical and emotional stress evident in *Le penseur* (*The Thinker,* 1881), the famous piece by Auguste Rodin (1840–1917)—the preeminent French sculptor of the 19th century—led to a new appreciation of Renaissance masters such as Michelangelo (1475–1564) and exercised a profound influence on 20th-century sculpture. National pride—in two nations—inspired sculptor and architect Frédéric-Auguste Bertholdi (1834–1904), whose massive *Le lion de Belfort* (1880), carved into a mountainside in Alsace, commemorates French fighting efforts in the Franco-Prussian War, and whose *Statue of Liberty* (*La liberté éclairant le monde*), given as a gift to the United States in 1886, remains his most famous work.

The stress on scientific method so evident among the realists is fully revealed in the work of pure and applied science, which counts many outstanding achievements. Louis Pasteur (1822–95) helped to discover vaccines; Marcelin Berthelot (1827–1907) synthesized methane and researched dyestuffs and explosives; Henri Poincaré (1854–1912) founded analytic geometry as the country's foremost 19th-century mathematician. Nobel laureates Pierre (1859–1906) and Marie (1867–1934) Curie isolated the element radium in 1898 and worked with Henri Becquerel (1852–1908), who

Marie Curie (Library of Congress, LC-USZ62-100303)

241

had discovered radioactivity in 1896. The daughter of the Curies, Irène Joliot-Curie (1897–1956), together with her husband, Frédéric Joliot-Curie (1900–58), would later win the Nobel Prize in chemistry in 1935 for their discovery of artificial radioactivity. In psychopathology, Jean Charcot (1825–93) studied hypnosis, hysterics, and other neurological conditions at his Paris clinic, where Sigmund Freud (1859–1939) became his most famous student.

Science of the fiction variety emerged fully in the works of Jules Verne (1828–1905), a writer considered to be the father of the genre. Born in Nantes, he moved to Paris to study law; instead, he spent his time learning science at the National Library. Verne won immediate success with *Cinq semaines en ballon* (*Five Weeks in a Balloon*, 1864), and many of his novels (*Le tour du monde en 80 jours* [*Around the World in 80 Days*], 1873; *De la Terre à la Lune* [*From the Earth to the Moon*], 1865; *Vingt-mille lieues sous les mers* [*Twenty-thousand Leagues under the Sea*], 1870) feature variants of future real-world inventions, such as submarines, space flights, and motion pictures.

Even at the height of positivism and scientism in the 1870s and 1880s, however, trends from the past and portents of the future appeared. The exotic romanticism that pervades the books of Pierre Loti (1850–1923), the pseudonym of Julien Viaud, proved popular with readers. In his best-selling novel *Le disciple* (*The Disciple*, 1889), Paul Bourget (1852–1935) challenged positivism in trumpeting the family and spirituality as the traditional social foundations. Human relationships form the core of the stories penned by Sidonie-Gabrielle Colette (1873–1954), who, by the early 20th century, had emerged as France's leading female novelist. The bittersweet tale of an older woman's love affair with an egotistic youth, *Chéri* (1920), epitomized her work, which memorably included *Gigi* (1944), a novella that later served as the basis of a U.S. movie.

Collectively identified as belonging to a new group labeled symbolism, a school of poets—Paul Verlaine (1844–96), Stéphane Mallarmé (1842–98), and Arthur Rimbaud (1854–91)—rebelled against both the aridity of realism and the sentiment of romanticism in seeking to provide neither exact images nor lucid ideas but only to express verbally pure states of consciousness. Inspired by the work of Charles Baudelaire, whom they regarded as their father, the symbolists sought to free poetry from prose. Poets did not tell stories, debate, or explain; rather, they used words to impart the musings of the mind.

To the symbolists, the meaning of words meant less than the sound they conveyed. Thus, although they aspired to reproduce that condition,

Cover for De la Terre à la Lune (From the Earth to the Moon) *and* Autour de la Lune (Around the Moon) *from the Voyages Extraordinaires series by Jules Verne, with a picture of the author in the center, ca. 1896* (Oxford Science Archive/HIP/Art Resource, NY)

only music was completely pure. Symbolism influenced such composers of music as Claude Debussy (1862–1918), whose composition for orchestra *Prélude à l'après-midi d'un faune* (1894), with its trendsetting sense of floating, ethereal harmony, was based on a poem by Mallarmé, and whose harmonic innovations, including his status as the first composer to exploit the whole-tone scale, would strongly influence 20th-century music. Though it exerted a less strong impact on artists in prose and painting, and though it faded as an original force after 1900, symbolism had a liberating effect on the arts for decades. It inspired writers such as Paul Claudel (1868–1955), whose novels often centered on themes of spiritual conflict, and André Gide (1869–1951), who won acclaim fully after World War I.

In painting, also the new styles that flourished from the 1890s on—cubism, fauvism, and others often joined together under the label of postimpressionism—reflected the general revolt against science. Uninterested in investigating nature with the precision of a scientist and finding it futile to try to reproduce light pictorially, artists such as Vincent van Gogh (1853–90), Paul Gauguin (1848–1903), and Henri de Toulouse-Lautrec (1864–1901) sought rather to express on canvas their own emotions and perceptions, including the irrational play of the subconscious. Artists came to employ stronger colors and mixed media and laid greater stress on abstract forms in place of formal linear design. A retrospective showing in Paris of the works of Cézanne in 1907, a year after his death, proved revelatory. His influence impacted painting for the next two decades, most profoundly seen in the canvases of innovators such as Henri Matisse (1869–1954), André Derain (1880–1954), and Georges Braque (1882–1963), pictorial artists who broke with traditions in developing fauvist and cubist styles distinguished by distorted forms and unconventional perspective. Pablo Picasso (1881–1973), a Spaniard who worked in France, created a sensation with his *Demoiselles d'Avignon* (1907), whose flat, two-dimensional picture plane and rendering of angular, distorted body shapes exerted a major influence on future art.

In philosophy, Henri Bergson (1859–1941) and Maurice Barrès (1862–1923) became the leading lights in the revolt against positivism. From Lorraine, Barrès was a brilliant, complex author who, both as a dedicated republican who advocated authoritarianism and as a believer who admired the church, defied precise labeling but whose exaltation of intense patriotism in works such as *Le roman de l'énergie nationale* (The novel of national energy, 1894–1902) proved highly influential. Bergson made a much deeper impact. Born in Paris and a professor at the Collège de France from 1900 to 1914, Bergson shifted the focus of attention from rational to nonrational drives and to intuition and not reason as the right road to truth. He asserted that one can comprehend life through instinct rather than through intellect. In his phrase *élan vital* (vital urge), he identified the life force, arising from the depths of the subconscious, that makes evolution creative and that constitutes the true genius of both individual human beings and nations. In *L'évolution créatrice* (*Creative Evolution*, 1907) in a famous simile, Bergson depicted life as a great cavalry charge: ". . . the whole of humanity, in space and in time, is one immense army galloping beside and before and behind each of us in an overwhelming charge able to beat down every resistance and to clear many obstacles, perhaps even death" (Bergson, 1911, 270–271). His ideas pervaded intellectual discussions at the same time that his lectures drew overflow crowds in the years just before 1914.

In political theory Bergson's outlook influenced Georges Sorel (1847–1922), a retired engineer and an ex-Marxist who renounced his earlier convictions to draw up the working-class doctrine of symbolism. Rejecting political parleying and theoretical planning, Sorel held that only direct action by workers could advance their just demands, and that, to succeed, such action needed to be backed up by a "great myth," which for the laboring masses should be the general strike. Operating at the far extremes of society—both as it existed and as they hoped it to be—others preferred the most radical beliefs of all. Drawing on German and Russian philosophic theorists, nihilists concluded that values of any kind do not exist, and anarchists rejected law and order of any sort in proclaiming war on the state and society itself. Ideologues put thoughts into action all across Europe at the close of the 19th century and the opening of the 20th in a spate of political assassinations, including President Marie-François Sadi Carnot (1837–94), who was stabbed to death by an Italian anarchist at Lyon in June 1894.

Anarchists remained isolated, individual activists, and Sorel's prescription was already put into practice by workers. But positivism never lessened its grip on the university elites, its continuing appeal reinvigorated by new thinkers, most especially Émile Durkheim (1858–1917), who proclaimed once again that reason, not emotion, imagination, or faith, accounts for humankind's emergence from primitive superstition to rational understanding. The enduring power of such beliefs testified to a widening gap, at the turn of the 20th century, between the world of education, business, and politics, which clung to the old nostrums, and that of an intellectual avant-garde alive to new ideas. The revolt against science and rationalism would spread through the wider society, but it would take another generation to do so and only after a war of unprecedented dimensions shook loose old mental beliefs. In 1900, the ruling elites, marveling at the advances science produced seemingly at a nonstop pace, looked ahead with confidence and optimism to a future they saw as bright with the promise of unbridled progress.

The Republic Now Secure, 1899–1914

The government that took office under René Waldeck-Rousseau (1846–1904) in 1899 marked a turning point in Third Republic politics. Though a moderate himself, key posts in the cabinet were held by Radicals and even, for the first time, a Socialist. Henceforth, the Radicals would replace the moderates as the cornerstone of ruling coalitions. They would do so under an organization officially constituted in 1901 as the Parti Républicain, Radical et Radical-Socialiste (Republican, Radical and Radical-Socialist Party, PR), which continues to exist today in claiming the status of France's oldest political party. Until the end of the Third Republic in 1940, the Radicals—or the Radical-Socialists—were rarely out of power and were usually the largest party in the Chamber of Deputies. After World War I, they would dominate the Senate.

Though the Radicals now assumed pride of place in the ruling driver's seat, they brought no sharp switch in the government's guiding spirit. Once fiercely egalitarian republicans whose chief strength was found in the cities, the Radicals had mellowed over time, coming to represent the interests of the lower middle classes, especially in rural areas and small towns, where, for many, individual rights trumped equal rights. Though organized in a party structure, they remained in fact a very loose amalgamation of shifting allegiances, and in ruling they adopted a willingness to compromise.

In doing so, the Radicals moved to the center of the political spectrum, a switch resulting partly from the responsibility that came with governing, which required a willingness to make concessions, and partly from the rise to their left of socialism. The Parti Socialiste Français (French Socialist Party)—its formal French title, Section Française de l'Internationale Ouvrière (Section of the Workers' International, SFIO)—emerged formally in 1905, having evolved from several organizations active in pushing laborers' rights after 1877. The party brought together the diverse strands of the workers' movement, uniting moderates led by Jean Jaurès (1859–1914), who advocated socialist participation in bourgeois governments, with committed Marxists such as Jules Guesde (1845–1922), who rejected any accommodation with the capitalist state. These two leaders frequently clashed, but the participation of Socialist Alexandre Millerand (1859–1943) in the 1899 government indicated the ascendancy of the moderates. Their willingness to cooperate gave the country two almost identical left-wing coalitions—of Radicals, Socialists, and moderates—from 1899 to 1905, the longest stretch of governmental stability to date.

Ever ready to attack their historical opponents, republicans at the turn of the 20th century went on the offensive against the church. They passed a Law of Associations in 1901, which put the power of authorizing "associations"—that is, religious orders—in the hands of the government. In 1904, all teaching by religious orders was forbidden, and in 1905, complete separation of church and state was decreed under which both the state and religions abstained from involvement in each other's affairs and the government was legally prohibited from recognizing any religion (laïcité). The concordat of 1801 was abrogated, priests ceased to be salaried by the government, funding for religious groups ended, and churches became the property of the state, which put them at the disposal of religious organizations at no expense provided they were used for purposes of worship.

The Socialists withdrew from the coalition in 1906, launching a period of Radical-moderate cooperation that lasted with interruptions until 1936. Radical politician Georges Clemenceau (1841–1929) came to office in 1906 promising a sweeping 17-point program of reforms, including a graduated income tax and enactment of social welfare measures. Only a few proposals succeeded in becoming law, however, in failing to win the support of Socialists in the Chamber of Deputies, angry with the government over its authorization of military force to break up a miners' strike in 1909.

Just as the Socialists represented a new and growing power on the left, so, too, new forces began to appear on the right, which surged in strength in the first two decades of the 20th century. The old conservatives—the ex-nobility and landowners ousted from politics, the church, and the army—remained active, but growing numbers came from new industrial and commercial circles, who, with abundant funds with which to get attention, gave voice to their dislike of popular democracy and their dread of socialism. Much right-wing sentiment came to coalesce around the newspaper L'Action Française, founded at the end of the 19th century, which became a daily in 1908 under the editorship of Léon Daudet (1867–1942) but whose guiding spirit was provided by literary critic Charles Maurras (1868–1952). An anti-Semite, a xenophobe, and at least in theory a royalist, Maurras waged relentless war

247

against the Revolution of 1789 and all that it stood for. He founded an Action Française movement in 1908 whose motto, "Classicism, Monarchy, Catholicism" appealed to the most conservative elements among the bourgeoisie.

With the working class pulled to the far left and the well-off drawn to the right, the old left—the moderates under whose stewardship the republic had been consolidated and the Radicals who were now entrusted with guaranteeing the perpetuation of that republic—had to find a way to accommodate the new forces engendered by modern industrial society to which the extremes exerted so much appeal. Polarizing currents blurred the nation's sense of political direction in the years before 1914, but in foreign affairs, at least, the country focused on clear-cut objectives.

Empire and Alliance Building, 1870–1914

At the start of the Third Republic, France stood alone in Europe, without friends or allies; thanks to the efforts of Germany's chancellor Bismarck, the country remained diplomatically isolated for 20 years after 1871. Preoccupied with domestic issues, the public displayed widespread indifference to international relations, leaving the field to a few politicians and interest groups.

French public opinion never forgave Germany for the loss of Alsace-Lorraine—the outstanding legacy of the Franco-Prussian War that still rankled—though only a minority, albeit a vocal one, remained bent on a war of revenge, a goal that emerged in organized form with the founding of the Ligue des Patriotes (League of Patriots) by Paul Déroulède (1846–1914) in 1882. The majority of the citizenry, however, while they could not countenance renouncing forever the lost provinces, grew increasingly less enthused with the passing of the years about an armed crusade to get them back.

Largely shut out from European statecraft, France embarked on a new course of imperial expansion in Africa, Asia, and the Pacific. Only scattered remnants were left of a once great overseas empire, though a start at rebuilding had already been made. Under Louis-Philippe the whole of Algeria had been absorbed, and France also took possession of Tahiti (1842) and the Comoro Islands (1841–1912), off Madagascar. In 1853, Napoléon III's regime annexed New Caledonia in the South Pacific as part of an effort to match Britain, which held a predominant presence in the region in Australia and New Zealand. Emulating the British in Australia, the French gained a foothold here in establishing penal colonies. On the Asian mainland, France added Cochin China (modern-day southern Vietnam) when a small force landed at Saigon (Ho Chi Minh City) in 1859 to protect Catholic missionaries and began a piecemeal conquest. The real goal was to secure a naval base and to gain a territorial foothold adjacent to the expected lucrative Chinese market. Protests at the high cost almost led the French to withdraw when pressure from the navy, the clergy, and Bordeaux shipping interests aborted the move, leaving the way open to acquisition of additional territory. A French protectorate was proclaimed over Cambodia in 1863.

A markedly more activist policy that began in the 1880s appears to have reflected mainly noneconomic motives, namely, to Christianize and "civilize" backward peoples and to rebuild French prestige by channeling the nation's energies, blocked in Europe, elsewhere. The pursuit of overseas territories is associated most closely with statesman Jules Ferry (1832–93), who held office as premier in 1881 and, though hesitant at first—he reluctantly agreed to occupy Tunisia in 1882—soon became an enthusiastic expansionist. During his second ministry (1882–85), he dispatched a series of major African expeditions to follow up small-scale ventures by French traders, explorers, and army officers that had already been launched. Pierre Savorgnan de Brazza (1852–1905) carved out a vast empire in central Africa. In West Africa, the French had been present since the 17th century, when they arrived in Senegal in 1677 to operate a minor slave depot. From the coast, they had moved inland in the 1850s, then proceeded eastward into the hinterlands to gain the immense Sahara wastelands. Djibouti on the Red Sea was acquired as a coaling station. Off southern Africa, a French army invaded the large island of Madagascar in 1883 to wage a protracted war against the local ruler. In 1896, France annexed the island, exiling the native royal family to Algeria. A French army also launched a war of conquest in 1883 in Tonkin China (northern Vietnam), completing acquisition of the territory in 1886.

Popular support for imperialism began to broaden in the 1890s, and economic interests, especially textile exporters and investment bankers, grew more enthusiastic. Almost complete by 1900, the empire grew to become the second largest in territory after that of Great Britain, though it neither earned, nor cost, the country much money. Most of the colonial budget went to pay for army expenses and the salaries of administrators. Private capital stayed away, intent on investing in more developed areas—North America and Russia—while the colonies themselves furnished little beyond foodstuffs.

249

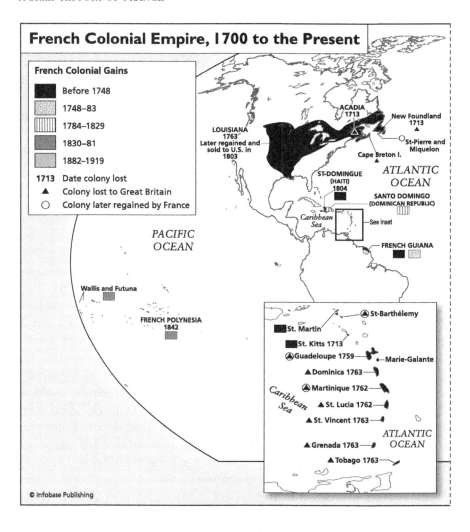

France built its empire at the same time that it won a major diplomatic victory in Europe. Intent on breaking its continental isolation, the country signed a political accord with Russia in 1891. Moving swiftly to take advantage of a growing rift between Germany and Russia, which had been linked under Chancellor Bismarck's statesmanship in the 1870s and 1880s, the French government followed up the diplomatic pact with a formal military alliance in 1894 in which each nation pledged to come to the other's defense in the event either was attacked.

The alliance was enthusiastically supported by all except those on the extreme left, the Socialists aghast at the oddity presented by a treaty between the democratic republic and the czarist autocracy. Ties were

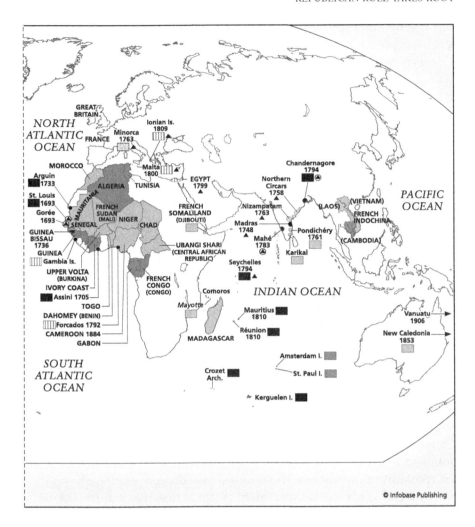

tightened in 1899 at the same time that diplomats searched for arrangements with others among the major powers, either an understanding
with Britain or a reconciliation with Germany. The possibility of a
rapprochement with the latter came closest to fruition in 1898 when a
small French force led by Captain Jean-Baptiste Marchand (1863–1934)
encountered a British expedition at the town of Fashoda on the Nile
River and the two nations came close to clashing over rival imperial
claims. In the end, cooler heads prevailed, and Britain and France
reached the conclusion that Germany posed the greater threat to both.

Under the impetus of French foreign minister Théophile Delcassé
(1852–1923), a Franco-British Entente Cordiale (friendly understanding)

251

was reached in 1904. The Germans set out at once to protest—and to test—the new accord in insisting on protection for German interests in Morocco, where France held a preponderance of influence. Emperor Wilhelm II (r. 1888–1918) was sent—much against his will—on a formal visit to Tangier, Morocco, at the conclusion of his annual Mediterranean cruise in March 1905. The French took offense at what they perceived to be intrusion into their sphere of influence, and Delcassé threatened action. French troops were moved to the German border. France then sought to open talks, which the Germans agreed to, though only on condition that the government dismiss Delcassé, with whom, as the architect of the Entente Cordiale, they would have nothing to do. The foreign minister was duly sacrificed, though this apparent victory for Germany turned to defeat at the international conference held at Algeciras, Spain (January–April 1906), where the assembled powers, distrustful of Germany, gave the victory to France, both in the short term—French control over Moroccan political and financial affairs was upheld—and in the long term—France's two diplomatic partners, Britain and Russia, reached an understanding between themselves in 1907. In 1911, Germany provoked another Moroccan crisis when the gunboat *Panther*—to Europe's astonishment—appeared suddenly in the port of Agadir on July 1 to back up German demands for compensation following French and Spanish suppression of a rebellion and, their intention clear to control the country fully, occupation of coastal regions. Insisting that it be given the whole of the French Congo—something France had no intention of granting—Germany obtained a large slice of the area at a subsequent settlement in return for recognition of France's protectorate in Morocco.

A wave of anti-German sentiment swept across the country, the public outraged at what was perceived to be backing down to German saber rattling, and the government fell partly in response to it. A new surge of nationalist spirit surfaced. Whatever hopes may have lingered for peaceful coexistence with France's eastern neighbor vanished, the public by turns puzzled, upset, and then resentful at what was perceived to be bullying behavior by Germany.

Raymond Poincaré (1860–1934) became premier at the beginning of 1912 and president a year later. A lawyer and a cautious, nondoctrinaire but intensely ambitious politician—at 26, the youngest member of parliament and, at 52, the youngest-ever president—he assumed a dominant position in foreign policy formulation. Though a member of a prominent family from western Lorraine, Poincaré did not pursue a course pivoted solely on recovery of the lost provinces. Rather, he strove to keep the lines of communication open with Germany, a stance symbolically in evidence in January 1914 when he attended a dinner at the German embassy—the first French president since 1870 to do so. At the same time, he oversaw a program of enhanced preparedness, one that centered on France's alliances. Under his leadership, the country built both its military and its diplomatic strength. With a population only two-thirds that of Germany's, France managed to field an army almost equal in size to that of its potential foe—about 1.4 million men—due to stringent conscription measures, with few exemptions allowed. The army draft laws extended the period of service from two to three years. More precise commitments were sought from the British, who were persuaded to enter into staff talks with the Russians. Fearing Russia might desert France to turn to Germany once again as an ally, the government promised to support Russian diplomatic policies on the Balkan Peninsula, where Russia assumed a protective stance toward the small Slavic nations (Serbia, Bulgaria) in their relations with Germany's menacing ally, Austria-Hungary. The nation took pride, viewing the outcome as a sign of its effective fighting abilities, when, during the First Balkan War (1912–13), the armies of Serbia, Bulgaria, and Greece, trained and armed by France, defeated the forces of the Ottoman Empire, schooled and equipped by Germany. Better prepared militarily and with a tightened alliance system in place, France faced with confidence and resolve the crisis provoked by the sudden assassination on June 28, 1914, of the heir to the throne of Austria-Hungary.

10

YEARS OF TURMOIL
AND TRAGEDY
(1914–1945)

War followed quickly in August 1914, once Europe's interlocking alliance system had been set in motion. World War I, the "Great War," as the French still call it, tested the nation in unprecedented ways, both material and moral. Poised for defeat, France fought doggedly back to secure a stalemate, which endured through four long, miserable years. In a war of attrition, of man versus machine, France and its allies—their staying power superior to that of their opponents—emerged victorious, but the triumph proved at once both sweet and bittersweet. The cost had been horrific. No other nation suffered such high proportionate manpower losses, and the scars left as deep a psychic impression as the physical destruction that marred the landscape—turned to moonscape—of the battle-ravaged regions.

The Third Republic had shown sufficient flexibility to weather the wartime crisis, but it proved much less resilient in facing the domestic and foreign problems of the postwar years. Though prosperity marked the 1920s and national security remained not too worrisome with Germany weak and unstable through most of the decade, the calm facade only masked deep divisions within society, which the onset of the Great Depression and then the rise of Nazism in the country next door brought to the fore in the 1930s. Chronic political instability paralyzed the ability to act, fatally weakening the nation's capacity to meet the new challenges.

Cabinets both on the right and on the left fell with dismal regularity while Europe edged toward war. When it came in September 1939, France tragically lacked both the will and the means to fight effectively. Because never before in modern French history had defeat come so quickly—in a mere six weeks—and so completely, so never before was France so broken in spirit and so utterly humiliated. The shock of capitulation reopened old debates, some of which dated back to 1789, about liberty versus order and church versus state. The country was divided between occupied and unoccupied zones. Support for the puppet regime at Vichy, at first widespread, gradually shifted as the oppression of German rule grew increasingly onerous and the forces of the Allies—Free French units battling at their side—made steady headway. Resisters fought collaborators in brutal fratricidal fighting.

By the time Allied troops landed on the beaches of Normandy in 1944–45, most of the French rallied around liberation as cause for celebration. Unlike after past wars that were lost, the choice of the ruling regime—a republic—was easy. This time the hard task would be not only to rebuild the physical devastation left by unprecedented destruction but also to heal the wounds to the national spirit left by so much division.

A War Unlike Any Before, 1914–1918

Events moved rapidly following Austria-Hungary's determination to wage war on Serbia. Intent on settling accounts with its small, troublesome Balkan neighbor, suspected of complicity in the assassination of Austro-Hungarian archduke Franz Ferdinand (1863–1914) and his wife Sophie (1868–1914) in June 1914, Vienna secured a "blank check" from its ally Germany in which Germany guaranteed unconditional support. Hostilities between the two powers commenced on July 28. Propelled by the conviction among the military staffs that victory would go to the nation that mobilized first, with only minor alterations the alliance systems worked as they were supposed to. Across Europe a few pacifist voices, mostly among Socialists, strove desperately to rouse the working classes to refuse to fight in a war for which, it was claimed, only capitalist rulers would gain, but the assassination of Jean Jaurès on July 31 by an ardent nationalist symbolized in France the triumph of patriotic pride over international class solidarity. To back up Serbia, France's ally Russia mobilized. Russian mobilization induced Berlin to declare war on August 1. Two days later, Germany declared war on France and—its request for a right of transit having been refused— invaded Belgium. This violation of that country's internationally recognized neutrality brought Britain into the war on August 4.

The French went off to war united, determined, and enthusiastic, sharing the confidence among all the fighting peoples that the conflict would be a short one. Both France and Germany put their prewar battle plans into action, both relying on an immediate offensive. The German Schlieffen Plan was centered on a rapid, massive drive through Belgium

French troops are cheered as they march through Paris, August 1, 1914. (Time & Life Pictures, Getty Images)

and northern France to knock out the French army, leaving what were expected to be the more slowly mobilizing Russians in the east to be dealt with later. The French Plan XVII called for a speedy advance into Alsace and Lorraine.

The French offensive was quickly halted, but the Germans enjoyed more success. Their armies swept into northern France and were stopped just short of Paris only in early September in a last-minute move overseen by General Joseph Joffre (1852–1931), who shifted 10,000 reserve troops back to the capital, 6,000 of whom were transported to the front in 600 Parisian taxicabs and buses in an operation orchestrated by General Joseph Gallieni (1849–1916), the military governor of Paris. The makeshift measure caught the imagination of the public, becoming a symbol of national solidarity and resolve, and the effort proved successful. French forces checked the German advance at the Marne River just east of the city. After November, when the Germans failed to break through the British lines at Ypres, Belgium, the war in the west settled into stalemate. A parallel line of zigzagging trenches snaked across a 500-mile stretch from the English Channel to the Swiss border, leaving all of northeastern France behind the German advance. Enduring bitter cold, blazing heat, mud, rats, and lice, the soldiers could expect relief from the deadly dueling only when the generals, on one side or the other, could restart an offensive in a way that would give them the victory.

Because they were fighting a war of attrition, a war that no one had expected, planners devised new strategies and tactics only very slowly and only after learning hard, costly lessons. The French high command had shown little inclination before the war to experiment with new kinds of weapons. Airpower, while appreciated for its potential, was not vigorously developed. Placing complete faith in the small, mobile 75-mm field gun as the centerpiece of French armored strength, the officer corps preached the virtue of the *offensive à outrance* (all-out offensive)—attack by masses of infantry equipped with only a rifle and the will to win. In the early weeks of the war, the cavalry, wielding lances from which pennants fluttered, spurred their horses to the charge while the infantry marched forward bedecked in their famed bright red trousers, the color having become the very symbol of French martial might. The switch to sky blue came after the price of many lives lost. In a confrontation with an enemy defending deeply dug trenches with machine guns, mortars, heavy artillery, and asphyxiating gas, the folly of the doctrine of the offensive could be read in the mounting casualty lists. Tens or hundreds of thousands of dead, injured, or missing were incurred in charging into a veritable rain of steel, only to fall back or to advance a few yards. In three years, the front line moved no more than 10 miles.

At the outset of the war, both the public and the politicians placed their faith in the high command. All political spectrums from far right to far left united in a *union sacrée* (holy union), which, while it lasted, proved patriotically intense. Plans made before the war to arrest trade union and extreme leftist leaders, who were expected to oppose hostilities actively, were canceled as unnecessary.

Joffre's success on the Marne strengthened the high command's authority, allowing him to keep the post of commander in chief for a further two years. Over time, however, frictions developed, and by 1916, politicians recovered their roles as dissatisfaction with Joffre's conduct of the war grew. His policy of battling the Germans bit by bit—by launching limited attacks—bled the army dry without producing any significant results. Criticism arose in particular over his failure to bolster the defenses of the great fortress city of Verdun, a stronghold that served as a lynchpin in France's line of defenses and one that he believed would not be attacked. When the Germans struck in February

1916 and overran most of Verdun's outer defenses, Joffre proposed to abandon the city and retreat to a shorter line that would be easier to defend. The politicians angrily dissented, arguing that it might lead

THE BATTLE OF VERDUN

France's epic test of World War I, the Battle of Verdun began on February 21, 1916. In an opening bombardment of more than 1 million artillery shells, including poison gas, heard 100 miles away, German armies launched an assault against a series of 18 major forts and other batteries surrounding Verdun, which had been largely stripped of defensive works in the belief that fortresses were obsolete, having proved vulnerable to modern heavy siege guns. Under General Henri-Philippe Pétain, the French rushed in reinforcements and for 10 months—the longest battle of the war—the two sides clashed in a titanic struggle that turned the battlefields into a gigantic killing ground. Captured by the Germans in February, Fort Douaumont, the largest fort, was retaken in October 1916. In December, the Germans were finally driven back across their February starting lines. The battle became a symbol of French determination never to retreat no matter the cost. Pétain's stirring order of the day—*Courage! On les aura!* (Courage! We shall get them!)—became a patriotic rallying cry. The battle has also become a symbol of the horrific human cost of war. Amid the mud and debris, an estimated 378,000 French casualties, including 163,000 killed, along with 330,000 German casualties, including 143,000 killed, are recorded. Human remains are still being uncovered.

The following is an account in the aftermath of the first German attack on French entrenchments at Fort de Vaux taken from the preface of the journal of Captain Delvert of the 101st Infantry Regiment, who was wounded four times. The "Boches" is French slang for Germans.

The rocks are everywhere spattered with red droplets. In places, there are pools of blood. On the parapet, in the communications trench, cadavers, stiff in death, are covered in tent cloth. A thigh wound in one of them opens. Putrefying flesh, under the burning sun, bursts out of uniforms, and swarms of fat, blue flies buzz busily around. To the right, to the left, the ground is strewn with innumerable debris: empty tin cans, tattered knapsacks, helmets with gaping holes, broken rifles splattered with blood. An unbearable odor infests the atmosphere. To top it all off, the Boches send gas shells our way, which render the air unbreathable. And

to the disintegration of both the army's and the public's morale. The job of saving Verdun fell to the section commander, General Henri-Philippe Pétain (1856–1951), who, in arguably the war's most critical

This pile of human bones attests to the horrific harvest reaped during the Battle of Verdun. (Library of Congress)

the heavy, hammer-like thuds of the artillery shells strike incessantly around us.

The courage of the men never fails. When the Boches surge forward again, they find our troops standing at the ready.

What is the reason for this singular heroism? Their captain explains. They die at their posts "because it is their duty to be there; . . . because they are men and they would feel themselves less than men and worthy of being called weaklings if they flinched; because, in their own muddle-headed way, they are conscious of being citizens of a great, free country who prize their liberty."

Source: Captain Delvert, Histoire d'une Compagnie: Main de Massiges, Verdun, Novembre 1915–Juin 1916. Preface by Ernest Lavisse. Translated by author (Paris: Berger-Levrault, 1921), p. xi.

action, managed to blunt the German drive in a 10-month battle that earned for this anti-Dreyfusard son of peasants a reputation for military genius and patriotic steadfastness. He was made a marshal of France in November 1918.

Members of the Chamber of Deputies as well as government ministers resumed their involvement in military matters as the fighting progressed, some grumbling that the administration of the war effort went according to *le système D,* from the verb *se débrouiller,* meaning to muddle through, in effect, no system at all. In truth, the country faced innumerable challenges. It proved difficult to launch new factories from scratch to replace those lost behind the German lines, where much industry was located. Financing was inefficient and the tax system insufficient—an income tax was established only in 1916, but even so rates were low and it was widely evaded. Inflation became widespread.

The nation rallied valiantly. The vast scale of war induced an unprecedented mobilization of society. Factory and mine workers were recalled from the trenches, replaced by peasant conscripts. The term *home front* came into use in designating the central importance of civilians in the war effort. To meet the ever-growing demand for labor to replace those who were called to the colors, women entered the workforce in large numbers and took over jobs that heretofore had been the exclusive preserve of men. They worked in munitions plants, drove the buses and trains, delivered the mail, and cleaned the streets. For the first time, the government intervened in a major way to organize and direct the economy. Centralized controls proved necessary to ration scarce commodities for both industry and consumers. The press and the new medium of film were actively employed in producing propaganda, which emerged as a valuable tool in rallying national morale.

Late in 1916, Joffre was transferred to a desk job in the war ministry, his fall marking the full return of civilians to running the war. From late 1916 to late 1917, the Chamber and the Senate controlled both the military's headquarters and the government's cabinet. They waxed enthusiastic over General Georges-Robert Nivelle (1856–1924), a charming junior commanding officer whose vigorous plan for a series of large-scale, coordinated attacks struck a cord in a nation, though now weary of war, willing to try yet another all-out drive. Unfortunately, Nivelle failed to foresee that, for his plan to succeed, he would need large reserves of manpower, which by 1917 no longer existed. The attack launched in spring 1917 proved an utter failure, the huge sacrifice of lives so appalling that it led to a near collapse of morale in parts of the

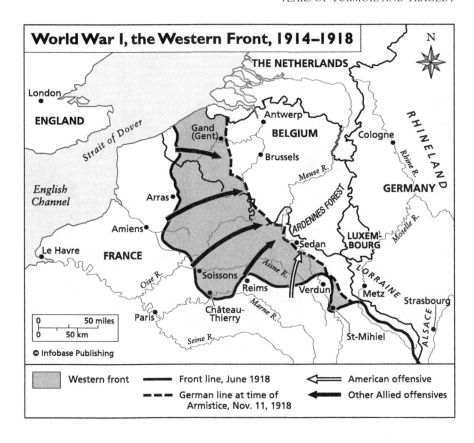

French army; whole companies willfully disobeyed orders in refusing to "go over the top" and charge the enemy defenses.

The fiasco led to Nivelle's ouster and Pétain's elevation to commander in chief. Using a mixture of repression and clemency, he quelled the mutinies and immediately canceled any further offensive actions, biding time until American men and matériel could arrive following U.S. entry into the war in April 1917.

While the low point in the army's fighting spirit peaked in spring 1917, civilian resolve cracked in the autumn. A serious wave of defeatism swept Paris, the sentiment strongest among the Socialists and left-wing Radicals. Antiwar attitudes had been building up slowly following the heady days of national solidarity in 1914, and those who, appalled at the seemingly never-ending cost, now came out in favor of a negotiated peace with the Germans rallied around the leadership of Radical Joseph Caillaux (1863–1944), an ex-premier who allegedly made several trips abroad to discuss a settlement. Squabbling and suspicions

Premier Georges Clemenceau (left) on the Somme front, ca. 1917 (Library of Congress, LC-USZ62-52292)

became so widespread that President Poincaré faced a dramatic choice: to form a government under either Caillaux or Georges Clemenceau (1841–1929), a politician with a steely determination to win who had been railing against defeatists for three years in his newspaper *L'homme enchaîné (The Chained-up Man)*.

A leader of the left in the Chamber of Deputies in the 1870s and 1880s who had acquired a reputation for his irascible stubbornness, Clemenceau contributed to the fall of so many governments that he earned the title *tombeur de ministeries* ("feller of ministries") and later, the *Tigre* (Tiger). A supporter of Dreyfus, he became a senator in 1902 and served as premier in 1909. Long having parted company with his leftist colleagues, Clemenceau returned to power backed almost entirely by the parties of the right and center. The *union sacrée* broke apart as the Socialists pulled out, unwilling to work with a politician remembered for his ruthless crackdown on strikers before the war. At the age of 76, having made so many enemies he cared little how many more he might score, Clemenceau vowed but one policy: "Home policy? he said: 'I wage war'! Foreign policy? 'I wage war'! 'All the time I wage war'!" (Brogan 1943, 536). Ruling as a virtual civilian dictator, he brought a harsh obstinacy to government that breathed a new fighting spirit into the nation. Compromisers and defeatists were brought to trial, and traitors, including the notorious spy Mata Hari (1876–1917), were shot, while he made regular visits to the front to shore up the fighting spirit of the troops and keep a check on the generals.

Morale revived just in time to allow France to withstand the great German spring and summer offensive of 1918. Once again, as in September 1914, the enemy advanced to the Marne. At the critical moment, Clemenceau persuaded Britain and the United States to accept the principle of a single command for all Allied forces on the western front. It was largely his decision that the choice fell to General Ferdinand Foch (1851–1929), who was named general in chief on March 26, 1918. The two argued fiercely, Clemenceau trying repeatedly to give Foch orders, but, to his credit, the premier usually let the general have the final say. In August, the Allies began an advance that proved unstoppable, an advance fueled by more and more fresh American troops along with their mountains of supplies. Germany and its allied Central Powers—Austria-Hungary, Bulgaria, and the Ottoman

The body of a French soldier lies in a trench near Châlons-en-Champagne (formerly Châlons-sur-Marne), September 1915. France lost virtually an entire generation in killed and wounded during World War I. (Adoc-photos/Art Resource, NY)

Empire—collapsed. On November 11—timed, with history in mind, to mark the momentous moment at exactly the 11th hour of the 11th day of the 11th month—an armistice was signed in Marshal Foch's railway car in the forest of Compiègne.

The Interwar Years
The Profits—and the Price—of Peace

France broke out in unalloyed joy at the conclusion of hostilities. An ordeal of monumental proportions had been endured, and the French took pride in the national spirit and stamina, and in the governing institutions, that had guided them to triumph. Widely criticized before the war for its instability, the Third Republic had managed to adapt itself to changing wartime conditions and had been shown to produce more competent leaders than had its autocratic enemies.

Euphoria was general, but some sensed that France could probably never again face another trial on so massive a scale. Indeed, reality proved sobering. Of the 8 million men mobilized, 5 million were killed or injured. An entire generation had been decimated; the dead alone totaled 10 percent of the working-age male population. Handicapped veterans were a common sight everywhere in the postwar years. Together with an already severe prewar demographic decline and a wartime plunge in the national birthrate, such losses threatened a population drop impossible to stop. In 1919, a further 166,000 were estimated to have been lost in the worldwide Spanish influenza outbreak that struck France.

Material devastation was substantial. The heavily shelled combat areas had been completely destroyed. All of northeastern France, where some of the best agricultural and all of the most developed industrial regions lay, had been ravaged. The franc fell from one of the world's most stable currencies to one of the shakiest. From one of the world's great banking and creditor nations, France became a postwar debtor, the government having relied on wartime borrowing, largely from the United States, rather than on a pay-as-you-go financing policy. Much of the country's overseas investment, including virtually all large amounts spent in prewar Russia, were lost. Inflation raged in the wake of skyrocketing expenditures and inadequate revenues gathered from low tax rates.

Cut off from its northeastern base, heavy industries shifted during the war to southern France and to the Paris area, where they joined small plants long located here. Industrial activities had switched in the course of the conflict from a concentration on textiles to metallurgy, the products needed to meet wartime demands. And they were made by a new kind of worker. Unskilled laborers had poured in from the countryside to work in war plants. Perhaps a million men joined the trade unions, bringing with them a new radicalization because none of them possessed long-time roots in the old craft institutions. Metallurgical workers became the most militant members of labor, and they made the red belt of industrial suburbs around Paris the base of Communist Party strength in the interwar years. For the entrepreneurial class, the war produced little expansion in the size of, or change in attitudes among, the business elite, who largely retained their traditional cautious approach to enterprise. The French peasantry suffered proportionally the highest casualty rates. Among the survivors, many never returned to the countryside, preferring urban to rural life. For those who stayed behind, the war years brought a new prosperity in meeting the high demand for foodstuffs, which enabled many farmers to pay off debts and buy more land.

The war having taken so staggering a toll, revenge occupied the mind's of most in the immediate aftermath. The French adopted the slogan "Germany will pay" for the losses, and French officials and diplomats, gathered at Paris with other Allied statesmen to draft peace terms, broached harsh conditions. The return of Alsace and Lorraine and payment of heavy reparations were taken as axiomatic. Concerned above all to ensure France's security from a resurgent Germany, Premier Clemenceau sought initially to dismember its former foe in establishing one or more buffer states on the west bank of the Rhine. Failing to achieve that, France supported the creation of independent states, including Poland and Czechoslovakia, on Germany's eastern border of sufficient strength to check a potential renewal of German ambitions in that region.

Yet, Clemenceau was enough of a statesman to realize that France could not dictate a peace, knowing that the British and Americans, whose aid had been indispensable to victory, had goals of their own and knowing, too, that permanent repression of Germany was impossible. He had little patience with the idealism behind many of the principles laid out by U.S. president Woodrow Wilson (r. 1912–20) in his famous Fourteen Points—God Almighty, he acidly remarked, had only 10—but he was willing enough to go along with commitments to freedom of the seas and creation of a League of Nations, and give up demands for French control of the Rhine, in return for mutual aid treaties with Britain and the United States promising military assistance in the event of an attack.

Thrashed out between January and June 1919 during negotiations in which the Germans were given no say and signed in a glittering ceremony in the Hall of Mirrors on June 28, the Treaty of Versailles gave France back its lost provinces. The west bank of the Rhine was to be permanently demilitarized and occupied by Allied troops for a period of 15 years. The Saar basin in Germany was likewise occupied and governed by Britain and France for 15 years, the coalfields ceded outright to the latter (the territory returned to Germany after a plebiscite in 1935). An Inter-Allied Commission would determine reparations figures, which, when set in 1921, the French declared to be too low. France acquired German colonies in Africa and administered Syria and Lebanon in the Middle East as mandates of the League of Nations.

The French ratified the treaty but only after a lengthy debate in the Chamber of Deputies that dragged on from August to October. The Socialists declared it to be too harsh. The center and right charged that it was too lenient, providing for no real assurances against German recovery and rearmament. They affirmed that aid treaties with Britain and the United States were of doubtful value—a fear borne out later when the U.S. Senate repudiated the entire treaty, including the League of Nations and the mutual security pact, and when Britain withdrew its aid pledge as well. Clemenceau defended his work, arguing that a less-than-perfect solution was inevitable, given the diplomatic compromises required by the involvement of so many actors. France would be compelled, he counseled, to maintain constant vigilance if it sought to keep the peace. It was an admonition that his war-weary countrymen, seeking to rest assured behind some invulnerable protective shield, were reluctant to hear.

The Search for Normalcy, 1919–1931

Anxious to return to the pursuits of peace, the French faced instead a stormy postwar start. A wave of strikes that began during the last years of the war continued through 1919, and violent clashes broke out in Paris on May Day (May 1). To mitigate labor unrest, some legislation was passed, including a law on collective bargaining (March 25, 1919) and one establishing an eight-hour workday (April 23, 1919), but tensions still simmered. In 1920, more than a million workers went on strike, most especially railway employees and miners in the north. Although a general strike called for May 1 proved disappointing, with barely half of railroad workers participating and fewer in other fields, the workers paid the consequences with thousands dismissed by railroad bosses and the CGT union losing half of its membership.

After the war, Parliament promptly resumed its prewar ascendancy over the executive. A striking change in the direction of power seemed in the offing as the 40-year trend to the left was reversed in November 1919, when the most rightist Chamber of Deputies since 1871 was elected, conservatives and moderates winning two-thirds of the seats. Called the Blue Horizon Chamber in reference to the military uniforms worn recently by many of the newly elected members, the body constituted the first in the Third Republic in which practicing Catholics made up a majority. The new regime proceeded to repair relations with the Vatican, which had been frayed, most especially over issues surrounding the separation of church and state.

But the political change proved more a momentary fluke than a future portend. A new electoral system in 1919 had given a fleeting advantage to parties that could organize effective electoral coalitions, which rightist groups were able to do under the title Bloc National. In fact, however, left-wing parties in 1919 scored vote totals higher collectively than those garnered in 1914, even if their main political vehicle, the SFIO party, was torn by bitter internal conflict occasioned by the 1917 Bolshevik revolution in Russia and the powerful pull the victory of the Communists there exerted on the far left.

Nothing really changed in the governing game after the war except that, whereas from 1899 to 1919 the Radicals had usually dominated right-center and left-center coalitions, from 1919 to 1936 the moderates would do so. The line dividing the two, however, was blurry. Both remained party groupings that were loosely stitched together. Although throughout most of the 1920s and 1930s, the Radicals constituted the largest single organized group in the Chamber, and they tightened their grip in the Senate, they remained, as they had been before the war, a confederation of middle-class individualists joined together more on the basis of personal interest than political principle. Politicians without firm convictions who could compromise best achieved the most success, notably Aristide Briand (1862–1932), who had already headed six cabinets before and during the war and who would form a record-breaking five more during the 1920s. His only serious rival during the decade was moderate Raymond Poincaré, a politician whose forte was finance. Poincaré broke precedent by returning to parliamentary politics after his presidential term ended in 1920 and held the premiership from 1922 to 1924 and again from 1926 to 1929.

By the end of the 1920s, the devastated areas had been rebuilt and industrial production rose well above the 1914 level. Women wartime workers having returned home, labor shortages were filled by immigration of some 2 million foreign workers. New industries—iron and steel, autos, petrochemicals, electrical equipment and production—boomed. Industrial firms modernized and grew larger. Finances, however, proved shaky. With the lifting of wartime currency controls, the franc lost more than 50 percent of its value within the first year of the armistice. In the early 1920s, wartime bonds fell due, which the government chose to repay with new issues bearing even higher interest rates. The interest burden consequently mounted at the same time that war loans from the United States went unpaid. Only a substantial tax increase, which politicians were reluctant to approve, could stem the revenue shortfall.

During the decade, a younger generation entered the political fray, including, on the right, Andre Tardieu (1876–1945) and Pierre Laval (1883–1945), and, on the left, Édouard Herriot (1872–1957) and Léon Blum (1872–1950). Herriot emerged as the spokesman of the Radical Party, while Blum sought to fill the gap in the Socialist leadership left by the assassination of Jaurès. The son of bourgeois Jewish parents and a brilliant student, a journalist, and a high civil servant, Blum won a seat in the Chamber in 1919 and strove first and foremost to stop the steady drift of the party into the Communist orbit. At a party congress in Tours in December 1920, his faction, which favored maintaining the tradition of working within the democratic system to effect change, lost a course-defining vote to the Communists. He and his supporters subsequently walked out, leaving almost everything—membership lists, electoral machinery, the party newspaper *L'humanité (Humanity)*—to the majority, which immediately renamed itself the Parti Communiste Français (French Communist Party).

Small in numbers and with little financial backing, the rump led by Blum fought its way back, retaining the SFIO title and gaining a dues-paying membership that by 1924 exceeded the Communists in attracting support from government bureaucrats and schoolteachers, among others. In 1922, Socialists in the Confédération Générale du Travail left as well to form a rival trade union, the Confédération Générale du Travail Unitaire (CGTU). In 1923, the party joined with the Radicals in creating a Cartel des Gauches (left-wing coalition), which together formed a government from 1924 to 1926.

During the 1920s, the Communists remained divided and quarrelsome, the members united around little more than an idealistic yearning for a Soviet-style government and kept in line by firm control from Moscow. After the mid-1920s, however, the party began to make slow but steady gains among voters, most especially in the Paris working-class suburbs, the departments of Cher and Lot-et-Garonne, and the "red crescent" area of the Massif Central, regions that would remain the core of Communist strength throughout the 20th century. But the party's steadfast refusal to cooperate with any other political group, viewing even the Socialists as "class" enemies, ensured its political isolation.

Though smaller, new movements also appeared on the center and moderate right. For the first time, Catholics engaged in organized political involvement. Christian democracy blossomed in the 1920s in a host of lay organizations, including young Christian worker and young Christian farmer groups and, especially, the Confédération Française de Travailleurs Chrétienne (CFTC), a new Catholic trade union founded in 1919. The Popular Democratic Party emerged in 1924, though it elected only a smattering of deputies, mostly in strongly Catholic Brittany and Alsace.

On the far right, the Action Française of Charles Maurras remained the most influential grouping. Its fervid nationalism and refurbished monarchism were now actively promoted by an armed militant wing, the Camelots du Roi, whose tacit encouragement of violence proved sufficiently off-putting for the Bourbon pretender to the throne to repudiate Maurras. In 1926, the Vatican instructed Catholics to abandon the movement, thus cutting out a major source of support. Its influence declined by 1930 when new protofascist and fascist groups outdistanced its appeal. Pierre Taittinger (1887–1965) founded the Jeunesses Patriotes, modeled after the fascists who succeeded to power in 1922 in Italy under dictator Benito Mussolini (1885–1945). Glorifying nationalism, one-man rule, and violence, fascism proved marginally attractive in the 1920s, but an increasing trend toward authoritarianism and a growing penchant for political action manifested themselves, most evident in the Croix de Feu, a nonpolitical organization of decorated war veterans formed in 1928 by Colonel François de la Rocque (1885–1946).

Stabilizing the currency and keeping France safe from a resurgent Germany were the two overriding concerns of the 1920s. The economy as a whole prospered and expanded. Agriculture lagged behind even as farming became slowly more efficient, especially in the northeast, where mechanized production of wheat and sugar beets became widespread, and as the number of rural workers continued to decline as they drifted to the cities.

Poincaré resumed the premiership in 1926 compelled to halt the by now almost permanent financial crisis, which, with nonstop inflation, threatened to collapse the value of the franc entirely. At long last, taxes were sharply increased and drastic cuts made in government expenditures. Capital returned from safe havens abroad or from hiding places at home to be invested or used to buy government bonds. The franc rose so fast that the government had to check its advance, but stability had returned.

In foreign affairs, France's postwar presence on the world stage grew more impressive than ever. The country's reach now extended over more than 4.5 million square miles with a population almost double that of the homeland. But while the prestige value was great, the gains in substance were few. With the exception of Algeria and, to a lesser extent, Tunisia and Morocco, none of the colonies attracted large-scale European settlement. French public spending on railways, harbors, and schools remained low, while private capital preferred more lucrative locales in developed places. The colonies drew small volumes of French goods and supplied little except foodstuffs in return. The overseas territories were ruled firmly from Paris under a bureaucracy that sent out thousands of colonial administrators. In exchange for the old policy of "assimilation"—by adopting French language and culture anyone among colonial peoples could become French—a new one of "association" aimed to imbue only a small native elite with French cultural traits, who would then share with the French the job of governing. At no time, however, did notions of granting local autonomy to the colonies or giving substantial decision-making powers to the natives enter into consideration.

But in the number-one foreign policy preoccupation—the search for security against Germany—French planners largely failed. A solid continental alliance of the states around Germany—attempted in agreements with the so-called Little Entente powers of Czechoslovakia, Yugoslavia, and Romania—never emerged because most of the new countries of eastern and Central Europe were too small and weak, with the exception of Poland, which became the anchor of France's eastern alliance system. A mutual security pact with Belgium in 1920 was abrogated in 1936, the Belgians reverting to their traditional policy of neutrality. France's efforts to put some muscle into the League of Nations—it sought to spell out terms for imposing sanctions against rogue nations and to create an independent military force under league auspices—came to nothing, foundering on the need in the Council of the league to secure a unanimous vote on all important questions and on a lack of agreement with Britain, which viewed the international organization more as an instrument of conciliation than coercion. Britain remained leery of giving any binding commitment to aid France, while the United

States withdrew into isolationism. The Soviet Union was recognized in 1924 but relations were stony—the Soviet government used its Paris embassy for propaganda and espionage. Failing to forge a reliable international security system, the nation sought insurance in its own military strength, embarking on construction of a defensive wall of its own. Begun in 1929 and completed in 1940, the Maginot Line, named for its designer, André Maginot (1877–1932), consisted of a line of elaborate fortifications along the German border; however, a line that, though formidable, stopped, significantly, at the frontier with Belgium, which took offense at an armed extension to the sea along its border.

The problem of reparations led to a break with the British, who, adopting a more forgiving attitude soon after the war, sided with their former enemy in believing that compensation figures were set too high. Deciding to act with no other collaborators save for the Belgians, in January 1923, France sent troops to occupy Germany's Ruhr valley—its western industrial heartland—on grounds, which were legally valid, that Germany had evaded and postponed payments due. The Germans backed down and, by the end of 1923, agreed to start sending sums. The episode marked the high point of French independent action during the interwar years; henceforth, in European statecraft the French would hesitate to act without the support of Britain.

Foreign policy in the late 1920s was shaped almost entirely by Aristide Briand, who served as minister of foreign affairs practically without interruption from 1926 until 1932. He championed disarmament and the League of Nations and negotiated a host of agreements— the Locarno treaties (1926) guaranteeing Germany's western borders and the Kellogg-Briand Pact (1928) outlawing war as an instrument of national policy—and even drafted a scheme for a projected United States of Europe in an effort to effect a reconciliation with a Germany that, in the late 1920s, because it had grown increasingly prosperous and stable, appeared less menacing. Briand withdrew the last French occupation troops in 1930, five years ahead of schedule.

At the end of the 1920s, the "Locarno spirit" seemed to offer the prospect of a bright future. France was prosperous with a booming economy and a stable currency in a peaceful Europe. Paris saw itself as once again the glittering capital of the Continent. The city celebrated the outstanding feat of the decade in extending a rapturous welcome to U.S. pilot Charles Lindbergh (1902–74), who landed his *Spirit of Saint Louis* monoplane at Le Bourget Airport on May 21, 1927, having completed the first solo, nonstop transatlantic flight. The daring demonstration pointed the way to the future—Air France, the national carrier, was launched in October 1933. At the same time, it was a city and country enjoying a postwar resurgence of an ever-changing, vibrant culture.

The Cultural Scene in the Interwar Years

The cataclysm of the Great War profoundly upset accepted and established patterns of thought and action. The optimism so dominant in the positivist prewar era gave way, among some thinkers and writers, to a skepticism best exemplified by fringe movements labeled collectively as dadaism and surrealism. With their origins in avant-garde groupings such as fauvism and postimpressionism, already in full revolt against prevailing attitudes before the war, dadaist and surrealist artists and authors rejected scientism and rationalism in favor of a nonsensical irrationalism, which, they held, more accurately reflected the senselessness of a world that could plunge itself so readily into world war. Emerging in the midst of World War I as a protest against the slaughter, dadaism had its postwar center in Left Bank Paris under artists such as Marcel Duchamp (1887–1968), whose prewar move to cubism had caused an uproar when his *Nu descendant un escalier* (*Nude Descending a Staircase,* 1912) was shown at exhibitions in Paris and New York.

A man of action who worked as a military aviator and who died—his plane was never recovered—while on a reconnaissance mission for Free French forces in World War II, Antoine de Saint-Exupéry (1900–44) evoked the romance of flying in beautifully poetic works (*Vol de nuit* [*Night Flight*], 1931) in seeking to link the meditative peace he found in his vocation with exaltation of love and sacrifice for humanity. Love transcends intellect in his *Le petit prince* (*The Little Prince,* 1943), an immensely popular children's book read by adults for its allegorical meanings. Rejecting realism for a belief that the imagination is the source of all ideas, prewar poet, novelist, and art critic Guillaume Apollinaire (1880–1918) helped shape postwar attitudes in combining sentimentality and irony in his works (*Les mamelles de Tirésias* [*The Breasts of Tiresias*], 1917), and he is believed to have coined the term *surrealism.* The leader of the French surrealists, André Breton (1896–1966) sought to express in his writings (*Les champs magnétiques* [*The Magnetic Fields*], 1924) the subconscious at work, which drives human beings without interference from reason, and the power of love freed from all social and moral shackles. In both poetry and painting, surrealism exerted a powerful influence on budding artists. A member for a time of a surrealist group, Antoine

Arnaud (1896–1948) wrote a collection of essays in the 1930s that laid the groundwork for modern experimental theater. He was known equally as a film actor.

French filmmaking fell from its exalted prewar heights after World War I, and U.S. imports increased their hold throughout the 1920s. Hollywood served as the model for sentimental love stories, comedies, and historical dramas, but serious theorizing about filmmaking also took place during a decade when the term *cinéaste* (film producer) was coined. In addition to U.S. competition, financial constraints during the 1930s led to the collapse of major studios such as Gaumont and Pathé-Nathan, while rigorous censorship laws, in place since 1917, stymied creativity. Most films were made for mass-market entertainment, though quality artistic productions were also crafted. A versatile writer and poet and a leader of the surrealist movement, Jean Cocteau (1889–1963) made his first film, *Le sang d'un poète* (*The Blood of a Poet*), in 1930; it is regarded as instrumental in bringing surrealism to cinema. His post–World War II films, including *La belle et la bête* (*Beauty and the Beast*, 1945) and *Orphée* (*Opheus*, 1950), have become screen classics. Surrealism faded in the 1930s, while filmmaking turned increasingly toward social subjects. Director René Clair (1898–1981) became known for the saucy humor in his films. The comedy *Le million* (*The Million*, 1938) has endured as a classic among choreographed musicals. Arguably the French director who possessed the most versatile gifts, Jean Renoir (1894–1979) satirized the bourgeoisie in *Boudu sauvé des eaux* (*Boudu Saved from Drowning*, 1932) and exposed their shallow values in *La régle du jeu* (*The Rules of the Game*, 1939), while his *La grande illusion* (*The Grand Illusion*, 1937) remains a powerful paean against war. A galaxy of stars emerged in the interwar years, prominent among them actor Jean Gabin (1904–76), whose characters—small-time criminals and ordinary working-class types—are strong yet vulnerable, neither altogether guilty nor innocent.

In literature, the outstanding talents of the 1920s were Marcel Proust (1871–1922) and André Gide (1869–1961), both writers who centered their attentions on the human mind. Born in Paris into a wealthy bourgeois family, Proust began his multivolumed masterpiece *À la recherche du temps perdu* (*Remembrance of Things Past* [or, more recently, *In Search of Lost Time*], 1913–22) before the war, but its mood reflects clearly the more somber postwar temper. Writing in the first person by means of an interior monologue, Proust examines, using exquisite language, the details of a disappearing social world peopled by a rich variety of characters, whose psychological development, exemplifying his interest in the subconscious, he probes minutely. Preoccupied with the passage of time, he seeks to uncover eternal truths in an ever-changing world.

André Gide became a literary icon in the interwar period, his nostalgia for and, at the same time, rejection of what he saw as the solid and safe middle-class values of prewar society leading him on an introspective journey reluctantly to find new ones. For Gide, his search involved an exhaustive lifetime self-examination, striving to reconcile the complexities and contradictions inherent in his dual bourgeois Catholic and Protestant heritage as well as in his homosexuality. In works such as *L'Immoraliste* (*The Immoraliste,* 1902) and *La porte étroite* (*Straight Is the Gate,* 1909), Gide expressed his belief that it was up to the individual alone to make his or her destiny, which was neither predetermined nor divinely guided. A founder of an influential literary journal *La Nouvelle Revue française* and an author of books that proved instrumental in securing reforms in French colonial laws, he received the Nobel Prize in literature in 1947.

At the same time that writers and artists reflected the rebellious currents in vogue, others remained true to the old Enlightenment heritage and the rationalistic tradition based on Descartes's Cartesian process of logical deduction. While the universities might be the strongholds of the new spirit of irrationalism, the old virtues of order and clarity continued to be stressed in the secondary and elementary schools. Many artists also continued to work in the traditional vein. Essayist Julien Benda (1867–1956), a passionate defender of rationalism in works such as *La trahison des clercs* (*The Betrayal of the Intellectuals,* 1927), was widely read. André Maurois (1885–1967) wrote works reflective of the skeptical tradition of Anatole France, as well as histories and short science-fiction essays. French bourgeois family life is the distinguishing topic of writer Jules Romains (1885–1972), who wrote almost 100 titles (*Les hommes de bonne volonté* [*Men of Good Will*], 1932–46) and who founded a doctrine called unanimism, which held that human beings are not so much individual actors as they are social creatures. Georges Duhamel (1884–1966), who worked as a surgeon during World War I, wrote prolifically afterward, his works extolling a civilization based on compassionate concern for humanity rather than technological progress (*Confession de minuit* [Midnight confession], 1920–32). The towering poet of the period, Paul Valéry (1871–1945), a disciple of Mallarmé, sought an accommodation between acting and thinking in verses that express and, on occasion, join the sensations of the self within classical forms. Major Catholic novelists include François Mauriac (1885–1970) and Georges Bernanos (1888–1948), both of whose novels deal with basic moral conflicts, chiefly between good and evil.

The moral battles that had long preoccupied defenders of the old values held little appeal for a new generation of young writers in the 1930s. Emmanuel Meunier (1905–50) denounced modern capitalism, with its spiritual decay and crass individualism, and proposed to replace it with a synthesis of Christianity and socialism, which he called *personnelisme.* Some practiced what they preached. Blending politics and spirituality, the activist turned religious mystic Simone Weil (1909–43) supported striking workers and the unemployed as a writer on social and economic issues in the 1930s. Born to Alsatian agnostic Jewish parents, she was drawn to Roman Catholicism after experiencing a religious ecstasy in 1937. Weil espoused a philosophy in which obligations take precedence over rights, the obligation for individuals to love and respect others superseding all others. She put into practice her beliefs, dying in Britain after refusing to eat, as a gesture in solidarity with those suffering in World War II, just after completing *L'Enracinement (The Need for Roots),* a statement of her guiding principles that was published in 1949. Inspired early on by surrealism, André Malraux (1901–76) went to Indochina as an archaeologist but soon became immersed in the struggle against French colonial rule, which he used as material for his novel *La condition humaine (Man's Fate,* 1931). Passionately opposed to fascism, he fought against the Fascists in the Spanish civil war and in the French resistance during World War II, and served as minister for cultural affairs in the 1960s. Others were drawn to this new creed, however, which proved so attractive to so many in Europe in the 1920s and 1930s in offering the excitement of physical violence expended on behalf of both nationalism and socialism. Pierre Drieu la Rochelle (1893–1945) welcomed wholeheartedly the world being made next door in Italy and Germany. In the 1930s, it was a world in which the voices of the fascist dictators grew ever more shrill with each passing year, one that France, preoccupied with domestic dramas, would be compelled increasingly to confront.

Crisis Decade, 1931–1939

France remained prosperous for two years after the New York Stock Market crash in October 1929 brought economic havoc to most of the rest of the world's wealthy nations. The country's antiquated small farms and the traditionally conservative, cautious character of business cushioned the shock as it had, earlier in the 1920s, precluded the kind of feverish speculative financial gambling that had occurred in the United States. In the early 1930s, gold flowed into the country because the franc stayed strong, and hardly any banks failed throughout the decade.

When a downturn set in by 1932 with a rise in bankruptcies and unemployment, the country was psychologically ill-prepared to accept hard times. Under a system of government with a weak executive and a dominant legislature, the nation struggled to enact the strong economic measures needed. Convinced that economic change would not be possible without first implementing political reform, André Tardieu, the key politician of the period who headed three cabinets between 1929 and 1932, sought to reduce the chronic instability by modernizing the electoral system in introducing an Anglo-American scheme of electing deputies by simple plurality, eliminating the need for a runoff ballot. Defeated by the Radicals and the Socialists in elections in 1932, in which the left won its greatest electoral triumph since 1914 and went on to govern from 1932 to 1934 in a second Cartel des Gauches, Tardieu withdrew from politics, leaving the country—with six cabinets in 20 months in 1932–33—to return to the old ways. Eleven governments devised 14 economic recovery plans between 1932 and 1935. Policymakers were convinced that France needed only to seal itself off behind protective tariffs to prevent economic malaise. Quotas were put in place when world prices fell so low as to threaten France's high tariff walls with a flood of foreign foodstuffs. Producers cut production and the government increased taxes and slashed administrative expenses, military spending, and veterans' pensions. Foreign laborers, who in 1930 constituted about 7 percent of the workforce, were sent home.

With an ineffective government and a worsening economy, many were drawn increasingly to authoritarian alternatives, which proved especially attractive following Adolf Hitler's succession to power as chancellor of Germany in January 1933. The dynamism and boastfulness of the fascist dictators beckoned, and radical right-wing movements grew in strength.

In 1934, the right pounced with glee in an attack on the regime that, whether planned or not, as the left charged and the right denied, profoundly shook the political system. A scandal initiated by a shady financier, Serge Stavisky (1886–1934), led to rumors of government collusion in his protection from prosecution for a scheme that bilked hoodwinked investors. When Stavisky was found dead—a suicide or murdered—the story spread that his death had been engineered by compromised politicians. The government fell, but when a new one formed by Radical-Socialist Édouard Daladier (1884–1970) took little

276

action to investigate the case, groups on the extreme right hurried into action. "Down with the Thieves!" screamed the Action Française in its newspaper. Street demonstrations begun in January 1934 culminated on the night of February 6 with a massive rally of various right-wing groups on the Place de la Concorde. Tensions spilled over, leading to a violent melee that left 15 dead and more than 1,500 injured—the largest bloodletting in Paris since 1871. Determined to counter the rightist protesters, on February 9, Communist-led agitators struck back, battling the police in a confrontation that placed working-class districts under a virtual state of siege. The trade unions called a general strike for February 12.

Daladier had resigned on February 7, and the creation of a "national union" ministry led by conservatives calmed jitters, but not for long. The fall of the government convinced the right that street action could prove successful. Labeling the regime corrupt, rightist groups called for national regeneration by removing it. Fearful of a possible fascist coup, the left mobilized. Antifascist coalitions such as the Comité de Vigilance des Intellectuels Antifascistes (Vigilance Committee of Anti-Fascist Intellectuals) emerged. During the next two years, the nation seemed poised on the brink of civil war, while the government, after an abortive effort by Premier Gaston Doumergue (1863–1937) to alter the constitution to strengthen the executive, remained largely paralyzed.

In an atmosphere ripe with tension, the left made steady electoral gains, winning municipal elections in May 1935. Communist and Socialist trade unions merged in March 1936. Their respective political parties joined with the Radical Socialists in overcoming a 15-year-old division to unite in a Popular Front, which, campaigning under slogans such as "Bar the way to fascism" and "Bread, peace, and freedom," won a narrow but clear-cut victory in elections in May 1936.

The new government took office on June 5 in the midst of a rash of factory sit-down strikes. Headed by Léon Blum, the first Socialist and the first Jew to lead a cabinet, the Popular Front moved with an energy not seen since before the war. Bringing labor and management together, the government engineered the so-called Matignon Agreement, which compelled employers to accept an industrial settlement that included wage increases, compulsory collective bargaining, a 40-hour work week, and paid vacations. The state tightened its control of the Bank of France, and the armaments industry was nationalized.

But the left's victory, far from cowing the opposition, invigorated rightist forces, which lost no time in launching a campaign of invective against the government. Under the slogan "Better Hitler than Blum," journalists and politicians heaped abuse on the premier, whom right-ist hoodlums had savagely beaten earlier in the year. Blum banned the Croix de Feu and other right-wing leagues in June 1936, only to see these movements reemerge as political parties. More than a half-million members quickly joined the Parti Social Français (French Social Party), the successor to the Croix de Feu, while the Parti Populaire Français (French Popular Party), founded by Jacques Doriot (1898–1945), an ex-Communist mayor of the Paris suburb of Saint-Denis, mod-eled itself exclusively on Germany's National Socialists. In November 1937, extremist army officers assembled in a Comité Secret d'Action Révolutionnaire (Secret Committee of Revolutionary Action), famil-iarly known as the Cagoule, to plan a coup d'état.

In the end, their scheming proved unnecessary because continuing economic woes brought the regime down. The labor settlement proved inflationary, and rising costs along with rumors of deflation prompted speculators to withdraw funds from the country, which aggravated the trade deficit. The rumors came true when Blum, desperate to jump-start the economy, reversed an earlier promise and devalued the franc in October 1936. His hopes were dashed, however; the measure was ineffective in the face of a continuing drop in industrial produc-tion. Persistent unemployment led to a renewal of strikes in summer 1937. Rifts in the leftist alliance appeared, caused partly by disagree-ments over the government's policy of nonintervention in the Spanish civil war (1936–39). Blum asked for emergency powers to cope with the crisis, including strict controls on foreign exchange, which the Chamber granted but which the Senate, ever cautiously conservative, refused. Blum resigned on June 22, 1937. A second Blum ministry in March 1938 met with a virtual replay when the premier's proposals for exchange controls and a capital tax were turned down by the Senate, and his government fell in less than a month.

The center and center-right returned to power under Daladier. The euphoria engendered by the Popular Front among workers evaporated, a general strike in late 1938 failed dismally, and trade union member-ship plummeted. The government took no direct steps to modernize the economy and, in any case, by 1938, was fully preoccupied by inter-national events.

Since March 1936, when Hitler's armies had marched into the Rhineland in violation of the Treaty of Versailles and the government had failed to act, the regime fumbled about in search of an effective approach to blunt a resurgent Germany. Some held firm in the belief that any concessions to the Nazi regime would be dangerous. Some hoped Hitler might behave if given his way. Some saw no alternative except for France to renounce any independent role, give up claims to great-nation status, and make the best possible arrangement with continental Europe's rising power next door. French fascists sought a blatantly copycat totalitarian state.

The capitulation of Britain and France to the dismemberment of Czechoslovakia at Munich in October 1938 marked France's abandonment of its binding treaty commitments to the defense of that central European nation and its acquiescence to a policy of appeasement, which, while welcomed by much of French public opinion, was largely promoted, not by France, but by Britain, whose lead French statesmen now studiously followed. Surprised at the rapturous crowds that greeted him on his return from Munich, Premier Daladier held no allusions that the pact constituted a disastrous setback for the Western democracies, a setback made evident in March 1939 when Hitler absorbed the rest of Czechoslovakia and only months later put pressure on Poland.

All segments of opinion save for the far right now rallied behind a policy of firm resistance. From March to August 1939, the government pursued negotiations with the Soviet Union in an 11th-hour effort to contain Hitler with a strong East-West alliance. The announcement that Soviet premier Joseph Stalin (r. 1922–53) had concluded a pact with Hitler on August 23, 1939, stunned the country. Many concluded that it would be folly to fight for Poland now that France was left largely alone—Britain was not expected to be fully armed for several years. But reasoning that France would emerge from another Munich as nothing more than a German satellite, the government resisted the cries of the defeatists and joined promptly with Britain in declaring war on September 3, 1939, following Germany's invasion of Poland two days before.

War Once More, 1939–1940

No one foresaw the speed with which Poland would be defeated after a mere month of fighting during which the French provided no help to their beleaguered ally—a few border raids into the German Saar basin proved no more than diversions. With Poland no longer a cause to fight for, the government came under intense pressure to quit the war, both from leading politicians—sentiment strong among them that Germany, supported by the Soviet air force, would turn on a France left isolated by Britain, which would now stand aloof on its island ready to make a deal after France fell—and from Hitler himself, who offered to make immediate peace.

But the government held firm. The so-called *drôle de guerre* (phony war)—the autumn and winter of 1939–40—passed in squabbling with the British and bracing for an expected German attack, which did not materialize only because of bad weather. Gas masks were issued to the public in Paris, and the city's monuments and public spaces were ringed with protective sandbags.

The large, well-trained French army was still believed by many to be among the world's best. But it was led by men unable to recognize the changed conditions of warfare so amply demonstrated in Germany's "lightning war," or blitzkrieg, defeat of Poland. Lacking imagination and foresight, planners such as Marshall Pétain clung to the lessons learned in the last war, anticipating a repeat of the drawn-out defensive struggle of World War I, from which, they believed, equipped with the Maginot Line—its superb formidable instrument—France would emerge victorious.

Preparedness also suffered from a lack of enthusiasm for war among wide segments of the public. The patriotic sentiments so widely expressed in 1914 were much less in evidence; in 1939, there were no calls for a *union sacrée.* Widespread pacifism rippled through society throughout the 1930s. Many on the far right made more common cause with fascism abroad than they did with the Third Republic, which Action Française excoriated as *la gueuse* (the bitch). With war looming in the lead up to the Munich agreement in 1938, right-wing journalist Marcel Déat (1894–1955) argued in a newspaper article titled "Why Die for Danzig?" in favor of admiring, not fighting, Germany. After the Nazi-Soviet pact of August 1939, Communists denounced the war as a battle of one imperialist against another and, as such, of no concern to workers.

The military struggled to put itself in readiness. The deep demographic gap, aggravated by the losses incurred during 1914–18, which the French labeled the "hollow years," meant that veterans in their 40s and 50s had to be recalled to the colors to fill the ranks. Only in 1938 did the government adopt a plan to modernize the air force, and the onset of war caught the country in the midst of the conversion effort. In September 1939, the French had fewer than 500 fully modern airplanes available as opposed to the 4,000 at the disposal of the Germans. In November 1939, Premier Daladier wired U.S. president Franklin D. Roosevelt (r. 1933–45) in a desperate plea for 10,000 planes to be sold at once, saying he was prepared to mortgage the country itself as the price. Rejected, he sank into a dispirited temper that matched much of the general mood. The French possessed almost as many tanks as the Germans—2,300 versus 2,700—but, parceled out in small groups to support a large number of infantry divisions, they failed to pack the punch of the German's highly mobile armored (panzer) divisions. Again, a conversion into more effective fighting formations was under way, but it was only half completed by spring 1940.

And so the army stood ready, half of it lined up along the heavily fortified Maginot Line and half of it, from Sedan to the English Channel, deployed along the only lightly defended frontier with Belgium. While the soldiers waited, the politicians resumed their feuding. Rivals of Daladier sought to replace his lackluster leadership and also to remove the commander in chief of the Allied forces, General Maurice Gamelin (1872–1958), a learned but indecisive officer wedded to the doctrines of the past.

Daladier was thrown out in a cabinet crisis on March 19, 1940, in part because his government had failed to help Finland resist an attack during the previous winter from the Soviet Union. He was replaced by Paul Reynaud (1873–1966), a more spirited politician who, along with a few military mavericks such as Colonel Charles de Gaulle (1890–1970), advocated new battle concepts based on mechanized mobile armed forces backed up by increased airpower. Reynaud, too, proved unable either to clear up differences of opinion between government ministers and military leaders or to end the bickering among the politicians, forced to keep his rival Daladier in the cabinet to maintain the political balance of forces. Feuding between the two led to the government's collapse on May 9, the very day before Germany launched its long-awaited attack.

The shaky Reynaud government stayed in office to fight the battle occasioned by the German invasion of the Netherlands, Belgium, and Luxembourg in the predawn hours on May 10. Within one week after the initial assault, the French lines were pierced near Sedan. A German spearhead of fast-moving tanks swung west toward the Channel, bypassing the Maginot Line, disrupting French communications, and splitting the Allied armies in two. Bewildered by the speed of the offensive and incapable of improvising an effective counterattack, the army fell apart. Headquarters lost touch with the various commands, its efforts to wage war hampered by as many as 6 million refugees who choked the roads, their columns strafed by dive-bombing Stuka fighters, which added to the chaos. Britain held back the bulk of the Royal Air Force, bracing for an expected cross-Channel attack. The government turned down a proposal broached by de Gaulle to retreat to a redoubt in Brittany pending a transfer to North Africa. In a gesture indicative of the desperate national

Refugees fleeing Paris, June 1940 (Getty Images)

predicament, free-thinking anticlerical republicans turned to their old enemy—the next-to-last cabinet of the Third Republic attending a special high mass at Notre-Dame on May 19—to implore divine aid.

After the Battle of Dunkirk (May 26–June 4), when British and French troops evacuated the northern coast, the Germans turned south to face a French army that had largely disintegrated as an effective fighting force. Paris emptied out, 2 million of its inhabitants fleeing by any means possible to the south, the burning suburban fuel storage tanks blackening the skies at their backs giving an apocalyptic aura to the chaotic scene. On June 10, Italy pounced, launching an attack on a reeling France, and the government departed for Tours. On June 15, it fled yet again—to Bordeaux. The capital was occupied without a fight. A dispirited cabinet voted to ask for armistice terms; Reynaud submitted his resignation and requested President Albert Lebrun (1871–1950) to appoint Marshal Pétain premier. Pétain had been brought in to head the Ministry of War on May 18 in a desperate hope that he might be able to repeat the 1914 "miracle of the Marne." On June 22, the capitulation was signed in a ceremony—held in the forest of Compiègne in the same railway car where the 1914 armistice had been concluded—arranged deliberately to have the maximum humiliating impact. Stunned by the swift course of events, French men and women reeled in shock and—among many—genuine grief, the magnitude of the tragedy almost beyond their belief.

Division and Liberation, 1940–1945

France split in two, at once geographically and, over time, politically. Two-thirds of the country—the north and the entire Atlantic coastline—were occupied and ruled directly by Nazi Germany, which also incorporated Alsace-Lorraine directly into the Reich. The remaining one-third—the south and east—was governed by a regime headed by Marshal Pétain. Headquartered in the famous spa town of Vichy, the marshal, at 84, aged, stubborn, and sly, put in place a new authoritarian order. A competing version was offered at once by General de Gaulle, who, in disobeying orders, had fled in a British plane from Bordeaux to London. There, on June 18, 1940, he issued a call for continuing resistance. Few heard—or heeded—his message in the June confusion,

Marshal Henri-Philippe Pétain (center) and Minister of Defense Admiral François Darlan (left) greet German field marshal Hermann Göring (1893–1946) as he arrives for discussions at Saint-Florentin-Vergigny, 1941. (Library of Congress)

but in time it would serve as the nucleus for a revival of French esteem. The Free French movement that he began eventually attained the status of a de facto government in exile.

Many of those on the right saw their wishes fulfilled under Pétain, who ushered in the strongman regime they had sought for so long. On July 9 and 10, 1940, the National Assembly voted overwhelmingly to revise the 1875 constitution to give him full powers. In 1940, and again in 1942 and 1944, the principal executive power at Vichy was held by Pierre Laval, a wily politician who had held many cabinet posts in prewar governments and who, as Pétain's chief aide, engaged actively in collaboration with Nazi Germany. In the interval when Laval was out of favor with the marshal, the dominant minister was Admiral François Darlan (1881–1942), a naval officer who commanded Vichy's armed forces and who later joined the Allied side and was assassinated.

The republic was blamed for the defeat. Vichy aimed to replace it with a "National Revolution." "Liberty, Equality, and Fraternity" gave way to "Work, Family, and Fatherland" as national slogans. Educational reform and a return to the values of the Catholic faith—religious instruction was restored to the state schools—would undo the moral and social decadence that, the authorities held, had brought disaster under the anticlerical republic. Officials sought to establish a corporative-style state, with government, business, and labor joined together in premodern, guildlike cooperative enterprises. Labor unions were abolished and strikes outlawed. Special corporations were set up, each uniting industrial workers, farmers, employers, veterans, and even children. Resolved as it was to replace the corruption and instability of the Third Republic, in the end, however, Vichy exhibited many of the same weaknesses. The assortment of politicians, right-wing ideologues, patriots, and profit seekers gathered around Pétain fell to feuding, leaving reform efforts unfinished or never begun. The thoroughgoing corporative structure failed to emerge, and a constitution for the country remained in the drafting stage.

The central fact remained that Vichy operated under the shadow of the German conqueror, to which it owed its very existence and whose commands and demands it could never discount. Those demands grew increasingly harsh, and the regime sought to mitigate them, but usually to little effect. Seeking to replenish its shortage of workers drained away in fighting the Soviet Union, which it attacked in June 1941, Germany insisted on conscripting French laborers. Laval's efforts at evasion failed, and under the Service du Travail Obligatoire (Obligatory Labor

Jewish children at the Izieu Children's Home shortly before they were deported, on April 6, 1944, to death camps (AFP/Getty Images)

Service), some 700,000 French workers were recruited, or compelled, into service in German war plants.

In one particular policy, Vichy needed no prompting from the Germans. Anti-Semitism was dominant among many officials, who blamed the Jews—Léon Blum and other left-wing Jewish politicians were cited—for contributing to the 1940 defeat. On its own Vichy set up a General Office for Jewish Affairs in March 1941. Jews were required to register with the police, and, under its auspices, beginning in July, many were deprived of their businesses and homes and some were imprisoned. Thus, the institutional framework was already in place when the Nazi extermination policy began in earnest in 1942. Some 330,000 Jews lived in France at the start of the war, about half of them foreigners. A flood of German and Austrian refugees had arrived beginning in November 1938 after discriminatory Nuremberg Laws had been adopted, followed by Polish Jews in autumn 1939. Most lived in the Paris area. The first mass deportations began in the occupied zone on July 16, 1942, when some 13,000 foreign-born Jews were rounded up, confined in the Vélodrome d'Hiver sports arena in Paris, and then shipped to the concentration camp at Drancy before being sent on to the death camps in Poland. In Vichy, the government tried at first to delay and negotiate, agreeing to turn over foreign-born Jews in return for a pledge to spare native French citizens; in the end, however, efforts proved ineffectual. Although some Catholic voices were raised in opposition and some police units were less than zealous in carrying out orders, others cooperated fully. It is estimated that some 90,000 French Jews perished in the Holocaust, or some 26 percent of France's prewar Jewish population (Davidowitz 1986, 403).

Conditions of life steadily worsened as the war dragged on. Industrial and agricultural production plummeted to below Great Depression levels. Coal and heating oil grew scarce, gasoline largely disappeared, and essential food items were strictly rationed. Daily life in the cities revolved around waiting in long lines before butcher, bakery, and grocery shops. The Germans became increasingly rapacious, stripping the country—the richest in resources in western Europe—of everything from food stocks to raw materials to machinery to priceless artworks.

In response to growing dissatisfaction, Vichy adopted increasingly repressive measures. Arbitrary arrests became commonplace, and after August 1941, emergency courts were set up to try growing numbers of offenders. In 1943, the regime organized the Milice, a special security force. Torture became an accepted tool of state action.

Special courts and police were established in part to blunt the Germans' declared intention to seize at random and execute hostages as a deterrent to sabotage. Almost spontaneously, a whole series of small, isolated underground movements emerged gradually, beginning within two months of the 1940 surrender. Later, many young men fled potential labor conscription and hid away in remote areas of central and southeastern France, where they joined armed groups called the maquis. In the unoccupied zone, most resisters came from the left of the political spectrum—the Communists among the most virulent opponents of the Nazis after the invasion of the Soviet Union—while in the German-occupied north, a broader membership was recruited. Groups were organized separately in north and south, except for the Communists, whose Francs Tireurs Partisans Français (French Partisan Snipers, FPS) straddled both zones. To weld these diverse underground units into a nationwide federation, agents from de Gaulle's Free French were smuggled in from Britain. Seeking to forge a united movement to serve as the base from which to build a new postwar France, the general secured creation of a Conseil Nationale de la Résistance (National Council of the Resistance) in May 1943, made up not only of the major resistance groups but also of the chief political parties and trade unions.

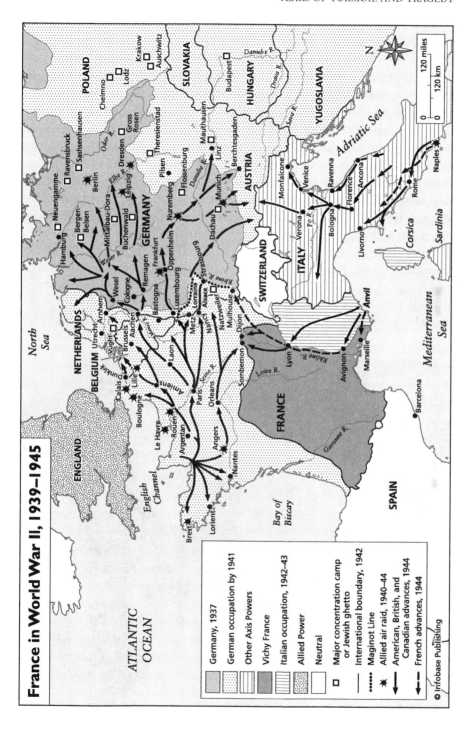

France in World War II, 1939–1945

POLAND
SLOVAKIA
HUNGARY
YUGOSLAVIA
AUSTRIA
GERMANY
SWITZERLAND
ITALY
NETHERLANDS
BELGIUM
FRANCE
SPAIN
ENGLAND

North Sea
Adriatic Sea
Mediterranean Sea
Bay of Biscay
English Channel
ATLANTIC OCEAN

Corsica
Sardinia

Krakow
Auschwitz
Lodz
Chelmno
Gross Rosen
Theresienstadt
Sachsenhausen
Ravensbruck
Neuengamme
Bergen Belsen
Hamburg
Berlin
Dresden
Leipzig
Buchenwald
Mittelbau-Dora
Weser R.
Oder R.
Elbe R.
Danube R.
Budapest
Mauthausen
Berchtesgaden
Linz
Munich
Dachau
Flossenburg
Pilsen
Nuremberg
Oppenheim
Frankfurt
Strasbourg
Rhine R.
Luxembourg
Remagen
Cologne
Wesel
Arnhem
Utrecht
Vught
Brussels
Aachen
Bastogne
Metz
Lorraine
Nancy Alsace
Natzweiler
Mulhouse
Dijon
Leon
Amiens
Seine R.
Paris
Orleans
Sombernon
Loire R.
Lyon
Rhône R.
Avignon
Marseille
Garonne R.
Barcelona
Dunkirk
Calais
Lille
Boulogne
Le Havre
Rouen
Argentan
Angers
Nantes
Lorient
Brest
Danube R.
Drau R.
Sava R.
Po R.
Monfalcone
Venice
Verona
Ravenna
Bologna
Florence
Ancona
Livorno
Rome
Naples
Anvil

120 miles
120 km

N

© Infobase Publishing

Legend:
- Germany, 1937
- German occupation by 1941
- Other Axis Powers
- Vichy France
- Italian occupation, 1942–43
- Allied Power
- Neutral
- □ Major concentration camp or Jewish ghetto
- International boundary, 1942
- Maginot Line
- ✳ Allied air raid, 1940–44
- ↓ American, British, and Canadian advances, 1944
- ↑ French advances, 1944

Clandestine paramilitary forces were united under a single command, titled Forces Françaises de l'Intérieur (French Forces of the Interior, FFI).

Throughout the war, the vast majority of the public sat on the sidelines—active collaborators and resisters were limited to a distinct minority—but opinion began inexorably to swing toward the Allied side. It started from a low point. In 1940, only a miniscule few rallied to de Gaulle's side. Finding it hard to believe that the war was not over, the vast majority expected that Britain would soon sue for peace. Most French reacted with rage when the British, fearing the French fleet would fall into the hands of the Germans, attacked and sank it at Mérs-el-Kébir, on the Algerian coast on July 3, 1940, killing or wounding more than 1,600. But sentiment gradually shifted, especially after Britain staved off defeat and after the United States entered the war in December 1941. Now fully aware that American power might tip the scales in favor of an Allied victory, Vichy adopted a fence-straddling attitude (*attentisme*), assuring the Germans of absolute loyalty but seeking wherever possible to distance itself from its overlord. Idealism for

Local resistance fighters wave their rifles overhead as they greet British troops arriving in their village, Quillebeuf, in August 1944. (AP Images)

288

a new order and popular support for Vichy steadily drained away after the Germans occupied the entire country in November 1942. Resisters fought collaborators in deadly clashes. Resistance by bands of partisans grew bolder, sparking harsh reprisals, most tragically carried out at the village of Oradour-sur-Glane in the Haute-Vienne Department, where, on June 10, 1944, 642 men, women, and children—including six unfortunates who happened to be cycling through the town—were rounded up and massacred, the men machine-gunned in barns and the women and children burned alive in the church.

De Gaulle moved his headquarters from London to Algiers following the successful Allied landings in North Africa in November 1942. From small colonial holdings in the Pacific, India, and Africa, Free French forces built up an independent territorial base with which to compete with the British and Americans, who in the beginning proved not especially welcoming. Before its entry in the war, the United States in particular kept its distance, hoping that by keeping lines open to Vichy, it might secure some degree of influence in blunting the latter's close collaboration with the Germans. In North Africa, the Americans chose to cooperate at first with Admiral Darlan and, after his assassination, with General Giraud as an alternative to de Gaulle, whom they found to be a difficult, egoistic man. Wrongly suspecting that de Gaulle's motives might be more dictatorial than democratic, President Roosevelt withheld legal recognition of his Free French government until October 1944.

By then, liberation of French soil was well under way. Informed of the D-day invasion (June 6, 1944) only after it had already begun, an incensed de Gaulle managed to soothe his ruffled pride by the time he made his triumphal entrance, marching on foot down the Champs-Élysées on August 25, 1944, into a jubilant Paris, where the honor of being the first to enter was given to the French 2nd Armored Division under General Philippe Leclerc (1902–47). Allied armies had moved swiftly, breaking out at Avranches from the Normandy beachheads and, after invading the Riviera coast, driving north in close coordination with FFI guerrilla units. In some areas, self-appointed resistance leaders, many of them Communists, moved quickly to fill the power vacuum left by the retreating Germans. Backed by a government infrastructure already in place, de Gaulle found it easy to appoint speedily his own regional representatives with orders to take over from these and other local groups.

By spring 1945, all of the country had been liberated. The human costs of the war were relatively light in comparison with the losses of

Crowds celebrate liberation from the Germans in front of the Hôtel de Ville, Paris, August 1944.
(Library of Congress)

World War I and, this time, borne more heavily by the civilian population, who made up some two-thirds of the approximately 600,000 casualties. More than 100,000 French citizens were deported to concentration and death camps, from which fewer than half—about 40,000—returned. But unlike the previous war, the physical devastation was much more widespread, encompassing virtually the entire country. More than 2 million buildings had been destroyed, rail and road systems ruined, and factories gutted. A massive increase in circulation of paper money during the war spawned rampant inflation.

But though ravaged in substance, the nation emerged from the war rejuvenated in spirit. The resistance movement had given the country a creditable cause for pride. Moved by idealism and patriotism, many thousands had risked or sacrificed their lives with a courage the memory of which still endures. The French military had been reconstituted based on Free French forces, to which some 100,000 volunteers from the FFI and FTP were added during the liberation campaign. The First French Army commanded by General Jean de Lattre de Tassigny (1889–1952), an escapee from interment in Germany, participated fully in the Allied invasion of the German homeland in driving deep into southwestern Germany. It was Tassigny who, on May 8, 1945, accepted the German unconditional surrender at Berlin on behalf of France. In Paris and elsewhere, surging crowds erupted in massive outpourings of joy. Feelings ran high that, out of the rubble, a revived nation under a wholly new republic—an incorruptible, long-lasting republic *(une république pure et dure)*—would arise.

11

REGENERATION AND TRANSFORMATION (1945–2000)

In the years immediately after World War II, it proved easier to mend the physical fabric of France than to put in place an effective governing system. The Fourth Republic emerged as nothing more than a revival of its predecessor, based also on a negative system of checks and balances, and its revolving door of cabinets brought a return of unstable government. At the same time, during the late 1940s and through the 1950s, the war damage was repaired, and the country inaugurated one of the world's first experiments in democratic economic planning. The economy thrived, and the downward population trend, so long a cause for worry, was reversed in a postwar baby boom. The welfare state was launched. The nation bound itself tightly to a Western alliance system in face of the Soviet threat, and a successful start was made, despite a costly war in Indochina, in letting go of colonial possessions.

As debilitating as its internal weaknesses were, it was a colonial war that destroyed the Fourth Republic. The crisis in Algeria brought a return to power of General Charles de Gaulle, who had left politics in the late 1940s but whose charisma as a war leader had never dimmed. The danger of civil turmoil proved so potent that the general's remedy—a completely new governing structure under a strong president—was overwhelmingly approved.

The 1960s were stamped entirely in the mold of France's chief executive. De Gaulle oversaw a settlement of the protracted Algerian war, the grant of self-rule to most of the country's colonies, a growing economy, and a more pronounced, independent foreign policy. The widespread rioting that marked the events of May 1968, though symptomatic of underlying economic, political, and social problems, failed to break the durability of the regime. The unrest weakened the authority of its architect, but de Gaulle's subsequent departure, too, left the Fifth Republic intact.

The 30-year unbroken record of economic growth came to an end in the mid-1970s, and high unemployment and a stubbornly persistent underclass remained to plague the country at century's end. Socialist prescriptions proved unworkable, but France became one of the world's most advanced social welfare states and one of its most fully modern nations, its economy and society reflective of the mass-consumer, high-technology world that tied together the developed West. Politics settled increasingly into a duel between two clearly defined right and left blocs. Europe became steadily more integrated, while the country strove to maintain a presence in international affairs befitting a power that, if no longer a player of the first rank, still possessed substantial means and an influential voice. France ended the 20th century as a country at peace abroad and, largely though by no means uniformly, prosperous at home.

The Fourth Republic, 1944–1958

De Gaulle and his advisers had laid plans to run the country and fashion a postwar government well in advance of liberation. During the interim months while the country was being cleared of the Germans and until some 2 million prisoners of war and conscripted workers could be repatriated, a provisional government made up of all parties, with de Gaulle president, ruled with virtually unrestricted authority. Plans for a plebiscite to win the public's approval were scuttled, de Gaulle acclaimed with virtual unanimity by a nation fired with renewed patriotic fervor. Idealistic, confident, and hungry for change, the public gave voice to the new mood in a referendum in October 1945, when more than 96 percent of voters rejected a return to the constitution of the Third Republic in favor of creating entirely new political institutions.

Scores with Vichy were settled. Collaborators were sought and punished, the severity of sentences corresponding to the degree and level of complicity. High-profile trials of Laval and Pétain resulted in verdicts of death, though de Gaulle commuted the old marshal's punishment to life imprisonment. Altogether, about 10,000 active German collaborators were executed (Agulhon 1993, 326). Minor officials and public servants were largely acquitted.

De Gaulle's one-man rule by consent lasted from the liberation of Paris (August 1944) until the election of a constituent assembly (October 1945). The assembly confirmed him in office, and the

CHARLES DE GAULLE

Charles de Gaulle (Library of Congress)

Born in Lille and educated at Saint-Cyr, Charles-André-Joseph-Marie de Gaulle (November 22, 1890–November 7, 1970) served with distinction at Verdun and was wounded and taken prisoner in World War I. Married in 1921 and the father of three, he gained prominence in the 1930s from his writings, in which he urged creation of a highly mechanized army. Made a brigadier general at the beginning of World War II, after the fall of France in June 1940, he escaped to Britain, where he announced the formation of a French National Committee in Exile, which won recognition by both the French resistance and Allied governments. De Gaulle led the Free French forces that wrested control of many French colonies from the Vichy

provisional government worked reasonably well. De Gaulle stood above and apart from the political parties, playing the role of the grand unifying leader he relished. Under his aegis, the coal, electrical, and gas industries, along with the airlines, many large insurance companies and banks, and the Renault automobile company—whose founder was an outspoken collaborator—were nationalized. Women were given the vote, a comprehensive social security system was enacted, labor unions reappeared, and workers were assigned places on panels that gave them a voice in industrial relations in enterprises that employed more than 1,000 laborers. But disagreements over policy issues and the structure of the draft constitution for a new republic led to the general's sudden resignation and his announced retirement in January 1946. This turn of events surprised public and politicians alike. A broad left-wing coali-

government and that formed France's organized fighting contingent that assisted in the liberation of the country.

Named provisional president in 1944, he served until resigning abruptly in a dispute over the failure to provide for a strong executive in constitutional drafts for the Fourth Republic. Active in politics briefly in the early 1950s, he retired, only to be recalled to power in June 1958, when the country was threatened by civil war over the Algerian crisis. Ruling by decree, de Gaulle supervised the drafting of a constitution that gave him the type of government he sought. He served two terms as president of the Fifth Republic, heading a government that initiated political and economic reforms, negotiated Algerian independence, relinquished most of the colonial empire, and sponsored the acquisition of nuclear weapons. Surviving a massive strike by students and workers in May 1968, de Gaulle won reelection in June, but in April 1969, after he suffered defeat in a national referendum, he retired to his country estate at Colombey-les-Deux-Églises, where he worked on his memoirs until his death.

Supremely confident, grand in gesture, occasionally inspiring, often petulant, and always attention-getting, de Gaulle dominated western Europe in the 1960s. A brilliant military commander and a strong political leader, he possessed a deeply felt patriotism. His effort to restore French pride and grandeur, though it often led to policies that irked his British and American allies, ultimately enhanced France's global image and position.

tion cabinet carried on the provisional government until a new constitution was ratified and promulgated in October 1946.

The old political parties had revived even before the liberation, and they were now joined by several new groups, which emerged from the resistance. The most prominent was the Mouvement Républicain Populaire (Popular Republican Movement, MRP), founded by a group of progressive Catholics and led by Georges Bidault (1899–1983), the president of the wartime National Council of Resistance. Its center-left program calling for social reform and government economic planning held out the promise of an alliance, or fusion, with the Socialists, led still by Léon Blum, who had returned in May 1945 from a German concentration camp. But a close association never came to be, the distrust inherited from the old church versus anticlerical divide carrying too many echoes for too many politicians whose attitudes remain wedded to the conceptions of their formative years. On the right of the political spectrum, dejection and disorder characterized the immediate postwar years. Many joined the MRP, having nowhere else to go in a country in which so many rightists had so readily signed on to the now reviled Vichy regime. Not until after 1950 would a conservative party of any strength emerge.

The left surged in the post-liberation months, the Communists especially winning support in proudly and loudly pointing to their record in the resistance and in basking in the reflected glory of the Soviet Union, now much admired for its overwhelming defeat of Hitler's Germany. De Gaulle helped to ease lingering fears of communism when he gave two Communists posts in his 1944 cabinet and when he traveled to Moscow in December 1944 to sign a 20-year treaty of alliance. But he remained wary, stubbornly refusing to give the Communists any key posts in his government, such as the armed forces or the police, from which they might launch an effort to seize power.

International communism proved increasingly worrisome, fed by growing evidence of Soviet expansionism, leading the government, conscious of the nation's weakened economic and political conditions, to align itself firmly with the U.S.-led Western alliance. The overthrow of a democratic regime in Czechoslovakia in February 1948 sent shivers through the nations that lay west of the by now firm Iron Curtain, and in April 1949, France joined unhesitatingly in creating the North Atlantic Treaty Organization (NATO), the postwar pact of Western powers formed to resist aggression by the Soviet bloc. Its headquarters were in Paris. France did so in having returned to the world stage as a major player, that status given expression in its holding both an occupation zone in Germany and one of the five permanent seats on the Security Council of the United Nations, the new world organization that replaced the League of Nations in 1945.

Awash with money, the Communists flooded the country with newspapers and pamphlets and set up a front organization to woo supporters. Winning 26.6 percent of the vote in the October 1945 elections for the constituent assembly, they emerged as the largest party. Together with the Socialists and the MRP, the left garnered three-fourths of all ballots.

Everyone acknowledged the need for change, but none could agree on what kind. Unwilling to accept either a strong executive or an all-powerful legislature, the French people had virtually nowhere to go but back to the past. After months of haggling, constituent lawmakers crafted a new constitution that amounted to not much more than a warmed-over version of the Third Republic. In the bicameral legislature, the new upper house—the Council of the Republic—held fewer powers than the old Senate, while the lower house, where real powered remained, simply changed names—the National Assembly replacing the Chamber of Deputies.

The new institutions became operational at the end of 1946, and tradition and habit quickly reemerged. Cabinets lasted an average six months, just as in the interwar period. The political equivalent of bread in a toaster, a total of 24 governments popped in and out of office during the Fourth Republic. The left's seemingly unassailable supremacy steadily shifted to the right. New parties—the Independent Republican and the Peasant—won enough votes to gain a place in a 1951 coalition after the Socialists pulled out of a "Third Force" government with the MRP and the Radicals. Governing was complicated by the periodic appearance of powerful right-wing movements hostile to the system, the first sponsored by de Gaulle himself, who reentered politics in 1947 in organizing the Rassemblement du Peuple Français (Rally for the French People, RPF).

While the politicians squabbled, the government moved to rebuild the economy. Deflected politically, the urge for change registered enormous success economically. A Planning Commission set to work immediately in 1946, headed for several years by Jean Monnet (1888–1979), the heir to a family cognac fortune, a technocrat who managed logistical supply during both world wars, and the former first deputy secretary-general of the League of Nations (1919–23). Drawing heavily on the advice of business and labor representatives, planners devised projects to channel investments, both public and private, into basic economic sectors, such as coal, electricity, steel, and farm machinery. Progress proved so substantial that by 1958 planning shifted to consumer needs, a sector long neglected. Monnet also guided the establishment of an École Nationale d'Administration (National School of Administration, ENA), which became a leading training institution for public servants and politicians. Growing numbers of French entrepreneurs shook off their traditional conservatism and spent funds freely, encouraged by young technicians, by the example of booming German business, and by U.S. missions financed through the Marshall Plan. Officially the European Recovery Program, the U.S. assistance scheme launched in 1948 pumped more than $2 billion, most of it in outright gifts of food, fuel, raw materials, and machinery, into the economy by the time aid ended in 1952. By the mid-1950s, French industry had entered a period of growth to a degree not seen since the 1850s. Production indicators had been restored to their 1929 levels—the high point during the interwar years—by 1949. Annual growth rates of approximately 5 percent were sustained from 1950 to 1958 while output soared. Expanding urban economies absorbed rural workers, who had been rendered redundant by a surge in agricultural productivity sparked at long last by widespread mechanization on the farms. The small farms and small shops of traditional France steadily declined. Rising prosperity encouraged a postwar baby boom that reversed longtime stagnant and downward demographic trends.

Marshall Plan guidelines mandated that Europeans cooperate in determining their recovery needs. But knowledgeable European planners, headed by Monnet, who had learned the lessons of the past, were also well aware that the economic well-being of each country was best advanced through the cooperation of all, and measures were set in motion to draw western European economies together. Monnet initiated the Declaration of May 9, 1950, which laid the basis for creation of the European Coal and Steel Community (ECSC), also known as the Schuman Plan, and he served as the first president of its High Commission (1952–55). France, West Germany, Italy, Belgium, the Netherlands, and Luxembourg pooled their coal and steel industries, which were placed under the binding control of a supranational high authority, a novel arrangement that, by putting German coal and steel under a multinational regime, ensured a balance of economic strength and broke the lingering fear among Germany's neighbors of its economic might, and the destructive potential that recent history had shown such power could wreak. The ECSC launched a drive to rationalize and modernize production in these key industries and, in replacing national governments with a regional authority in decision making, it marked a major step in postwar European integration. In 1955, Monnet founded the Action Committee for a United States of Europe, which played a leading role in the drafting of the Treaty of Rome (March 25, 1957), the founding document of the European Economic Community (EEC), or Common Market. Launched on January 1, 1958, the new organization cut internal customs duties and tariffs and extended aid to agriculture and industry among the six founding states (France, Italy, West Germany, Belgium, the Netherlands, and Luxembourg).

Prosperity arrived but problems persisted. Regional economic differences stayed stubbornly in place. Capital, labor power, and industry flowed more readily to the modern, dynamic areas—northeastern France from Paris to the Belgian border, leaving the center, south, and west underdeveloped. Many farmers remained obstinately individualistic, though progress was made in creating farmers' unions, the most successful being specialized groups such as growers of wheat and grape cultivators. Rival trade unions continued to compete. After the war, the CGT was reborn, and control was wrested by the Communists after 1945. Catholic workers flocked back to their own union, the CFTC. Anticommunists seceded from the CGT in 1948 to form the Force Ouvrière (Workers' Force), with unofficial ties to the Socialists.

Two outstanding political events marked the 1950s: The effort by Pierre Mendès-France (1907–82) to inject vigorous change into the system and the rise of a new ultra-rightist protest movement that appeared as a result of his endeavors. A lawyer who had served in the Free French air force and a member of the Radical Party, Mendès-France served as premier only from June 1954 to February 1955, but his brief cabinet had a dramatic impact. Seeking to convert the Radical Party into a forceful, disciplined political vehicle, he founded the Republican Front, a noncommunist leftist coalition. A maverick, he brought hardheaded realism to domestic affairs. Determined to rid the country of its antiquated small-scale business structure, he encouraged economic rationalization, eliminating tax subsidies for small shops in favor of the growth of large-scale enterprises. In doing so, he earned the wrath of small-town retailers and artisans, who formed the backbone of his Radical Party. Mendès-France's anti-alcoholism campaign, in which he urged the French to drink more milk in place of wine, served as a focal point, crystallizing the anxieties of his opponents, who feared for their livelihoods.

He lost the support of the bulk of his party, and he also engendered a new political movement. The Poujadist episode embodied an emotional protest against the kind of modernization that Mendès-France represented. A small-town shopkeeper from the Lot who had fought with de Gaulle's forces, Pierre Poujade

Pierre Mendès-France (Library of Congress)

299

(1920–2003) won notoriety when he led local merchants to resist government tax officials intent on uncovering tax evaders. He organized a national group that quickly ballooned in size, entering politics on a platform that, in opposing economic controls, taxes, and fiscal levies, upheld the interests of small-town, rural France. The Poujadists won a startling 3 million votes in the 1956 elections and more than 50 seats in the National Assembly. But just as suddenly, the bubble burst. Poujade showed no skill as a leader. More than half of the Poujadist deputies deserted to other right-wing parties during the next two years. Poujade himself lost in a Paris by-election, and the national organization disintegrated.

Mendès-France won his greatest success in foreign affairs. Calls for independence stirring throughout European colonial possessions after the war appeared in France's overseas territories first in Indochina. In 1941, France had been supplanted from its Southeast Asian territory by the Japanese and had never succeeded in reasserting control after 1945. A Vietminh guerrilla movement led by longtime Communist Ho Chi Minh (1890–1969) controlled most of the countryside, and its strength intensified, especially following its recognition by the Soviet Union and the People's Republic of China. France sent 200,000 troops, but by the mid-1950s, increasingly on the defensive and the war growing more unpopular at home, military leaders switched to building up a Vietnamese army, backed by huge increases in U.S.-supplied equipment. Under General Henri Navarre (1898–1983), French forces launched an offensive in the north to trap the Vietminh, a drive that ended with the French themselves encircled. Besieged at the fortress of Dien Bien Phu, the French army capitulated on May 7, 1954. The government fell, and the new ministry under Mendès-France, who favored divestment of the colony, reached a negotiated settlement in July under the Geneva Accords, which extended independence to Laos, Cambodia, and a Vietnam divided between a communist North and a noncommunist South.

The Indochina defeat proved humiliating to French army officers, who were determined never to lose another colonial war. Another such conflict soon broke out in Algeria, where a rebellion began with a string of bombings on November 1, 1954, launched by Arab insurgents grouped in a Front de Libération Nationale (National Liberation Front, FLN), intent on winning independence. Within a year, the revolt intensified to full-scale war. Settlement of the conflict posed challenges unlike those faced anywhere else. The formula adopted for Morocco and Tunisia, where potential strife had been averted in granting both

A French soldier shoots a fleeing nationalist rebel in a street in Constantine, Algeria, August 1955. (Library of Congress)

territories independence in 1956, proved impossible in Algeria because more than a million Europeans lived in the country, many born there (*colons*) in families who had been settled for many generations and who staunchly opposed independence. An attempt by Premier Guy Mollet (1905–75) in 1956 to negotiate with the rebels was greeted by threats of violence when he visited the country. The bulk of the army, including, unlike in Indochina, conscripts, was transferred to Algeria in an attempt to defeat an indigenous force that, though small, proved futile because it engaged in guerrilla tactics. The rebels' resort to terrorism, both in Algeria and in France, embittered the struggle and led to counteractions by French troops, both sides committing atrocities. Emotions ran deep, with public opinion becoming increasingly polarized.

Almost without precedent in modern French history, the French army played the key role in the emergence of the Fifth Republic in 1958. Traditionally remaining strictly aloof from politics, the army's officer corps, some of whom had been fighting almost without interruption since 1939 and had known more defeats than victories, was riddled with disaffection. Sentiment was widespread that the weak and scheming politicians and leftist intellectuals in Paris had burdened the

301

fighting forces with one thankless task after another and had failed to provide the material means to do the job successfully.

Plots against the regime began to brew as early as the mid-1950s. Made up mostly of civilians and ex-soldiers with a few active-duty officers, clandestine groups in Paris and Algiers sought revolutionary change. Some favored an army coup d'état and the establishment of a ruling military-civilian clique. Others looked to de Gaulle as both a symbol and a savior as the person under whose leadership the government could be reordered and the armed forces refortified.

A cabinet crisis in April 1958 offered an unexpected opportunity to take action. The premier-designate of the new coalition government, MRP deputy Pierre Pflimlin (1907–2000), was rumored to favor negotiating with the Algerian rebels. Fearing that possibility, demonstrators sought to intimidate the legislators in Paris by staging a riot outside the main government building in Algiers on May 13. Crowds invaded and sacked the premises and proclaimed a revolutionary Comité de Salut Public (Committee of Public Safety). Upheaval threatened to spread to metropolitan France. General de Gaulle announced on May 15 that he would accept power but not through a violent overthrow of the system or through constitutional processes. Ever desirous to project himself as above the fray, he was able to appeal to everyone by distancing himself from both sides. Negotiators debated for two weeks. Helped by key members of the army high command in Algiers, Gaullist agents maneuvered their way into control of the Committee of Public Safety, avoiding thereby a complete break with Paris and making possible a peaceful transfer of power, though a resort to force was only narrowly averted with plans in place for a march on Paris. Desperate to prevent civil war and believing that the Fourth Republic's constitution needed revising, President René Coty (1882–1962) persuaded Pflimlin and his cabinet to resign on May 28, and the next day he called on de Gaulle to form a new government. On June 1–2, the National Assembly voted to accept de Gaulle's government, granting the general and his entourage full powers for six months. Then it adjourned, never to reconvene.

The Fifth Republic under de Gaulle, 1958–1969

Entrusted with drafting a new constitution to be approved by popular referendum, de Gaulle fulfilled the aim he had sought, and failed, to obtain in 1946—to give the republic the firmness of leadership that would prevent any further turns to authoritarian regimes or threats of civil war. For the first time in French history, the writing of the document was entrusted not to an elected assembly but to an appointed committee, chaired by Minister of Justice Michel Debré (1912–96), who became the new constitution's principal author.

Announced by de Gaulle on the place de la République on September 4, 1958, the anniversary of the proclamation of the Third Republic, the new ruling blueprint of the Fifth Republic departed significantly from that which had guided both of its predecessors. Encompassing a blend of both parliamentary and presidential systems, it was designed to strengthen the executive branch without eliminating its responsibility to the legislature. Legislative powers were reduced. Parliamentarians could not serve as cabinet ministers, and sessions were limited to six months a year. Assemblies could no longer overthrow cabinets with the ease that had so bedeviled politics in the two previous republics. The prime minister chose the members of his cabinet, but the president appointed them. This reflected a change under which the president now became the centerpiece of executive authority, endowed with enhanced prestige and greater independent power.

The presidential office was tailor-made to fit the pretensions of de Gaulle, whose standing stood so high that, in the referendum held in September to ratify the new system, almost 80 percent of voters expressed approval, despite a vigorous negative campaign by the Communists, a minority bloc of Socialists, and assorted individual leftist leaders such as Mendès-France, who feared that the new constitution was designed to ensure that the left could never regain power.

Strengthened by a display of public confidence that surprised even the Gaullists, de Gaulle put in place the institutional framework of the Fifth Republic. During winter 1958–59, a reorganized two-house parliament consisting of a lower-chamber National Assembly and an upper-chamber Senate was elected. The new Assembly was dominated by just shy of a clear majority of Gaullists, who had hurriedly organized a new party, the Union pour la Nouvelle République (Union for the New Republic, UNR) to serve as the general's political vehicle. De Gaulle was named to a seven-year term as president by a broadened electoral college and, as president, chose Debré to be the Fifth Republic's first premier.

In an imaginative plan that forestalled the chance that Algerian-type revolts might spread, de Gaulle gave electors in the colonies the opportunity to vote on the new constitution. Voters everywhere but in Algeria, where the ongoing turmoil barred balloting on the issue, could win immediate independence if they rejected it. If they approved, they were given a choice to become an integral part of the republic, to retain their current status, or to become self-governing republics within a new French Community, which would replace the French Union, an organization created in 1946 that had aimed to bind France with its colonies on a more equitable basis in replacing the French Empire. Except for Guinea, which opted for outright separation, the 12 largest African colonies chose the latter path. But the winds of change moved faster than expected, and decolonization drives appeared so rapidly that the reordered relationships proved short-lived. By 1960, the new African republics were already demanding full independence, which France conceded by amending the constitution so that self-determination could be combined with continued membership in the French Community.

Only Algeria defied an easy solution. The guerrilla war continued; rebels raided the hill country and mounted terrorist strikes in the cities. Having reluctantly come to accept that self-government was, in the end, inevitable, in 1959, de Gaulle offered full independence at the end of four years. The plan outraged Europeans in Algeria, rightists at home, and elements within the army command. Extremists rioted in Algiers in January 1960, but with de Gaulle firmly in control, the army backed down and the rebellion collapsed. In April 1961, four disaffected senior officers led by generals Maurice Challe (1905–79) and Raoul Salan (1899–1984) raised the standard of revolt. In the gravest challenge to his authority during the Algerian war, de Gaulle—his military stature recalled in the World War II uniform he wore—broadcast an impassioned speech to the nation on April 23, denouncing the coup in the making, in which he convinced conscripts to refuse to back their rebellious leaders. Salan went into hiding to emerge as titular head of the Organisation Armée Secrète (Secret Army Organization, OAS), which would launch indiscriminate terrorist attacks across Algeria and in Paris, including several attempts to assassinate the president. But the extremists' efforts proved futile, de Gaulle's success in securing the loyalty of the majority opening up sufficient divisions within the army to put to rest any prospect of Algeria remaining French. Officials opened talks with the provisional government of Algeria, the political wing of the FLN, at Évian in May 1961, which led to a grant of independence in accords signed on March 18, 1962, which 91 percent of French voters accepted in April. The revolt-turned-quagmire had cost the French in excess of 17,000 soldiers and 10,000 civilians killed and the Algerians many more—the new government claimed 1 million. Amid tragic scenes, a million Europeans (*pieds noirs*) fled across the Mediterranean Sea to France, their fate mitigated in part by their successful assimilation into metropolitan society thanks to the prospering economy.

His status now secure, de Gaulle further implanted his stamp on French politics. In a referendum in September 1962, voters approved election of the president by universal suffrage, a move designed to enhance the legitimacy of the officeholder. Any parliamentary opposition was squelched when elections to the National Assembly (November 18–25, 1962) returned record levels of support for the Gaullists. The center parties—Radicals, MRP—were crushed, while the left managed to poll respectable results. Political restructuring began to take place, leading gradually to a more bipolar system under which parties tended to coalesce into Gaullist and opposition groups. The process was largely forced on the politicians by a new electoral system that required alliances to succeed and by polling in single-member districts in two rounds, which discouraged the proliferation of parties: Only the two leading survivors confronted each other in the runoff.

While Gaullism took command on the right, on the left, the Communists kept their core constituency; but, clinging to rigid pro-Soviet positions, they failed to grow and so remained on the political sidelines, opening the way for the Socialists to rise to the fore, albeit slowly. At first closely associated with the failure of the Fourth Republic, the moderate left rebuilt its fortunes as the 1960s progressed in opposing what it decried as the excessive personal power of the president and the social injustices of the regime. Under the leadership of François Mitterrand (1916–96), mainstream Socialists, Radicals, and various splinter groups formed a Fédération de la Gauche Democrate et Socialiste (Federation of the Democratic and Socialist Left, FGDS). Mitterrand ran a close race with de Gaulle, forcing the president into a humiliating second round of balloting in presidential elections in December 1965, and in legislative elections in March 1967, the Socialists improved their showing.

During the Algerian crisis, de Gaulle appealed to the French to support his efforts to end the conflict, in part because the war damaged France's international prestige. The maintenance and enhancement of French grandeur—as he defined it—became an overarching goal of French foreign affairs. This policy arena under the Fifth Republic emerged—based on de Gaulle's trailblazing efforts—as one entrusted largely to the president to shape and direct. By the early 1960s, European integration had become an accepted fact, but the general sought to mold the nascent continent-wide institutions in his own image. In May 1962, he declared his opposition to tighter links, favoring instead cooperation within a much looser supranational "Europe of the Nations," in which the nation-state, not regional bodies, would remain preeminent. In October 1963, he vetoed Britain's membership bid to the EEC on the grounds that admitting the British, who were so closely tied to the Americans, would facilitate increased U.S. cultural and economic influence in Europe at the expense of that of France.

The decision followed logically from the president's deeply held suspicions of the "Anglo-Saxons." Based partly on his belief that French greatness depended on the adoption of as independent a role as possible in world affairs and partly on never-forgotten snubs by Allied leaders during World War II, de Gaulle's policies distanced the country increasingly from the Western alliance and, in particular, U.S. foreign policy. France withdrew from the NATO military command structure in March 1966, compelling the organization to move its headquarters to Belgium. To give the nation greater freedom to maneuver between the rival superpower blocs that defined the postwar cold war, substantial resources were poured into building an independent nuclear capability, which was launched when France exploded its first atomic weapon in February 1960, followed by its first hydrogen bomb in August 1968. Its own *force de frappe* (strike force) would provide the nation with the means to protect itself from nuclear blackmail by any state in the event that the United States, which remained the ultimate nuclear protector, might prove unwilling to risk all-out war in defense of the country.

Seeking to redirect French foreign policy from an Atlantic to a continental focus, de Gaulle pursued reconciliation with France's old foe, a policy reciprocated by West German chancellor Konrad Adenauer (r. 1949–63). A strong link between continental Western Europe's two largest states could serve as a "European Europe" counterweight to both the Atlantic and the Soviet powers. Tying West Germany firmly to its European neighbors would strengthen German democracy, the foundation on which its economic and military prowess could proceed, which would in turn accrue to the benefit of all of Western Europe. The seal was set on reconciliation and the long, bitter history of Franco-German hostility at last laid formally to rest with the signing by the two leaders of the Élysée Treaty on January 22, 1963, which put in place mechanisms for consultation on issues of defense and education.

De Gaulle delighted in stirring the international waters, even if only oratorically. The president criticized the U.S. war in Vietnam and later hosted peace talks, he rebuked Israel during the Arab-Israeli War of 1967, and that same year he voiced support on a visit to Quebec, Canada, for that province's separatist movement in a remark *Vive le Québec libre!* that, while he never elaborated on his exact meaning, sparked outrage from his hosts.

Efforts were taken to secure closer relations with the Communist bloc. The administration recognized the People's Republic of China in 1964. Improved ties were sought with the Soviet Union, de Gaulle broaching vague ideas about a Europe from the Atlantic to the Ural Mountains, even while the reality of current events compelled the country, when faced with potential flash points, such as the Cuban missile crisis (October 1962) and the Soviet-led Warsaw Pact invasion of Czechoslovakia (October 1968), to declare its solidarity with the Western alliance.

The active foreign policy was backed by a more powerful military, which in turn depended closely on a prosperous, modern economy. A slight dip in economic expansion in the late 1950s led the new government to cut a budget deficit by decreasing subsidies to nationalized industries and agriculture. Indirect taxes were raised, and a new franc was introduced to replace the old. Tariffs were lowered, and some currency exchange controls ended to make the domestic market more accessible to international business. Political stability during the 1960s together with the government's firm anti-inflationary policies helped to sustain rapid growth, interrupted by a brief period of rising prices in 1963, which continued into the mid-1970s. The opening of economic frontiers within the EEC forced French firms to become competitive, while large subsidies and tax incentives aided business expansion. Urbanization and industrialization proceeded, and the standard of living steadily rose, per capita income climbing by an annual average of 4.5 percent between 1959 and 1973. In the immediate postwar years, Paris regained its reputation as a world capital of romance, glamour, and haute couture.

Amid this auspicious scene, however, widespread discontent simmered, due in part to persistent inequalities in the distribution of wealth made all the more glaring in light of the widening prosperity and in part to government policies that, to curb inflation, cut expenditures on housing, schools, and hospitals and placed controls on wages. A boom in postwar housing construction, intended to remedy a shortfall that had been building since the post–World War I period, made significant progress. But much of it was poorly built, deteriorating within a generation into slums. Large, high-rise complexes, built in suburban places without the social spaces—cafés were disallowed as a measure to fight alcoholism—that were so much a feature of urban working-class neighborhoods, bred isolation. Workers lagged behind the middle classes in social benefits, such as paid vacations, and their discontent found expression in the growing strength of the Socialists.

HAUTE COUTURE

Haute couture ("high sewing" or "high dressmaking") began in the mid-1800s in referring to custom-fitted clothing made to order for a specific customer using high-quality, expensive fabrics. French styles had been setting fashion standards since at least the late 17th century, but couturier Charles Frederick Worth (1826–95) is widely believed to have founded modern French haute couture. Born in Britain, Worth moved in 1846 to Paris, where he revolutionized dress-making, turning it into a design statement. Opening a gallery in 1858 on the rue de la Paix, Worth fashioned one-of-a-kind creations made to order for titled wealthy patrons. He also prepared a portfolio of designs that were displayed by his live models at his premises—the House of Worth—from which a customer would make a choice and specify the color and fabric. A duplicate was then made in his workshop.

Worth combined individual tailoring with standard ready-to-wear production, which was then emerging. His techniques were followed by others in the early 20th century, including Jeanne Lanvin (1867–1946), Gabriel Bonheur "Coco" Chanel (1883–1971), Elsa Schiaparelli (1890–1973), Cristóbal Balenciaga (1895–1972), and Christian Dior (1905–57). French designers were the acknowledged best, and genuine Paris creations were considered the ultimate fashion acquisition.

In the 1960s, a younger generation that had trained in these and other fashion houses, including Yves Saint Laurent (1936–2008), Pierre Cardin (1922–), and Emanuel Ungaro (1933–), left to start their own businesses. They were joined at the end of the 20th century by, among others, Thierry Mugler (1948–), Christian Lacroix (1951–), and Jean-Paul Gaultier (1954–).

The great fashion houses no longer earn the bulk of their income from custom-designed clothing; rather, mass-produced ready-to-wear apparel and accessory luxury products, such as perfumes and

Unexpected though they were, the massive riots of May 1968 laid bare an undercurrent of pent-up resentment against those in authority—not only in politics but also in society in general—and against the inequality and injustice their policies allegedly bred. Students sparked the unrest, driven by anger at the elitism of a university system dominated by exclusive, highly selective universities (grandes écoles), at over-crowded and poorly equipped teaching facilities, and at an international capitalist order whose immorality they believed was clearly evident in

Fashion designer Yves Saint Laurent, flanked by his models, following presentation of the new Christian Dior line, July 30, 1959. Saint Laurent designed for Dior at the time. (Associated Press)

shoes, together with licensing ventures, earn much greater returns for them. The internationalization that set in beginning in the 1960s, both in styles—with the revolt in favor of convenience and uniformity at the expense of cost and exclusivity—and in locales—with the rise of competing fashion centers in New York, London, Milan, and elsewhere—has made Paris, while still a recognized fashion capital, no longer the sole arbiter of tastes and trends.

the Vietnam War. Unrest began in March on the Nanterre campus on the outskirts of Paris. Orchestrated by small fringe groups of anarchists led, most prominently, by Daniel Cohn-Bendit (1945–), a sociology student, the son of German Jewish refugees, and—to avoid the French draft law—a West German citizen, activists admired revolutionaries such as Leon Trotsky (1879–1940), Mao Zedong (r. 1949–76), and Che Guevara (1928–67), and they drew inspiration from, among others, the doctrines of the Situationists, artists and intellectuals who called for

Police rush student demonstrators near the Sorbonne in Paris, on May 6, 1968. (AP Images)

social revolution and individual liberation. The disturbances spread due to the incompetence of university administrators and police brutality. When Nanterre was closed on May 2, militants moved their protest to the Sorbonne, and demonstrators swarmed through the Latin Quarter. On the night of May 10–11, the "night of the barricades," students imitated their revolutionary forebears in tearing up cobblestones, uprooting trees, and overturning cars in battles with police, who responded with batons, tear gas, and water hoses. Rioting spread to the provinces. An estimated 10 million workers joined the protest, launching strikes, occupying factories, and essentially shutting down the economy. A general workers' strike in Paris on May 13 found 800,000 marchers calling for de Gaulle's departure. The protesters gave expression to a loss of confidence in institutions deemed part of an overly centralized political system run by an aging head of state incapable of adjusting to change. France seemed on the verge of yet another revolution.

Taken by surprise, the government vacillated. Prime Minister Georges Pompidou (1911–74) made concessions, allowing the Sorbonne to reopen, its courtyard and the nearby Odéon theater promptly turning into a nonstop teach-in at which students and teachers debated social theory. Having left on a state visit to Romania on May 14, de Gaulle returned on May 19. He proposed a referendum on workers' participation in industry, and Pompidou offered wage increases and the promise of better conditions, which were rejected. Left-wing leaders Mendès-France and Mitterrand offered to head a provisional government. Encouraged by the military, de Gaulle recovered his nerve and addressed the nation, bluntly declaring that France faced two choices: either himself or anarchy. He was helped by disunity among his foes, the trade unions in particular seeking limited gains in wage and working improvements and anxious for disorder not to proceed too far, and by the lack of any among the government's opponents willing to take the lead and try to seize power. Gleeful at the course of events, which it had not foreseen, the Communists nevertheless staunchly respected the bounds of law and order, refusing to countenance extralegal action.

No matter, the president charged the Communists with harboring plans to take power. De Gaulle dissolved the National Assembly on May 30 and called for the country to rally to the government's support. Campaigning on a law-and-order platform, the Gaullists won a resounding victory in elections on June 23 and 30. The extreme left was marginalized, and unrest subsided. But the election proved more a victory for the system—the voters clearly expressing their firm decision to have done with social revolution—than for its leader. De Gaulle's authority had been considerably weakened, his indecision and seeming indifference at the outset of the crisis standing in contrast to the better leadership skills shown by his prime minister. Moreover, the president's sudden, unexpected dismissal on July 10 of Pompidou, who had served loyally as prime minister in five governments, seemed a ruthless, petty-minded attempt to eliminate a potential rival.

De Gaulle's new education minister, Edgar Faure (1908–88), began reforms that addressed some of the worst problems in the schools, including overcrowding. Judging the moment right to relaunch reforms of the regime, the president placed before the public a series of proposals to decentralize local government by transferring some limited powers to regional authorities and to reduce the power of the Senate, which had served all too often as a venue for his critics. But the public balked, 53 percent of voters rejecting the moves in a referendum on April 27, 1969. His former vitality clearly no longer evident in the months after May 1968, de Gaulle delivered a terse statement, announcing that he would resign by noon of the following day. He returned to private life, leaving the nation to wonder: Would the regime survive the departure of its founder?

Left and Right Compete for Power, 1969–2000

The Gaullists offered a meager program and little unity beyond loyalty to their founder, but the party remained in power due to the determination of the general's successors to exercise fully the governing powers bequeathed by the system he created and to the willingness of all the parties to respect the constitution.

The son of a schoolteacher and a banker who had served in the resistance, Pompidou was virtually unknown to the public when de Gaulle made him prime minister in April 1962, but his status as heir apparent was sufficiently well earned for him to win handily the presidential election in June 1969. Politics developed gradually into a more "normal" pattern in contrast to the one-man leadership of de Gaulle. Pompidou based his support on the Gaullist UNR, which rapidly adapted to the political system in becoming one among several parties of the moderate right that included non-Gaullist groups, most notably the Républicains-Indépendents (Independent Republicans) led by Valéry Giscard d'Estaing (1926–   ), a career civil servant who joined Pompidou's government in 1969 as minister of finance and economic affairs. For the first time in modern French history, a powerful federation on the right had been forged.

Credited with the restoration of social order in 1968 and with the by now almost 30-year stretch of glorious prosperity (*les trente glorieuses*) marked by low inflation, a balanced budget, and rising living standards, the Gaullists, who, in 1971 had created a new party—the Union des Démocrates pour la République (Union of Democrats for the Republic, UDR)—joined with other conservatives in winning the 1973 legislative elections. Under Pompidou, they showed that they could govern despite the absence of de Gaulle's personal charisma.

The economy hummed ahead of all those of France's neighbors, while the government sought to ease strains through governmental price supports for farmers and restrictions on supermarket growth, the latter to abet the worries of small shopkeepers that the competition could put them out of business. Large sums of money were committed to prestige projects such as the Concorde and the European Airbus planes. In Paris, extensive urban renovation, including clearing slums, constructing more expressways, transferring the historic old central market (Les Halles) to the suburbs, and building high-rise complexes (notably La Défense), made the capital a more modern city though at the expense of greater congestion and, in places, loss of traditional ambiance.

The government continued the educational reforms begun under de Gaulle, and it achieved a longtime goal of greater administrative decentralization in a reform that, for the first time since their creation in the 1790s, deprived the departments of certain powers, which were transferred to regional assemblies. A more cooperative spirit toward European integration was reflected with admission of Britain, Denmark, and Ireland to the EEC in 1973.

And then in 1974, the economy turned sour with a recession precipitated by the sudden jump in oil prices resulting from embargoes put in place by Arab supplier nations during the 1973 Arab-Israeli war. Inflation and unemployment rose, growth fell, and the balance of trade posted negative numbers consequent to the higher costs of oil imports. Ill with leukemia, Pompidou failed to provide the strong direction needed to counter the general malaise.

The Gaullists surrendered their hold on the post of head of state when the prime minister, Pierre Messmer (1916–2007), declined to run and their candidate, Jacques Chaban-Delmas (1915–2000), lost in the first round of balloting in the presidential election of May 1974. The win in the second round went to fellow rightist Giscard d'Estaing. A shift away from the formerly dominant Gaullists toward the non-Gaullist conservatives set in at the same time that the left showed growing strength, the Socialist Mitterrand having won just under half of the votes cast.

Giscard sought to restore business confidence by reducing government expenditures and the balance of payments deficit and by practicing a more hands-off approach, relying on the market to restore the country's global competitiveness; however, social reforms and social welfare measures were also enacted. The age of consent and of voting were lowered to 18 in 1974, and in 1975, abortion was legalized, divorce procedures simplified, and the sale of contraceptives authorized. Social security payments were made more generous, and access to secondary schooling improved. Inflation was stabilized but at the price of high unemployment. The move away from the traditional distaste of Gaullists for stronger European, at the perceived expense of French, power continued with an initiative by France and Germany that led to elections by universal suffrage to the European Parliament. France joined the European monetary system in 1979, establishing the écu—the Common Currency Unit—as the basis for currency union.

The conservatives held the legislative majority, but divisions became increasingly apparent. The Gaullists under Jacques Chirac (1932–), a minister in Pompidou's government and Giscard's prime minister, grew restive. He resigned in August 1976 and reorganized his party under a new title, the Rassemblement pour la République (Rally for the Republic,

RPR), a more popularly based political vehicle. Chirac increased pressure on the non-Gaullists by standing for and winning the newly created office of mayor of Paris in March 1977 in defeating Giscard's own candidate. The president responded in February 1978 by organizing the non-Gaullist conservatives into the Union pour la Démocratie Française (Union for French Democracy, UDF), a party that placed more stress on individual rights and on the government's responsibility to ensure social justice in contrast to the Gaullists penchant for strong leaders. Conservatives managed to retain their legislative majority in elections in March 1978, despite a drop in Giscard's popularity occasioned by a program of economic austerity launched by the prime minister, Raymond Barre (1924–2007), only because self-interest in not wishing to lose power motivated them to pull together sufficiently to win, and because the left, despite some efforts at unity, remained divided.

Since the mid-1960s, attempts by the Socialists and Communists to establish an alliance had been made, notably in 1972 with establishment of the Union de la Gauche (Union of the Left) and a Common Programme of Government. However, the determination of both parties to retain their ability to act independently coupled with the ambition of leaders in either party to take a principal role stymied efforts to establish closer links. The Communists clung to their Soviet model of socialism, a prescription that proved increasingly less attractive in a country grown wealthy under capitalism. Their share of the vote dropped—from 28 percent in 1946 to 20 percent by 1978—and it fell to only 9.8 percent in 1986. Overseeing a tiny remnant of a once impressive force, the party's secretary-general since 1972, Georges Marchais (1920–97), resigned in January 1994, at the same time that the party shed its doctrinaire ideology, which had been shown to be no longer viable following the collapse of communism in Eastern Europe and the demise of the Soviet Union itself in 1991.

The Communists' decline was matched by the corresponding rise of the Socialists. The Parti Socialiste (Socialist Party, PS) had emerged in its modern form after the splintering in 1968 of the SFIO, its having grown steadily more decrepit, and after the Left's disastrous loss in the 1969 presidential election. The Socialists drew increasing strength due both to the abilities of its leadership—largely that of Mitterrand, chosen first secretary in 1971 who proved to be an excellent organizer and a tireless campaigner—and to its doctrines. The party's moderate, pragmatic, left-of-center principles beckoned more than did communist ideology to left-leaning supporters, who, while anxious to further social welfare programs, sought to do so within a democratic state.

The appeal of such a program proved sufficiently strong for the moderate left to prevail in the presidential elections of 1981. The Communist vote collapsed on the first ballot, and François Mitterrand led the Socialists to victory through a carefully planned campaign in which he presented himself to voters as the upholder of traditional values and, to counter fears of a radical turn to the left, as a *force tranquille* (tranquil force) who stood for limited reform. He was helped by less than enthusiastic support for Giscard, who suffered as the president of a country in which inflation stood at 14 percent and unemployment at 8 percent.

Mitterrand immediately carried through on a campaign promise that, if elected, he would dissolve the National Assembly to draw quickly on the victory to secure a legislature favorable to the government. His hopes were realized when the legislative elections in June 1981 produced a major shift in power. Divided and discouraged by the presidential loss, conservatives stayed away from the polls, while the Communists lost more than half of their seats, giving the Socialists an absolute majority.

No matter the soothing reassurance exuded by Mitterrand during the campaign, in power for the first time in the Fifth Republic, the left was encouraged to put in place not the more cautious program promised by the president-elect but rather the Socialist Party's official, much more doctrinaire plans. While retaining the commitment of their conservative predecessors to economic modernization and closer European integration, the government raised the minimum wage and increased welfare payments through fiscal measures that included a wealth tax and reform of the inheritance tax. Although levied only on the top tier of the most well off, the tax, together with rhetoric that attacked the rich, roused sufficient worries as to shake business confidence and provoke a flight of capital. To improve the quality of life, the working week was reduced to 39 hours, and a fifth week of paid vacations was added to workers' benefits, along with enactment of early retirement and retraining programs. The death penalty was abolished. Through increased public spending and easier availability of credit, it was hoped to redress unemployment, a goal that also drove increased nationalization. State ownership of the major steel companies, all close to bankruptcy, and of manufacturing firms in fields such as aeronautics, chemicals, and information technology would, it was believed, facilitate the adoption of a rational investment program, which would lead to greater hiring.

In practice, the program had little impact on lowering unemployment. Instead, imports rose, the balance of payments declined, and inflation soared. After two years, having learned that only by encouraging private business initiative could economic growth return, the government switched tactics, its interventionist formulas renounced by Prime Minister Pierre Mauroy (1928–   ) in March 1983. To stem the mounting public debt, officials froze wages, prices, and welfare spending and raised taxes. Public confidence plummeted. In a bid to restore its image, the administration sought to advance local democracy by implementing a major shift away from the centuries-old centralizing tradition of government. A 1982 law on decentralization led to creation of elected assemblies endowed with considerable powers, especially over economic planning, in the 22 planning regions that had been created a decade earlier. Executive authority in the departments was transferred from the prefect to the president of the elected department council, and the latter body was given independent powers in areas such as social services, health, and transportation infrastructure.

The government's poor economic performance, manifested in a drop in the popularity of the president and the left's loss of municipal elections in 1983 and European Parliament elections in 1984, reinvigorated the parties on the right, though their persistent divisions impaired their prospects. These divisions widened further in the early 1980s when a third party appeared in force beside the UDF and the RPR. A former Poujadist, Jean-Marie Le Pen (1928–   ) had founded the Front National (National Front, FN) in 1972. A decade later, its platform, infused most prominently by an ugly racism that called for restrictions on immigration especially from North Africa, which it blamed for high crime and unemployment, appealed to those on the far right, including former Vichyites, monarchists, anti-Semites, and Catholic fundamentalists.

Divided though it was, the right's prospects in the legislative elections of March 1986 were improved due to the by now weak position of the Socialists. Prime Minister Mauroy had resigned in 1984, replaced by Laurent Fabius (1946–   ), and the economic downturn boded ill for their chances. To minimize an expected electoral drubbing, Mitterrrand implemented a controversial proposal to change the electoral system by replacing single-member constituencies with a form of proportional representation on a departmental basis. In the elections, though the Socialists and their allies remained the largest single group in parliament, they failed to prevail by the slimmest of margins, the UDR and RPR together winning an absolute parliamentary majority by a mere two seats.

The president was constitutionally obliged to call on the RPR's Jacques Chirac, as the leader of the largest party, to serve as prime minister. For the first time ever, a president and a prime minister from two opposing parties would be serving together. In working out the rules for what was dubbed "cohabitation," an uneasy division emerged in which Mitterrand reserved for himself the chief policymaking role in foreign affairs and defense, in line with the clear intent of the constitution, while Chirac presided over domestic matters. The president began to redefine his image, projecting himself as the head of state who stood above party politics, and assuming a pose of grandeur that, together with the attention he garnered on the world stage, gave him an opportunity to remain constantly in the public eye.

Determined to break with Socialist policies, Chirac carried out widespread deregulation and privatization, although not of traditional public-sector holdings in gas, electricity, telecommunication, or aerospace. Still, the economy remained in the doldrums. In the presidential campaign of April–May 1988, no one took to advocating, or defending, a left-wing program. By then, the Socialist Party had dumped all of its Marxist references in favor of business-friendly prescriptions. Mitterrand secured 54 percent of the vote, mostly from the unemployed, industrial workers, public employees, and the young, against Chirac, who was forced to defend a mixed record and faced a formidable challenge in the first round of balloting from Raymond Barre (1924–   ) of the UDR and the FN's Le Pen.

Socialist Michel Rocard (1930–   ) took office as prime minister. After the dissolution of the National Assembly in May 1988 and subsequent elections, the PS won enough seats to forge a ruling coalition with center deputies. Mitterrand continued to distance himself from the daily doings of government, leaving domestic affairs to Rocard, who presided over a resumption of economic growth until just before his resignation in May 1991. To succeed him, the president appointed Édith Cresson (1934–   ), who became France's first female prime minister. She proved to be an outspoken, polarizing figure forced to deal with a succession of public-sector strikes that damaged the government's image as a friend of organized labor. The failures of the early 1980s were well remembered, and little government interference in the market took place, but left-wing militants grew increasingly concerned that, in giving the fight against inflation top priority, the administration was pursuing policies that betrayed Socialists' interventionist traditions, which, as a consequence, were producing stagnant real wage growth and a widening gap between rich and poor. The discovery of government corruption and illicit political funding led to scandals that added to the discontent.

The country also faced an irksome campaign by groups seeking independence for the island of Corsica. Sporadic bombings and occasional assassinations, usually targeted at buildings and officials representing the government, had begun in the 1970s. Several deaths occurred in the 1990s during an especially violent internecine war between two rival groups. Discontent still simmers, and since 2000, governments have promised increased autonomy, including the grant of greater protection for the island's indigenous language (Corsu). In 2008, Corsu and all regional languages were recognized as belonging to the heritage of France.

Battling a public image that associated it with strikes and faulty economic solutions, the left met with electoral disaster in the legislative elections of March 1993, when together with independents, conservatives took 83 percent of the seats in the National Assembly. Another period of cohabitation followed with a prime minister, banker Édouard Balladur (1929–   ), who soon emerged as a rival of the RPR's leader Chirac. Mitterrand carried on as before, striving to stay above the fray in overseeing foreign and defense policies and seriously ill with the prostate cancer that would take his life after leaving office. His personal image besmirched by revelations of his youthful right-wing flirtations and Vichy past and his political legacy damaged by the shady financial dealings of some among his entourage, he would depart in 1995, his tenure remembered most favorably in bequeathing to Paris an impressive architectural legacy that included the Pyramide du Louvre, the Arche de la Défense, the Opéra de la Bastille (Bastille Opera), and the new Bibliothèque Nationale (National Library).

Jacques Chirac had long made known his ambition to win the presidency, an aim he achieved in May 1995, when he defeated rival Balladur on the first ballot and, on the second, Lionel Jospin (1937–   ), who had served as the Socialist Party's first secretary and minister of education under Mitterrand. Eschewing the stately pose of his predecessor, Chirac practiced a more open, relaxed style. The political right ended the 20th century controlling the presidency, the National Assembly, and a majority of the regional councils and departments.

But the problems faced by the previous government plagued the new one as well. The popularity of the administration soon collapsed when it failed to deliver on all its electoral promises. Chirac dismissed 13 ministers within six months of taking office in searching to find a way to deliver on broken pledges and after revelations of sleazy practices by some officials. Measures to reduce government spending, promulgated by decree rather than through parliament, prompted cries of an autocratic ruling style. Unemployment stayed stubbornly high at about 10 percent of the working population, while growing international competitiveness and technological innovation encouraged mergers and downsizing across the private-industry and service sectors. Welfare expenses called for cuts that sparked social unrest. At the same time, across the decades, while government policies and players changed, France maintained its proud status as one of the world's preeminent, prolific cultural places.

Contemporary Culture and Leisure
Literary and Intellectual Trends

The dislocations of World War II proved no less shattering than those that followed World War I. The most significant force in thought and literature to emerge after the trauma was existentialism, whose influence proved the most profound since surrealism. It was born in the late 1930s, brought to France from Germany by the young philosopher, teacher, and novelist Jean-Paul Sartre (1905–80), who became its chief French representative. In *La nausée* (*Nausea,* 1938), his first novel, Sartre traces the path of a rootless, alienated intellectual who drifts aimlessly through an existence that has neither meaning nor reason. In his major philosophic work, *L'être et le néant* (*Being and Nothingness,* 1943), he outlines his principles. The pessimism and despair so readily apparent in Sartre's writings are counterbalanced by his call for individuals to engage in actively shaping their lives, which resonated with the demands of a world that needed reconstruction. Beyond the doctrine's highly technical philosophical underpinning, existentialism could be understood in its assertion that humankind's past and future, indeed, its very existence, are in fact incomprehensible. Human beings could know only that they do indeed exist, and that being so, they are free to make choices, to shape their lives as they will. The universe may be irrational, but Sartre and his disciples preached the need for individuals not to run away from the world; rather, one must lead a life of involvement in whatever way one sees fit.

Sartre's life and thought were linked to those of his lover, Simone de Beauvoir (1908–86). Her existential analysis of women's place and status in modern society, *Le deuxième sexe* (*The Second Sex,* 1949) proved highly influential in feminist theory, which would emerge in coming decades. Another writer, Jean Genet (1910–86) drew on his own life as an imprisoned homosexual in novels and plays (*Notre dame des fleurs* [*Our Lady of the Flowers*], 1949) in which the characters confront issues of identity and alienation and in which traditional values are scorned as absurd and hypocritical. Born in Algeria into a family of modest means, Albert Camus (1913–60) became a journalist in Paris and joined the resistance during World War II. His novel *L'étranger* (*The Stranger,* 1942) earned him instant renown, but it was his postwar work *La peste* (*The Plague,* 1947) that best expressed his search for a collective morality behind which humanity could rally in the face of evil.

Existentialism faded as an innovative force by the 1970s, but even at its height there were voices that rejected its precepts. Marxists trumpeted their scientific materialism, while Catholics clung to their faith's traditional values. Others drew inspiration from a type of Christian existentialism espoused before the war by Gabriel Marcel (1889–1973), who substituted faith in the divine for Sartre's atheism (*Être et avoir* [*Being and Having*], 1935). Neopositivism looked to a faith in science and technology, while the old Enlightenment tradition still beckoned to some. Structuralism emerged to challenge existentialism in affirming that underlying structures form, limit, and affect society, language, and the human mind, evolving into schools of poststructuralism by the end of the 20th century. Postmodernism appeared, defined by Jean-François Lyotard (1924–98) as a disbelief in all general theories and grand schemes. His assertions were echoed by Michel Foucault (1926–84), who also proclaimed a distrust of absolutes and universal ideologies, such as Marxism, that had entranced so many past thinkers. Jean Baudrillard (1929–2007) affirmed that there are no truths in a given field, but that society, by means of what he called simulacra, conceals that fact, leading in the end to an inability to distinguish between reality and illusion. Jacques Derrida (1930–2004) founded deconstruction, a process of rigorously examining the meaning of a text to show that such meanings are unstable and hence capable of highly original interpretations.

Communism lost its intellectual appeal even before the collapse of the Soviet Union in 1991. Suspicion of bourgeois capitalism remained, but writers and thinkers were open to new currents in pacifism and ecologism, while at the same time they continued to approach old issues via moral principles, using ethical and humanitarian responses to global problems and conflicts. Universal theories have retreated in the face of pragmatic solutions to individual issues as they arise. France's intellectual elite, always a robust and never to be ignored source of ideas and argument, now offers prescriptions less for general, and more for individual, social and moral ills.

No clearly defined schools in literature and the arts emerged to rival existentialism. Experimental novelists of the 1950s and 1960s worked as individuals rather than as members of any specific school or tendency. Fiction evolved from a concentration on the somber times in the 1930s to a stress on personal and group involvement in the 1940s to a postwar emphasis on literature as totally uncommitted to anything but the freedom for writing to follow its own logic. This new outlook advanced in *Tel Quel*, a journal that guided mid-century intellectual currents. Prose comic writing most especially surged in the postwar years, dominated by Raymond Queneau (1903–76) and Georges Perce (1936–82).

Coined in 1957 by poet, novelist, and literary critic Émile Henriot (1889–1961), the term *nouveau roman* (new novel) designated a theory of experimental fiction that did away with traditional elements such as sequential plots and character analysis in favor of a noninterpretive, nonjudgmental recording of objects and sensations, though critics labeled the term more a marketing slogan than a mark of major innovation. Writers associated with the style include, most especially, Alain Robbe-Grillet (1922–2008) (*La Jalousie [Jealousy]*, 1957), whose collection of essays *Pour un nouveau roman* (*For a New Novel*, 1963) helped delineate the attributes of the nouveau roman, as well as Nathalie Sarraute (1900–99) (*Les fruits d'or [The Golden Fruits]*, 1963) and Michel Butor (1926–) (*La modification [Second Thoughts]*, 1957). Joining autobiography and fiction in a paradoxical combination, so-called *autofiction* features the use of fiction by a writer in quest of individual identity. Authors couch autobiographical details in fictionalized accounts and use of third-person characters. The term originates with Serge Doubrovsky (1928–), who used it to define his novel *Fils* (Son, 1977). Autofiction is associated with other contemporary autors such as Guillaume Dustan (1965–2005) (*Dans ma chambre [In My Room]*, 1996), Annie Ernaux (1940–) (*La Place*, 1994), and Catherine Millet (1948–), who used the techniques to explore her sexual experiences in *La vie sexuelle de Catherine M* (*The Sexual Life of Catherine M*, 2002).

The novel is much more nonideological today, characterized by both traditional structural and innovative nonstructural narratives. It remains a versatile outlet for philosophers, social critics, and the socially marginalized, including spokespersons for the poor, immigrants, and the gay, lesbian, and transgendered communities. The recipient of the 2008 Nobel Prize in literature, the novelist Jean-Marie Gustave Le Clézio (1940–), Nice-born and widely traveled, has written more than 40 books. His breakthrough came in 1980 with publication of *Désert* (*Desert*), winner of the Grand Prix Paul Morand, a novel that, in recounting the experiences of a young Moroccan boy and girl, regales the reader with splendid images of the North African desert.

Women writers are now fully representative among the literary lights. Marguerite Yourcenar (1903–87), who had been writing since the 1920s, made her reputation with *Les mémoires d'Hadrian* (*The Memoirs of Hadrian*, 1951), a multidimensional depiction of the Roman emperor. In 1980, she became the first woman to be elected to the Académie Française. Perhaps the most original French woman writer of the later 20th century, Marguerite Duras (1914–96), wrote novels characterized by the absence of traditional narrative structures and plots (*Moderato Contabile*, 1958). Novelist and playwright Hélène Cixous (1937–) pens works not only as a committed feminist but also as a woman who affirms that each human being expresses both femininity and masculinity (*Le rire de la Méduse* [*The Laugh of the Medusa*], 1975).

Cixous writes for the Théâtre du Soleil, one of many theatrical companies that reinvigorated the French theater after the late 1960s. Eugène Ionesco (1909–94) inspired creation of the Theater of the Absurd movement in writing his first play, *La cantatrice chauve* (1950), which reflects on the lack of direction in human life. The plays of Jean Anouilh (1910–87) embody the author's search for reasons why idealism so often fails in the face of reality, an inquiry that led him to seek explanations for human failures in Greek mythology in a trilogy of famous works (*Medea*, 1937; *Eurydice*, 1942; *Antigone*, 1942). Theatrical experimentation suffers in an age in which drama must compete with radio, television, and film and when appeal must be made to mass audiences. But new playwrights succeed nevertheless in combining elements of popular theater with innovative scripts and stage techniques.

Film

Exiles from the film world returned after the war to a French cinema that, during the 1940s and 1950s, remained more conventional than experimental. Only the documentary exhibited some adventurous spirit, filmmakers combining sensitivity with authenticity. Competition from Hollywood was intense, while a new medium appeared in television. Attendance at films started falling in the late 1950s.

Moviegoers could find classic films playing in the national chain of cinema clubs or, in Paris, in the Cinémathèque Française, where director Henri Langlois (1914–77) had assembled a vast collection of French and foreign films. It was here that François Truffaut (1932–84), Eric Rohmer (1920–2010), Alain Resnais (1922–), Jean-Luc Godard

(1930–), and other aspiring directors, producers, and cinematographers acquired detailed knowledge of filmmaking. They developed a new concept of film that they tried out in directing documentaries and narrative shorts, making use of lightweight cameras and faster film that made location shooting easier. They achieved commercial and artistic success when they fully utilized their talents to produce a *nouvelle vague* (New Wave) of feature films. Influential worldwide, between 1958 and 1963 about 100 New Wave films were made, including stellar productions such as Truffaut's *Les quatre cent coups* (*The 400 Blows*, 1959), Resnais's *L'année dernière à Marienbad* (*Last Year at Marienbad*, 1961), and *Bande à part* (*Band of Outsiders*, 1964) and *À bout de souffle* (*Breathless*, 1960) by Godard, considered by many the most influential and innovative New Wave figure. They rejected the strong narrative tradition of classic French cinema in favor of a heavy fictional symbolism to make adventurous, highly personal (*auteuriste*) statements that were the antithesis of the stylized films that New Wave replaced. Though working with small budgets, producers achieved success such that a new galaxy of film stars appeared, including Yves Montand (1921–91), Jeanne Moreau (1928–) Jean-Paul Belmondo (1933–), Alain Delon (1935–), and Catherine Deneuve (1943–). Screenwriter, director, and producer Roger Vadim (1928–2000) went to court in defense of his *Les liaisons dangereuses* in 1959, judged to have besmirched French literary repute, but he is best remembered for launching the career of Brigitte Bardot (1934–), whose appearance in *Et dieu créa la femme* (*And God Created Woman*, 1956) made her an international sex symbol.

By the mid-1960s New Wave had become orthodoxy, its techniques increasingly routine. A more politically

Actress Brigitte Bardot popularized the bikini worldwide in the 1950s. (AP Images)

323

committed cinema appeared in the aftermath of the May 1968 events, but established directors soon returned to their preoccupation with traditional subjects. Pornography flooded the market following a relaxation of the censorship laws in 1974, and the explicit treatment of sexual subjects moved into mainstream film. Financing troubles gave rise to coproductions and participation by television companies, while innovative efforts continued to receive support from the Centre National Cinématographique, an important source of state monies since the 1940s.

Quality began to be redefined in commercial terms in the 1980s when forceful marketing campaigns sought to woo viewers to films that, because television monopolized the market for family fare, dealt with violence and sex and that featured big budget productions. Films celebrated the youth culture (*Subway,* 1985; director Luc Besson [1959–]) and also the past (*Le retour de Martin Guerre [The Return of Martin Guerre]*, 1982; director Daniel Vigne [1942–]).

Nostalgia for the past continued to appeal in the 1990s (*Indochine [Indochina]*, 1991; director Régis Warnier [1948–]), but audiences were also drawn to current issues. The rise of a multicultural society and the problems it has engendered are reflected in films such as *Douce France* (1996; director Malik Chibane [1964–]) and *La haine* (*Hatred,* 1995; director Matthieu Kassowitz [1967–]), which exemplify a new style of cinema verité. Crime films moved away from detection toward psychological examination, while comedy offered both popular farce and high-brow black comedic fare.

At the beginning of the 21st, century France remains Europe's leading film producer and, after the United States, the second-largest film exporter in the world. State funding remains vital for the production of "quality" films since television companies can dictate what they want, given their position as the industry's biggest customer, a status they possess because 60 percent of films shown on TV are legally required to be European-made. The viewing public has remained high, a loyalty explained by pride both in France's long record as a film pioneer and in its cultural traditions, manifested especially in defending the French language against encroachments by English. But audiences are also drawn consistently to Hollywood films. American dominance is today conceded, even if reluctantly, and some actors and directors have argued for a cinema that embodies European values but speaks English. At the same time, the electronic revolution of videogames and DVDs offers contemporary hurdles once posed by television. Despite the challenges, an international market still exists for innovative, beautifully crafted

French films. The motion picture continues to provide entertainment and to serve as a vehicle both to shape attitudes at home and to convey French culture abroad.

Painting and Music

Paris lost its preeminent place as the center of the art world when, after World War II, innovative artists could be found working in many other venues, but Paris-based painters have shaped the course of art, most especially Pablo Picasso, who remained an active, and by now a world-renowned, artist into the 1960s, and Georges Braque (1882–1963), whose career also spanned many years. Both men's styles, emerging from experiments with the pictorial values of composition, color, and form, changed the direction of painting. In architecture, Charles-Édouard Jeanneret, or Le Corbusier (1887–1965), pioneered function-alism in breaking with historical forms to construct buildings made of modern materials designed for practical use. He contributed greatly to the emergence of an international style, whose unadorned, simply formed low-lying buildings are on display in the palace of the League of Nations in Geneva, Switzerland (1927–28), and at the headquarters of the United Nations in New York (1953).

In popular music the chanson experienced a golden age during the 1950s and 1960s with an array of major stars, including Édith Piaf (1915–63), Charles Trenet (1913–2001), Charles Aznavour (1924–   ), and Belgian-born Jacques Brel (1929–78). International forms were popular, especially American and British music, but indigenous varia-tions achieved equal if not greater success. American rock and roll made inroads in the 1950s, but no star won greater acclaim than Johnny Hallyday (1943–   ), a rock and roll singer as well as an actor who has achieved iconic standing in a career that has spanned half a century. Hallyday's wife, Sylvie Vartan (1944–   ), the most productive of the popular yé-yé girls of the 1960s, is an active artist of rock and roll, jazz, and soul music. Singer-songwriter Serge Gainsbourg (1928–91) began as a jazz musician in the 1950s and became a prolific performer of everything from rock to pop to disco.

New artists modernized the chanson in the 1970s and 1980s, and French variants of rock and other forms of music spawned a myriad of styles in succeeding decades, just as international trends—punk rock, disco, heavy metal—found listeners. Folk music enjoys success, none more so than that of Brittany. The documented history of its distinctly Celtic sounds began in 1839 with publication of a collection of folk songs, and assembly of material along with its popularization—Lorient hosts a major festival—continues. In the early 1970s, Breton musician Alan Stivell (1944–) launched French folk rock by combining Breton styles with progressive rock sounds. France's greatest contribution to recent musical innovation is a form of computer-assisted composition called "spectral music," based on analysis of sound spectra. Practitioners have included Gérard Grisey (1946–98) and Tristan Murail (1947–).

Science

French scientists have worked in the forefront of developments in many fields. In 1939, the government established the Centre National de la Recherche Scientifique (National Center for Scientific Research) as a publicly funded organization to carry out investigative work. Measured by receipt of Nobel Prize awards, French scientists have excelled especially in work in physics, chemistry, and physiology or medicine. Jean-Marie Lehn (1939–) helped develop the field of supramolecular chemistry, and Louis Néel (1904–2000) worked as a pioneer in the study of the magnetic property of solids. Pierre-Gilles de Gennes (1932–2007) developed an important theory of polymer dynamics.

French medical researchers were among the earliest to investigate the outbreak of acquired immune deficiency syndrome (AIDS), and Françoise Barré-Sinoussi (1947–) and Luc Montagnier (1932–) won the Nobel Prize in physiology or medicine in 2008 as codiscoverers of the human-immunodeficiency virus (HIV).

World-renowned oceanography and filmmaker Jacques-Yves Cousteau (1910–97), together with French-Canadian engineer Émile Gagnan (1900–79), perfected the Aqua-Lung, which enabled underwater divers to remain submerged for several hours at a time. Using his ship *Calypso,* Cousteau undertook aquatic research and promoted environmental awareness, and he showcased his efforts in producing award-winning films.

France plays a leading role in the European Space Agency, founded in 1975. In 2000, the country launched a joint program with the U.S. National Aeronautics and Space Administration for exploration of the planet Mars.

Sports

France helped launch the world of modern sports in the person of educator Pierre Frédy, baron de Coubertin (1863–1937), who founded

TOUR DE FRANCE

Watched by a handful of spectators, the men flourishing their hats and the ladies their parasols, at precisely 2:15 P.M. on July 1, 1903, some 60 cyclists pedaled away from the starting point near the café Réveil-Matin in Montgéron, a Paris suburb, bound for Lyon, more than 290 miles (467 km) away over poorly paved roads on the first of six designated stages of the first Tour de France. Nine days later, after riding day and night, Maurice Garin (1871–1957) entered the Parc des Princes in Paris, having covered 1,510 miles (2,430 km) at an average speed of 15.9 miles (25.6 km) per hour.

A rivalry between two Parisian weeklies launched the race, sports journalist and amateur cyclist Henri Desgranges (1865–1940) seeking revenge for a successful lawsuit against him and getting it when the circulation of his newspaper soared after the race. He remained the patron and sponsor of the tour until his retirement in 1937.

The tour took on its modern form gradually over the years. The first races were for individuals and members of sponsored teams. National squads replaced sponsored ones from 1930 to 1961, when trade teams returned, the race sponsors fearful that the bicycling industry, then undergoing a slump, would die if manufacturers and

(continues)

Louis "Louison" Bobet (1925–83) of France wins the 21st stage of the Tour de France between Épinal and Nancy, July 30, 1954. Bobet won the Tour de France that year. (Associated Press)

327

TOUR DE FRANCE *(continued)*

others were deprived of the publicity engendered by the tour.

Early distances, which reached a maximum of 3,570 miles (5,745 km) in 1926, have been reduced to a more modest length, set in 2009 at 2,150 miles (3,459.5 km), and the number of daily stages has declined from about 30 to about 23. Strenuous mountain stretches began in the Pyrenees in 1910 and in the Alps in 1911. Riders had to carry their bicycles over unmade tracks. Early winners sported a green armband, the famed *maillot jaune* (yellow jersey) first appearing on July 18, 1919, worn by Eugène Christophe (1885–1970), the winner of that day's stage, who disliked it because spectators lining the road from Grenoble to Geneva called out "canary" as he sped by. Original routes remained within French territorial bounds, but today portions often run through neighboring countries. For the first five years, the course ran through Alsace, but in 1906, German authorities prohibited the race because roadside crowds began singing the Marseillaise.

After World War I, foreign riders began to participate, and although French riders have won the most overall tours (36), modern-day victors, such as five-time winners Belgian Eddy Merckx (1945–) and Spaniard Miguel Induráin (1964–) and seven-time champion American Lance Armstrong (1971–), attest to the event's international appeal. Both winning speeds—the 2009 figure stood at 25 miles (40.3 km) per hour—and the number of contestants—180 in 2009—have risen progressively. While the Tour de France has been plagued by scandals involving use of endurance-enhancing drugs, it remains France's most famous sporting event.

the International Olympic Committee in 1896, which sponsored the modern revival of the ancient games. Coubertin served as president until 1925. The country's athletes have won many awards, including winning the most medals of all the participating nations in the 1900 games, held in Paris. France hosted the first winter Olympic games in Chamonix in 1924. Notable modern-day French Olympians include triple-medal-winning alpine skier Jean-Claude Killy (1943–) and track racer Marie-José Pérec (1968–). Football (soccer) remains the most popular sport, but practitioners and spectators of all the major athletic endeavors abound. A distinct national game, boules, is played with metal balls in parks and open spaces across the nation. Pétanque, reputedly invented in La Ciotat in 1907, is a variant played in southern France. Launched in Paris as a national competition in 1891, the French Open, or the Roland Garros Tournament—named for a noted French aviator (1888–1918) killed in World War I—has become one of the most prestigious international events in the sport of tennis. The Tour de France has become the world's premier event in bicycle racing. The lure of sports draws millions today, reflecting a society endowed with an abundance of leisure time, one measure of the prosperity enjoyed by French citizens at the end of the 20th century.

329

12

FRANCE IN THE TWENTY-FIRST CENTURY: THE POWER OF PRESTIGE

France enters the 21st century under a form of government that, since the Revolution of 1789, has withstood the test of time longer than any previous regime, save for the Third Republic. Politics is well ordered, its participants at peace with the system. The country is today a modern nation with a capitalist, market-oriented economic system, albeit with a major public presence, that has made it one of the world's wealthiest societies. Agriculture is mechanized, business is streamlined, and high-technology and service industries are fully functional.

Republican government is now a fact of life, but the governments that come to rule are beset by tensions stemming both from conditions peculiar to the country and from problems that confront Western societies in general. Prosperity is widespread, but unemployment is persistent. The welfare system is generous but too expensive. Farmers demand protection for their markets, business elites insist on open markets. Rising crime rates are blamed on immigrants, who counterclaim that built-in racism prevents them from fully assimilating into mainstream society. Cultural differences induce strains. Avenues to jobs, schools, and political influence are blocked for too many. Threats of potential terrorism, both domestic and international, require constant vigilance. A united Europe beckons, while the glories of a sovereign, fully independent France are cherished in a country with a continuing strong sense of national identity.

The extent to which governments succeed—or fail—to deal with these and other issues will determine the future course of the nation. Unpredictable events and stresses may produce shocks that could profoundly transform the system. Challenges lie ahead, but France can look back to its past, to its long history—a record that includes revolutions, wars, numerous regime changes, and economic and social crises—as a source to guide, inspire, instruct, and warn.

Will the Fifth Republic Endure?

The mixed system of presidential and parliamentary government of the Fifth Republic has brought a far more stable regime than its cabinet-style predecessors, the Third and Fourth Republics, and it has proved far more durable than the latter. It has survived the powerful personality of its founder, General de Gaulle, and it has remained the governing system under the Socialists, many of whom opposed its creation. Worries that rule by a president and a prime minister of two different parties could not be sustained have been shown to be unfounded.

The longest period of such cohabitation to date came in April 1997 when the left, led by Socialist Party leader Lionel Jospin, won a solid National Assembly majority. The government of President Chirac had been damaged by massive strikes that virtually shut down the country in November and December 1995, called to protest free-market reforms that would have cut social spending.

The period of joint rule ended following Chirac's decisive defeat of Jospin in presidential elections in April and May 2002, the first to be held following approval in a referendum to reduce the president's term of office from seven to five years. Divided into three political parties, the right moved to unite behind Chirac in the lead-up to the elections in founding the Union en Mouvement (Union on the Move). After Chirac's victory, preparations to wage a united effort to win the upcoming legislative elections led to establishment of the Union pour un Mouvement Populaire (Union for a Popular Movement, UMP), which emerged as a permanent political party. Created through the merger of the Gaullist (RPR), Liberal (DL), Christian Democrat (UDF), and Radical Parties, the UMP embodies the fusion of the four major center-right French political traditions into a single vehicle.

The new party won the subsequent legislative elections in June, and a government was formed led by Jean-Pierre Raffarin (1948–). Raffarin resigned in May 2005 following the defeat by French voters of a referendum on a treaty establishing a proposed constitution for Europe, which the government had backed. To replace him, President Chirac appointed as prime minister Dominique de Villepin (1953–), who had served as French foreign minister. Villepin quickly earned the public's ire in introducing in 2006 a so-called First Employment Contract (CPE), a series of amendments that would have created a special employment contract allowing employers to hire and fire workers freely under age 26. Aimed at reducing high unemployment among youth by easing workplace rules, the proposal raised a storm of protest, opponents claiming that it unfairly singled out the young instead of tackling the general issue of unemployment and that its passage would weaken workers' rights. The scheme was withdrawn.

Villepin had been considered a contender for the 2007 presidential elections, but the failure of the CPE dashed his hopes. A total of 12 candidates ran in the first round of presidential balloting on April 22, none winning more than 50 percent. In the runoff, the two major contenders—Nicolas Sarkozy (1955–) of the UMP and Ségolène Royal (1953–) of the Socialists—battled for the top French political prize. The son of a Hungarian immigrant, Sarkozy headed the UMP and served as minister of the interior in Raffarin's and Villepin's governments. The first woman to be nominated for president by a major party, Royal held office as a government minister, a member of the National Assembly, and as president of the Poitou-Charente regional council. In a spirited, 10-day campaign that contained all the drama and market sophistication of American-style electioneering, both candidates embodied a new generation of leadership. Sarkozy promised to revitalize the country through modernization reforms, lower taxes, and initiatives to make the economy more globally competitive. Royal pledged to ensure protection for cherished employee and welfare rights and to introduce a breath of change by shaking up the male-dominated world of French politics. During the campaign, the Socialists suffered from political blunders and internal party disputes, and enthusiasm for Royal, initially very high, declined by a margin sufficient enough to give the victory, on May 5 and 6, 2007, to Sarkozy by a 53 to 47 percent vote. A near record 84 percent of 44.5 million voters cast ballots.

Outgoing president Jacques Chirac (background) and incoming president Nicolas Sarkozy before the 2007 elections (Patrick Kovarik/Associated Press)

National Assembly Elections 2002 and 2007		
Party	2002 Seats	2007 Seats
Union for a Popular Movement (UMP)	357	313
Union for French Democracy (UDR)	29	–
New Center (NC)	–	22
Miscellaneous right-wing (DVD)	8	8
Movement for France (MPF)	1	2
Liberal Democracy (DL)	2	–
Rally for France (RPF)	2	–
Total "Presidential Majority" (Right)	**399**	**345**
Socialist Party (PS)	140	186
French Communist Party (PCF)	21	15
Miscellaneous left-wing (DVG)	6	15
Left Radical Party (PRG)	7	7
The Greens (VEC)	3	4
Total "United Left"	**177**	**227**
Democratic Movement (MoDem)	–	3
Regionalists and Separatists	–	1
Miscellaneous (DIV)	1	1
National Front (FN)	–	–
Hunting, Fishing, Nature, Traditions (CPNT)	–	–
Other Ecologists	–	–
Other Far-Right (ExD)	–	–
Other Far-Left (ExG)	–	–
Total	577	577

In the subsequent legislative elections held on June 10 and 17, the right retained its majority in the National Assembly, although it lost some 40 seats to the Socialists. Political parties continue to proliferate, while at the same time, the trend toward amalgamation in favor of two strong parties—one on the center-right and one on the center-left—bodes well for future political stability. The two current major party contenders—the UMP and the Socialists—draw substantial voter support, attracting 39.5 percent and 24.7 percent in the 2007 legislative elections, respectively.

Sarkozy's win reflected in part voters' concerns about the country's economic condition. Technological change, in the form of an explosion in information technology—computers and cell phones are as omnipresent here as elsewhere in the West—and the growth of robotics and biotechnology, has led to major gains in productivity and in national income and wealth, but it has failed to dent high unemployment, which has persisted, especially among the young, for more than 30 years—hovering around 10 percent since the mid-1980s and rising from a 7.4 percent in 2008 to nearly 10 percent in 2009 ("France Unemployment" 2009)—or to shrink the growing gap between those who possess the marketable skills needed in the new economy and those who do not. Unequal access to educational and employment opportunities and to avenues to wealth creation and political power carry the potential for internal conflict.

At the same time, government expenditures for unemployment payments and funding for a welfare state characterized by lavish pensions and long vacations are among the most generous in the world. They have given the country a first-rate social security system. The World Health Organization ranked the nation's health care the best in the world in a 2000 survey ("World Health" 2000). But the benefits have come at a price. Expenditures produce large budget deficits and impede French international competitiveness, while unemployment reduces tax income. High spending is especially troublesome given the slow growth of the French economy. The economy expanded by a mere .03 percent in the second quarter of 2009 and is forecast to move up slowly to about 1 percent, a lower rate than those expected in the United States and Asia ("French PM Warns of Lingering Economic Risks" 2009). Ongoing globalization with its shift of jobs to low-cost countries in Asia and elsewhere imposes worrisome strains on a country, with an aging population, high salaries, and lavish social services, that must confront a shortfall in revenue earnings. The Sarkozy government has created an 18 billion euro investment fund to be used to protect French companies from foreign takeovers.

Sarkozy has declared that France must not only lower taxes—at nearly 50 percent of GDP one of the highest in Europe—but also change its work ethic to generate new jobs and compete in the global economy. Efforts by the administration to convince some among the public to work longer hours and to settle for a less beneficent public largesse have not been easy. In 2007, under a program titled Révision générale des politiques publiques (General Revision of Public Policy, RGPP), the government announced plans to cut government salaries and jobs and reduce state services, which led to widespread disruption of public services in November when civil servants took to the streets in protest, joined by workers from transport and energy industries. The global financial crisis struck France in 2008, compelling the government to inject 10.5 billion euros to shore up the reserves of the country's six largest banks and to launch a series of stimulus measures totaling 25.5 billion euros in February 2009. More buoyant consumer and government spending and a reduced exposure to the downward trend in demand occasioned by the crisis has lessened its impact in the country. Adding to concerns, the increasingly integrated economies of EU members, all of which use the euro as their currency, requires nations whose economies are large and relatively healthier to contemplate stepping in with bailout programs to calm the jitters of stock and corporate bond markets fearful of default by heavily indebted countries, a scenario that France faces in dealing with massive budget shortfalls in 2010 in Greece, Spain, and Portugal. Since 2008, France's own budget deficit has soared, reaching 8.2 percent of GDP in 2010. Intent on carrying out public-sector reforms, the Sarkozy administration in February 2010 unveiled plans for cutting public spending. Given the need to save money and because the deficit threatens the viability of the pension system, which is losing money, the government in June raised the retirement age from 60 to 62, effective in 2018. The stability program is intended to reduce the deficit to 3 percent—the threshold set by the EU—by 2013 ("French government cites European debt crisis," 2010).

Can the American capitalist model of less government and a less regulated private market—elements of which President Sarkozy seeks to adopt—be applied in a country long accustomed to a major role of the state in economic participation and regulation and in social protection? Should France even wish to proceed in that direction? While Socialist prescriptions of large-scale nationalization and public-sector spending, which proved disastrous in the 1980s, have not been broached, a lively debate continues between those on the right, who advocate greater market freedoms, and those on the left, who are anxious to preserve the social safety net and advance wealth redistribution. The Fifth Republic has so far successfully accommodated these economically driven strains. The system has been far more threatened by recent tensions arising from social and ethnic divisions.

Will Assimilation of Immigrants Advance or Retreat?

The prospering post–World War II economy attracted growing numbers of immigrants, who began to arrive from southern Europe and Turkey in the late 1950s and from former French colonies in North and West Africa beginning in the 1960s to take low-paying jobs. Europeans repatriated from Algeria and elsewhere were easily assimilated, but others, those who were poor and possessed an alien religion and customs, met with discrimination and, from some quarters, outright racial hatred. The French have prided themselves on their nation's reputation as an open, tolerant society. Touting its status as Europe's leading nation of immigration, they point to a tradition of welcoming newcomers in the name of liberty that dates to the French Revolution. That tradition dictates that a united, homogeneous citizenry is sought as the patriotic ideal in which ethnic, religious, and cultural differences are submerged in favor of these universal attributes. Recent years have witnessed public acknowledgment of instances in which the ideal has been violated. President Chirac in 1995, Roman Catholic bishops in 1997, and the Council of State in 2009 have issued apologies for the nation's shameful active participation in the deportation of Jews under the Vichy regime during World War II. Historically, the French have considered not race but rather a failure to assimilate culturally, to adopt French social norms and the French language, as barriers to national integration. Provided newcomers professed loyalty to the nation and acquired these attributes, immigrants and their children born in France could easily obtain French citizenship. However, recent arrivals from Islamic nations have profoundly tested accepted attitudes and practices. Prior to the 1970s, few regulations impeded entry into the country, but the recession of that decade compelled the government to place a moratorium on immigration and initiate repatriation policies. These were not entirely successful, and numbers continued to rise. By the 1990s, France hosted at least 4 million Muslim immigrants, giving it western Europe's largest Islamic community.

Many new arrivals found themselves confined to public housing projects built beginning in the late 1960s as replacements for the *bidonvilles*—shantytowns that had sprung up in the 1950s on the outskirts of major cities, so-called for the makeshift shacks with roofs of corrugated iron (*bidon*) built by immigrants. Large immigrant families, mostly Muslim, reside in these now aging low-rent complexes (*habitation à loyer modéré*, HLM) in working-class areas in distant suburbs. In these virtual ghettoes where unemployment, especially among the young, is startlingly high, the immigrants live apart, separated by religion, customs, and class from the French, many of whom fear and shun them, blaming them for high crime and poverty.

Anti-immigrant attitudes explain in large part the success of Jean-Marie Le Pen's National Front Party. The party has won governing posts at local and regional levels, and Le Pen emerged as Chirac's sole contender in the 2002 presidential runoff campaign, which, even if it was made possible only because of divisions on the left, sent shockwaves through the country.

A major avenue for assimilation into the mainstream is sought through the secular education system, but insistence by immigrants that they be allowed to retain cultural markers—first made manifest in October 1989 when three teenage girls appeared at a local school in the town of Creil dressed in the traditional Muslim head scarf and were turned away by the headmaster—has met fierce resistance in being seen as a deliberate rejection of the nonsectarian character long cherished in French public education. The headmaster declared that the head scarf was a religious symbol and as such inappropriate in a state-run school. In June 2009, the government set up a parliamentary commission to study wearing of the burka (the full-length veil with a mesh screen for the eyes) and the niqab (the full-length body garment) by Muslim women. "I say it solemnly," President Sarkozy told parliamentarians, "the burka is not welcome in France" in calling it a "problem of liberty and dignity for women" as a "symbol of servitude and humiliation" ("Burka is not welcome in France," 2009). The commission reported in January 2010 that Muslim women should not be permitted to wear burkas in public institutions, such as government buildings, banks, and schools, as well as on public transportation. It called for educational programs designed to counteract fundamentalist Islamic teaching. In summer 2010, the National Assembly debated imposition of fines for those found in violation, should recommendations be enacted into law.

At the same time, calls for a modification of precepts and attitudes have gathered strength in recent years. In 2007 President Sarkozy ran on an election platform advocating modernization of the 100-year-old principle of *laïcité* in which the government would recognize the contributions of religious institutions to French culture, history, and society, open up the public discourse to allow for wider participation by religious authorities, and extend government subsidies to faith-based groups.

For their part, recent immigrants affirm that French society has long made a practice of hiding, or least looking away, from signs and symptoms of racism and hatred of foreigners. Pent-up feelings exploded in late October 2005. Riots erupted that were triggered by the death of two Muslim teenage boys in Clichy-sous-Bois, a poor township in an eastern suburb of Paris. Expressing their rage mainly by burning cars and public buildings, the demonstrators spread havoc, which soon engulfed poor housing projects all over France. At least one individual

337

Firefighters try to extinguish blazing cars set alight by rioters in La Reynerie housing complex in Toulouse, November 10, 2005. Arson and rioting broke out across France by protesters angered at perceived injustices and discrimination. (Remy Gabalda/Associated Press)

was killed and more than 2,900 were arrested. Public authorities under then interior minister Sarkozy alleged that provocations had been deliberately launched by organized gangs and drug dealers, while the rioters claimed that police brutality and harassment compelled them to strike back. The government invoked a state of emergency, which lasted until January 2006, and the rioting subsided.

But the massive civil unrest laid bare social tensions and evoked serious questionings not only about how best to alleviate the poverty endemic among immigrants, but also about the reality behind French social and cultural assumptions. Some who assumed their country to be tolerant and welcoming have been rudely disabused, while others affirm that no tolerance should be extended to newcomers who refuse to adopt fully national customs and standards. The emergence of radical Islam and of the weapon of choice employed by some of its adherents—acts of international terrorism of the type and on a scale so horrifically enacted on September 11, 2001, in the United States—have raised anxieties and hardened attitudes among those who fear for the safety of a country where millions of Muslims live. The alleviation of poverty will go a long way toward integrating impoverished immigrants into French society, but cultural attributes stemming from religious and social differences will constitute hurdles to overcome. Antiforeigner sentiments remain strong, and no one can be certain how events will unfold. France shares the problem with most of its neighbors, which, while it does not lessen the gravity of the situation, may prove important in alleviating it. The nation's relations with other European countries constitute another important contemporary issue.

Will Ties to Europe Tighten or Loosen?

European integration has been a core goal of France since the early 1950s at the same time that the nation has advanced its individual sovereign stance and the French have cherished a vigorous patriotism. The wish, indeed, the need to forever banish the resort to war, which had ravaged the Continent so brutally twice in the 20th century by uniting, first, the economies, and later, the social, political, and security systems of Europe launched the drive for continental cooperation, whose goal was to ensure peace and prosperity for all. The basis for progress rested with close French and German cooperation, because reconciliation between the two old enemies was an essential precondition for efforts to prove successful. Today that foundation remains the lynchpin for progress, because the two possess Western Europe's largest continental economies.

Two of the founding fathers of the European Union (EU), Jean Monnet and MRP politician and twice premier (1947–48) Robert Schuman (1886–1963), were in the forefront of initial efforts at regional integration. In the 1950s, the European Coal and Steel Community, the European Atomic Energy Agency, and the European Economic Community were all created with active French participation, and the country played a vital part in the subsequent history of cooperative efforts. France welcomed new member states; instigated the Single European Act in 1986, which ensured the free movement of people, goods, and capital; negotiated the Maastricht Treaty in 1992, which widened supranational powers within the new institutional framework of the EU; and adopted the euro, which replaced the franc, as its currency in 2002.

But, countercurrents against stronger cooperative efforts in defense of specifically French self-interests continue to exert a strong influence. Politicians on both extremes of the political spectrum, including Le Pen on the right and Jean-Pierre Chevènement (1930–   ), a former minister of defense (1988–91) and minister of the interior (1997–2000) on the left, have advocated a reassertion of French independent prerogatives. General de Gaulle attempted to shape integration in his own image as a Europe of loosely linked sovereign states, and today the union that ardent integrationists foresee as a Europe ruled by a powerful central authority to which nations have abdicated significant powers is a vision by no means shared by all. Significant segments of public opinion balk at too great a surrender of sovereignty to a supranational European authority. Resentment runs deep at unelected bureaucrats at EU headquarters in Brussels making decisions with no accountability to constituents and, critics assert, no knowledge of local conditions or concerns. Only just more than 51 percent of voters approved ratification of the Maastricht Treaty in a referendum in September 1992. In 2005, a referendum on the treaty to establish a constitution for Europe was rejected by the public by a margin of 55 percent to 45 percent. In 2007, the constitutional project was abandoned, and existing treaties were amended instead.

While governments of both left and right have supported closer integration since the 1970s, they have never hesitated, when they deemed it necessary, to interject strong defense of what they perceive to be French national interests. President Sarkozy's opposition to the admission of Turkey, considered insufficiently ready in terms of economic strength and democratic political maturity, testifies to the country's determination to shape the future EU in what it sees to be France's best interests.

The ongoing debate between those who wish to maintain a strong national independence and those who see France's future in a strengthened European Union is starkly evident in the realm of national defense and security, issues of particular pride to advocates of French self-identity. Long a larger player in international affairs, France has proved reluctant to allow the EU to speak for itself in these matters, making it difficult to move ahead in the professed goal of common EU foreign and defense policies. While a broad consensus accepts that the country's future lies within the EU, debate continues on the kinds and the amount of power—on the overall future course—of continental institutions. Although it will always have a large voice in policy determination within a united Europe, France will inevitably have to yield some greater degree of sovereignty if political and military integration is to deepen. Reality rules as well in considering the country's future status in world affairs.

Will France Have a Central Place on the Future World Stage?

France no longer wields the diplomatic and military power that made it one of the world's most active nations around the globe for most of its modern history. However, though its presence has receded, the country remains a committed participant in the international theater. France has taken a position, and sometimes played a major role, in all the major issues that have shaped global affairs since 1945. A staunch ally of the Western alliance, the nation joined all of the organizations aimed at countering the Soviet threat in the early cold war years.

An early, close ally of the state of Israel, France joined with that country and Britain in 1956 to battle Egypt after its leader Gamal Abdel Nasser (1918–70) seized the Suez Canal. In the mid-1950s, France cooperated closely with Israel in a mutual effort to develop both countries' nuclear capabilities, signing a secret agreement in 1957 in which the French agreed to build a nuclear reactor for the Israelis, and scientists and technicians from the two nations worked together to design and test weapons. Paris later adopted a more balanced approach to the Middle East's ongoing central dispute in calling for a settlement between Israel and its Palestinian neighbors that recognizes the rights of the latter to self-determination. France has shown special interest in the affairs of Lebanon, a country where it has a long record of involvement as protector of the Christian population in the 19th century and where it ruled under a League of Nations mandate between the world wars. Troops were dispatched as part of a multinational peacekeeping force during the protracted Lebanese civil war (1975–90) in October 1983, though they were speedily withdrawn after 58 service personnel were subsequently killed in a suicide bombing of a French barracks.

France retains close commercial, cultural, and military ties with most of its former colonial possessions in central and West Africa. Over the decades, the French have routinely extended military and material aid. The CFA franc is the currency of 12 former French-ruled African colonies. Franco-African summits have been held regularly for 50 years among heads of states as part of a continuing dialogue. The nation's role has not gone without criticism. Some have decried assistance given to secure beneficial trade relations that has helped to prop up corrupt, unelected leaders. France's continued support of Rwanda's former Hutu-dominated government in the early 1990s after evidence emerged that a plan was underfoot to wipe out the country's Tutsi minority, which was carried out in 1994, has left a black mark on the nation's diplomatic record. The country maintains three military bases in Africa—in Djibouti, Chad, and Senegal—as well as in Abu Dhabi on the Arabian Peninsula, which opened in May 2009. French forces stand at the ready to intervene in places—46 military operations have been launched in France's former colonies in Africa between 1960 and

2005—although since the 1980s, overt military measures have been replaced increasingly by an emphasis on mutually cooperative means, and defense of human rights has assumed a greater policy role. In Côte d'Ivoire (Ivory Coast), French military forces battled national troops after the besieged government of President Laurent Gbagbo (1945–) launched a military raid that killed nine French peacekeepers in 2004. French troops remaining in the country strive to maintain the peace in a nation torn by rival claimants to power.

Since the start of the Fifth Republic, France tended to depart increasingly from its tight ties to its Western partners in seeking to play a more independent role in the world. De Gaulle's policies represented that stance at its most extreme, but subsequent presidents also sought to distance the country specifically from U.S.-directed policies, when they thought it was correct to do so. Oftentimes an irritant to Washington, France's positions stemmed less from deep-seated anti-Americanism than from a commitment to keep the country's voice in play in world events. It joined fully in the 1991 Gulf War to oust Iraq from Kuwait, but its opposition to the U.S. invasion of Iraq in March 2003 earned it disdain from the George W. Bush (1946–) administration and outright hostility from some American congressional lawmakers. Nevertheless, the so-called war on terror finds the nation fully cooperating with its NATO partners in the provision of troops in Afghanistan to battle Taliban insurgents there and in working closely with other Western security agencies in detecting and counteracting international terrorism. President Sarkozy has sought a closer relationship with the United States, a policy in evidence with the return of France to NATO's integrated military command structure in 2008.

The legacy of France's former colonial presence remains in what the French call the "confetti of empire"—scattered bits of territory that include French Polynesia, New Caledonia, and Wallis and Futuna in the South Pacific, the islands of Saint-Pierre and Miquelon off Newfoundland, French Guiana in South America, and Martinique, Guadeloupe, Saint-Martin, and other islets in the Caribbean. These remnants of a once vast empire remain French, based partly on centuries-old treaties and traditions and partly on the wishes of the inhabitants. They produce commodities such as codfish in the North Atlantic and nickel ore in the Pacific. The islands in Polynesia have served as testing grounds for French nuclear weapons. The detonations have drawn the ire of peace activists and neighboring nations (New Zealand), while French Guiana hosts the launching pads for European Space Agency explorations.

Problems plague several of these places. Despite massive subsidies funded by French taxpayers, unrest has broken out in Guadeloupe and Martinique, where the islanders are fighting for enhanced benefits to compensate for the higher cost of living in these tiny markets, which are heavily dependent on imports from faraway France. In the late 1980s, New Caledonia broke out in open insurrection launched by those seeking independence. The unrest led to the grant of greater local powers and the promise of a referendum on independence sometime after 2014. Mayotte has caused no end of trouble. An island in the Indian Ocean that remained a French dependence after the rest of the Comoros archipelago voted for independence in 1974, it has been plagued by illegal immigration from the other islands. The independent Islamic Republic of Comoros claims Mayotte as a part of its territory, a claim backed by the United Nations.

National defense remains an important issue. The nation's independent nuclear force is a source of pride even as the financial strains posed by its maintenance prove burdensome, a fact made embarrassingly evident during the Gulf War when French conventional forces suffered from lack of up-to-date equipment. The ending of the cold war, while it did not remove the nuclear threat, facilitated moves toward creation of a more mobile, professional military, which the phased abolition of conscription has also promoted. President Chirac's decision in 1995 to resume nuclear testing in the face of widespread international criticism is indicative of the continued determination to assert the primacy of French national interests.

In the cultural realm, public and private agencies work assiduously to promote French products and productions as well as the French language. Founded in 1883 by a group of eminent writers and scientists, including Jules Verne and Louis Pasteur, the Alliance Française is a privately financed institution, though it also receives a small government subsidy, that offers French-language courses and cultural exhibits for foreign students in France and at locations in more than 100 countries. The government operates some 150 individual French Cultural Institutes abroad. The language is a source of special pride. After World War II, efforts were begun to combat the increasing use of English, steady growth of which was viewed by some as an attack on the identity of the nation itself. Measures enacted to stem the adoption of English words for which no French equivalent exists (*franglais*) have included financial support for French-language dubbing industries and for French films, while public authorities such as the Académie Française remain vigilant, ever-ready to propose alternatives for English

343

loanwords. The effort remains formidable given the steady importation of U.S. products and the realities of modern telecommunications, notably the explosive growth of the Internet, on which English is the language overwhelmingly in use.

France's economic and military resources dictate that it will remain a power of the middle rank; but if the past is any indication, the country will not soon abandon a determination to maintain some portion of its former glory. History—indeed, the history of France itself—shows that economic wealth and military might can be matched, and surpassed, by other nations. In the end, France's influence will endure through the prestige won for it from its splendid political and cultural achievements. The human rights so eloquently enshrined in the Declaration of the Rights of Man and of the Citizen, the quest for liberty that has marked its modern history, the cultural brilliance on display in the country's architectural, artistic, literary, and philosophical heritage, the renowned reputation earned in fields from food to fashion and in science and technology, and the country's continuing contributions to this record, because they have played so significant a role in advancing the world's well-being, will ensure for France a prominent place on the global stage.

APPENDIX 1

RULERS OF FRANCE: 987 TO THE PRESENT

Capetian Dynasty

987–996	Hugh Capet
996–1031	Robert II (the Pious)
1031–1060	Henry I
1060–1108	Philip I
1108–1137	Louis VI (the Fat)
1137–1180	Louis VII (the Young)
1180–1223	Philip II Augustus
1223–1226	Louis VIII (the Lion)
1226–1270	Louis IX (St. Louis)
1270–1285	Philip III (the Bold)
1285–1314	Philip IV (the Fair)
1314–1316	Louis X (the Stubborn)
1316	John I
1316–1322	Philip V (the Tall)
1322–1328	Charles IV (the Fair)

Valois Dynasty

1328–1350	Philip VI
1350–1364	John II (the Good)
1364–1380	Charles V (the Wise)
1380–1422	Charles VI (the Mad, Well-Beloved, or Foolish)
1422–1461	Charles VII (the Well-Served or Victorious)
1461–1483	Louis XI (the Spider)
1483–1498	Charles VIII (Father of His People)
1498–1515	Louis XII
1515–1547	Francis I

1547–1559	Henry II
1559–1560	Francis II
1560–1574	Charles IX
1574–1589	Henry III

Bourbon Dynasty

1589–1610	Henry IV
1610–1643	Louis XIII
1643–1715	Louis XIV
1715–1774	Louis XV
1774–1792	Louis XVI

First Republic

1792–1795	**National Convention**
1795–1799	**Directory** (directors)
1795–1797	Lazare-Nicolas-Marguerite Carnot
1795–1797	Étienne Le Tourneur
1795–1799	Paul-François-Jean-Nicolas de Barras
1795–1799	Jean-François Reubell
1795–1799	Louis-Marie La Revellière-Lépeaux
1797	François, marquis de Barthélemy
1797–1798	François de Neufchâteau
1797–1799	Philippe-Antoine-Merlin de Douai
1798–1799	Jean-Baptiste, comte de Treilhard
1799	Emmanuel-Joseph, comte de Sieyès
1799	Roger, comte de Ducos
1799	Jean-François-Auguste Moulins
1799	Louis Gothier
1799–1804	**Consulate**
1799–1804	Napoléon Bonaparte (First Consul)
1799	Emmanuel-Joseph, comte de Sieyès (Second Consul)
1799–1804	Jean-Jacques Régis de Cambacérès (duc de Parme) (Second Consul)
1799	Pierre-Roger Ducos (Third Consul)
1799–1804	Charles-François Lebrun (Third Consul)

First Empire (emperors)

| 1804–1814 | Napoléon Bonaparte |
| 1815 (March–June) | Napoléon Bonaparte (restored) |

Bourbon Dynasty (restored)

1814–1815	Louis XVIII
1815–1824	Louis XVIII (restored)
1824–1830	Charles X

Orléans Dynasty

1830–1848	Louis-Philippe I

Second Republic (presidents)

1848	Louis-Eugène Cavaignac
1848–1852	Louis-Napoléon Bonaparte

Second Empire (emperor)

1852–1870	(Louis-Napoléon Bonaparte) Napoléon III

Third Republic (presidents)

1870–1871	Louis-Jules Trochu (provisional)
1871–1873	Adolphe Thiers
1873–1879	Edme de Mac-Mahon
1879–1887	Jules Grévy
1887–1894	Sadi Carnot
1894–1895	Jean Casimir-Périer
1895–1899	Félix Faure
1899–1906	Émile Loubet
1906–1913	Armand Fallières
1913–1920	Raymond Poincaré
1920	Paul Deschanel
1920–1924	Alexandre Millerand
1924–1931	Gaston Doumergue
1931–1932	Paul Doumer
1931–1940	Albert Lebrun

Vichy Government (chief of state)

1940–1944	Henri-Philippe Pétain

Provisional Government (presidents)

1944–1946	Charles de Gaulle
1946	Félix Gouin

| 1946 | Georges Bidault |
| 1946 | Léon Blum |

Fourth Republic (presidents)

| 1947–1954 | Vincent Auriol |
| 1954–1959 | René Coty |

Fifth Republic (presidents)

1959–1969	Charles de Gaulle
1969–1974	Georges Pompidou
1974–1981	Valéry Giscard d'Estaing
1981–1995	François Mitterrand
1995–2007	Jacques Chirac
2007–	Nicolas Sarkozy

APPENDIX 2

BASIC FACTS ABOUT FRANCE

Official Name
French Republic (République française)

Government
A unitary mixed presidential/parliamentary republic. The executive branch consists of the president of the republic, who is head of state and is elected by universal adult suffrage every five years, and the prime minister, who is appointed by the president and heads the government. The legislative branch consists of a bicameral parliament, which passes legislation and votes on the budget. The lower house, the National Assembly, determines the makeup of the government based on party strength in the chamber and can dismiss the cabinet. It shares roughly equal powers with the upper house, the Senate. A civil law system operates based primarily on written statutes.

Political parties are numerous. The two largest parties currently are the Socialist Party on the left and the Union for a Popular Movement on the right.

Political Divisions
France is divided into 100 departments, each headed by a prefect. There are also 26 administrative regions, subdivided into districts.

Capital	Paris (approx. 2.2 million [11.7 million metro region], 2009 est.)

Geography

Area	212,935 square miles (551,500 sq. km) (metropolitan France, including Corsica)

Boundaries	bounded by the Atlantic Ocean and the English Channel on the west; by Belgium, Luxembourg, and Germany on the north; by Germany, Switzerland, and Italy on the east; by the Mediterranean Sea, Andorra, and Spain on the south
Topography	mostly flat plains or gently rolling hills in north and west; mountainous in south (Pyrenees), east (Alps), and southeast (Massif Central)
Highest Elevation	Mont Blanc at 15,771 feet (4,807 m)
Longest River	Loire at 628 miles (1,102 km)
Largest Lake	Lac Léman at 92 square miles (239 sq. km)
Climate	Temperate in north and northwest with cool winters and mild summers; mild winters, warm summers, and rain in west; mild winters and hot summers in southeast; mild summers and cold winters in high mountains

Demography

Population	62,793,432 (metropolitan) (2010 est.); population density: 299 persons per square miles (115 per sq. km); urban: 77%; rural: 23% (2008 est.)
Major Cities	Paris, Lyon, Marseille, Toulouse
Language	French
Religion	Roman Catholic (approx. 83–88%); Muslim (8–10%); Protestant (2%); Jewish (1%)

Economy

Currency	euro (€) = 100 cents
GNP per capita	$28,500 (OECD 2007 est.)
Agricultural Products	wheat, cereals, sugar beets, potatoes, wine, cheese; beef, dairy products; fish
Industrial Activity	machinery, chemicals, automobiles, metallurgy, aircraft, electronics, textiles, food processing; tourism
Trade	
Main Exports	machinery and transportation equipment, aircraft, plastics, chemicals, pharmaceutical products, iron and steel, beverages, consumer goods
Main Imports	machinery and equipment, vehicles, crude oil, plastics, chemicals

350

| Labor Force | agriculture (3.8%); industry (24.3%); services (71.8%) (2005 est.) |

Media

Newspapers	the four largest daily newspapers are *Le Monde* (centrist), *Le Figaro* (conservative), *Libération* (center-left), and *Ouest-France* (centrist); Agence France Presse, founded in 1835, is the largest news agency.
Television	approx. 584 TV broadcast stations
Web Sites	general information: www.franceguide.com public services: www.service-public.fr city of Paris: www.paris.org French presidency: www.elysee.fr culture: www.frenchculturenow.com

APPENDIX 3

CHRONOLOGY

Beginnings to the Land of the Gauls

ca. 950,000–80,000 B.C.E.	End of the Ice Age. *Homo erectus*—first humans in France
ca. 80,000–30,000 B.C.E.	Neanderthal Man
ca. 33,000–10,000 B.C.E.	*Homo sapiens* appears as Cro-Magnon Man
ca. 17,000 B.C.E.	Lascaux cave paintings
ca. 4,000–2,500 B.C.E.	Neolithic Period; farming begins
ca. 2,500–50 B.C.E.	Celts dominate in Gaul
ca. 600 B.C.E.	Massilia (Marseille) founded by Greeks

Roman Gaul

58–51 B.C.E.	Julius Caesar wages Gallic Wars. Roman rule begins
52 B.C.E.	Lutetia (Paris) is founded
43 C.E.	Lug(o)dunum (Lyon) is founded
100s C.E.	Christianity makes its first inroads in Gaul
275	Barbarian invasions begin
406	Franks and other Germanic tribes invade and settle
476	Roman Empire in the West ends

The Kingdom of the Franks

481	Clovis converts to Christianity
508	Clovis selects Paris as his capital
ca. 600	The name "France" emerges
732	Charles Martel defeats the Moors near Poitiers

751	Pepin the Short becomes first Carolingian ruler
800	Charlemagne crowned emperor by Pope Leo III
843	Treaty of Verdun lays territorial basis for French state
911	Foundation of the future duchy of Normandy
980s	Castles and knights begin to appear in the sources
987	Louis V, the last Carolingian ruler, dies

France in Embryo

987	Hugh Capet crowned king
1095	Pope Urban II calls for the First Crusade at Council of Clermont
1115	Bernard of Clairvaux founds his first monastery
ca. 1120	Abelard writes *Sic et non*
1163	Construction of Notre-Dame in Paris begins
1180	Philip II Augustus ascends the throne
ca. 1200	University of Paris founded
1204	Normandy is acquired by Philip
1208–13	Crusade against the Albigensians
1226	Louis IX (Saint Louis) becomes king
1285	Philip IV "le Bel" ascends the throne

The Making of the Monarchy

1337	Philip VI confiscates Gascony from Edward III of England; start of Hundred Years' War
1348–50	Black Death ravages France
1413	Cabochien rising at Paris
1428–29	Joan of Arc liberates Orléans from the English; Charles VII crowned at Reims
1438	Pragmatic Sanction of Bourges
1449–53	Charles conquers Gascony; end of Hundred Years' War
ca. 1470	Printing press introduced in France
1481	Louis XI adds Provence, Anjou, Maine, and Bar to royal domains
1491	Brittany acquired by Charles VIII
1526	Construction of Chambord launches château building in the Loire valley
1530	Collège de France founded
1532	Rabelais composes *Pantagruel*

1539	Decree of Villers-Cotterêts, French made compulsory language in all court documents
1541	Calvin translates *Institutes of the Christian Religion* into French
1562–98	Wars of Religion

The Monarchy Made Majestic

1589	Henry IV ascends the throne as the first Bourbon monarch
1598	Edict of Nantes grants religious toleration
1608	Quebec founded
1635	Académie Française founded; France enters the Thirty Years' War
1648	Peace of Westphalia; Paris rises against Anne of Austria
1648–53	Fronde revolts
1667–1713	Wars of Louis XIV
1680	Comédie-Française founded
1681	Louis XIV seizes Strasbourg; Four Gallican Articles
1682	Royal court established at Versailles; Louisiana founded
1685	Revocation of the Edict of Nantes
1725–43	Ministry of Cardinal Fleury
1734	Voltaire's *Lettres philosophiques* published
1756–63	Seven Years' War
1762	Rousseau's *Du contrat social* published
1763	Peace of Paris: France loses Canada, Louisiana, and Senegal
1766–68	Annexation of Lorraine and Corsica
1778	French ally with the United States of America in the War of the American Revolution
1783	Peace of Paris: France recovers Senegal; Montgolfier Brothers' balloon flight
1787	Meeting of first Assembly of Notables
1788	Meeting of second Assembly of Notables

The Great Revolution and the Grand Empire

| 1789 | Estates General opens (May); fall of the Bastille (July 14); ancien régime abolished (August); |

	Declaration of the Rights of Man and of the Citizen (August 26); royal family forcibly brought to Paris (October)
1790	Civil Constitution of the Clergy; France divided into departments
1791	Flight to Varennes (June 20–21); metric system introduced
1792	End of the monarchy (August 10); war against Austria and Prussia; September Massacres (September 2–6); declaration of the republic (September 21)
1793	Execution of Louis XVI (January 21); war against Great Britain and Netherlands (February 1); *Levée en masse* (mass conscription) (August 23)
1793–94	Reign of Terror
1795–99	The Directory
1798	Annexation of Mulhouse; de facto annexation of left bank of the Rhine; war against the Second Coalition
1799	Coup d'état of 18 Brumaire: Napoléon becomes effective ruler of France (November 9–10)
1799–1804	The Consulate
1804	Civil Code promulgated (March 21); Napoléon crowned emperor (December 2)
1805	War against the Third Coalition
1806	War against the Fourth Coalition
1809	War against the Fifth Coalition
1812	French invade Russia; Napoleonic empire at its height
1814	Allies invade France; Napoléon abdicates; First Restoration: monarchy reinstated with Louis XVIII
1815	Napoléon's exile to Elba and return; One Hundred Days; Battle of Waterloo (June 18); Second Restoration

The Search for Stability

1815–16	White Terror
1820	Assassination of the duke of Berry; Ampère formulates laws of electromagnetism

1824	Niépce inaugurates photography
1830	Revolution (July 27–29); Louis-Philippe I crowned king of the French; conquest of Algeria begins
1830–40s	Realism school of painting begins
1831	French Foreign Legion formed
1833	Guizot Law establishes primary education system
1835	Honoré de Balzac publishes *Père Goriot*
1836	Arc de Triomphe in Paris formally inaugurated
1837	Railway line opens between Paris and Saint-Germain-en-Laye
1840–48	Guizot ministry
1848	February revolution: Second Republic proclaimed; workers' insurrection in Paris (June); Louis-Napoléon becomes president (December)
1850	Falloux Law; Electoral Law
1851	Coup d'état of Louis-Napoléon, proclaimed as Napoléon III (December 2)
1852	Proclamation of Second Empire
1853	Haussmann begins to redesign city of Paris
1857	Gustave Flaubert's *Madame Bovary* and Charles Baudelaire's *Les fleurs du mal* published
1858–63	Indochina occupied by the French
1860s	Liberal period of Second Empire begins; impressionism school of painting begins
1860	Annexation of Savoy and Nice; free trade treaty with Great Britain
1862	Victor Hugo's *Les misérables* published
1862–67	Expedition to Mexico
1864	French workers win right to strike

Republican Rule Takes Root

1870–71	Franco-Prussian War
1871	Paris Commune (May)
1872	Alsace-Lorraine annexed by Germany
1875	Constitution of Third Republic approved; George Bizet's *Carmen*
1877	Monarchist coup fails; consolidation of republic begins

1880–1901	French expansion in West and Equatorial Africa
1884	Trade unions legalized
1885	Louis Pasteur discovers antirabies vaccine; early automobiles appear
1887–89	Eiffel Tower built
1894	Dreyfus affair begins; De Coubertin launches International Olympic Committee
1895	Lumière brothers inaugurate motion pictures; Confédération Général du Travail (General Confederation of Labor, CGT) founded
1900	Pierre and Marie Curie discover radium
1903	Tour de France begins
1904	Entente Cordiale with Britain; 10-hour workday law
1905	Law of separation of church and state; Section Française de l'Internationale Ouvrière (SFIO) founded
1907	Triple Entente
1909	Sergey Diaghilev's Ballets Russes in Paris; Louis Blériot flies across the English Channel
1913	First part of Marcel Proust's *À la recherche du temps perdu* (*Remembrance of Things Past* [or *In Search of Lost Time*]) published

Turmoil and Tragedy

1914–18	World War I
1914	Battle of the Marne (September)
1916	Battle of Verdun
1918	Armistice (November 11)
1919	Paris Peace Conference; Treaty of Versailles (June 28)
1920	Communist Party formed
1923–25	French occupation of the Ruhr
1928	Social Security Law; Maurice Ravel's *Boléro*
1930	Maginot Line begun
1936–38	Popular Front government
1940–45	World War II
1940	France overrun by Nazi Germany; Vichy regime established in southeast France

| 1943 | Jean-Paul Sartre's *L'être et le néant* (*Being and Nothingness*) is published |
| 1944 | D-day landings (June 6); liberation of Paris (August 25) |

Regeneration and Transformation

1945	Referendum ends Third Republic (October 21); French women vote for first time in municipal elections
1945–75	Thirty years of sustained economic growth
1949	North Atlantic Treaty signed; Simone de Beauvoir's *Le deuxième sexe* (*The Second Sex*) published
1954	Fall of Dien Bien Phu (May); Algerian revolt erupts (November)
1956	Independence granted to Morocco and Tunisia
1957	Common Market treaty ratified
1958	De Gaulle forms a government (June 1); referendum approves establishment of Fifth Republic (September 28)
1960	Introduction of "new franc" (January); first French atomic bomb exploded (February); 14 French colonies in Africa granted independence
1962	Independence for Algeria; referendum approves direct election to the presidency
1968	Strikes by students and trade unionists (May)
1969	De Gaulle resigns (April); Pompidou elected president (June)
1971	Socialist Party founded at Épinay
1974	Giscard d'Estaing elected president (May)
1975	Weil Law legalizing abortion passed
1976	Rassemblement du Peuple Français founded
1981	François Mitterrand elected president (April–May)
1986	First summit of Francophone countries; first "cohabitation" government (March)
1988	Mitterrand reelected president
1991	First female prime minister (Édith Cresson) forms government (May); Treaty of Maastricht (December 10)

1993	Landslide victory of center-right in legislative elections and second "cohabitation" government (March)
1994	Paul Touvier is first Frenchman found guilty of crimes against humanity
1995	Jacques Chirac elected president (April–May); French nuclear tests in the Pacific draw international condemnation (June); terrorist bombs in Paris (July)
1997	Left wins legislative elections and third "cohabitation" government

France in the Twenty-first Century: The Power of Prestige

2001	Compulsory military service abolished
2002	The euro replaces the franc as the official currency (January 1); Chirac reelected president (May); Union pour un Mouvement Populaire (UMP) formed
2003	Constitutional revisions devolve powers to regions and departments; heat wave kills thousands (August)
2005	Proposed European Union (EU) constitution defeated in referendum (May); massive urban rioting (October–November)
2006	Youth unemployment laws scrapped after mass protests (March–April); new immigration laws toughen restrictions (June)
2007	Nicholas Sarkozy elected president (May); public services disrupted by civil servants protesting pay cuts and pension reforms (November)
2008	Lisbon Treaty ratified (February); France assumes EU presidency (July); Jean-Marie Le Clézio wins Nobel Prize for literature (October)
2009	Government unveils stimulus program to revitalize the economy (February)
2010	France dismantles illegal Roma camps and deports their residents to Romania and Bulgaria (August); government decrees raising the retirement age from 60 to 62, effective 2018 (September); parliament approves ban on veils that cover the face, effective 2011 (September)

Appendix 4

Bibliography

Agulhon, Maurice. *The French Republic, 1879–1992.* Translated by Antonia Nevill. Oxford: Basil Blackwell, 1993.

Bergson, Henri. *Creative Evolution.* New York: H. Holt, 1911.

Brogan, Denis W. *The Development of Modern France (1870–1939).* London: H. Hamilton, 1943.

"Burka Is Not Welcome in France, Says President." Irish Times. June 23, 2009. Available online. URL: http://www.irishtimes.com/newspaper/world/2009/0623/1224249339255.html. Accessed March 10, 2010.

Burke, Edmund, and Thomas Paine. *Reflections on the Revolution in France and the Rights of Man.* Garden City, N.Y.: Anchor Books, 1973.

Burley, P., ed. *Witness to the Revolution: American and British Commentators in France, 1789–94.* London: Weidenfeld & Nicolson, 1989.

Caesar, Julius. *Ceasar's Commentaries on the Gallic and Civil Wars.* Translated by William Alexander McDevitte and W. S. Bohn. Vols. 1 and 3. New York: Harper & Brothers, 1872.

Chateaubriand, F. R. *Mémoires d'outre-tombe.* 3 vols. Paris: Flammarion, 1948.

Davidowitz, Lucy S. *The War against the Jews, 1933–1945.* New York: Bantam, 1986.

"Declaration of the Rights of Man and of the Citizen." Available online. URL: http://www.constitution.org/fr/fr_drm.htm. Accessed August 11, 2009.

Delvert, Captain. *Histoire d'une compagnie: Main de Massiges, Verdun, Novembre 1915–Juin 1916.* Preface by Ernest Lavisse. Paris: Berger-Levrault, 1921.

Descartes, René. *Discourse on Method and Meditations.* Translated by L. Lafleur. Indianapolis, Ind.: Bobbs Merrill, 1960.

Durant, Will, and Ariel Durant. *The Age of Napoleon.* New York: Simon & Schuster, 1975.

Elisabeth Charlotte, duchess of Orléans. *A Woman's Life in the Court of the Sun King: Letters of Liselotte von der Pfalz, 1652–1722.* Edited and translated by E. Fortser. Baltimore, Md.: Johns Hopkins University Press, 1984.

Flanner, Janet. *Paris Journal.* 2 vols. New York: Atheneum, 1965–71.

Fletcher, Charles Robert Leslie. *The Journal of a Spy in Paris during the Reign of Terror: January–July 1794.* By Raoul Hesdin. London: John Murray, 1895.

"France Moves toward Partial Ban on Full Veil." *Hindustani Times.* January 27, 2010. Available online. URL: http://www.hindustanitimes.com/rssfeed/europe/France.html. Accessed March 14, 2010.

"France Unemployment Rate—Economy." Available online. URL: http://www.indexmundi.com/france/unemployment_rate.html. Accessed September 30, 2009.

"French Government Cites European Debt Crisis to Slash Spending." World Socialist Web Site. Available online. URL: http://www.wsws.org/articles/2010/feb2010/fran-fl17.shtml. Accessed March 14, 2010.

"French Prime Minister Warns of Lingering Economic Risks." Associated Press. Available online. URL: http://www.msnbc.msn.com/id/32705911/ns/world_news. Accessed September 29, 2009.

Girling, John. *France: Political and Social Change.* New York: Routledge, 1998.

Gregory of Tours. *The History of the Franks.* Translated by Lewis Thorpe. New York: Penguin Books, 1974.

Gwatkin, H. M., et al., eds. *The Cambridge Medieval History.* Vol. 7. Cambridge: Cambridge University Press, 1932.

Hargreaves, Alec G. *Immigration, 'Race' and Ethnicity in Contemporary France.* New York: Routledge, 1995.

Institut National de la Statistique et des Études Économiques (INSEE). Government of France. "Pyramide des âges au 1er janvier 2009." Available online. URL: http://www.insee.fr/fr/ppp/basesde-donnees-detaillees/bilan-demo/df/pyramide-des-ages-2009.xls. Accessed August, 14, 2009.

Joinville, Jean. "Life of Saint Louis." In *Chronicles of the Crusades.* Translated by Margaret R. B. Shaw. New York: Penguin, 1963.

Millingen, J. G. "The Revolutionary Tribunal, Paris, October 1793." In *Eyewitness to History.* Edited by John Carey. Cambridge, Mass.: Harvard University Press, 1988.

Monnet, Jean. *Mémoires.* Paris: Fayard, 1976.

Morris, Gouverneur. *A Diary of the French Revolution.* 2 vols. Edited by B. Cary Davenport. Boston: Houghton Mifflin, 1939.

Padover, Saul K. *The Life and Death of Louis XVI*. New York: D. Appleton-Century, 1939.

Pernoud, Regine. *Joan of Arc by Herself and Her Witnesses*. Lanham, Md.: Rowman & Littlefield, 1994.

Persico, Joseph E. *Eleventh Month, Eleventh Day, Eleventh Hour: Armistice Day, 1918*. New York: Random House, 2004.

Phillips, Rod. *A Short History of Wine*. New York: HarperCollins, 2000.

Population Reference Bureau. "Population Basics." Available online. URL: http://www.prb.org/TopicsPopulationBases.aspx. Accessed September 6, 2009.

Roberts, William J. *France: A Reference Guide from the Renaissance to the Present*. New York: Facts On File, 2004.

Saint-Simon, Louis de Rouvroy, duc de. *The Memoirs of the Duke de Saint-Simon on the Reign of Louis XIV and the Regency*. Translated by Bayle St. John. London: Allen & Unwin, 1900.

Sauvigny, G. de Bertier de. *La restauration*. Paris: Flammarion, 1955.

Sévigné, Mme de. *Selected Letters*. Edited by L. Tanock. London: Penguin, 1982.

Suger, Abbot of Saint-Denis. *Abbot Suger on the Abbey Church of St.-Denis and Its Art Treasures*. Edited and translated by Erwin Panofsky. Princeton, N.J.: Princeton University Press, 1946.

Voltaire. *Memoirs of the Life of Monsieur de Voltaire Written by Himself*. Translated by Andrew Brown. London: Hesperus, 2007.

Wight, Orlando Williams, ed. *Lives and Letters of Abelard and Heloise*. New York: M. Doolady, 1861.

Williams, Helen M. *An Eye-Witness Account of the French Revolution, by Helen Maria Williams: Letters Containing a Sketch of the Politics of France*. Edited by J. Fruchtman, Jr. New York: Peter Lang, 1997.

World Health Organization. "World Health Organization Assesses the World's Health Systems." Available online. URL: http://www.who.int/whr/2000/media_centre/press_release/en/. Accessed August 11, 2009.

Wright, Gordon. *France in Modern Times*. Chicago: Rand McNally, 1960.

Young, Arthur. *Travels during the Years 1787, 1788 and 1789*. 3 vols. London: W. Richardson, 1794.

APPENDIX 5

SUGGESTED READING

General

Aldrich, Robert. *Greater France: A History of French Overseas Expansion.* Basingstoke, England: Macmillan, 1996.

Alexander, Martin S., ed. *French History since Napoleon.* London: Arnold, 1999.

Allport, Alan. *Jacques Chirac.* New York: Facts On File, 2007.

Blunt, Anthony. *Art and Architecture in France, 1500–1700.* 5th ed. New Haven: Yale University Press, 1999.

Brynes, Joseph F. *Catholic and French Forever: Religious and National Identity in Modern France.* University Park: Pennsylvania State University Press, 2005.

Bryson, Norman. *Tradition and Desire: From David to Delacroix.* Cambridge: Cambridge University Press, 1984.

Buss, Robin. *French Film Noir.* London: M. Boyars, 1994.

———. *The French through Their Films.* London: Batsford, 1988.

Chadwick, Kay, ed. *Catholicism, Politics and Society in Twentieth-Century France.* Liverpool: Liverpool University Press, 2000.

Charle, Christophe. *A Social History of France in the Nineteenth Century.* Oxford: Berg, 1994.

Collins, James B. *From Tribes to Nation: The Making of France, 500–1799.* Washington, D.C.: Georgetown University Press, 2001.

Conklin, Alice L. *A Mission to Civilize: The Republican Idea of Empire in France and West Africa, 1895–1930.* Stanford, Calif.: Stanford University Press, 2000.

Coward, D. *A History of French Literature: From Chanson de Geste to Cinema.* Oxford: Basil Blackwell, 2002.

———. *The State in Early Modern France.* Cambridge: Cambridge University Press, 1995.

Crook, Malcolm, ed. *Revolutionary France, 1788–1880.* Oxford: Oxford University Press, 2002.

Dewald, J. *Aristocratic Experience and the Origins of Modern Culture, France 1570–1715.* Berkeley: University of California Press, 1993.

Duby, Georges. *France in the Middle Ages, 987–1460: From Hugh Capet to Joan of Arc.* Translated by Juliet Vale. Cambridge, Mass.: Basil Blackwell, 1991.

Dunbabin, Jean. *France in the Making, 843–1180.* Oxford: Oxford University Press, 2000.

Evans, Martin, ed. *Empire and Culture: The French Experience, 1830–1940.* New York: Palgrave Macmillan, 2003.

Galliou, Patrick, and Michael Jones. *The Bretons.* Hoboken, N.J.: John Wiley & Sons, 2002.

Gildea, Robert. *Children of the Revolution: The French, 1799–1914.* New York: Allen Lane, 2008.

———. *The Past in French History.* New Haven, Conn.: Yale University Press, 1994.

Green, Christopher. *Art in France, 1900–1940.* New Haven, Conn.: Yale University Press, 2000.

Haywood, Jack E. S. *Fragmented France: Two Centuries of Disputed Identity.* Oxford: Oxford University Press, 2007.

Higonnet, Patrice. *Paris: Capital of the World.* Translated by Arthur Goldhammer. Cambridge, Mass.: Harvard University Press, 2005.

Hodge, Susie. *Claude Monet.* New York: Franklin Watts, 2002.

Hoffmann, P. *Growth in a Traditional Society: The French Countryside, 1450–1815.* Princeton, N.J.: Princeton University Press, 1996.

Hollier, Denis, ed. *A New History of French Literature.* Cambridge, Mass.: Harvard University Press, 1989.

Jordan, William. *The French Monarchy and the Jews.* Philadelphia: University of Pennsylvania Press, 1989.

Judt, Tony. *Blum, Camus, Aron and the French Twentieth Century.* Chicago: University of Chicago Press, 1998.

Kelly, Michael, ed. *French Culture and Society: The Essentials.* London: Edward Arnold, 2001.

Macmillan, James. *Twentieth Century France: Politics and Society, 1898–1991.* London: Arnold, 1992.

Mason, Haydn. *French Writers and Their Society, 1715–1800.* Basingstoke, England: Macmillan, 1982.

McPhee, Peter. *A Social History of France, 1789–1914.* 2d ed. New York: Palgrave Macmillan, 2004.

Mullarky, John. *Bergson and Philosophy.* Edinburgh: Edinburgh University Press, 1999.

Oscherwitz, Dayra. *Historical Dictionary of French Cinema.* Lanham, Md.: Rowman & Littlefield, 2007.

Pitte, Jean-Robert. *French Gastronomy: The History and Geography of a Passion.* Translated by Jody Gladding. New York: Columbia University Press, 2002.

Pitts, Jennifer. *A Turn to Empire: The Rise of Imperial Liberalism in Britain and France.* Princeton, N.J.: Princeton University Press, 2005.

Rubin, James H. *Impressionism.* London: Phaidon, 1999.

Shennon, Andrew. *De Gaulle.* London: Longman, 1993.

Sutcliffe, A. *Paris: An Architectural History.* New Haven, Conn.: Yale University Press, 1996.

Troy, Nancy J. *Couture Culture: A Study in Modern Art and Fashion.* Cambridge, Mass.: MIT Press, 2003.

Trubeck, Amy B. *Haute Cuisine: How the French Invented the Culinary Profession.* Philadelphia: University of Pennsylvania Press, 2000.

Vale, Malcolm G. A. *The Ancient Enemy: England, France and Europe from the Angevins to the Tudors, 1154–1558.* London: Hambledon Continuum, 2007.

Walter, Henriette. *French Inside Out: The Worldwide Development of the French Language in the Past, Present and the Future.* Translated by Peter Fawcett. New York: Routledge, 1994.

Williams, Charles. *Last Great Frenchman: A Life of General de Gaulle.* Hoboken, N.J.: John Wiley & Sons, 1997.

Willms, J. *Paris: Capital of Europe from the Revolution to the Belle Epoque.* Translated by E. L. Kanes. New York: Holmes & Meier, 1997.

Zdatny, Steven M. *Fashion, Work, and Politics in Modern France.* New York: Palgrave Macmillan, 2006.

Beginnings to the Land of the Gauls

Aujoulat, Norbert. *Lascaux: Movement, Space, and Time.* New York: Harry N. Abrams, 2005.

Clark, Peter, ed. *Bronze Age Connections: Cultural Contact in Prehistoric Europe.* Oxford: Oxbow Books, 2009.

Curtis, Gregory. *The Cave Painters: Probing the Mysteries of the World's First Artists.* New York: Random House, 2007.

Henderson, Jon. *The Atlantic Iron Age: Settlement and Identity in the First Millennium BC.* New York: Taylor & Francis, 2007.

Hodge, A. Trevor. *Ancient Greek France.* London: Duckworth, 1998.

White, Randall Keith. *Dark Caves, Bright Visions: Life in Iron Age Europe.* New York: W. W. Norton, 1986.

Wilcox, Peter. *British and Gallic Celts.* London: Osprey, 1996.

Roman Gaul

Drinkwater, J. F. *Roman Gaul: The Three Provinces, 53 BC–AD 260.* London: Croom Helm, 1983.

Ebel, Charles. *Transalpine Gaul: The Emergence of a Roman Province.* London: E. J. Brill, 1976.

Février, P.-A. "The Origins and Growth of the Cities of Southern Gaul." *Journal of Roman Studies* 63 (1973): 1–28.

Hatt, Jean-Jacques. *Celts and Gallo-Romans.* Translated by James Hogarth. London: Barrie & Jenkins, 1970.

Raymond, N., ed. *From the Sword to the Plough: Three Studies on the Earliest Romanisation of Northern Gaul.* Amsterdam: University of Amsterdam Press, 1996.

Van Dam, Raymond. *Leadership and Community in Late Antique Gaul.* Berkeley: University of California Press, 1985.

Woolf, Gregory. *Becoming Roman: The Origins of Provincial Civilization in Gaul.* Cambridge: Cambridge University Press, 1998.

The Kingdom of the Franks

Barbero, Alessandro. *Charlemagne: Father of a Continent.* Translated by Allan Cameron. Berkeley: University of California Press, 2004.

Butt, John J. *Daily Life in the Age of Charlemagne.* Westport, Conn.: Greenwood Press, 2002.

Halsall, Guy. *Barbarian Migrations and the Roman West, 376–568.* Cambridge: Cambridge University Press, 2007.

James, Edward. *The Origins of France: From Clovis to the Capetians, 500–1000.* London: Macmillan, 1982.

MacLean, Simon. *Kingship and Politics in the Late Ninth Century: Charles the Fat and the End of the Carolingian Empire.* Cambridge: Cambridge University Press, 2003.

Mathison, Ralph W. *Roman Aristocrats in Barbarian Gaul: Strategies for Survival in an Age of Transition.* Austin: University of Texas Press, 1993.

Mathison, Ralph W., and Danuta Shanzer. *Society and Culture in Late Antique Gaul: Revisiting the Sources.* Burlington, Vt.: Ashgate, 2001.

Nelson, Janet L. *The Frankish World, 750–900.* London: Hambledon Press, 1996.

Nicolle, David. *Poitiers AD 732: Charles Martel Turns the Islamic Tide.* London: Osprey, 2008.

Scherman, Katherine. *The Birth of France: Warring Bishops and Long-Haired Kings.* New York: Random House, 1987.

Wemple, Suzanne. *Women in Frankish Society: Marriage and the Cloister, 500 to 900.* Philadelphia: University of Pennsylvania Press, 1981.

Wood, Ian N. *The Merovingian Kingdoms, 450–751.* London: Longman, 1993.

France in Embryo

Baldwin, John W. *The Government of Philip Augustus: Foundation of French Royal Power in the Middle Ages.* Berkeley: University of California Press, 1986.

Bradbury, Jim. *The Capetians: Kings of France, 987–1328.* New York: Hambledon Continuum, 2007.

Burge, James. *Heloise and Abelard: A Twelfth-Century Love Story.* London: Profile, 2003.

Clanchy, M. T. *Abelard: A Medieval Life.* Oxford: Basil Blackwell, 1997.

Costen, M. D. *The Cathars and the Albigensian Crusade.* New York: St. Martin's Press, 1977.

Crouch, David. *The Birth of Nobility: Constructing Aristocracy in England and France, 900–1300.* London: Longman, 2005.

Duby, Georges. *The Legend of Bouvines: War, Religion and Culture in the Middle Ages.* Translated by Catherine Tihanyi. Cambridge: Polity Press, 1990.

Gaposchkin, M. Cecilia. *The Making of Saint Louis: Kingship, Sanctity, and France in the Later Middle Ages.* Ithaca, N.Y.: Cornell University Press, 2008.

Hallam, Elizabeth M., and Judith E. Evarard. *Capetian France, 987–1328.* 2d ed. London: Longman, 2001.

Lambert, Malcolm D. *Cathars.* Hoboken, N.J.: John Wiley & Sons, 1998.

LeGoff, Jacques. *Saint Louis.* Translated by Gareth Evan Gollrad. Notre Dame, Ind.: University of Notre Dame Press, 2009.

Nolan, Kathleen, ed. *Capetian Women.* New York: Palgrave Macmillan, 2003.

Read, Piers Paul. *The Templars.* London: Weidenfeld & Nicolson, 1999.

Strayer, Joseph. *Albigensian Crusades.* Ann Arbor: University of Michigan Press, 1992.

Weir, Alison. *Eleanor of Aquitaine: A Life.* New York: Random House, 2001.

The Making of the Monarchy

Baumgartner, Frederic J. *France in the Sixteenth Century*. New York: St. Martin's Press, 1995.

———. *Henry II: King of France, 1547–1559*. Durham, N.C.: Duke University Press, 1988.

Frieda, Leonie. *Catherine de Medici: Renaissance Queen of France*. New York: HarperCollins, 2006.

Knecht, Robert J. *The French Civil Wars, 1562–1598*. London: Longman, 2000.

———. *Renaissance Warrior and Patron: The Reign of Francis I*. Cambridge: Cambridge University Press, 1994.

Le Roy Ladurie, Emmanuel. *The Royal French State, 1460–1610*. Oxford: Basil Blackwell, 1994.

Major, James R. *From Renaissance Monarchy to Absolute Monarchy: French Kings, Nobles, and Estates*. Baltimore, Md.: Johns Hopkins University Press, 1994.

Neillands, Robin H. *The Hundred Years War*. Rev. ed. London: Routledge, 2001.

Pitts, Vincent J. *Henri IV of France: His Reign and His Age*. Baltimore, Md.: Johns Hopkins University Press, 2008.

Wolfe, M. *The Conversion of Henri IV*. Cambridge, Mass.: Harvard University Press, 1993.

Wood, James B. *The King's Army: Warfare, Soldiers and Society during the Wars of Religion in France, 1562–1576*. Cambridge: Cambridge University Press, 1996.

The Monarchy Made Majestic

Bergin, Joseph. *The Rise of Richelieu*. New Haven, Conn.: Yale University Press, 1991.

Bluche, François. *Louis XIV*. Translated by M. Greengrass. Oxford: Basil Blackwell, 1990.

Brecher, Frank W. *Losing a Continent: France's North American Policy, 1753–1763*. Westport, Conn.: Greenwood Press, 1998.

Furbank, Philip N. *Diderot: A Critical Biography*. New York: Knopf, 1992.

Gray, John. *Voltaire*. New York: Routledge, 1999.

Hardman, John. *French Politics, 1774–1789. From the Accession of Louis XVI to the Fall of the Bastille*. London: Longman, 1995.

Kleinman, Ruth. *Anne of Austria, Queen of France*. Columbus: Ohio State University Press, 1985.

Le Roy Ladurie, Emmanuel. *The Ancien Régime: A History of France, 1610–1774.* Cambridge, Mass.: Basil Blackwell, 1996.

———. *Saint-Simon and the Court of Louis XIV.* Translated by Arthur Goldhammer. Chicago: University of Chicago Press, 2001.

Levi, Anthony. *Cardinal Richelieu and the Making of France.* New York: Carroll & Graf, 2000.

Love, Ronald S. *The Enlightenment.* Westport, Conn.: Greenwood, 2008.

Murphy, Antoin E. *John Law: Economic Theorist and Policy-Maker.* Oxford: Clarendon Press, 1997.

Nolan, Cathal J. *Wars of the Age of Louis XIV, 1650–1715.* Westport, Conn.: Greenwood, 2008.

Pérouse, de Montclos, Jean-Marie. *Versailles.* Translated by John Goodman. New York: Abbeville Press, 1991.

Pevitt, Christine. *The Man Who Would Be King: The Life of Philippe, d'Orléans, Regent of France, 1674–1723.* London: Weidenfeld & Nicolson, 1997.

Rapley, E. *The Devotes: Women and Church in Seventeenth-Century France.* Montreal: McGill-Queen's University Press, 1990.

Riley, Patrick, ed. *The Cambridge Companion to Rousseau.* Cambridge: Cambridge University Press, 2001.

Treasure, Geoffrey R. *Mazarin: The Crisis of Absolutism in France.* London: Routledge, 1995.

Wilkinson, Richard. *Louis XIV.* New York: Routledge, 2007.

The Great Revolution and the Grand Empire

Asprey, Robert. *The Rise of Napoleon Bonaparte.* New York: Basic Books, 2000.

Bell, Madison Smartt. *Lavoisier in the Year One: The Birth of a New Science in an Age of Revolution.* New York: W. W. Norton, 2005.

Bruce, Evangeline. *Napoleon and Josephine: The Impossible Marriage.* New York: Scribners, 1995.

Doyle, William. *The Origins of the French Revolution.* Oxford: Oxford University Press, 1980.

———. *The Oxford History of the French Revolution.* Oxford: Oxford University Press, 1989.

Forrest, Alan I. *Conscripts and Deserters: The Army and French Society during the Revolution and Empire.* New York: Oxford University Press, 1989.

Fraser, Antonia. *Marie Antoinette.* New York: Knopf, 2002.

131819202122232425262728293031323334353637383940

Godeschot, Jacques. *The Taking of the Bastille: July 14th, 1789*. Translated by Jean Stewart. New York: Scribner, 1970.

Jones, P. M. *The Peasantry in the French Revolution*. Cambridge: Cambridge University Press, 1988.

Lewis, Gwynne. *The French Revolution: Rethinking the Debate*. London: Routledge, 1993.

Lyons, Martyn. *Napoleon Bonaparte and the Legacy of the French Revolution*. Houndmills, England: Macmillan, 1994.

Schama, Simon. *Citizens: A Chronicle of the French Revolution*. New York: Knopf, 1989.

Schom, Alan. *Napoleon Bonaparte*. New York: Harper Perennial, 1997.

Smith, William H. C. *The Bonapartes: The History of a Dynasty*. London: Palgrave Macmillan, 2005.

Sutherland, Donald. *France 1789–1815: Revolution and Counter-Revolution*. New York: Oxford University Press, 1985.

Thomson, David. *The Babeuf Plot: The Making of a Republican Legend*. Westport, Conn.: Greenwood Press, 1975.

The Search for Stability

Agulhon, Maurice. *The Republican Experiment, 1848–52*. Translated by Janet Lloyd. Cambridge: Cambridge University Press, 1983.

Bierman, John. *Napoleon III and His Carnival Empire*. New York: St. Martin's Press, 1988.

Carmona, Michel. *Haussmann: His Life and Times, and the Making of Modern Paris*. Chicago: Ivan R. Dee, 2002.

Charlton, D. G. *The French Romantics*. Cambridge: Cambridge University Press, 1984.

Collingham, H. A. C. *The July Monarchy, 1830–48*. London: Longman, 1988.

Howarth, T. E. B. *Citizen-King: The Life of Louis-Philippe, King of the French*. London: Eyre & Spottiswoode, 1961.

King, Ross. *Judgment of Paris: The Revolutionary Decade That Gave the World Impressionism*. New York: Walker & Co., 2006.

Mansel, Philip. *Louis XVIII*. Stroud, England: Sutton, 1999.

———. *Paris between Empires, 1814–1852*. London: John Murray, 2001.

McMillan, James F. *Napoleon III*. London: Longman, 1991.

Petrey, Sandy. *In the Court of the Pear King: French Culture and the Rise of Realism*. Ithaca, N.Y.: Cornell University Press, 2005.

Pilbeam, Pamela. *The French Revolution of 1830.* London: Macmillan, 1991.

Price, Roger. *Napoleon III and the Second Empire.* New York: Routledge, 1997.

Wawro, Geoffrey. *The Franco-Prussian War: The German Conquest of France in 1870–1871.* New York: Cambridge University Press, 2003.

Republican Rule Takes Root

Abel, Richard. *The Ciné Goes to Town: French Cinema, 1896–1914.* Berkeley: University of California Press, 1994.

Begley, Louis. *Why the Dreyfus Affair Matters.* New Haven, Conn.: Yale University Press, 2009.

Brian, Denis. *The Curies: A Biography of the Most Controversial Family in Science.* Hoboken, N.J.: John Wiley & Sons, 2005.

Bury, John P. T. *Gambetta and the Making of the Third Republic.* London: Longman, 1973.

Cronin, Vincent. *Paris on the Eve, 1900–1914.* New York: St. Martin's Press, 1991.

Eichner, Carolyn J. *Surmounting the Barricades: Women in the Paris Commune.* Bloomington: Indiana University Press, 2004.

Elliot, Brian A. *Blériot: Herald of an Age.* Stroud, England: Tempus, 2000.

Gildea, Robert. *France 1870–1914.* 2d ed. London: Longman, 1996.

Goldberg, Harvey. *The Life of Jean Jaurès.* Madison: University of Wisconsin Press, 1962.

Harding, James. *The Astonishing Adventure of General Boulanger.* New York: Scribner, 1971.

Herbert, Robert L., et al. *Impressionism: Art, Leisure, and Parisian Society.* New Haven, Conn.: Yale University Press, 1991.

Horne, Alistair. *The Terrible Year: The Paris Commune, 1871.* 2d ed. London: Macmillan, 2004.

Jonnes, Jill. *Eiffel's Tower.* New York: Penguin Books, 2009.

Mayeur, Jean-Marie, and Madeleine Reberious. *The Third Republic from Its Origins to the Great War, 1871–1914.* Translated by J. R. Foster. Cambridge: Cambridge University Press, 1982.

Smith, Hillas. *The Unknown Frenchman: The Story of Marchand and Fashoda.* Sussex, England: Book Guild, 2001.

West, Richard. *Brazza of the Congo: European Exploration and Exploitation in French Equatorial Africa.* London: Cape, 1972.

Years of Turmoil and Tragedy

Adamthwaite, Anthony P. *Grandeur and Misery: France's Bid for Power in Europe, 1914–1940*. London: Arnold, 1995.

Andrew, Christopher M., and A. S. Kanya-Forstner. *France Overseas: The Great War and the Climax of French Imperial Expansion*. London: Thames & Hudson, 1981.

Christofferson, Thomas R. *France during World War II: From Defeat to Liberation*. New York: Fordham University Press, 2006.

Clayton, Anthony. *Paths of Glory: The French Army, 1914–18*. London: Cassell, 2003.

Collins, Larry, and Dominique Lapierre. *Is Paris Burning?* London: V. Gollancz, 1965.

Cronin, Vincent. *Paris: City of Light, 1919–1939*. London: HarperCollins, 1994.

Jackson, Julian. *France: The Dark Years, 1940–1944*. Oxford: Oxford University Press, 2001.

Keiger, John F. V. *France and the Origins of the First World War*. New York: St. Martin's Press, 1983.

Knight, Frieda. *The French Resistance, 1940 to 1944*. London: Lawrence & Wishart, 1975.

Knowles, Dorothy. *French Drama of the Interwar Years, 1918–39*. London: G. G. Harrap, 1967.

Lloyd, Christopher. *Collaboration and Resistance in Occupied France: Representing Treason and Sacrifice*. Houndsmill, England: Palgrave Macmillan, 2003.

Ousby, Ian. *The Road to Verdun: World War I's Most Momentous Battle and the Folly of Nationalism*. New York: Doubleday, 2002.

Martin, John W. *The Golden Age of French Cinema, 1929–1939*. Boston: Twayne, 1983.

Martin, William. *Verdun 1916*. London: Osprey, 2001.

Paxton, Robert O. *Vichy France: Old Guard and New Order, 1940–1944*. London: Routledge, 1972.

Rearick, Charles. *The French in Love and War: Popular Culture in the Era of the World Wars*. New Haven, Conn.: Yale University Press, 1992.

Stewart, Mary Lynn. *Dressing Modern Frenchwomen: Marketing Haute Couture, 1919–1935*. Baltimore, Md.: Johns Hopkins University Press, 2008.

Trachtenberg, Marc. *Reparation in World Politics: France and European Diplomacy, 1916–1923*. New York: Columbia University Press, 1980.

Warner, Philip. *The Battle of France: 10 May–22 June 1940. Six Weeks Which Changed the World.* London: Simon & Schuster, 1990.

Weber, Eugen. *The Hollow Years: France in the 1930s.* London: Oxford University Press, 1995.

Webster, Paul. *Pétain's Crime: The Full Story of French Collaboration in the Holocaust.* London: Macmillan, 1990.

Williams, Charles. *Pétain.* London: Little, Brown, 2005.

Regeneration and Transformation

Aron, Raymond. *The Elusive Revolution: Anatomy of a Student Revolt.* Translated by Gordon Clough. New York: Praeger, 1969.

Austin, Guy. *Contemporary French Cinema: An Introduction.* Manchester, England: Manchester University Press, 1996.

Berstein, Serge, and Jean-Pierre Rioux. *The Pompidou Years, 1969–1974.* New York: Cambridge University Press, 2000.

Clayton, Anthony. *The Wars of French Decolonization.* New York: Longman, 1994.

Duchen, Claire. *Feminism in France from May '68 to Mitterrand.* London: Routledge & Kegan Paul, 1986.

———. *Women's Rights: Women's Lives in France, 1944–1968.* London: Routledge, 1994.

Fallaize, Elizabeth. *French Women's Writing: Recent Fiction.* Basingstoke, England: Macmillan, 1993.

Gildea, Robert. *France since 1945.* 2d ed. Oxford: Oxford University Press, 2002.

Gough, Hugh, and John Horne. *De Gaulle and Twentieth-century France.* London: Edward Arnold, 1994.

Horne, Alistair. *A Savage War of Peace: Algeria, 1954–1962.* Rev. ed. New York: Penguin, 1987.

Kelly, Michael. *The Cultural and Intellectual Rebuilding of France after the Second World War.* New York: Palgrave Macmillan, 2004.

Neupert, Richard. *A History of the French New Wave Cinema.* Chicago: University of Chicago Press, 2007.

Nuenlist, Christian, Anna Locher, and Garret Martin. *Globalizing de Gaulle: International Perspectives on French Foreign Policies, 1958–1969.* Lanham, Md.: Rowman & Littlefield, 2010.

Penniman, Howard R., ed. *France at the Polls, 1981–1986.* Durham, N.C.: Duke University Press, 1988.

Raymond, Gino, ed. *France during the Socialist Years.* Brookfield, Vt.: Dartmouth, 1994.

Rioux, Jean-Pierre. *The Fourth Republic, 1944–1958.* Translated by Geoffrey Rogers. Cambridge: Cambridge University Press, 1987.

Thody, Philip M. W. *The Fifth French Republic: Presidents, Politics and Personalities.* New York: Routledge, 1998.

———. *Le Franglais: Forbidden English, Forbidden American. Law, Politics, and Language in Contemporary France.* Atlantic Highlands, N.J.: Athlone, 1995.

France in the Twenty-first Century

Cole, Alistair, Jonah Levy, and Patrick le Gale, eds. *Developments in French Politics 4.* New York: Palgrave Macmillan, 2008.

Gueldry, Michael R. *France and European Integration: Toward a Transnational Policy.* Westport, Conn.: Greenwood, 2001.

Hudson, David L. *Nicolas Sarkozy.* New York: Facts On File, 2009.

Maclean, Mairi, and Joseph Szarka, eds. *France on the World Stage: Nation-State Strategies in the Global Era.* New York: Palgrave Macmillan, 2008.

O'Shaughnessy, Martin. *The New Face of Political Cinema: Commitment in French Film since 1995.* New York: Berghahn Books, 2007.

Sarkozy, Nicolas. *Testimony: France, Europe, and the World in the Twenty-first Century.* Translated by Philip H. Gordon. New York: HarperCollins, 2007.

Serfaty, Simon. *Architects of Delusion: Europe, America, and the Iraq War.* Philadelphia: University of Pennsylvania Press, 2007.

INDEX

Note: **Boldface** page numbers indicate primary discussion of a topic. Page numbers in *italic* indicate illustrations. The letters *c* and *m* indicate chronology and maps, respectively.